NANNAU

❧ A RICH TAPESTRY OF WELSH HISTORY ❧

NANNAU

❧ A RICH TAPESTRY OF WELSH HISTORY ❧

Philip Nanney Williams

First published in Great Britain in 2016
A Llwyn Estates Publication, Llwyn, Manafon, Welshpool, Powys. SY21 8BJ.
www.nannauhistory.com
ISBN 978-0-9955337-0-7

Cover and internal design by jenksdesign@yahoo.co.uk
helped by Sion Williams

Printed and bound by 1010 Printing International Ltd. China

Photograph on previous page
Nannau from the slopes of Moel Offrwm (2015)

To Pauline, whose incredible support
& encouragement
made this book
possible.

&

To the memory of my mother,
Eleanor, a gifted and inspirational
teacher whose influence was
immense.

FOREWORD I

*I*f this beautiful and engrossing book had celebrated a famous old English family and illustrated in vivid detail its generations of success, setbacks and eccentricity, it would have found a home in a well-stocked bookcase with many others. But as a story from Wales, it has too few companions. Biographies of great houses and their dynasties here have been rare. The Welsh outlook for most of the last century was very different: events, circumstances and national sympathies directed the attention of our many historians and narrators elsewhere, or at least until the most recent decades.

Perhaps this is because the old Welsh gentry as a social class are now nearly an extinct species. No longer a threat or even an influence in national affairs, they can be studied without biting back against criticism, if unsympathetic conclusions are drawn or long stifled secrets fall out of the archive. They and their households led a life that no longer exists, while the last depleted generation which has any actual (now childhood) memory of old country house days is fast passing on.

 How rapidly things change. We live now in an era suddenly and fervently gripped by a fascination for the past. Whole television channels are devoted to nothing else. Vast amounts of historic information are available at the press of a button at home. Never has the past been more easily at hand, and with it an acute appreciation of what has slipped through the fingers and been forgotten forever. New organisations are springing up to reclaim lost understandings of past society, most relevant to mention in the context of this book being the newly formed Institute for the Study of Welsh Estates at Bangor University, where a magnificent collection of country house archives is being put to use to show how profoundly the old landed estates and their owners shaped the lives and indeed the landscape of the whole breadth of society in the days prior to the Industrial Revolution, and to a surprising extent in rural areas right up to the First World War. And clearing one's way through the smokescreen of political ill-feeling directed toward the gentry in the early part of the last century, it becomes very evident that these old landlords generally (though not always) made a far better fist of their role as leaders of local society, promoters of their tenants' welfare, patrons of local artists, craftsmen and writers and concerned with the common good than they have had credit for to date.

No better example of this can be offered than through an exploration of the lives of the great inter-related families of Nanney and Vaughan of Merioneth and their many kinsmen. Putting together a narrative of one constantly distinguished clan over a thousand years is an exacting, almost heroic task, but Philip Nanney Williams – a descendent as his name implies - has spent years delving into the family papers (personally rescuing and making available an important chunk of them), and traversing across north Wales to find the places where they lived or fought and where their bodies lie. Moreover he has gone to great length to put all this in the broader context of the history of their times, so that after reading all that he has written, the reader of his fast-moving text will have gained a deeper knowledge of places and people of our past. Many illustrations show portraits and other treasures never put into the public record before, so that a sight of these things will never now be lost to scholarship, wherever the originals may now be or in the future go. For indeed, the sad recent history and current abandonment of the house (empty now for above a decade) makes a mournful endpiece to this centuries-long story.

Above all this book is about great characters whose lives have been born again for our appreciation. What finer Welshman was there ever than Sir Robert Williames Vaughan Bt., of Nannau, a man of huge frame, huge generosity and huge industry; the builder of miles of new roads, much at his own expense, earning him the nickname of The Colossus of Roads. To have his life set out for us here is a joy (and a debt that he has been owed for two hundred years). But this book is positively hopping with characters spanning the whole gamut from patriot to traitor. It will not rest on any bookshelf for long.

Thomas Lloyd

Wales Herald of Arms Extraordinary

FOREWORD II

My father, God bless him, was a practical man. He knew neither the blessings nor the burdens of ancestors (I mean 'Ancestors'), but, in 1965, newly returned from the colonies with his young wife and baby son, he was sufficiently aware of his wife's illustrious forebears to suggest attendance at the Nannau contents auction (p. 289). By all accounts my mother was ambivalent, but the timing was perfect as they had a nearly empty house to furnish. As a teenager she had spent a summer or two living at the old mansion ('cold and damp'), whose name she shared, but at that tender age my mother was far more interested in the horses under her care than Nannau's historic interiors.

Looking back, I see how Nannau entwined itself, like a web of romantic ivy, through the consciousness of my maternal relations and deeply into my own. In the small library of old books at Llanfendigaid (p. 362) was one special volume to which I frequently returned as a boy. 'Haunted Homes and Family Legends' (1897) had a shroud-clad ghost on the spine and my great-grandfather's name on the title page. It was here that I first read the story of Howel Sele and Ceubren Yr Ellyll, Nannau's haunted tree. In Llanfendigaid's drawing room there was a fine copy of Colt Hoare's watercolour of the famous oak (p. 32), painted by my great-grandmother. She borrowed the original from John & Ellinor Vaughan whose portraits she had painted in miniature (p. 193 & 212) prior to her marriage. Set over the fireplace in the same room was a boldly painted panel with the Nanney and Wynn arms, and in a garden wall there was a curious stone tablet, carved with the arms and names of 'Hughe & Anne Nanne' (p. 87 top left & p. 197). This had been rescued from the rubble during the demolition of the wings and rear ranges, which took place after the sale of Nannau to Mr and Mrs Morrison (for a mere £8000) in 1965 (p. 290). Thus I grew up with the material confetti of the Nanneys at both my parents' home in England, and my maternal grandparents' home in Wales. My father 'adapted' (this was the '60's ...) a late 17th-century oak deuddarn from the Nannau sale to fit his hi-fi, and my sister was born in an elegant Regency four-poster bed bought at the same auction. In a show of inverted snobbery, my parents enjoyed retelling the story of bidding for two very shabby armchairs, beds for the Vaughans' dogs in the Nannau kitchens. Subsequently re-covered, they were upgraded to my father's study and considered rather good. I can still bring to mind my father's refrain: 'Oh, those came from Nannau', and I am now using the deuddarn to store my gallery's papers and tools.

My memories of Nannau as a private house are limited to a vague recollection of drinks with the Morrisons in an upstairs drawing room, in the mid-1970s. There were reports of ghosts. The contrast between the cavernous rooms, bereft of their long-accustomed furnishings, and the newly compact living-quarters of the Vaughans, decamped to nearby Maesybrynner (p. 295), was stark. The latter house, long and low, was filled from floor to ceiling with dozens of family portraits as every object associated with the history of the Nanneys and the Vaughans had been retained for later distribution to the Vaughans' daughters. Their tenure at Nannau had been all too short and yet it had been characterised by a late flowering of family pride which saw the house opened to the public, with all the historic contents researched, catalogued and displayed coherently for the first time. The prime force behind this was the Hon. Mrs 'Plum' Vaughan, who took up the cause of sorting out the complex and muddled genealogy of her husband's ancestors with alacrity, imagination and a stoic humour. The knowledge she accumulated in the process was remarkable and it was her nature to share it generously. She would have been absolutely delighted by the publication of this book.

It was my great good fortune to have had a lengthy correspondence with 'Mrs V', as she liked to be addressed. This began in 1985, when I was at Cambridge and when my obsessive interest in old sealed wine bottles (another story) led me to write to her to enquire about the possible availability of those I remembered seeing at Maesybrynner some years before. It was some years before I was able to buy one of Sir Robert Williames Vaughan's late 18th-century magnums (bearing his seal embossed simply 'R.W.V.') but within five years, Mrs Vaughan's daughters had begun to sell off the Nannau heirlooms, some privately and some via auction. In June 1990, the day before a picture sale at Phillips in Bath where the best 17th-century Nanney portraits were to be sold, I travelled down to Wiltshire to stay with Mrs Vaughan and one of her daughters. Down from the attic came Col. Huw Nanney's drum (p. 110), a very fine pencil portrait of the 2nd Vaughan Baronet and various other tempting bits and pieces. The next day I returned to London, with not only these remarkable items, but also with portraits of four Nanney heirs (p. 88, 105, 106 & 108). This was just the start of many purchases lasting until the final big sale in 2008, which took place following the untimely death of the eldest of the Vaughan daughters, Susan Muirhead. That final auction was held at a minor saleroom in Somerset and, though well advertised in the antiques trade press, it was poorly attended and represented a rather ignominious end for the treasures of Nannau.

But treasures they were. One of the many services Philip Nanney Williams has rendered in compiling this book is putting on record a range of the most important contents, especially the pictures. It is now clear that Nannau had one of the most interesting and important country-house collections in Wales. The original contents included two fine Welsh landscapes by Richard Wilson (1714-1782) commissioned by William Vaughan of Corsygedol (p. 114). These were sold by General Vaughan at Christie's in 1930 and soon entered the collection of the National Museum of Wales. There was a complete run of family portraits from the early 17th to the mid 20th centuries, including the most extensive surviving group of pictures in private hands by the pre-eminent Welsh painter William Parry (p. 132, 134, 138-140). As well as Parry's family commissions for Robert Howel Vaughan, the house also contained the artist's remarkable group portrait of 'Omai, Joseph Banks and Dr Solander', which is now in public ownership. Nannau also contained the 2nd Baronet's complete commission to Daniel Clowes, central to which was his celebrated image of the 'White Ox' (p. 153 & 168-169). The art collection was greatly enhanced and complimented by a wide variety of associated objects (p. 133, 140 & 170). Amongst these were Robert Howel Vaughan's Jacobite relics, including a possibly unique set of 12 'Cycle of the White Rose' drinking glasses of c. 1771 (p. 135), the extensive collection of items fashioned from Ceubren Yr Ellyll (p. 32, 33, 39, 155, 167 & 171) and locally-made oak furniture (p. 165 & 172).

Despite the Hon. Mrs Vaughan's sterling work in researching and cataloguing the Nannau papers and collections, the cultural importance to Wales of the house and its contents were far less appreciated in the 1960s than is the case now. The significance of some of the best items had yet to be recognised (including all the family portraits by Parry) and the Welsh country house, with contents intact, was not yet the critically endangered species it has sadly become.

The story of the house since 1965 has been a sorry one and Nannau continues the long wait for a sympathetic owner with both resources and integrity. However, it is perhaps some consolation that many of the best contents are now held in both public and private collections where they are properly catalogued and where they serve as a reminder of the past glories of a truly historic Welsh estate.

Miles Wynn Cato

Ludlow. April 2016

CONTENTS

INTRODUCTION

$\int$tanding in the shadow of Moel Offrwm, two miles north east of Dolgellau, amid Snowdonia's majestic scenery, lies the historic mansion of Nannau. Its classical lines hark back to Georgian times, and reveal little if anything of the four earlier dwellings that have stood on the site, the earliest dated from the eleventh century when descendants of Cadwgan ap Bleddyn, Prince of Powys, first settled the territory.

Nannau, the plural of Nant (a mountain stream), is a name clearly derived from its setting. The two mountain streams, running north and south of the site, gave birth to not only the house but the township of Nannau and the family who, in the sixteenth century, adopted the name.

From its ancient origins the family of Nanney arose to become one of the most eminent families in North Wales. With Nannau at the core of their extensive estates, lands were transmitted in unbroken descent for almost 900 years. Nannau was also renowned for its patronage of the bards; the wealth of poetry that emanated from these connections reveal much valuable insight if interpreted skilfully.

E.D. Jones (later Librarian of The National Library of Wales), in a lecture delivered at Nannau in 1952, noted:

Indeed the most cursory examination of the bardic remains of the seventeenth-century eulogy of the Nanneys is in itself a course in Welsh history.

A family as old as Nannau inevitably has many illustrious members, with a number having played a significant part in Welsh history. Represented amongst its family members are some of the most well-known and infamous characters in the history of North Wales. From 'treacherous traitors' to 'murderous judges', with a liberal dose of benefactors and public-spirited individuals thrown in for good measure, the family's prominence has developed throughout the centuries.

Nannau's sons and occasional daughters have figured strongly in the history of Merioneth and beyond, as the succeeding chapters will demonstrate. I hope they will also justify my choice of title:

Nannau – A Rich Tapestry of Welsh History.

The seeds of this book were sown in my childhood: I inherited the family name of Nanney Williams and have always been aware of its historical importance. I vividly recall, at the tender age of 9 years, 'lecturing' a family associate (the then High Sheriff of the county) about the tragic story of my 18th great grandfather, Hywel Sele, and his demise at the hands of his cousin Owain Glyndŵr and his subsequent incarceration in a hollow oak! A fascination with the more colourful members of the Nannau family first led me to research the family's history.

ACKNOWLEDGEMENTS

*I*n retirement, the last eight years have afforded me the opportunity to finally produce a definitive account of the House of Nannau. None of this would have been possible without the considerable assistance of many institutions and individuals, in particular Mrs Janey Allen (née Vaughan), daughter of Brigadier C.H.V. Vaughan (late of Nannau), whose assistance and encouragement has been a constant source of inspiration throughout the work. Others deserving of special thanks include:

Rhiannon Jones and Staff of the Hugh Owen Library, Aberystwyth University; Staff of the Merioneth Records Office, Dolgellau; Staff of the National Library of Wales, Aberystwyth; Staff of the Royal Commission on Ancient and Historical Monuments in Wales, Aberystwyth; Mr Einion Thomas and Staff of Bangor University Archives, Oliver Fairclough and Staff of the National Museum of Wales; Staff of St. Fagans: National History Museum; Miles Wynn Cato (Welsh Art); Dr Stephen Briggs; Joan Harris; Brian Slyfield; Gemma Williams; Paul Hett; David Brown; Tom Morrison; Richard Pillinger; Aled Thomas; Ann Thomas; Peter Ogden; Dr Helen Pendry; Thomas Lloyd; Dr Mark Baker; Dr Shaun Evans; Robert Nanney Williams; Alan Ludovic Nanney Williams; Isobel Nanney Williams; Vaughan Gaskell; Christopher Quail; Spencer Smith; Major Richard Hargreaves MC; Staff of the National Archives, Kew; Staff of the Northumberland Archives, Woodhorn; Staff of Horse Power: The Museum of the King's Royal Hussars; Molly Bartle (née Vaughan); Anne Hughes; Heulwen Watts; Jack and Kath Smith; J. Owen & Sons; Phylis Jones; Eirlys Price; Gladys Thomas; Gerallt Hughes; Fleur Richards; Susan C. Passmore; Ruth Tudor-Swift; Edmund Bailey; Sherril Kelly.

And finally, to all the many people that have so generously allowed access to their houses, a special note of thanks. Visiting the many properties with such intimate family connections has been a truly fascinating experience. The words of Simon Jenkins certainly ring true in this respect:

The best guides to any house are the people who occupy it.

(England's Thousand Best Houses, 2003)

1

1018-1128

A ROYAL DYNASTIC DESCENT

The foundations of the House of Nannau are immensely ancient; its roots permeate to the very core of Welsh history.

Counted amongst its ancestors are many of the early Welsh kings and princes who fought, often brutally, to maintain Welsh independence through the turbulent 11th and 12th centuries.

One such ancient and heroic warrior, Bleddyn ap Cynfyn, is widely acknowledged as the seed of the Nannau family, a proud and formidable King of Gwynedd and Powys, who died in 1075.

He was aptly described as:

the most amiable and merciful of all kings ... he injured no one; he was gentle to his kinsmen; just to the poor, and merciful towards Pilgrims, orphans and widows; he was the defender of the weak and the strength of the wise, the honour of the churches, and the foundation and delight of the bards, generous towards everybody, terrible in war, amiable and gentle in peace, and a protector for everyone.
(Chronicle of the Princes)

Bleddyn ap Cynfyn had been recognised as 'king of the Britons', the leading Welsh king of the time. To say that Bleddyn's rise to such heights was fortunate is an understatement, as history could well have dealt him a less favourable hand. His father was Cynfyn ap Gwerystan, a Powysian nobleman whose fortunate marriage to Angharad of Wales, the widow of Llywelyn ap Seisyll, King of Gwynedd, was the prime reason for Bleddyn's 'meteoric' rise to power.

Llywelyn ap Seisyll was first referred to as a king in 1018, but by 1022 he was acknowledged by the Chronicle of the Princes as being

king of Gwynedd and the supreme and most praiseworthy king of the Britons,

with his ambitions set on ruling Deheubarth. His astute marriage with Angharad, the great - granddaughter of Hywel Dda, whilst not giving him the legitimate right to rule Deheubarth, would have conferred that right on a son of the union. That son was to become the most successful king Wales was ever to see, the renowned Gruffudd ap Llywelyn.

3. The Descent of **Bleddyn ap Cynfyn**

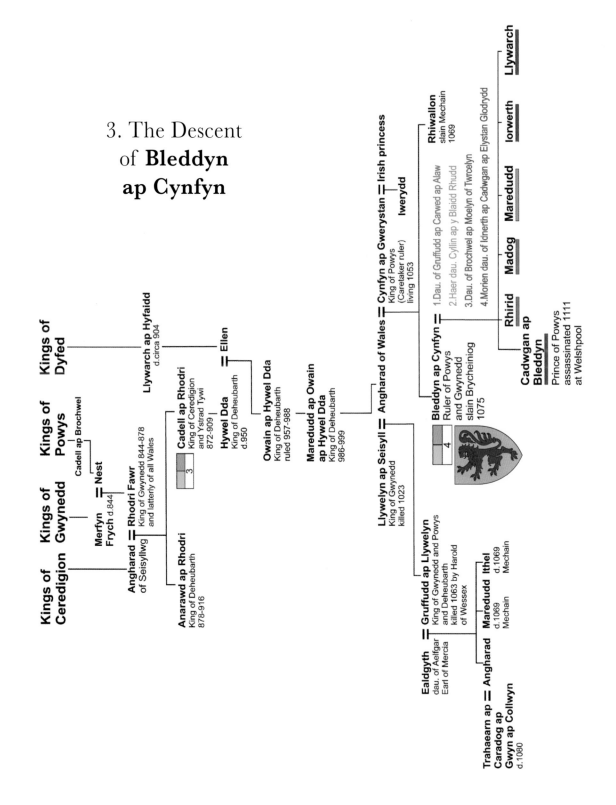

Kings of Ceredigion

Kings of Gwynedd

Kings of Powys

Kings of Dyfed

Cadell ap Brochwel

Merfyn Frych d.844 = Nest

Angharad of Seisyllwg = Rhodri Fawr
King of Gwynedd 844-878 and latterly of all Wales

Llywarch ap Hyfaidd
d.circa 904

Anarawd ap Rhodri
King of Deheubarth
878-916

Cadell ap Rhodri
King of Ceredigion and Ystrad Tywi
872-909

Hywel Dda
King of Deheubarth
d.950

= Ellen

Owain ap Hywel Dda
King of Deheubarth
ruled 957-988

Maredudd ap Owain ap Hywel Dda
King of Deheubarth
986-999

Llywelyn ap Seisyll =
King of Gwynedd
killed 1023

Angharad of Wales =

Cynfyn ap Gwerystan = **Irish princess**
King of Powys
(Caretaker ruler)
living 1053

Iwerydd

Ealdgyth
dau. of Aelfgar
Earl of Mercia

= **Gruffudd ap Llywelyn**
King of Gwynedd and Powys and Deheubarth
killed 1063 by Harold of Wessex

Bleddyn ap Cynfyn
Ruler of Powys and Gwynedd
slain Brycheiniog
1075

Maredudd
d.1069
Mechain

Ithel
d.1069
Mechain

1.Dau. of Gruffudd ap Carwed ap Alaw
2.Haer dau. Cyllin ap y Blaidd Rhudd
3.Dau. of Brochwel ap Moelyn of Twrcelyn
4.Morien dau. of Idnerth ap Cadwgan ap Elystan Glodrydd

Rhiwallon
slain Mechain
1069

Trahaearn ap Caradog ap Gwyn ap Collwyn
d.1080

= Angharad

Rhirid **Madog** **Maredudd** **Iorwerth** **Llywarch**

Cadwgan ap Bleddyn
Prince of Powys
assassinated 1111
at Welshpool

Tragically, in 1023 Llywelyn ap Seisyll was killed, and a dangerous power vacuum occurred. His son and heir Gruffudd ap Llywelyn was still a minor and consequently Gwynedd passed back to the hands of Iago ab Idwal, a member of the northern branch of the line of Merfyn (hereditary rulers of Gwynedd).

Under Iago's rule Gwynedd posed little territorial threat to Powys, which was now being ruled by Cynfyn ap Gwerystan, who had married Angharad the widow of Llywelyn ap Seisyll. Cynfyn was acting as 'caretaker king' whilst the legitimate heir Gruffudd ap Llywelyn was too young to rule.

When eventually Gruffudd ap Llywelyn came to power in 1039 he immediately set about overthrowing Iago ab Idwal, King of Gwynedd, causing him and his son Cynan to flee to Ireland. He then turned his attention to Deheubarth, believing his right to rule implicit, as did his father. He attacked the monastery of Llanbadarn and ejected Hywel ab Edwin, King of Deheubarth, from his territory, forcing him into exile. Fired up with his military successes Gruffudd looked east and at the Battle of Rhyd y Gors on the River Severn, he fought and killed Edwin, brother of Leofric, Earl of Mercia. His territorial appetite knew no bounds.

In 1041 Hywel ap Edwin returned, attacking Deheubarth in an attempt to reclaim his lands. In the ensuing Battle of Pencadair, Gruffudd, although victorious, did not succeed in holding Deheubarth, but as a mark of defiance, he abducted Hywel's wife and took her for himself.

However, by 1055 Gruffudd ap Llywelyn was King of Deheubarth, Gwynedd, Powys and possibly Morganwg and powerful enough to ally himself with the Mercians against Harold Godwinesson of Wessex. When Aelfgar became Earl of Mercia in 1057, Gruffudd negotiated a treaty with him and consolidated this by marrying his daughter Ealdgyth. He had become a major player in the power struggles of the time and a major force on the border region.

The death of Aelfgar in 1062 deprived Gruffudd of a powerful ally and Gruffudd's long-standing adversary Harold Godwinesson attacked Gruffudd at Rhuddlan at Christmastide. Gruffudd was fortunate to escape, but was hunted mercilessly. Eventually his supporters dwindled and he was assassinated by one of his own household - an ignominious end to what had been a glorious reign. As was often the tactic after a victory, Harold then took Gruffudd's widow Ealdgyth of Mercia as his wife.

Gruffudd ap Llywelyn's place in history had been established: never again would a Welsh ruler enjoy such great influence and power. Many would attempt to emulate him, none would succeed. He is recognised as:

> *the only Welsh king ever to rule over the entire territory of Wales ... a feat with neither precedent nor successor.* (John Davies, 1993)

Gruffudd's successors, his maternal half-brothers Bleddyn and Rhiwallon, were waiting in the wings and took on Gruffudd's mantle, submitting to the Saxon king of England, Edward the Confessor, and later to his successor Harold as

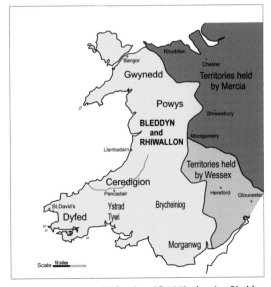

4. above: **Wales circa AD 1063, showing Bleddyn and Rhiwallon's territories**

vassals. At the onset of the Norman invasion the territorial map of Wales had been rewritten, with Bleddyn and Rhiwallon being given Gwynedd and Powys but having lost the hard-fought Deheubarth.

Despite their submission to Harold Godwinesson, Bleddyn and Rhiwallon's alliance with the Mercians was still robust, as in 1065 they were known to have lent Welsh troops to Morcar, the younger son of Aelfgar, to secure his earldom in Northumbria. In the wake of the Norman conquest, Bleddyn and Rhiwallon proved their independence and fortitude on more than one occasion, backing up Mercian rebellions against the Conqueror's forces if their borders were in any way threatened.

Gruffudd ap Llywelyn's ambition to found a dynasty had failed. In 1069, when both of his sons came of age, they rose up against their uncles, Bleddyn and Rhiwallon, to regain Gwynedd. In the ensuing Battle of Mechain, Ithel and Maredudd were both killed, together with Rhiwallon, leaving Bleddyn ap Cynfyn in the early years of the Norman Conquest sole ruler in North Wales.

Over the next few years Bleddyn was seen to consolidate his position in the north of Wales until 1075 when he, emulating Gruffudd ap Llywelyn, had designs on the south of Wales and attacked Deheubarth. The Welsh Chronicles recall that:

> *Bleddyn ap Cynfyn was killed through the evil-spirited treachery of the princes and nobility of Ystrad Twyi...being killed by Rhys ap Owain.*

Bleddyn's cousin Trahaearn ap Caradog, a Powysian nobleman, took up the gauntlet and sought to avenge his death, defeating Rhys ap Owain in the Battle of Goodwick in 1078 and banishing him into exile. Bleddyn's dynastic ambition regarding Deheubarth had been a recurring theme throughout the last decades of the 12th century, and his sons certainly followed the family line in this respect.

Bleddyn is not only remembered as a warrior, but as an administrator who, probably based at his ancestral seat of Mathraval in Powys, took advantage of less turbulent times to revise the Laws of Hywel Dda. It is said that he also issued regulations for the better government of the Order of Bards. He was the founder of one of the five Royal Tribes of Wales and also of the 2nd Dynasty of Powys - a truly worthy founder of the House of Nannau.

Interestingly, some of the most important Welsh leaders, namely Llywelyn the Great, Llywelyn the Last and Owain Glyndŵr, were all direct descendants of the family of Bleddyn ap Cynfyn.

On the death of Bleddyn ap Cynfyn in 1075, none of his sons were old enough to succeed him. Trehaearn ap Caradog, a ruler of part of Powys and cousin of Bleddyn, rose to the ascendancy and seized Gwynedd and Powys.

Another legitimate contender for Gwynedd arrived in the form of Gruffudd ap Cynan, whose grandfather Iago ap Idwal of Gwynedd had been unseated by Gruffudd ap Llywelyn in 1039.

5. above: **Wales circa A.D. 1080, showing Marcher Lord incursions**

6. above: **Mathrafal - near Welshpool - the seat of the Kings and Princes of Powys from the 9th century**

Gruffudd ap Cynan had been raised in Ireland in his father's period of exile from Wales. His father had married Ragnhildir, daughter of Olaf, Viking King of Dublin. Gruffudd brought with him a strong force of Viking mercenaries from Dublin and raided Anglesey. He later confronted the usurper Trahaearn in battle, but it was to take a further six years for Gruffudd to regain his inheritance. In 1081 victory was his: he defeated and killed Trahaearn in the Battle of Mynydd Carn, a victory only achieved by an alliance with Rhys ap Tewdwr, King of Deheubarth.

The balance of power in the latter part of 11th century Wales was not clearly defined, mostly due to aggressive Norman incursions at that period. Gruffudd ap Cynan had been imprisoned by the Normans whilst returning from his victory at Mynydd Carn, and Rhys ap Tewdwr was firmly in control of the South. It was at this volatile period that the sons of Bleddyn made their appearance, with a vengeance and determination characteristic of this warrior dynasty.

RISE OF THE Sons of Bleddyn

In 1088 the sons of Bleddyn - Madog, Rhirid and Cadwgan, now of fighting age, burst into Deheubarth. They were no doubt aware of their father's claim to the area and sought to extend their territory, which had very much dwindled as a result of the Normans. Rhys ap Tewdwr was taken by surprise and was driven into exile. He fled to Ireland, where he set about recruiting a Viking mercenary fleet who would later engage Bleddyn's sons at the Battle of Llech y Crau. Here Madog and Rhirid were killed and Cadwgan was forced to retreat, defeated but, by default, the undisputed sole ruler of Powys.

Cadwgan has often been styled as the Prince of Powys and first Lord of Nannau. However, I believe this is erroneous. It is more likely that the first Lord of Nannau was his son, named Madog. Prince Cadwgan certainly exercised rule over Merioneth and thus the Nannau area, but sought for most of his life to devolve power to his vassal Uchdryd ap Edwin, a family member who

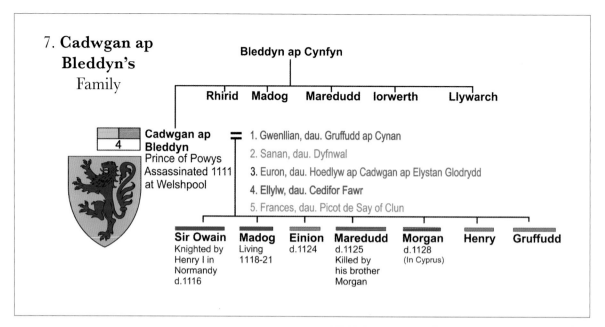

7. Cadwgan ap Bleddyn's Family

Bleddyn ap Cynfyn

Rhirid   Madog   Maredudd   Iorwerth   Llywarch

Cadwgan ap Bleddyn
Prince of Powys
Assassinated 1111
at Welshpool

1. Gwenllian, dau. Gruffudd ap Cynan
2. Sanan, dau. Dyfnwal
3. Euron, dau. Hoedlyw ap Cadwgan ap Elystan Glodrydd
4. Ellylw, dau. Cedifor Fawr
5. Frances, dau. Picot de Say of Clun

Sir Owain
Knighted by
Henry I in
Normandy
d.1116

Madog
Living
1118-21

Einion
d.1124

Maredudd
d.1125
Killed by
his brother
Morgan

Morgan
d.1128
(In Cyprus)

Henry

Gruffudd

had fought valiantly with him in many battles. Interestingly, Cadwgan is considered the only example of a Welsh prince ever to have a vassal lord ruling on his behalf.

In 1093 Rhys ap Tewdwr was killed in an attempt to halt Bernard Neufmarche, a Norman Lord, from annexing Brycheiniog. Rhys's death precipitated a 'free for all in Wales', with the Normans attempting to over-run large swathes of the country.

Likewise, Cadwgan reacted and quickly became the focus of Welsh resistance to the Norman invaders, a veritable thorn in the side of the enemy for a decade. *The Chronicles of Ystrad Fflur* describe the start of his retaliations thus:

In this year (1094) the Britons being unable to bear the tyranny and injustice of the French, threw off the rule of the French, and they destroyed their castles in Gwynedd and inflicted slaughter upon them. And the French brought a host to Gwynedd and Cadwgan ap Bleddyn drove them to flight with great slaughter at Coed Yspwys.

The rebellion, masterminded by Cadwgan, gathered pace, rising initially in Gwynedd and spreading to Deheubarth. By 1095, William Rufus,

Illustration: T. Prytherch in 1900

8. above: **Gruffudd ap Cynan escapes from Chester**

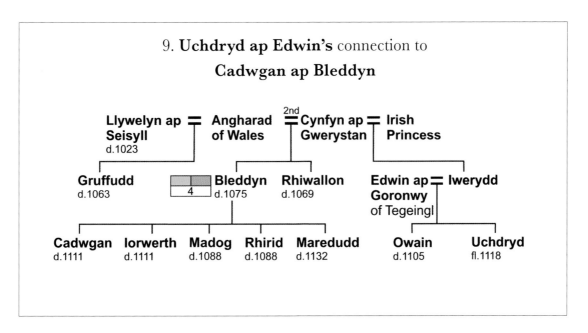

9. **Uchdryd ap Edwin's** connection to **Cadwgan ap Bleddyn**

now King of England, had returned from Normandy and set about quelling the rebellion but with little success. Cadwgan's warband struck relentlessly, despoiling Pembroke and terrorising the countryside. The rebellion grew, becoming a nationwide uprising that spread beyond the borders of Wales as Cadwgan's force

burned many vills and seized booty in Cheshire, Shropshire and Herefordshire; and put to death many of the English and Normans.

Gruffudd ap Cynan, now recently escaped from imprisonment in Chester, became allied to Cadwgan forming an effective fighting partnership.

By 1098 the rebellion in South Wales had petered out, the tide turning against the Welsh. The Earls of Chester and Shrewsbury, both confusingly called Hugh, drove Cadwgan and Gruffudd's forces back to Gwynedd, trapping them in Anglesey, from where they fled to Ireland. On their return in 1099 Cadwgan and Gruffudd brokered a peace with William Rufus, which resulted in the confirmation of Cadwgan as ruler of central Powys and Ceredigion, and Gruffudd was given Anglesey. During this period of calm, Cadwgan consolidated his position by marrying Gwenllian, daughter of Gruffudd ap Cynan.

It was around this time Cadwgan probably established Dolgellau as a serf town, populated by slaves captured in the various offences. He established a similar settlement at Llanfachreth.

The death of William Rufus in 1100 shattered the possibility of continued peace; his younger brother Henry I was a more formidable and ruthless opponent, as Cadwgan was to shortly discover. Henry, however, had to deal with discontent amongst his own barons who had favoured the claim of his elder brother, Robert of Normandy, to the Crown of England. Cadwgan and his brothers Iorwerth and Maredudd allied themselves with Robert de Bellême, the new Earl of Shrewsbury, and his brother Arnulf, Lord of Pembroke, against the King.

Henry was successful in the ensuing engagement with the rebellious barons and immediately employed a strategy that would become a hallmark of his dealings with the Welsh, that of divide and conquer. He offered Cadwgan's brother Iorwerth ap Bleddyn all of Robert de Bellême and Arnulf's lands in Wales in return for his support. Iorwerth, as was typical of the time, switched allegiances and delivered his own brother Maredudd into Henry's hands as a hostage! The King's plan worked beautifully and the rebellion soon collapsed.

Henricus primus

ultimate downfall and his son Owain would be directly responsible.

Cadwgan's feast of 1109 would be eclipsed by Owain's daring abduction of the beautiful Princess Nest of Wales, the Welsh equivalent of Helen of Troy. To quote *The Chronicle of the Princes* from Peniarth MS 20:

Cadwgan ap Bleddyn prepared a royal feast for the leading men of the land. And he invited Owain, his son, from Powys to the feast. And he held that feast at Christmas in honour of Jesus Christ. And when the feast was ended, Owain heard that Nest, daughter of the Lord Rhys ap Tewdwr, wife of Gerald the officer, was in the said castle, and when he heard, he went, and with him a small force, to visit her as though she were a kinswoman-and so she was, for Cadwgan ap Bleddyn and Gwladus, daughter of Rhiwallon, who was mother to Nest, were first cousins: for Bleddyn and Rhiwallon were brothers, sons of Cynfyn by Angharad, daughter of King Maredudd. And after that, at the instigation of the Devil, he was moved by passion and love for the woman, and with the small company with him – about fourteen men – he made for the castle at night. And unknown to the watchers, he came into the castle over the wall and ditch, and surrounded the building where Gerald and Nest, his wife, were sleeping. And he raised a shout around the building and set fire to the buildings and kindled them. And Gerald awoke from his slumber and was afraid when he heard the shout, and knew not what he should do. And his wife said to him, 'go not to the door, for there are thine enemies around it, but come with me.' And thus he did. And she led him to the privies which adjoined the building. And through the pit of the privies he escaped, she shouted from within and said, 'Why do you shout in vain? He whom you were seeking has escaped.' And they came inside and searched everywhere. And when they did not find him, they seized Nest and her two sons and the third son, whom Gerald had by a concubine, and a

Henry, however, reneged on his promises, imprisoning Iorwerth in Shrewsbury. The scene was set for a decade of bluff and counter bluff between Henry and Cadwgan, when Cadwgan would be more than once well and truly defeated, not by force but by subterfuge. Henry manipulated the Welsh princes as if they were pawns in a game of chess; Cadwgan would be the next recipient of Henry's deviousness, but in the meantime he was left as sole ruler of Powys.

Cadwgan's hold on his territories seemed secure. His son Owain was beginning to cut his teeth in the military sense, assisting his father on raids in the Norman-held territories of Deheubarth. In an attempt to demonstrate his power and authority in the area, Cadwgan held a great feast at Cardigan for the nobles of South Wales. The events that unfolded were to be Cadwgan's

11. left: **The Chronicle of the Princes - Brut y Tywysogion**
(Peniarth Manuscript 20)

daughter. And they utterly pillaged the castle and burned it. And he violated Nest and lay with her and then returned home.

Cadwgan, his father, was not in the place, for he had gone to Powys to pacify some men who were opposed to Owain his son, and had deserted him.

And when Cadwgan heard that story, he was grieved and was frightened for two reasons; because of the violation of the lady, and because of fear of King Henry on account of the injury to his officer. And when he returned, he sought in every way to restore the woman and the spoil, but he was not allowed. And Owain, because the woman was for ever saying unto him, 'I thou wilt have me true and keep me for thyself, release my sons to their father,' – and in his infatuation for the woman, he released the two sons and the daughter.

The fact that this brutal act occurred is unquestionable, having been recorded by a number of contemporary sources. Authorities on the era have cast doubts on the accuracy of some versions of the event, *The Chronicle of the Princes* being a case in question. On close analysis it has been revealed that the original material had been altered to give a more informed view of the account. It is known at this time that the Chronicler exhibited some bias towards portraying the Powys Princes in a more heroic light.

Without doubt Owain is widely regarded as one of the more colourful characters of Welsh history, being aptly described as:

> *... dashing, but utterly irresponsible.*
> (R.R. Davies)

Owain was born into violent times, characterised by bitter dynastic rivalries, tempered with hatred of the Norman invader. It is not surprising that he burst violently into historic prominence in 1106, achieving notoriety through the killing of two of his cousins, Griffri and Meurig ap Trahaearn - a typical way of dealing with potential claimants to the throne. Cadwgan, by 1109, had submitted to the King and was playing a more subtle game in

12. above: **The Teifi Gorge, immediately below Cilgerran Castle**

13. above: **Cilgerran Castle - probable site of the abduction of Nest, and in her time a wooden castle**

terms of territorial advancement in Deheubarth. It is likely that Owain resented his father's apparent cooperation with the Normans, and driven by a desire for retaliation, planned the abduction of Nest as the ultimate insult to Gerald de Windsor, the King's representative in Dyfed. The fact that Nest had previously been a favourite mistress of Henry I and had borne an illegitimate child by him, Henry Fitzroy, could well have added fuel to Owain's fire and been an additional reason for the abduction.

The likely scene for this historic abduction was Cilgerran castle, strategically placed close to the river Teifi and just up river from Cardigan Castle. Gerald had constructed the wooden castle of Cilgerran in 1108 as part of the Norman colonisation of the area, and was known to have fortified it in anticipation of an attack by the Welsh.

Many have questioned the motives of Cadwgan in holding his feast in 1109. Did he have an ulterior motive, or was it simply a lavish demonstration of hospitality? Holding a feast for the 'leading men of the land' might indicate that Cadwgan was exploring the idea of gaining overlordship of these petty rulers? Heroic poems of the era have shown that feasts were often a prelude to a military campaign, to fire up the troops and recruit supporters. If this were so, Gerald would be imminently expecting an attack, but why was his wife Nest placed in such a vulnerable location?

The chronicles describe at length Gerald's escape through 'a privy hole', a most embarrassing exit for an accomplished Norman warrior! It begs the question: was Gerald even there at the time of the abduction? The later stone castle built at Cilgerran certainly would have incorporated a latrine channel; whether the earlier wooden

14. **Nest** and **Owain ap Cadwgan's**
family relationship

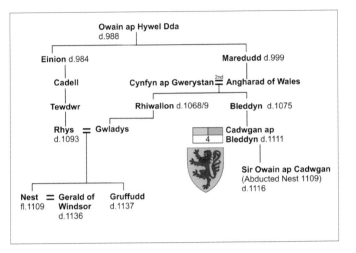

Owain ap Hywel Dda
d.988

Einion d.984

Maredudd d.999

Cadell

Cynfyn ap Gwerystan ══ Angharad of Wales
2nd

Tewdwr

Rhiwallon d.1068/9

Bleddyn d.1075

Rhys
d.1093

Gwladys

Cadwgan ap
Bleddyn d.1111

4

Sir Owain ap Cadwgan
(Abducted Nest 1109)
d.1116

Nest ══ Gerald of
fl.1109 Windsor
d.1136

Gruffudd
d.1137

structure possessed one is debatable. As far as insulting the Norman invaders with the ignominious retreat of one of their leaders, it made for good propaganda.

Nest was second cousin to Owain and one might assume safe from an attack by her own kinsfolk. If Gerald thought this way, he was not prepared for Owain's actions. If left to Cadwgan, Nest would not have come to any harm, this fact clearly demonstrated by his reactions on hearing of the abduction. The seizing of wives from defeated kings was commonplace in Medieval Wales, but Cadwgan positively condemned it.

The retaliation was swift and powerful. Owain had not only earned the wrath of Gerald; Henry I was likewise outraged. A chain of events was unleashed, beginning with Bishop Richard, the King's representative in Shrewsbury, summoning Owain's cousins Madog and Ithel ap Rhirid. He laid a deal on the table: if they could capture Owain and his complicit father, they would be rewarded with the perpetrators' lands in Powys and Ceredigion. The devious cousins were up to the challenge and recruited Llywarch ap Trahaearn, another family member with a grudge against Cadwgan, and launched a fierce attack on Powys, driving both Cadwgan and Owain to ground. Owain fled to Ireland, and Cadwgan lay

low possibly in the safety of his lands in the Clun area, having recently married the daughter of Picot de Say, a Marcher lord.

It is known that Nest and her children were returned to her husband at some point in time, but Owain remained an outlaw. Cadwgan must have drawn heavily on his skills of diplomacy to once more receive the King's favour. Cadwgan was returned to his lands by the end of the year, having paid a fine of £100, but with an important caveat:

... that there was to be no association or friendship between him and Owain, his son, and he was not to allow him to come into the land, and that he was not to give him either counsel or advice, either support or help.
(Thomas. Jones, ed. & trans. *Brut y Tywysogyon*)

The renegade Owain, on his return, continued to ravage Ceredigion with his usual flair for violence, by now allied to Madog ap Rhirid,

15. above: **Princess Nest of Wales in bed with Henry I**
(British Library Add. MS 10292 f. 21 v)

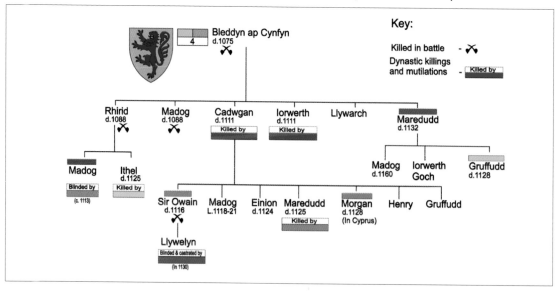

previously his bitter enemy but now his ally in adversity. Together they

made for the land by night and burned and slew all they found in it, and plundered others and took others with them in fetters and sold them to their folk or sent them bound to the ships.
(Brut y Tywysogyon)

In 1111, Cadwgan decided to make his seat of government in Welshpool, having

brought his country to some state of quietness, and saw right and justice ministered therein, he came to Trallwn (now called the Poole), and the elders of the country with him, and minding to dwell there, began to build a castle.
(Caradoc of Llancarvan)

Perhaps he was seeking a quieter life, maybe inspired by time spent at Clun? Whatever the reason, he started to build a castle of his own in Wales. He was not apparently prepared for the actions of his renegade nephew Madog ap Rhirid,

who was still on the rampage. Earlier that year Madog had killed Cadwgan's brother Iorwerth in nearby Caereinion, but now had his sights on Cadwgan:

Madoc sent spies to learn where Cadogan might be found, and they returned and said that the person they were in search of was far and near. And he and his men immediately came upon Cadogan, and Cadogan not imagining any mischief, conducted himself weakly, and would not flee, and without being able to fight (all his men having fled), he being alone was put to death.
(Brut y Tywysogyon)

Retribution followed swiftly, with Maredudd ap Bleddyn capturing the assassin who was delivered to Owain ap Cadwgan. He then quickly settled the score, blinding and castrating Madog, a punishment noted by contemporaries as being 'kind', as opposed to death! The mutilators then shared Madog's territory in Powys.

On hearing of Cadwgan's untimely death, Henry I, no doubt requiring a strong leader, reinstated Owain as ruler of Powys. The chronicles show that Owain accompanied Henry on an expedition to Normandy about 1112, where he was knighted for service to the King.

Sir Owain's fate was sealed in 1116. Whilst on a mission for the King to subdue a rebellion in South Wales, he was killed by the arrow of a Flemish soldier in the employ of no other than Gerald de Windsor. Revenge had been enacted.

Owain's brother Einion succeeded as Prince of Powys, supported by his brothers Madog and Maredudd and their uncle Maredudd ap Bleddyn. The death of Owain must have prompted Cadwgan's vassal Uchdryd ap Edwin to break his vow of homage and claim the territory of Merioneth as an independent lord. This clearly was unacceptable to Einion, and with the assistance of his cousin Gruffudd ap Maredudd, they swept across the country attacking Uchdryd's castle at Cymer near Dolgellau and sending him fleeing to Chester to seek safe refuge with the Normans.

Einion seems to have based himself in Merioneth after this time until his death in 1124, when disputing factions caused Gruffudd ap Cynan to send his sons, Cadwaladr and Owain, to annex the territory.

In a generation, virtually the whole of Cadwgan's family had been exterminated. It had been a bloodbath on an unprecedented scale and the self-destruction was almost complete.

The dynasty sank to an all time low in 1125 when Maredudd ap Cadwgan was killed by his own brother Morgan as a result of a quarrel. The murder weighed so heavily on Morgan's conscience that he embarked on a penitential pilgrimage to Jerusalem, dying in Limassol, Cyprus, on the journey home in 1128.

Maredudd ap Bleddyn's family took over control of Powys with little opposition from family rivals.

2

1129-1400

FOUNDATIONS OF THE HOUSE OF NANNAU

With the demise of Cadwgan ap Bleddyn, Wales had lost a decisive figure in the fight against the Norman invader. The *Anglo-Saxon Chronicle* stated that:

the Welsh ... chose many leaders from among themselves, one of them was called Cadwgan, who was the finest of them.

He was the undisputed leader and architect of the rebellion against Norman rule certainly, but less formidable in his ability to curb the family violence that plagued the end of his reign.

Upon his death in 1124, Cadwgan's son Einion had bequeathed Merioneth and parts of Powys to his brother Maredudd, but enjoyment of his inheritance was to be short lived as his uncle Maredudd ap Bleddyn aggressively annexed his territory. On hearing of Maredudd ap Bleddyn's actions, Gruffudd ap Cynan dispatched a 'mighty host' into Merioneth under the command of his sons Cadwallon and Owain Gwynedd. Maredudd was decisively weakened, but it would take a few more years before Merioneth and the lordship would be back in the hands of the Princes of

Gwynedd. The death of Maredudd ap Cadwgan in 1125, slaughtered by his own brother Morgan, was no doubt precipitated by the family's loss of lands.

Madog ap Cadwgan was now the sole Welsh survivor of Cadwgan's sons. He does not seem to have taken part in the expulsion of Uchdryd ap Edwin from Merioneth in 1116; that seems to have been carried out by his brother Einion and his cousin Gruffudd ap Maredudd. The two cousins shared Uchdryd's lands: Einion received Merioneth and half of Penllyn; Maredudd received Cyfeiliog, Mawddwy and the remainder of Penllyn.

We now enter a period of family history where the historical record is very limited and one has to resort to careful scrutiny of the genealogical record in an attempt to follow the intrigue and subterfuge. No mention is made of Madog ap Cadwgan receiving any portion of the spoils after the ejectment of Uchdryd, but he is later styled as 'Lord of Nannau', whilst his brother Einion is 'Lord of Merioneth'. This attribution effectively establishes Madog ap Cadwgan as the first Lord of Nannau.

After the annexation of Merioneth by Gwynedd in 1124, it is likely that Madog ap Cadwgan or his son Cadwgan ap Madog, made a pact with the Gwynedd dynasty, and the family tree gives a snapshot of the intricacies of these dynastic alliances.

Revealingly, it can be seen that Cadwgan ap Madog married Gwenllian, a daughter of Owain Gwynedd, thus entering into a pact with the conqueror. The aggression of his uncle Maredudd ap Bleddyn was the probable catalyst for such a union. With the existence of such an alliance, Cadwgan ap Madog and his father were brought into the orbit of Owain Gwynedd, and possibly fought alongside him and his family. Owain was an effective military leader, adept at controlling his headstrong warrior sons. He

made intelligent use of his resources, relying on the skills and loyalty of his family to control lands in Merionydd and Ceredigion.
(Kari Maund, 2000)

*19. above: **Cymer Castle, 1.5km north of Dolgellau - site of Uchdryd ap Edwin's stronghold.** (Inset - close-up of 18th-century summerhouse associated with the Hengwrt estate)*

By allowing his son-in-law Cadwgan ap Madog to control a portion of his territory in Merioneth, as Lord of Nannau, he had shrewdly placed a family member who had a natural distrust of the neighbouring Powys dynasty. Owain was living up to his reputation as a skillful governor and diplomat. The fact that he responded swiftly to family dissension with the removal of territories, meant that he kept his family in line. His legacy was a strong and stable kingdom, as opposed to Powys, which was becoming increasingly fragmented. Merioneth would be held as a vassal lordship of Gwynedd, occupied by major

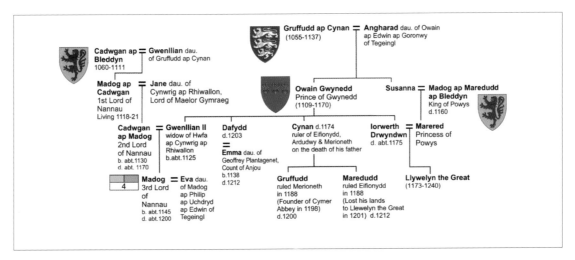

members of the dynasty, and considered strategically important to Gwynedd in the defence of its kingdom. Later castles built in this area, such as Castell y Bere, demonstrate the significance of this territory.

Cadwgan's son Madog likewise made a desirable marriage, his wife Eva being the great-granddaughter of Uchdryd ap Edwin, the vassal Lord of Merioneth created by Cadwgan ap Bleddyn. Eva was Uchdryd's heiress and a union would have conferred Madog with lands in the Cymer area, and of course, in the vicinity of Nannau. Madog would have been in a fairly secure position, with lands in Cymer and with a mother who was daughter of Owain Gwynedd himself. He now had a foothold in the scattered 'gwely' lands of Nannau and was on course to establish the beginnings of an estate. Cadwgan ap Bleddyn's family had carried out the first of many fortuitous marriages that would in future result in the family gaining control of vast land holdings.

During the tenure of Meurig ap Madog, 4th Lord of Nannau, the Cistercian Abbey of Cymer was founded under the patronage of Maredudd ap Cynan, the then Lord of Merioneth. Maredudd was a grandson of Owain Gwynedd and cousin to both Meurig ap Madog of Nannau and Llywelyn the Great. The *Chronicle of the Princes* outlined that:

> *in that year (1198) a community from Cwm-hir went to reside at Cymer in Nannau in Merionydd.*

This community was of Cistercian monks from the Abbey of Cwmhir, who Maredudd ap Cynan had possibly induced to set up a new foundation. Later, in his capacity as Lord of Lleyn, he further endowed Cymer Abbey with lands in the Lleyn Peninsula at Neigwl and elsewhere. Other benefactors of the abbey included Prince Llywelyn ap Iorwerth (Llywelyn the Great) and Gwenwynwyn, Lord of Lower Powys. Generations of the Nannau family would associate themselves with this peaceful abbey, situated in the beautiful Mawddach estuary, one and a half miles north west of Dolgellau.

Sometime in the mid-12th century, Merioneth, in common with other parts of Wales, witnessed a fundamental change as far as its population was concerned. This change was possibly orchestrated

21. above: **Artist's impression of Cymer Abbey in the 13th century** *(Robert Nanney Williams - 2012)*

by a number of Welsh princes, who were known to have encouraged free tribesmen to change their lifestyle from being nomadic to living a settled existence. Princes were known to have given lands to their followers and their descendants, but the ownership would be devolved to the family as a whole, not to individuals, and became known as a 'gwely', literally a resting place. These freemen began, in family groupings, to settle upland areas. The Nannau Township was to become such a settlement, occupied by one extended family and destined to be the largest populated township in Merioneth by the time of the Edwardian conquest. These nomadic freemen chose sparsely populated areas to settle. Nannau was certainly sparsely populated before their arrival; indeed the *Chronicle of the Princes* alludes to Merioneth, after 1124, as being totally desolate. As mentioned previously, Gruffudd ap Cynan was known to have sent his sons Cadwallon and Owain Gwynedd with a 'mighty host' into Merioneth where they

carried off all the people of that land and all their chattels with them into Llyn.

The term 'gwely' is allocated to landholdings owned by people bound together by common blood relationships, all of free status. They initially established themselves around the original settlement of the common ancestor, adjacent lands becoming enclosed and farmed. When the head of a family died, his wealth and land was subdivided equally among all his sons, and later grandsons. After four generations new family groupings were formed and land redistributed. This often led to the fragmenting of land holdings and the only way to increase your land was to bring into cultivation previously wild areas. Increasing your holding by purchase was impossible as the selling of gwely land was forbidden. Knowing your family's tree was a vital pre-requisite to claiming your rightful inheritance, hence the Welsh preoccupation with genealogy.

Cadwgan ap Madog and his son Madog were established in the Nannau Township precisely when this change from nomadic to permanent

settlement took place. It is likely that the settlement of Nannau developed from the extended family of Cadwgan ap Madog, and this original settlement became the sprawling mass of seventy tythynods (small holdings), all with a common ancestor. Amongst one of these units was Tythyn Cefn Llanfair, which in Tudor time would become the site of Plas Nannau, the centre of an expanding estate.

Meurig, the 4th Lord of Nannau, is a historically elusive character, with the exception of his marriage to Gwenllian, daughter of Iorwerth ap Peredur ap Ednywain ap Bradwen. Gwenllian's great-grandfather was Lord of Merioneth, having married Margred, daughter of Cynan ap Owain Gwynedd - further proof of Owain Gwynedd's strategy of placing his family as vassal lords of Merioneth. Ednywain ap Bradwen is acknowledged as the founder of the '15th noble tribe' of North Wales and the ruins of 'Llys Bradwen', his father's court, are clearly visible today in Cregennan, near Dolgellau.

Ynyr, the 5th Lord of Nannau, is often referred to as Ynyr Hên (old Ynyr) to distinguish him from his son, Ynyr Fychan. He 'exists' only as a name in a dusty manuscript, but his legacy lives on in the extraordinary lives of his offspring, a son who was destined to become one of the greatest of all the medieval Welsh bishops, and a grandson who became a poet of national renown. It is likely that Ynyr Hên kept a low profile in these turbulent times. In 1256 he would have seen the rightful heir of the Lordship of Merioneth ejected by Llywelyn ap Gruffudd (Llywelyn the Last) for betraying him to the English. No doubt as Lord of Nannau, Ynyr would have felt more vulnerable than previous members of his family who had secured marriages with Gwynedd princesses. Ynyr's family links to Llywelyn were much more distant, although it is evident that Ynyr's wife Gwerful was a second cousin to Llywelyn the Last.

Ynyr Fychan, the 6th Lord of Nannau, was head of the family at the time of the Edwardian conquest. He was the first of the family to be authenticated by archival records, allowing us to track his activities in this important phase of estate building. Ynyr, as was typical of his class, joined a large body of noble familes who worked with the English administration. He was astute enough to realise that cooperation with the new regime would benefit his family, laying a firm foundation for the future prosperity of the Nannau dynasty.

Edward I is thought to have issued a proclamation that all who submitted to him would retain their lands. Ynyr Fychan is known to have been one of the local tribal leaders who paid homage to Edward in May 1295 when the King visited Dolgellau.

To reap the benefits of cooperation with the Crown, Ynyr needed to join the 'elite'

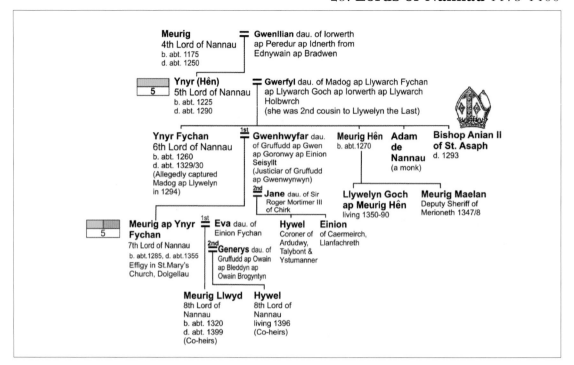

office-holding class, and secure one of the posts such as 'rhaglaw'. In 1295 Ynyr seized the opportunity for betterment by claiming that he had been the captor of the rebellious Madog ap Llywelyn, and that he had been promised the Rhaglawry of Talybont rent-free as a reward for this loyal act.

The previous year Madog ap Llywelyn had risen up in revolt against the oppressive English rule in Wales. Madog was a direct descendant of the Lords of Merioneth, and had served Edward I faithfully. He naturally expected to be reinstated with his ancestral lands, but found himself instead palmed off with a small landholding in Anglesey. He obviously bitterly resented this and used his personal grievance to enact revenge by leading the rising against the English. The time was right; the country was ready for revolt and Madog, as a direct descendant of Owain Gwynedd, became its natural leader.

The first thrust of the rebellion began in Anglesey and quickly spread to Caernarfon, the administrative centre of Edward's Principality, where the rebels seized and burnt important

documents and records. The town walls and castle defences were destroyed and Sir Roger de Puleston, the less-than-popular sheriff, was allegedly hanged in the doorway of his own house.

The rising spread to the Conway valley, with vicious attacks on the Welsh who were known to have cooperated with the English administration. Edward was not taking this lightly; he had been informed of the rebellion whilst waiting at Portsmouth for a favourable wind to sail to France. He completely changed his plans, intent on crushing the rebellion that had already destroyed one of his castles.

Madog's rebel force was now safely ensconced in Snowdonia waiting for the expected retaliation. Edward, taking personal command of the situation, arrived at Chester on the 5th December 1294 where his large forces were to muster. On the 8th December, he led his army into Wales, arriving at Conway on the 26th December with little opposition. After enjoying the Christmas festivities, the army commenced their advance to Bangor. For some unknown reason Edward retreated to Conway, possibly thinking that his

24. right: *A stone bridge that leads to 'Llys Bradwen',
the remains of the residence of Ednywain ap
Bradwen, a 12ᵗʰ-century Welsh chieftain*

advance force might be compromised. He took refuge in the castle, but not before the rebels had attacked and captured vital supplies. Edward's situation was dire: he was held up in Conway Castle, separated from the main bulk of his army due to the flooded river, and devoid of food and resources. The flood subsided and Edward rejoined his army but the offensive was not started again until the following April, when a major effort was made to bolster the castles of Criccieth and Harlech in preparation for a renewed invasion.

Madog, by the beginning of 1295, had moved his army southwards, only to encounter William Beauchamp, the Earl of Warwick. Their forces met at the Battle of Maesmadog in Caereinion. Madog was decisively crushed and became a fugitive, hunted from pillar to post. Edward was to continue his incursions, but with no more Welsh resistance. In order to ensure that Anglesey would not be overrun again, he set about building the castle at Beaumaris.

Meanwhile, Madog had been tracked down to a dense wood in Ardudwy, but he managed to evade capture on this occasion. He had returned to his home territory, but, unfortunately for him, it was also Ynyr Fychan's territory. Edward left Anglesey, arriving in Dolgellau on the 12ᵗʰ May 1295, and received the homage of the nobles of Merioneth. Edward left the Principality with Madog very much at large, but with a five hundred marks reward for his capture.

The rebel Madog was in captivity by the first week of August 1295. Records show that he was still imprisoned in the Tower of London in 1312. Ynyr Fychan's claim to have captured Madog is entirely feasible: he seemingly did not hesitate to promote himself at the expense of Madog ap Llywelyn. Considering the petitions made by contingents of Merioneth men repudiating Madog, others were also well disposed to betray his cause. Ynyr Fychan's claim for the post of rhaglaw by virtue of a reward was initially unsuccessful, but miraculously by 1304 an 'Eyngon

Vagghan' was named in the sheriff's account for Merioneth as Rhaglaw of Talybont, and he held it until 1329/30, when his own son Meurig Fychan took over.

Ynyr Fychan's second marriage is something of an enigma, in that he married Jane, the daughter of Sir Roger Mortimer III of Chirk. Historical accounts reveal that Ynyr's allegiances lay firmly with the King, having taken part in an attack on the town of Ruthin in 1322, with Sir Gruffudd Llwyd, the Sheriff of Merioneth and a contingent of county men. What is surprising is that whilst Ynyr was aiding the King through his actions, his father-in-law was the leader of an anti-royalist faction, family ties clearly losing precedence over alignment with the Crown. Ynyr had realised that his future lay in unwavering royal allegiance, a strategy that would assist the family's rise to prominence, but on occasion would be catastrophic. Ynyr's great-grandson would pay the ultimate price for his support of the English Crown.

THE BLACK BROTHER of Nannau

Whilst Ynyr Fychan was carving a niche for himself at the county level, his brother Einion was becoming a major player at a national level. Having followed an ecclesiastical career, Einion, better known as Anian II, or the 'Black Brother of Nannau,' rose to prominence in the latter half of the 13ᵗʰ century as the Bishop of St. Asaph.

Anian's upbringing at Nannau would no doubt have brought him into contact with the brethren at Cymer Abbey and possibly it was they who inspired him to take his chosen path. He was known to have joined the newly established

25. *above:* **The rugged landscape of Llys Bradwen, near Arthog, Merioneth**

Dominican friary at Rhuddlan with his brother Adam de Nannau. On the 21st October 1268, Anian, now the Prior of Rhuddlan, was consecrated Bishop of St. Asaph at Southwark by Bishop Boniface, Archbishop of Canterbury.

At the time of his elevation the diocese was under the control of Prince Llywelyn ap Gruffudd, the Last Prince of Wales. Anian and the Prince were initially on amicable terms, but Llywelyn was yet to witness Anian's wrath when his bishopric was in any way threatened. By the end of 1273, the relationship had soured, Anian having reportedly made representations to Pope Gregory X accusing Llywelyn of interfering with matters that lay within the jurisdiction of the ecclesiastical courts, and depriving the Church of its rights. Llywelyn vigorously denied the accusations and elicited the support of abbots from seven of the Welsh

Cistercian houses who all protested Llywelyn's innocence to the Pope. Anian's relationship with Llywelyn was at an all time low, and by January 1276 it appears that Anian sought the support of Edward I. Anian was now becoming embroiled in the increasingly bitter relations that were developing between the King and Llywelyn. Anian's presence at the declaration of war against Llywelyn, issued on the 17th November 1276, was a telling indicator of his allegiance. Llywelyn was declared a rebel and Anian returned to St. Asaph and put his hand to a further catalogue of grievances against the Prince.

The subsequent Treaty of Conway, on the 9th November 1277, removed Anian's diocese from the control of Llywelyn to the Crown. Anian's dealings would henceforth be with Edward I. No longer in dispute over rival interests, Anian

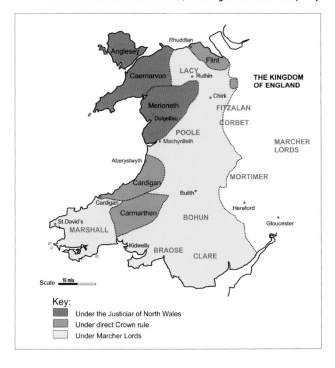

Rhuddlan

Anglesey

Flint

LACY

Caernarvon · Ruthin

THE KINGDOM
OF ENGLAND

· Chirk

FITZALAN

Merioneth

Dolgellau

CORBET

POOLE

· Machynlleth

MARCHER
LORDS

Aberystwyth

MORTIMER

Cardigan

Builth ·

Cardigan

Hereford ·

Carmarthen

BOHUN

St.David's

Gloucester ·

MARSHALL

Kidwelly

BRAOSE

CLARE

Scale 10 mls

Key:

▪ Under the Justiciar of North Wales
▪ Under direct Crown rule
☐ Under Marcher Lords

and Llywelyn returned to a more amicable understanding, with Anian acting as intermediary for Llywelyn on a number of occasions.

At the outbreak of the Welsh war in 1282, St. Asaph was burnt to the ground by English soldiers in the bitter fighting. Anian responded angrily, immediately quitting his diocese and further refusing to excommunicate Llywelyn for his actions. This earned him the wrath of Edward, who now suspected Anian of being a rebel sympathiser and who ordered the immediate confiscation of his property. Even the tragic downfall of Llywelyn did not see Anian restored to his diocese. It took the diligent diplomacy of Archbishop Peckham to return the bishop to his beloved See, which was accomplished in 1284. Anian eventually received a small grant from Edward to rebuild the damaged cathedral along with the return of his personal property.

Anian II died on the 5th February 1293. He had been a strong personality of noteworthy intentions, totally dedicated to the interests of his diocese against any possible threat. He was a

27. below: **Southerly view of Conway Castle**

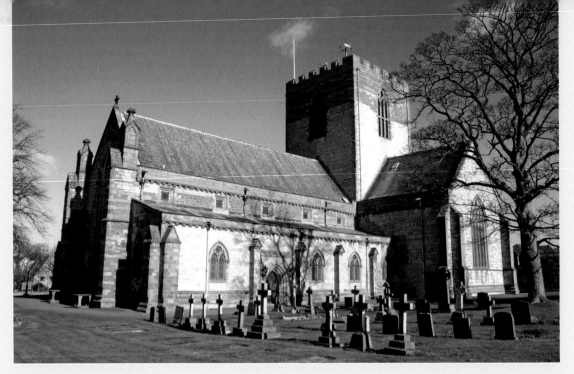

28. above: **St. Asaph's Cathedral, the earliest part dating to the 13th century**

politically adept bishop who had walked the tightrope between two of the most powerful individuals of the era, Edward I and Llywelyn the Last, and in this tenuous process, had probably earned the respect of both.

In accordance with his will, he was buried at the Dominican friary at Rhuddlan, his brother Adam de Nannau being one of his executors. He died a wealthy individual, giving much of his wealth away to worthy causes, mostly, as one would expect, ecclesiastical.

In his will Anian II bequeathed:

- *to King Edward, one of his palfreys, and another to the Archbishop of Canterbury;*
- *to Griffith, Archdeacon of St. Asaph, one of his best colts and a silver cup;*
- *to Adam de Nannew (his brother), his Bible;*
- *the rest of his theological books to the Friars Preachers;*
- *the silver vessels of his kitchen to the fabric of the Church of St. Asaph;*

- *a third part of his corn & c. in granary to be distributed between the fabric of the Church of St. Asaph and Bangor, the Friars Preachers and Minor of the Dioceses of St. Asaph and Bangor; the remainder to his poor relations and other poor persons of the Diocese of St. Asaph;*

- *growing crops to pious uses and to poor persons of Wales at the discretion of his executors;*

- *various money (marks) to religious orders;*

- *100 cows to be distributed amongst his servants, according to their respective length of service;*

- *100 cattle (veria consimilia) to be distributed amongst his poor relations;*

- *his stud of horses to the work (opera) of the Church of St. Asaph;*

- *his pigs to his poor relations;*

- *to the White Nuns of Brewode, eight oxen.*

The Will was proved 1st May 1293, before Prior Henry of Eastry, in the Church of St. Mary at Bow.

It is interesting to note that Anian's name appears in the Lay Subsidy for Talybont of 1292/3, where he was evidently leasing lands in Brithdir from Cymer Abbey, the tax being paid on moveable goods, in this case livestock. Anian paid four times as much tax as the Abbot of Cymer, an indicator of the amount of livestock, and the amount of land leased. He must have leased virtually the whole of the Abbey grange at Brithdir Uchaf and other nearby lands. Anian's presence as lessee of Cymer Abbey lands demonstrates that, from the 13th century, the descendants of Cadwgan ap Bleddyn were already taking advantage of monastic lands in their area; subsequent centuries would see them acquired freehold.

Anian's bequest of cattle and pigs to his poor relations could possibly appertain to his family at Nannau - although gaining in stature at the time, they were certainly poor compared to Anian. Such a bequest would have made a considerable difference to the family, at a time when wealth equated to the quality and number of livestock a person owned. Anian II's effigy lies proudly on a stone plinth in the south aisle of his beloved cathedral, as a proud testament to his achievements. This remarkable stone edifice is regarded as one of the finest pieces of medieval carving to survive in North Wales and is a worthy tribute to the 'Black Brother of Nannau', son of Ynyr Hên, the 5th Lord of Nannau.

A KNIGHT in armour

Ynyr Fychan's son Meurig, 7th Lord of Nannau, followed his father's example and cooperated with the English administration, taking over the office of Rhaglaw of Talybont in 1332, a post which he held until 1340. It is also noted that he received the Bailiwick of the bond vill of Dolgellau in 1338. Consolidating the family's hold on Crown offices, Meurig's brother Hywel held the post of Coroner of Ardudwy, Talybont and Ystumanner from 1337 to 1343, and Meurig's cousin, Meurig Maelan, topped the family's achievements by being elected as Deputy Sheriff of Merioneth in 1347/8.

Although busily acquiring minor crown offices, Meurig found time to cultivate an important marriage alliance by marrying Generys, the daughter of Gruffudd ap Owain Bleddyn of Dinmael (son of Owain Brogyntyn, a member of the Powys ruling dynasty). Whilst on one hand increasing their wealth and position in society, the Nannau family was not yet the greatest freeholder in the township. They had seen their estate fragment as both Ynyr Fychan and Meurig's generation each split their patrimony amongst six sons. The serious accumulation of land, which was to form the foundation of the Nannau estate, was yet to occur; subsequent generations with only one son to inherit would fortuitously leave undivided successions.

Meurig ap Ynyr Fychan's public life is clearly established through surviving records. His personal life, however, is shrouded in mystery and poses somewhat of a dilemma. His fine recumbent effigy survives to this day, lying in a window sill of St. Mary's Church, Dolgellau. He is depicted as a warrior, clad in the medieval armour of his day. Edward Lhuyd the antiquarian is known to have visited St. Mary's Church in 1698, before the church was rebuilt in its present form in 1716. He described the effigy as standing under an arch on the north side of the chancel. The effigy is one of the oldest found in North Wales, dated to around 1345. One may wonder why he was represented as a warrior? The answer may lie in the exploits of his father, Ynyr Fychan. Ynyr, as mentioned previously, was involved in the attack on Ruthin in 1322. An entry in the Close and Patent Roll of 14th February 1322 calls for a

commission to Griffin ap Rees and Giles de Bello Campo to array 2,200 footmen in the following counties, viz. 800 in Angleseye, 800 in Karnarvan, and 600 in Merionyth, and to march them to Coventry to the King by Friday after the first Sunday in Lent for service against the Scots and rebels.

Sir Gruffudd Llwyd was known to have led a force of some 1,907 men from the counties mentioned above. It is likely that Ynyr or possibly

his son Meurig took part in this campaign, hence the military effigy. The 1322 Scottish campaign led by Edward II ended in a crushing defeat of the huge English army at the Battle of Byland. As both Ynyr and Meurig continued as loyal crown representatives, they must have survived the onslaught.

Certain tenuous references seem to show that Meurig ap Ynyr's son, Meurig Llwyd, may have been born in Pas-de-Calais in France, circa 1320. If this is correct, Meurig ap Ynyr could well have fought for the King at the onset of the Hundred Years War.

Close scrutiny of Meurig ap Ynyr's effigy also reveals further interesting possibilities, in that the medieval stone carver was bound by rigid rules as to how the individual should be represented in the effigy. Of particular interest is the depiction of his sword, this being unsheathed and held across the thighs. According to the medieval convention, such a depiction would indicate an individual who

died victoriously in battle. Nobles were also allowed this depiction if they died in their own lordship, as was probably the case with Meurig ap Ynyr Fychan.

A further anomaly exists: why is Meurig ap Ynyr Fychan's effigy in Dolgellau Church? Considering the Nannau family links with Cymer Abbey, surely this location would be a more fitting resting place for our illustrious warrior! There are several examples of 14th-century effigies known to have been located in Cistercian monasteries, but perhaps because of the dissolution, were moved to the safety of nearby parish churches. Gruffudd ap Llywelyn ap Ynyr's effigy circa 1320, now in the Church of St. Garmon, Llanarmon-yn-Ial, Denbighshire, was originally located in the Cistercian Abbey of Valle Crucis. A final tantalising shred of evidence exists in an ancient record which recalls that:

the Abbot of Bardsey, placed him (Meurig) together with his wife, parents and issue under the special protection of the holy place.
(Arch. Camb.,1860)

Meurig ap Ynyr Fychan must have been a pious man and it would seem not indisposed to purchasing such temporalities. By seeking burial at Cymer Abbey, through some beneficial means, Meurig would have secured the monks to pray for him in perpetuity. The fact that subsequent members of the Nannau family, in the 15th century, chose Cymer Abbey as the family's preferred burial location adds weight to the suggestion that Meurig ap Ynyr possibly initiated this trend.

Of the six sons of Meurig ap Ynyr Fychan, only two rise to historical prominence: Meurig Llwyd and Hywel, both Lords of Nannau. These brothers were noted patrons of the bards in the latter part of the 14th century.

THE BEGININGS OF NANNAU'S
bardic traditions

With the demise of the Welsh princes, the courtly poets turned their attention to the 'uchelwyr', the men of noble birth, and sought patronage from this surviving class of Welsh nobility. They practiced 'Clera', the name given to the practice of plying their skill between these illustrious households in an attempt to earn a living through the practice of their art. Nannau was well known for the magnificent hospitality awarded to these itinerant bards, with the Nannau brothers, Meurig Llwyd and Hywel, being particularly benevolent.

33. below: **Meurig ap Ynyr Fychan's stone effigy in St. Mary's Church, Dolgellau**

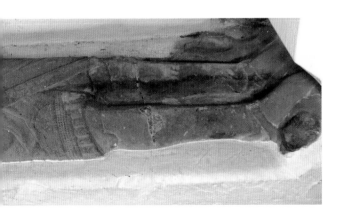

34. below: **Plan of St. Mary's Church, Dolgellau, with location of Nanney memorials**

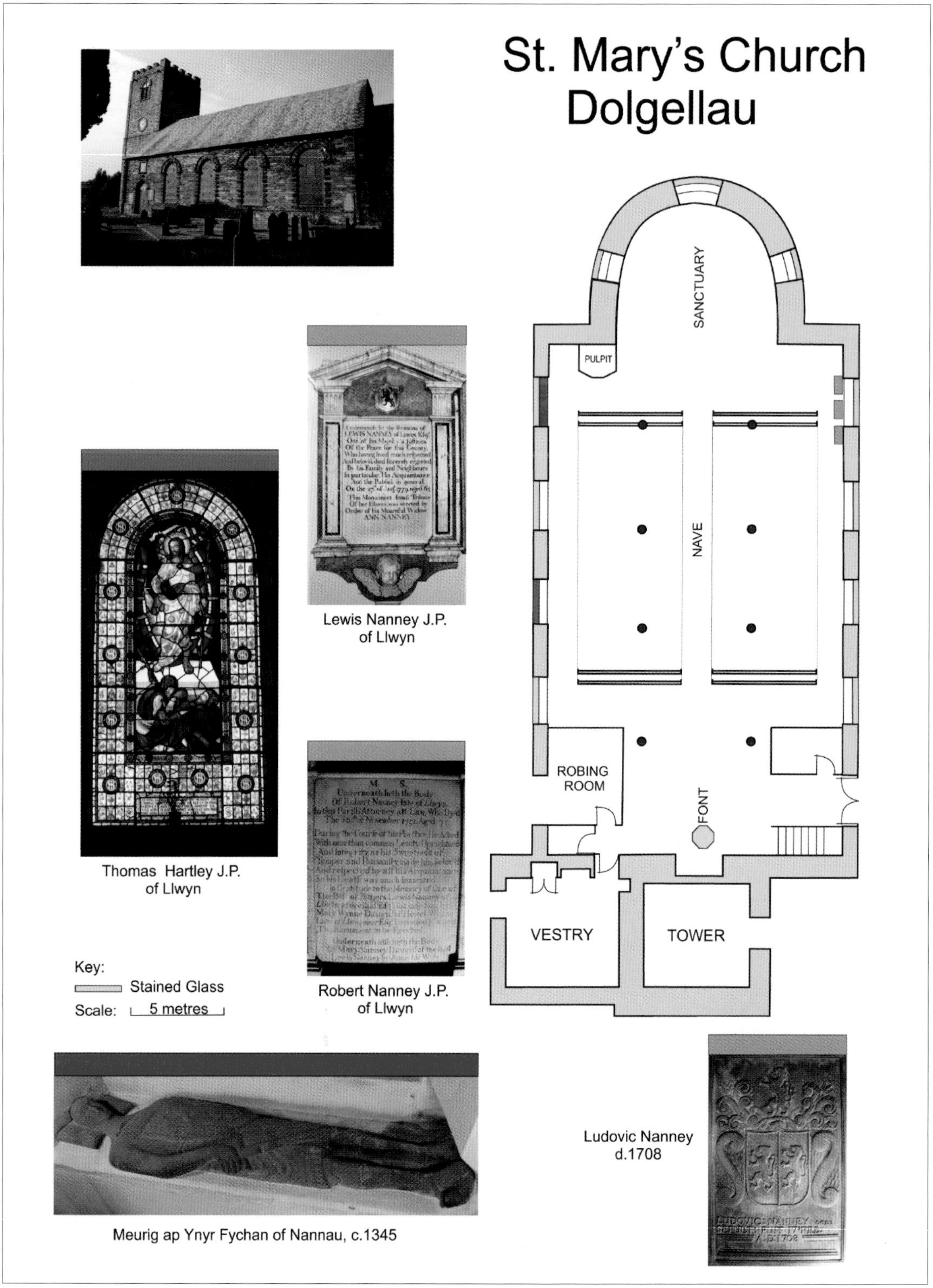
St. Mary's Church
Dolgellau
SANCTUARY
PULPIT
NAVE
ROBING ROOM
FONT
VESTRY
TOWER
Lewis Nanney J.P. of Llwyn
Thomas Hartley J.P. of Llwyn
Robert Nanney J.P. of Llwyn
Key:
Stained Glass
Scale: 5 metres
Meurig ap Ynyr Fychan of Nannau, c.1345
Ludovic Nanney d.1708

The Powys poet, Gruffudd Llwyd noted that:

It is easy for me to give a greeting,
It was my treasure, in exchange for much gold;
And easily did they give me
Ample gold on the edge of the hill.
It is blameless for me, when I consider it, to
receive
Good in exchange for good, I am a man without
sadness,
I receive gold from Meurig's sons
Without an hour's vexation.
I received their bountiful gifts,
They get a greeting from their poet.

There was no need for the brothers to trawl far for poets to heap praise on the family as they had within their ranks a poet of national significance, their uncle, Llywelyn Goch ap Meurig Hên. Llywelyn is widely regarded as one of the best poets of the 14th century, and it is entirely possible that some of his most beautiful elegies were composed whilst staying at Nannau.

Llywelyn is best known for his famous eulogy written on the death of his lover, Lleucu Llwyd of Pennal near Machynlleth, a celebrated beauty of her time. This eulogy has been aptly described as having 'art in every line' and is profoundly moving. The beautiful Lleucu Llwyd was the beloved of the bard Llywelyn Goch ap Meurig Hên, but her father objected to the match. When Llywelyn was away, possibly eliciting patrons, the scheming father convinced his daughter that her lover had married someone else. The poor girl, beside herself with grief, pined away and died. Llywelyn then returned hoping to marry her, but tragically found her dead. He spent hours at her graveside composing what has become one of the most beautiful elegies in the Welsh language.

An indicator of the powerful nature of the eulogy is evident from the following extract:

Beauteous lady bound in oak,
Angry purpose, dusty cloak,
Gwynedd's candle her image,
Hours of the grave her age,
My soul, rise upward once more,
Open darkest earthen door,
Don't lie there in the dirt and cold,
Face to face please be as old.
Longing for our bygone days,
Above your grave the sun's rays,
And ashen faced without you.
Llywelyn Goch tolls your due,
Grieving bard, adversity,
The passion and the pity.
I am more and more your slave,
Two days since, above your grave,
My tears torrents falling,
On its cold face a taught string.
You my beauty are silent,
Caverned life from body rent.

(Translated by Dr. Myron Evans)

This poem, amongst others, clearly established Llywelyn as a love poet, his work being hugely popular in 14th-century society. Llywelyn was also the bardic teacher of Iolo Goch, who was harpist and poet to Owain Glyndŵr.

Through Llywelyn's work we gain glimpses of the characters of his nephews, Meurig Llwyd and Hywel:

their common delights – reading the law, and
the old Welsh chronicles, playing on the crwth,
and following greyhounds.

Of the life in a late medieval court we witness:

This is my task with my lords,
And I am also their aged relative:
To read civil law to my kinsmen
(There is need of a fluent voice);
To dress myself in their fine gifts,
Green clothing from the splendid hand of each;

To satirise loudly that furious crew,
You can hear their commotion, the dunghill
minstrels;
Gift after gift I've received,
Earnestly comparing my love, Lleucu Llwyd,
To a fair, blooming rose in a beautiful garden,
To the noble Virgin Mary, or to the brilliant
sun.
It's delightful for this scrawny old man
(There is a good time to be had on Sunday)
To hear the sounds which Christmas brings:
Cooks slicing into meat,
Barking of shaggy hunting dogs, I know for
sure,
Straining at their chains,
The harmony of the lively crwth and the
bagpipes,
The voices of peacocks in unison,
And the Sanctus bells, and laughter,
And the calling of men to wine.

Llywelyn Goch ap Meuring Hên

(Translated by the Centre for Advanced
Welsh & Celtic Studies)

Both Meurig Llwyd and Hywel each named one of their daughters Lleucu, illustrating a mark of respect for their now famous uncle and his unrequited love. In St. Eurgain and St. Peter's Church, Northop, Denbighshire, local tradition has it that an effigy of a medieval lady is a depiction of Lleucu Llwyd. Both Meurig Llwyd and Hywel are known to have died around 1400, leaving Meurig's son Hywel Sele as the 9th Lord of Nannau at the onset of the Glyndŵr rebellion.

36. above: **Close-up of 'Lleucu Llwyd's' face**

37. right: **St. Eurgain and St. Peter's Church, Northop**

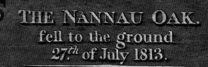

THE NANNAU OAK.
fell to the ground
27th of July 1813.

This frame is made of the real wood.

Sketched by Sir Richd C. Hoare.
on the morning preceding
the night on which it fell.

·209·

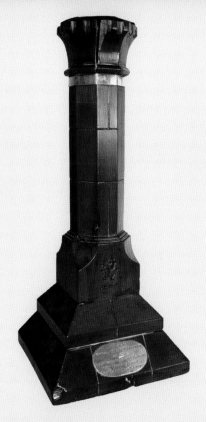

3

1401-1402

NANNAU'S BLASTED OAK

Meurig Llwyd's son, Hywel Sele, the 9th Lord of Nannau, continued the family's links with the English administration, holding various local offices, being granted the Farm of the Amobor of Talybont and the Piscary (fishing rights) of Barmouth in 1399/1400 at a rent of £7 a year. Hywel Sele's father, grandfather and uncle had all served the Crown through minor offices, and evidently Hywel was intent on following the family line. His marriage to Mali, the daughter of Einion ap Gruffudd of Corsygedol, Sheriff of Merioneth, helped to propel Hywel to the pinnacle of local gentry. His social climbing however would be tragically curtailed in brutal circumstances so very typical of the times.

Lack of documentary evidence has not prevented Hywel Sele achieving notoriety, his name being immortalised in a romantic legend that surrounds his involvement with his distant cousin, the legendary Owain Glyndŵr.

Hywel Sele, in common with many members of the gentry, was wary of the revolt led by Glyndŵr and was unwilling to take up arms against the Crown. Two powerful local lords holding such diverse loyalties, one a Lancastrian the other a staunch Yorkist, would invariably collide, as was the case in 1401 when our tragic tale begins.

In June of 1401, Henry Hotspur, the Governor of North Wales, marched into Merioneth and confronted Glyndŵr's forces near Cader Idris. Hotspur was to retreat unsuccessfully, but it is believed that Hywel Sele had been complicit in inviting him to the area. Glyndŵr's retaliation was swift and brutal, attacking his antagonistic cousin's house at Nannau, burning it to the ground and carrying off its beleaguered lord.

The defiant Sele would have been a thorn in Glyndŵr's side, in the very heart of his territory. Sele was well connected and of similar princely descent and seemingly a threat that needed to be neutralised. The act of burning the house of a 'traitor' was a common ploy used by Glyndŵr when dealing with individuals who supported the Crown. By taking his kinsman a prisoner, one could deduce that he hoped to change Sele's mind and have him agree to join the rebellion.

40. *above:* **Llanelltyd Bridge, scene of the encounter where Hywel Sele's son-in-law tried to to rescue him from Owain Glyndŵr**

Hywel's plight was comprehensively outlined in *The Story of Two Parishes: Dolgelley & Llanelltyd* by T.P. Ellis, published in 1928. In it he describes the aftermath of the battle with Hotspur near Dolgellau:

> *In the meantime, Glyndŵr was dealing with Hywel Sele. As he was a dangerous man to be at liberty, Glyndŵr determined on capturing him; and in the beginning of 1402 he collected a few men together, attacked Nannau suddenly, and made Hywel Sele a prisoner. Returning to Dolgelley by the road north of Moel Cynwch, and down to the Ganllwyd valley, Glyndŵr found his way blocked at Llanelltyd bridge by Griffith ap Gwyn, the son-in-law of Hywel Sele, who had come down by a short cut with 200 men to rescue the captive. A terrible fight took*

41. *above:* **Close-up of Owain Glyndŵr's magnificent statue at Corwen**

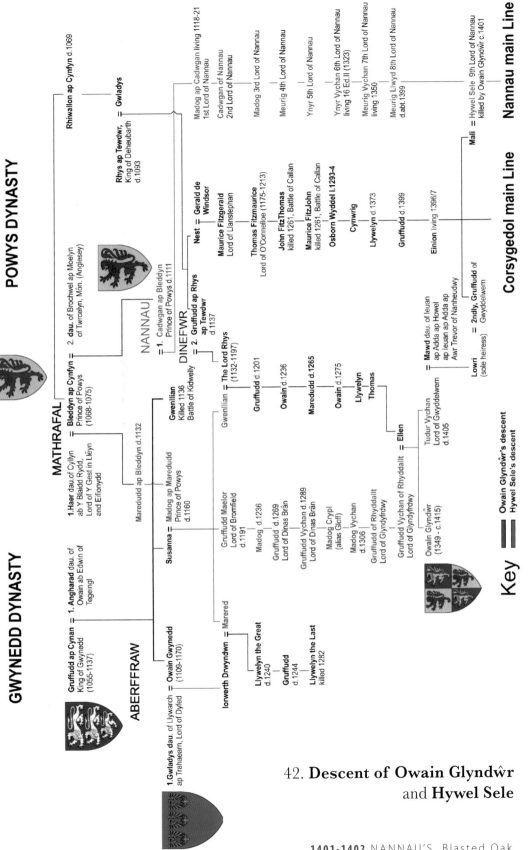

42. **Descent of Owain Glyndŵr**
and **Hywel Sele**

hollow trunk of an old oak tree, inside which it remained for something like 40 years. For centuries after the tree was looked upon as haunted, and it was known as Ceubren yr Ellyll, the Hollow Tree of the Ghost, and no one would go near it at night.

It was blown down at last in a terrible storm on the night of the 27th July 1813, when its trunk, three feet from the ground, was found to measure 27 feet in circumference. Its site, in the kitchen garden of Nannau, is still marked with a sundial and a brass plate, on which is engraved a sketch of the tree, made the very day it fell.

Such highly romanticised accounts were typically found in many publications printed in the 18th and 19th centuries. They appealed to the tourists of the time who visited Nannau on their Welsh tours in search of the picturesque. Although elements of Hywel Sele's plight undoubtedly occurred, certain details do not seem to have any foundation. It is necessary to disentangle fact from fantasy and elaboration.

Arranging each version of the encounter on a continuum highlights the way the story has developed through the centuries:

1650 - Robert Vaughan, the Antiquarian of Hengwrt, copying an ancient manuscript, portrays Hywel Sele as a powerful individual with local connections, not willing to pay homage to Glyndŵr. Incensed with such defiance, Glyndŵr attacks Nannau, burning it to the ground, and takes Hywel hostage. Hywel's son-in-law, Griffri ap Gwyn, intercepts the hostage party near Llanelltyd bridge and a fierce battle ensues, with sixty of Griffri's men slaughtered. Glyndŵr emerges victorious and nothing is heard of Hywel Sele again.

place on the bridge, Owain Glyndŵr eventually cutting his way through his interceptors, of whom some 60 were left dead on the field.

The worthy abbot of Cymer (a nearby Cistercian Abbey), whose sympathies were entirely with Glyndŵr, appears to have intervened then, and to have patched up an agreement under which Hywel Sele agreed to support Glyndŵr, or at any rate, not oppose him, and he was set at liberty in consequence.

A short while after Glyndŵr visited Nannau probably to discuss terms of support, and he and his former captive went into the woods together. While out walking, a deer was espied, and Hywel Sele, pretending to draw upon it, wheeled round suddenly and shot his arrow at Glyndŵr. Thanks to his coat of mail, the latter escaped injury, and in revenge for the treacherous assault, he slew Hywel Sele on the spot, and, carrying the corpse a little distance, he thrust it into the

44. above: **Stourhead in Wiltshire, the seat of Sir Richard Colt Hoare**

1660 - Robert Vaughan adds the caveat that Hywel Sele was killed by Owain Glyndŵr and his body dropped into the hollow of an oak tree.

1778 - Thomas Pennant visits Nannau whilst researching his *A Tour in Wales* publication and further adds that the Abbot of Cymer had brokered a peace between Sele and Glyndŵr. Later, consolidating their pact, they are seen enjoying the thrill of the hunt in Nannau forest. Sele is portrayed as an assassin, turning his bow on Glyndŵr rather than the espied deer. We are told that Sele's arrow failed to kill Glyndŵr as he had armour hidden beneath his clothes. Incensed with such treachery, Glyndŵr killed his cousin, disposing of the body in an old oak tree. Further venting his anger, Glyndŵr burnt Sele's house to the ground and departed.

Subsequent versions tell of Sele's distraught widow Mali grieving for forty years, until she is notified of Hywel's demise. She finds her husband's body, complete in rusty armour, with his sword still grasped in his fleshless hand, as he had fallen forty years previously. Conclusive documentary evidence however reveals that Mali remarried Owen ap Meredith ap Gruffudd Fychan of Neuadd Wen, county Montgomery, and had further children.

A well-known Victorian poet described Hywel's magnificent burial in Cymer Abbey:

They bore the corpse to Vanner's shrine,
With holy rites and prayers addressed;
Nine white-robed monks the last dirge sang'
And gave the angry spirit rest.

(An extract from *The Spirit's Blasted Tree* by Rev. George Warrington, published circa 1800)

45: *Moses Griffith, 1798*　　46: *John Parry for Sir Robert Williames Vaughan after 1808*　　47: *Sir Richard Colt Hoare, 1813*

The legend of the Ceubren spread far and wide, with stories circulating that it was haunted. Numerous artists were drawn to the site and many depictions were made of the now badly decayed tree. The earliest drawing was by Moses Griffith, Thomas Pennant's friend and artist, who had accompanied him on his tours and places of interest which were later used as illustrations in Pennant's *A Tour in Wales*.

On the 26ʰ July 1813, Richard Fenton, the Antiquarian, arrived at Nannau with his friend Sir Richard Colt Hoare, an accomplished artist from Stourhead in Wiltshire. Sir Richard was from a wealthy banking family and together with Fenton he spent many summers touring Wales. He had previously visited Nannau on the 5th August 1808, when he had noted in his journal:

We also rode up to Nannau, the residence and park of Sir Robert Vaughan who has lately built a large solid mansion house, not in the most appropriate style of architecture.

At this time Sir Richard had recently completed extensions to his own elegant family seat at Stourhead, and it is understandable that he found the rebuilt Nannau a rather unrefined block.

But now in 1813 he was back and set about sketching the infamous Nannau Oak. Fenton, writing in his journal on the 26th July 1813, noted that:

The gardens are at a good distance from the house, in a sheltered hollow to the south east of the house ... in them stands the celebrated old oak called Ceubren-yr-Ellyll, a most venerable relic, and yet not so decayed but that it has a few branches productive of foliage, and within these 5 years, of acorns, from which Sir Robert Vaughan shewed me two or three thriving young plants. Sir Richard employed his pencil on this curious survivor of the old foresters, and made a charming drawing.

Curiously, a storm blew up on the very night Sir Richard had made his drawing and the following morning they awoke to hear that the celebrated oak had toppled. Salvaging some of the sound timber from the tree, Sir Robert Vaughan utilised it to make a range of wooden artifacts, such as candlesticks, boxes and beautifully carved cups, shaped like acorns and trimmed with silver. Sir Richard Colt Hoare, in keeping with tradition, mounted his Ceubren drawing in a wooden frame also made of the venerable tree, which is still to be seen hanging in the library at Stourhead. An etching was

later made of Sir Richard's drawing by George Cuitt and many copies were circulated to friends and family by Sir Robert Vaughan. Sir Richard's sketch has also been reproduced on silver discs that adorn the Ceubren artifacts, demonstrating their authenticity. The brass plaque marking the Ceubren's position in the walled garden was similarly engraved, though it is no longer in existence. The Ceubren achieved national notoriety in 1808 when Sir Walter Scott alluded to it in his poem *Marmion*.

To further commemorate the 9th Lord of Nannau, Sir Robert Vaughan built Hywel Sele Lodge in 1820, a majestic gothic folly on the site where Sele's house once stood. Now recently renovated, it looks deliciously mysterious and romantic, complete with turrets and sculptured mullioned windows. It stands defiantly on the crest of a hill, overlooking Nannau's ancient deer park. Sir Robert went on to build numerous gothic lodges and quaint cottages on his extensive estate.

Clearly, Hywel Sele's story has become an elaborately woven legend with successive generations adding their own embellishments. I believe that the only version that has any credibility is Robert Vaughan's 1650 transcription. It is the only documentary evidence that exists. Tenuous evidence exists to support the burning of Nannau in the form of an article in the *Cornhill Magazine* in 1884 which noted that:

> *the blackened ruins of his (Hywel Sele's) burnt castle were cleared away some years ago to build a lodge for Nannau deer park.*

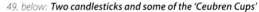

50. *Hywel Sele Lodge after restoration (2012)*

51. above: **Owain Glyndŵr's Mound at Sycharth (2015)**

52. right:
**Remains of
fishponds at
Sycharth**

I believe the assassination attempt on Glyndŵr is highly improbable. Hywel Sele was recognised as one of the best archers of his day. George Agar Hansard, in *The Book of Archery* (1841) stated that:

Howel Sele was of gigantic stature, and enjoyed the reputation of being the strongest and most skillful bowman, where excellence in archery was an accomplishment possessed by many. Rarely was he seen to launch a second arrow at the same object; the twang of his bowstring sounded as the knell of his victims, whether in war or in the chase.

According to legend, Glyndŵr wore chain mail or armour beneath his tunic, which caused the alleged arrow to be deflected. Modern day experiments have proven that neither armour nor chain mail provides defence against an arrow expelled from a longbow.

Whether or not Sele's body was placed in a decaying oak is a matter of conjecture. It is entirely feasible that a decaying oak, hollowed and rotten in 1400, could still be standing four hundred years later. The change from a solid to a hollow trunk often enables an aged tree to withstand a gale better than a younger healthy specimen. In the ancient hunting parks of England, it is not uncommon to discover hollow oaks, four or five hundred years old, still standing after a storm, when younger ones have been blown over. Careful scrutiny of the drawings made of the Ceubren show signs of pollarding. This procedure would have also prolonged its life and made it less susceptible to being toppled by the wind. With some imagination, one could possibly accept Robert Vaughan's assertion, that Hywel's body was deposited in such a tree.

It is debatable whether or not Hywel's house was burnt by Glyndŵr; the evidence is weak, as is our knowledge of his house. But once more our illustrious antiquarian Robert Vaughan comes to the rescue, in that he states that Hywel Sele's house was

the stateliest structure in all North Wales.

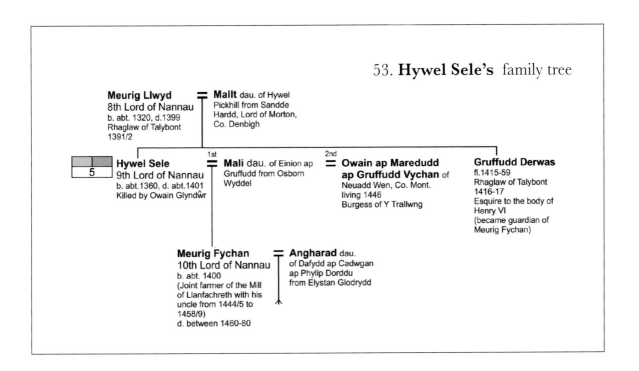

53. **Hywel Sele's** family tree

Meurig Llwyd
8th Lord of Nannau
b. abt. 1320, d.1399
Rhaglaw of Talybont
1391/2

= **Mallt** dau. of Hywel
Pickhill from Sandde
Hardd, Lord of Morton,
Co. Denbigh

1st

Hywel Sele
9th Lord of Nannau
b. abt. 1360, d. abt.1401
Killed by Owain Glyndŵr

5

= **Mali** dau. of Einion ap
Gruffudd from Osborn
Wyddel

2nd

= **Owain ap Maredudd
ap Gruffudd Vychan** of
Neuadd Wen, Co. Mont.
living 1446
Burgess of Y Trallwng

Gruffudd Derwas
fl.1415-59
Rhaglaw of Talybont
1416-17
Esquire to the body of
Henry VI
(became guardian of
Meurig Fychan)

Meurig Fychan
10th Lord of Nannau
b. abt. 1400
(Joint farmer of the Mill
of Llanfachreth with his
uncle from 1444/5 to
1458/9)
d. between 1460-80

= **Angharad** dau.
of Dafydd ap Cadwgan
ap Phylip Dorddu
from Elystan Glodrydd

Such a description does not allow us to build up a comprehensive picture of the house, but careful analysis of the immediate surroundings reveal some remarkable medieval features. Such evidence points to a house of high status. Immediately to the side of Hywel Sele Lodge there exists the outline of four pillow mounds which are remains of artificial rabbit warrens used for the farming of rabbits in medieval times. It is likely that the Cistercian monks of Cymer Abbey introduced such structures to the area.

The field just below the lodge is called 'Y Winllan Bach' (the small vineyard), a field name stretching back to ancient times. Brigadier Vaughan, the last beneficial owner of the Nannau estate, argued that this was the site of a medieval vineyard and was noted as the warmest spot on his estate. A few hundred yards beyond the lodge and into the deer park are the remnants of two fishponds. Likewise

medieval in origin, these would have provided a supply of fresh fish for the lord's table. Such facilities would have been needed to support a lord's household.

Through the work of Iolo Goch, Owain Glyndŵr's domestic bard, we get a glimpse of life at 'Sycharth', Glyndŵr's castle near Llansilin. Widely regarded as one of the best known of all medieval Welsh poems, it provides many insights into Welsh court life in the early 15th century. It is a 'snapshot' that yields many similarities to Hywel Sele's Nannau.

Iolo describes Sycharth's great medieval hall, ancillary buildings, roof tiles and chimney. Such chimneys were a real innovation for the time, a considerable advance on a hole in the roof for smoke to escape. He clearly described the vineyard, rabbit warren, deer park and fishponds.

Iolo describes Sycharth as,

*The court of a baron, a place of
refinement, where many poets frequent,
a place of the good life.*

(Gruffydd Aled Williams, 2010)

I believe that the scene described at
Sycharth could well have been emulated at
Nannau. As distant cousins, from the same
princely descent, Hywel might have been
inspired by his kinsman's lifestyle or vice
versa.

Using Iolo's poem as a guide, we have
recreated Hywel Sele's house in its most
likely setting, at the entrance to his beloved
deer park, with majestic Cader Idris providing
a perfect backdrop.

That Hywel's life was cut short is indisputable,
and it is doubly tragic that his son Meurig
Fychan was left fatherless at the age of two.
Fortunately for Meurig, Hywel's brother
Gruffudd Derwas was to take up the
guardianship of the young heir through the
exceedingly challenging times that followed the
Glyndŵr wars.

55. right: **Hywel Sele Lodge
from Nannau Deer Park**

4

1403-1573

THE EMERGENCE OF A GENTRY FAMILY

The devastation suffered by Merioneth in the wake of the Glyndŵr revolt was immense. The whole area erupted into violence and lawlessness with much feuding between rival factions. It became an outlaw-ridden area where cattle rustling and attacks on the population were common-place. The turmoil in the area was described by Sir John Wynn of Gwydir as

nothinge but killing and fightinge.

Against the backdrop of such social chaos, the emerging Nannau dynasty miraculously survived the turbulent times, later rising to the pinnacle of Tudor gentry. The family's future was in the balance, Hywel Sele's death had left them bereft of leadership, and their son and heir Meurig Fychan II was only an infant.

Fortunately, Hwyel's brother Gruffudd Derwas filled the void and steered the now fractured family through what must have been extremely difficult times.

Little is known of the plight of the Nannau family in the early years of the 15th century.

Hywel Sele's widow's marriage to Owen ap Maredudd of Neuadd Wen, a well-known Glyndŵr supporter, is somewhat perplexing, following on so closely after the death of her husband in such devastating circumstances. It is possible that she was carried away as a hostage in 1401/2.

Gruffudd Derwas probably spent the early years of the Glyndŵr rebellion lying low in Gwanas near Dolgellau, not wishing to experience the wrath of Glyndŵr. He would have been aware of the fate of his niece Lleuci's matrimonial home of Ystumcegid, which had been razed to the ground by Glyndŵr.

By 1410 however, Glyndŵr's revolt was in decline, Harlech Castle had fallen to the English and Glyndŵr's wife and two daughters had been captured and imprisoned in the Tower of London. Glyndŵr became a fugitive hiding in the hills, possibly finding refuge with one of his daughters at the end of his life.

Significantly, the Nannau family soon reappear. The Ministers' accounts of 1414/15 reveal that

Gruffudd Derwas, now Rhaglaw of Talybont, is living at Nannau, tutor and guardian to young Meurig. By this time, presumably Nannau had been rebuilt after the earlier house had been destroyed some ten years previously. Gruffudd, true to family traditions, followed three generations of the Nannau clan into local Crown offices, some more profitable than others. Such was Gruffudd's appetite for power that he was to amass a veritable collection of offices, these being:

1414/15 -Rhaglaw of Talybont
-Farm of the Fridd of Penantigi
-Farm of the office of Woodward of Talybont
-Farm of the Amobor
1424/5 -Rhaglaw and Mill of Talybont
-The Court, Toll and Mill of Dolgelley

Such was his status in Merioneth that Robert Vaughan, the Antiquarian of Hengwrt, was to describe him as

the chiefest man of command in our country all his tyme

A Woodward was responsible for the guardianship of the Prince's hunting rights, dealing with timber sales and arranging rights of passage through the forest. It was potentially a lucrative post as officers were able to recoup the rent through levies of various kinds and timber sales. The ability to raise levies often led to office holders collecting money unjustly to line their own pockets; many such 'extractions' were highlighted in 14th century Court Rolls, though to date, no evidence has been found of Nannau office holders misappropriating funds.

During these troubled times many families demonstrate conflicting loyalties. Mallt, a daughter of Hywel Sele of Nannau, is known to have married Gruffudd ap Jenkin of Llwydiarth, who was implicated in the Glyndŵr rebellion, but later pardoned by King Henry V.

Nannau was probably rebuilt between 1410/15, after a decade of desolation. The estate was possibly abandoned by the family who may have sought safe refuge elsewhere. By 1419, when Meurig was about twenty, he became co-heir with Gruffudd Derwas and others to a 'gwely' of land in the Extent of Merionethshire.

Meurig Fychan II is honoured as being the first member of the family to be mentioned in the Nannau Manuscripts as early as 1436, when he leased land in the Township of Llwyngwril. By 1438, Meurig Fychan II received the farm of a bond township and was well placed to secure estate expansion into Crown territory. Thirteen years later he significantly made the first ever recorded purchase of Nannau land,

58. left: **Picture from 'Livre de le Chasse' depicting a forest hunting scene**

when he bought two tenements in Garthgynfawr from no less a person than his uncle Gruffudd Derwas for forty shillings. This purchase marks the beginning of the Nannau estate expansion. The period from 1450 to 1540 would be remarkable in the furious manner in which the Nannau family aggressively purchased tribal lands that came on the market, often at the expense of their less fortunate neighbours.

There is no record of Meurig Fychan taking part in the Wars of the Roses. His cousin Dafydd ap Ieuan ap Einion, however, played a significant role, most notably as Commander of Harlech Castle which he famously held for the Lancastrians. In common with many Welshmen of his time, Dafydd served in the English army in France during the later stages of the Hundred Years' War, returning to England when the English lost Normandy.

Dafydd is noted as holding Harlech Castle for King Henry VI, and it is where his Queen, Margaret of Angou, and her young son took refuge in 1460, after the Battle of Northampton. Later Dafydd and his Lancastrian entourage were besieged by Yorkist forces under the command of Sir William Herbert who was sent by Edward IV to lay waste to the castle. Despite numerous requests to surrender, Dafydd resisted the powerful Yorkist forces until he eventually submitted on the 1st August 1468 and received a pardon due to the insistence of Sir William Herbert.

61. Family tree of **Dafydd ap Ieuan ap Einion,** Constable of Harlech Castle

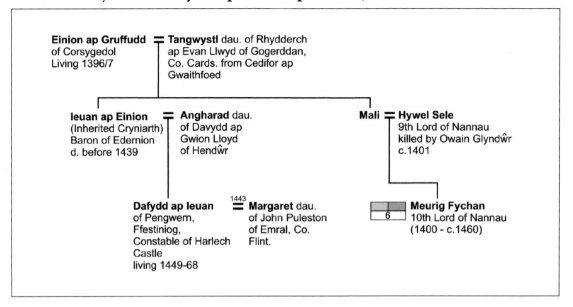

Einion ap Gruffudd
of Corsygedol
Living 1396/7
= **Tangwystl** dau. of Rhydderch
ap Evan Llwyd of Gogerddan,
Co. Cards. from Cedifor ap
Gwaithfoed

Ieuan ap Einion
(Inherited Cryniarth)
Baron of Edernion
d. before 1439
= **Angharad** dau.
of Davydd ap
Gwion Lloyd
of Hendŵr

Mali = **Hywel Sele**
9th Lord of Nannau
killed by Owain Glyndŵr
c.1401

Dafydd ap Ieuan
of Pengwern,
Ffestiniog,
Constable of Harlech
Castle
living 1449-68
=1443 **Margaret** dau.
of John Puleston
of Emral, Co.
Flint.

| 6 | **Meurig Fychan**
10th Lord of Nannau
(1400 - c.1460) |

*62. below: **Detail of Harlech Castle by cartographer John Speed** 1616*

According to legend Dafydd is thought to have claimed that:

> *He had once in his youth maintained a castle so long in France that every woman in Wales had heard of it, and in his old age had held a castle in Wales for so long that every old woman in France had heard of it.*

Three of Meurig's cousins are mentioned as being part of the Harlech Castle's garrison during the siege, but Meurig being very elderly by now, probably watched from the sidelines. Meurig's Lancastrian leanings are evident when in 1468 he is known to have issued a request to the Constable of Harlech Castle (along with other landed proprietors of the county), for pardons for twenty-five men of Talybont who were involved in the Lancastrian defence of the castle.

To commemorate the longest known siege in the history of the British Isles and the brave

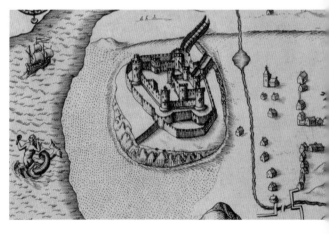

defence by the small Welsh garrison commanded by Dafydd ap Ieuan, the stirring music 'March of the Men of Harlech' was first published in 1794. Many lyrical versions have followed over the centuries. Perhaps one of the best-known is to be found in a version written especially for the 1964 film 'Zulu' and sung by the soldiers of the South Wales Borderers, to lift their spirits as they braved the Zulu attack:

Men of Harlech stop your dreaming
Can't you see their spear points gleaming
See their warrior's pennants streaming
To this battlefield
Men of Harlech stand ye steady
It cannot be ever said ye
For the battle were not ready
Stand and never yield
From the hills rebounding
Let this war cry sounding
Summon all at Cambria's call
The mighty force surrounding
Men of Harlech on to glory
This will ever be your story
Keep these fighting words before ye
Cambria (Welshmen never) will not yield.

Stirring words for our gallant hero of over five centuries ago, but still remembered.

PATRONS of the bards

During the tenure of Meurig Fychan and his uncle, Nannau became a prime venue for many of the itinerant bards. Many had lost the patronage of noble families who had turned their back on Welsh culture in the wake of the Glyndŵr Revolt and its feared repercussions. The Nannau family fortunately managed to remain loyal to the Crown whilst not compromising their Welsh heritage, maintaining this stance through to the 17th century, and they were to be the last Welsh family to have a 'live-in bard', a worthy distinction to hold.

Meurig Fychan was particularly noted for his hospitality, being praised by the esteemed poet Guto'r Glyn:

Meurig is not like the men of England,
the descendants of earls, with his wine.
A lord who wants to give a great feast
will bolt the gate and call the gatekeeper;
and the blessed hall of white and grey-

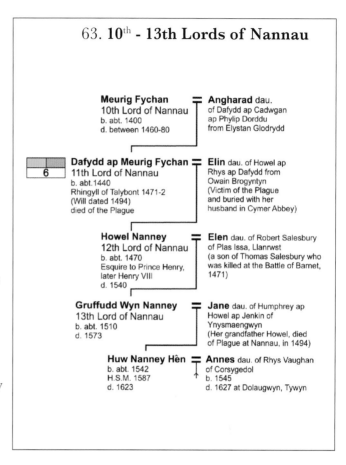

63. 10th - 13th Lords of Nannau

Meurig Fychan
10th Lord of Nannau
b. abt. 1400
d. between 1460-80
= **Angharad** dau.
of Dafydd ap Cadwgan
ap Phylip Dorddu
from Elystan Glodrydd

Dafydd ap Meurig Fychan
11th Lord of Nannau
b. abt.1440
Rhingyll of Talybont 1471-2
(Will dated 1494)
died of the Plague
= **Elin** dau. of Howel ap
Rhys ap Dafydd from
Owain Brogyntyn
(Victim of the Plague
and buried with her
husband in Cymer Abbey)

6

Howel Nanney
12th Lord of Nannau
b. abt. 1470
Esquire to Prince Henry,
later Henry VIII
d. 1540
= **Elen** dau. of Robert Salesbury
of Plas Issa, Llanrwst
(a son of Thomas Salesbury who
was killed at the Battle of Barnet,
1471)

Gruffudd Wyn Nanney
13th Lord of Nannau
b. abt. 1510
d. 1573
= **Jane** dau. of Humphrey ap
Howel ap Jenkin of
Ynysmaengwyn
(Her grandfather Howel, died
of Plague at Nannau, in 1494)

Huw Nanney Hên
b. abt. 1542
H.S.M. 1587
d. 1623
= **Annes** dau. of Rhys Vaughan
of Corsygedol
b. 1545
d. 1627 at Dolaugwyn, Tywyn

haired Meurig
is forever without a lock, not hiding
the food.
The son of Hywel Selau never bothered with
gatekeeping
when he was younger, a generous court.
The feast will come to the side of Y Lan
and food to feed the whole of Gwynedd.

... Whoever desires to live a long life,
may he go with one leap to Nannau;
whoever desires heaven, a home where he
will endure,
let him go to die in Meurig's house.

(Translation by Guto'r Glyn.net)

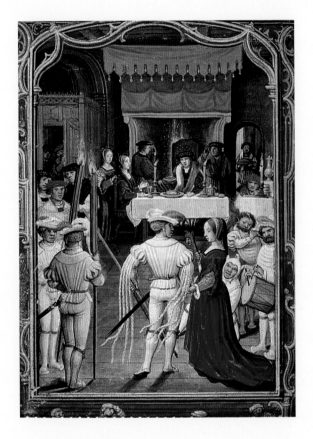

Guto further states that Meurig Fychan and his wife Angharad were laid to rest in nearby Cymer Abbey along with other members of the family. Guto suggests that both Meurig and his wife Angharad were victims of the plague, which was prevalent in Wales during that period.

Meurig Fychan's son Dafydd first appears in records in 1471/2 as Farmer of the Mill of Llanfachreth and Rhingyll of Talybont, perfectly aligned with his family's Lancastrian sympathies. It is surprising, however, to find him serving a Yorkist dynasty under Edward IV, clearly not averse to sacrificing his principles for self-advancement. His 'turncoat ways' however, must have been noticed by officers of the Principality as he held no office whatsoever under Henry Tudor.

Lack of office did not hamper Dafydd in his quest to expand the estate. He is seen purchasing two tenements in 1480 and encroaching on Crown lands in Llwyngwril in 1489, seizing every possible opportunity to enlarge his landholding. So eager was he to purchase this land that in 1490 he had to present a petition at the Great Sessions held in Caernarfon praying the Prince's pardon for acquiring forty-five acres of land in Llwyngwril without first having obtained the Prince's licence. The petition was granted, but with a hefty fine of ten shillings!

The purchasing of tribal land was prohibited under Welsh laws, but to circumvent this obstacle, lands were acquired by a process known as 'tir prid'. This was a form of lease where lands were held for an initial term of four years, to be renewed quadrennially until the property was redeemed by the alienator. This veiled means of purchase was used extensively by the Nannau and other gentry families and contributed immensely to the breakdown of the tribal lands.

A later elegy for Meurig and his wife Angharad states:

Great was the lament for the Three Generous Men,
the grieving for generous Meurig was greater.
The weeping is a deluge, like a lake,
the death of a unique man is agonising.
I have a memory and I will put it to song,
a long memory, alas, Meurig Fychan,
a supporting son of wealthy Hywel,
the chieftain of the great death.
The chief of his people, it's painful to sing,
he was a sovereign over Llanfachreth;
Dolgellau and Nannau together,
their two roots have been uprooted.

(Translation by Guto'r Glyn.net)

*He runs well over two parks, sure his
footing,
very good is his trot carrying a blind man.*

(Translated by Guto'r Glyn.net)

The fact that Dafydd understood three
languages is interesting; it indicates that he
must have had some education, perhaps
provided by a tutor or even a bard. The poem is
dated to around 1480, with Dafydd obviously a
young man, yet he was to die in 1494, quite
possibly contracting the plague as it is well
documented that Howel ap Jenkin (a grandson
of Gruffudd Derwas) died at Nannau in 1494 of
plague. Dafydd's son and heir Howel was
probably left a minor on the death of his father
but was extremely well provided for in his
father's will, as was the rest of the family.

Dafydd ap Meurig's will is very enlightening in
many ways. It reveals the considerable wealth
and status of the Nannau family. Indeed in 1873
W.W.E. Wynne of Peniarth noted that:

*Dafydd ap Meurig Vychan of Nanney (now
Nannau) was the representative, of his day,
of probably the greatest family in the county
of Merioneth.*

In total Dafydd bequeathed:

- *thirteen shillings and four pence to the Abbot
and Convent of Cymer for ten oblations
(offerings to God);*

- *six shillings and eight pence towards the
construction of Llanfachreth Church;*

- *ten shillings towards the buildings of Cymer
Abbey;*

- *four nobles for the construction of St. Mary's
Church Dolgelley;*

- *ten shillings to the friars of Bangor;*

- *ten shillings to the friars of Llanfaes;*

Dafydd, like his father Meurig, was a patron of
the bards and it is through the eyes of Guto'r
Glyn we gain the most insights into Dafydd's
life and times. A poem written to thank Dafydd
ap Meurig Fychan and his wife for the gift of a
horse is particularly interesting; Dafydd is
described thus:

*A modest lamb is Dafydd towards us,
but harsh and strong towards the wicked;
he would neither do wrong nor consider it,
his father would do no spite nor deceit.
He is a decent man, the best of his land,
fine, young and trustworthy;
a man great in his wide-ranging qualities,
a learned man, he knows three languages;
a man of more revenue beside the ebb of the
sea than ten, may God bless his houses.*

*... My lord, Dafydd, sends me a horse,
he has all but given me two horses.
Full of strength, that is his characteristic,
a red lion of the same colour as stags.*

❧*six shillings and eight pence towards glazing the windows of the Chapel of the Knights of St. John at Gwanas, and ten pounds for the celebration of masses for his soul for the space of two years;*

❧*six shillings and eight pence towards the repair of the bridge at Edyrn;*

❧*four marks to Ieuan ap Rynallt.*

He further bequeaths to his daughters various numbers of cattle, the total amounting to over three hundred, and the rest of his goods, both movable and immovable, he leaves to Howel ap Dafydd, his son.

Dafydd, according to his wishes, was buried in Cymer Abbey, as was the wish of his father Meurig Fychan, only fifteen years earlier. This is certainly the will of a wealthy individual for the times, someone well-placed financially

to purchase new lands that became available, ensuring the continued expansion of his family estate for the foreseeable future. Dafydd's legacy to his son and heir Howel Nanney was substantial, as intimated by the bard Tudur Aled in his 'cywydd' composed to celebrate the young heir's succession:

> *Mountain, woodland, you shall have them,*
> *cornland, meadowland, banquet-halls,*
> *Tenants in multitude like the snow of January,*
> *and your men about the heights of Moel Orthrwn.*

(Moel Orthrwn – a hill immediately in front of Nannau)

Howel Nanney's name occurs on a multitude of leases and purchase documents, first appearing in 1500. For four decades, his appetite for land was unwavering. A large transaction was

recorded in 1505, amounting to the sizeable sum of fifty pounds for three properties. The fact that he leased land from Gruffudd, Abbot of Cymer, in 1500 is also significant, as the family would in subsequent generations be well- placed to acquire further Abbey lands upon the dissolution of the monasteries in Henry VIII's reign.

Howel is noted as holding the office of Farmer of the Mills of Llanfachreth and Llanegryn in 1512/13 and is known to have been an Esquire to Prince Henry, later to become Henry VIII, but little else is known of the 'elusive' 10th Lord of Nannau. Fortunately, the bards once more come to the rescue and provide us with a valuable commentary on Howel Nanney. His diligence in attending to his estate and duties as a landlord caused Tudur Aled to note:

What ploughed lands and what cottages are there without a tenant?

Rhisiart Cynwal, commenting on the death of Howel, noted that his patron's rule in Merioneth had been worthy of his lineage and that his ability to interpret and practice the law noteworthy. Many poets lamented his passing as they saw the death of such an inspired leader of the county as being the death knell of law and order, giving

brigands and other malefactors an opportunity to perpetrate their criminal activities once more, particularly in a

remote and mountainous area such as Merioneth.

(J.G. Jones, 1984)

By the time of his death around 1540, Howel's family had well and truly emerged as Tudor gentry. Howel Nanney was the first member of the family to be referred to as 'generos' (gentleman) in 1538, quickly followed by the first use of the family surname by Tudur Aled who refers to Howel as Huw Nannau.

Howel Nanney was to leave three sons, the first of the Nannau family for four generations to leave more than one heir; up till now the undivided inheritance had enabled the Nannau estate to grow unfettered under Welsh laws of partible succession.

The Act of Union introduced English common law to Wales, affecting many aspects of Welsh society. No longer would the Welsh laws of partible succession apply; it would be replaced by the English laws of inheritance, that of primogeniture, the inheriting of property by the eldest male heir. Estate building could now proceed apace, irrespective of the number of male heirs. Younger sons of the gentry however, would now have to carve out their own way in life.

Howel Nanney was known to have provided well for his sons, but the eldest, Gruffudd Wyn, was identified as the heir. He made his

68. Cymer Abbey 2015

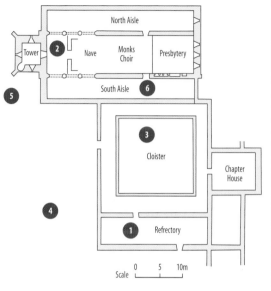

Plan labels: Tower, North Aisle, Nave, Monks Choir, Presbytery, South Aisle, Cloister, Chapter House, Refectory

Scale: 0 5 10m

1. South view across the remains of the cloister and the South Aisle

2. View through the arches to the North Aisle

3. The 14th-century tower at the Western end of the Nave

4. View of Abbey from across the road

5. North East view of the tower

6. South door from the Monks' choir

first appearance in a deed of 1536, coinciding with two landmark events, the first Act of Union and the Dissolution of the Monasteries. Both events would be crucial to the development of the estate and have far-reaching consequences.

In 1537, Gruffudd Wyn would no doubt have witnessed the tragic dissolution of nearby Cymer Abbey. In 1536, the first bill had been introduced in Parliament aimed at dissolving the smaller monasteries whose income was less than two hundred pounds per annum. Cymer, with a gross income of £58. 15. 4d., fell well below this threshold and was consequently dissolved in March 1537, three hundred and forty years after the small group of pathfinder monks left the Abbey of Cwmhir and crossed the Cambrian Mountains to establish their new abbey near Llanelltyd in 1198.

Today, the ruins of Cymer Abbey stand as a testament to the white-robed brethren who nine hundred years ago colonised this peaceful location. The words of T.P. Ellis evocatively describes the scene in the 1950s:

The abbey originally had a big church, remains of which still stand, a side chapel, now occupied as cattle-sheds, cloisters, a frater, a dorter, a chapter-house, and a few other buildings, all of which have now disappeared. Behind, under the slope of the hill rising just behind, lay their burial ground, Cae Fynwent as it is still called, where not so much as a stone remains, and where sheep and cattle graze peaceably. In the spring-time it is white with flowers, like no other field nearby is, a tribute, perhaps, by nature to a purity of life led in ancient days. The abbey spring can still be traced, and the steps leading down to it are covered with the slime of centuries.

The old 'angelus' bell, calling people to prayer for the ringing of which the farm of

Dol y Clochydd was assigned to the ringer, is silent, and ruin and decay is all round, where once was toil and praise. In the floor of the tower is the trunk of a great sycamore tree, the seed of which fell there long after the abbey fell into ruins. It grew and has been felled; like the thing of beauty in whose ruins it flourished for a time. But there is still some beauty left in the great cast window, festooned now with creeping ivy, in the graceful red sandstone pillars which separate the lancets of it, brought from Chester or Shrewsbury, in the ruins of the three sedilia, near where the altar stood, in the piscina adjoining, and in the arches which led into the side-chapel. It does not require much imagination to forget the farm-yard squalor, the penned-in sheep which occupy the ruins now, and go back to the days when the altar shone with lighted tapers, the sanctuary lamp was burning, and the monks were reciting the offices of the day from early morn till vespers.

(T.P. Ellis, *The Founding of Cymer Abbey*)

THE DOLGELLAU Chalice and Paten

The Crown stripped Cymer Abbey of its wealth
and property, but miraculously some of its
most prized possessions have survived through
the centuries and exist as exhibits in the
Museum of Wales. The chance discovery of a
chalice and paten in the hills above Dolgellau in
1890 caused great excitement at the time and
touched a number of people in the vicinity of
Nannau and Dolgellau.

The story broke in the *London Illustrated News*
on the 14th June 1890, having already appeared
in the *Western Mail* thus:

*DISCOVERY OF GOLD CHALICE AND
PATEN NEAR DOLGELLEY*

*A curious and what has proved to be valuable
find has just been made in North Wales.
While two men were proceeding across a
ridge near the residence of Mr. Pritchard
Morgan, M.P., Dolgelley, one of them
perceived what appeared to be a plate
embedded in a rock. After considerable
trouble they dislodged it and carried it home,
where it was found, after considerable
washing and scraping, to be a gold plate.
They did not know that their find was of any
value, but eventually it was shown to Mr.
Morgan. That gentleman, feeling interested
in the matter, instituted a stricter search
about the spot, which has not been useless,
for close by a vase-shaped vessel was
unearthed.*

*Both these articles, which were encrusted
with about 2 inches of vegetable matter,
appear to belong to each other, and it is
affirmed that they are an ancient
sacramental wafer-dish and wine-cup. The
vessels are beautifully hand-wrought,
chased, and engraved, weighing altogether
about forty-six ounces, and composed of gold
with an admixture of silver. The plate, which
is circular, bears the inscription,*

71. top: **Mrs E. A. Vaughan of Nannau, who initally
purchased the Chalice in 1890**

72. bottom: **Ellis Jones, one of the goldminers
who discovered the Chalice and Paten**

73. above: **The shop of T.H. Roberts, Ironmonger of Dolgellau -** *(The large building in the centre)*

"In Nomine Patris et Fili et Spiritus Sancti Am", accompanied by an engraving representing the figure of Christ with His right hand upheld, and the third and fourth finger closed. The other vessel is about 12 inches high, the cup being about 6 inches across. The pedestal is chased and hammered as well as the under-side, bearing the words "Nicolus de Herefordis me fecit."

Close to the spot where the articles were found is the ancient Monastery of Llanelltyd, and it is assumed that they at one time belonged to the monks who during the reign of Henry VIII buried them in the place from which they have now been unearthed. The vessels have been submitted to first-class London experts, who declare them to be of great value from an antiquarian point of view, dating back

to about the thirteenth century. Considerable excitement is felt in the district, and the search is still being continued in the hope of finding other relics. The land upon which the articles have been found is said to be the property of the Crown, and it is hoped that the State will purchase them for the country.

(Western Mail – 4th June 1890)

Both articles were brief and somewhat incomplete. A closer scrutiny reveals the intrigue and ramifications of this incredible discovery and how it captured the attention of the country.

Griffith Griffiths and Ellis Jones were two Llanfachreth gold miners in the employ of a consortium headed by T.H. Roberts, an ironmonger of Parliament House in Dolgellau. On the 13th February 1890, Griffith and Ellis were prospecting on a ridge called 'Garn' near Cwm Mynach, Dolgellau. Whilst on their way home to Llanfachreth they noticed a shiny object lying between some boulders. Closer inspection revealed two metal objects encrusted with soil and vegetation. The miners' initial reaction was to throw them away, not thinking that they would have any value, but then they decided to take their discoveries home.

Totally unaware of the value and rarity of their discoveries, the two miners took the objects to their landlord, Mrs E. A. Vaughan of Nannau. It is evident that she invited her nephew Reverend Davies, the vicar of Llanfachreth, to view the objects and in no time the items changed hands, Mrs Vaughan buying the chalice for forty shillings and Reverend Davies acquiring the paten for ten shillings. It is easy to imagine that the vicar and his aunt would have wished to acquire the relics for their much-loved church at Llanfachreth.

News of the find spread very quickly through the close-knit community and eventually to T.H. Roberts, who in his own words stated:

I heard of the find and we threatened to prosecute them for stealing them and they at once were repaid and the chalice and paten were returned.

According to T.H. Roberts, the items were sent to London to be sold some two years later in a sale at Christies Auction House. They were sold for £805, purchased by a dealer of the name of Mr Boore. Within a short while, he had resold them to Baron Schroder, an avid collector, for £3,000.

Within weeks of the final sale, Mr. T.H. Roberts and partners, Mr Boore and Baron Schroder, were all served with writs of recovery of the items, on the grounds that they

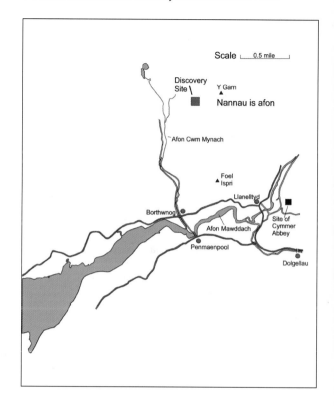

were Treasure Trove and hence the property of the Crown. Baron Schroder is known to have stepped in and offered to gift the items to the Crown in his will. This seems to have appeased the Crown and the litigation ceased.

The Baron died in May 1910 and his will stated:

... I bequeath the chalice and paten, or wafer dish, which was discovered near Dolgelley in the County of Merioneth, Wales, and which was some years since purchased by me, to his Majesty the King, his heirs and successors, to be disposed of for the public service in such a manner as His Majesty, his heirs and successors, or the Lords Commissioners of the Treasury for the time being on his or their behalf, shall direct.

The controversy was however not over as there was much discussion on where the items should be kept. Eventually the National Museum of Wales was selected, in line with the wishes of King George V.

It is interesting to speculate on how the chalice and paten came to be found in this remote and inaccessible spot in the barren wilds of Ardudwy. The most plausible explanation is that monks from Cymer Abbey hid them to avoid their most valuable items being confiscated at the time of the Abbey's dissolution.

The location of the finds in Cwm Mynach is significant because 'mynach' is the Welsh word for monk. It is likely that the area was associated with Cymer Abbey. The fact that the two items were found together effectively rules out that they were accidentally dropped or lost. The weight of evidence points towards them being deliberately hidden and never retrieved. The effect of erosion and weather exposed the carefully concealed treasure after more than three and a half centuries. Other theories have been postulated on the origins of the chalice and paten, such as them being stolen treasure from Edward I's retinue, but ultimately all that can be said with any degree of certainty is that the items in question are of the 13th century.

It is sad to think that neither Griffith Griffiths nor Ellis Jones got any form of reward or for that matter any real recognition for discovering these highly important artefacts.

On the dissolution of Cymer Abbey in 1537, very little of its land fell into the hands of the Nanneys, instead it passed to English speculators and only many decades later into local ownership. By 1584, in the tenure of Gruffudd Wyn's son Huw Nanney I, huge swathes of Abbey lands had been acquired, but during Gruffudd's time land purchases had slowed down to a trickle.

Gruffudd Wyn would have been the first Nanney to experience the direct effects of the

Acts of Union which were to have such an impact on Wales.

The 1536 Act of Union:

formed new Welsh counties from the old Marcher Lord territories, these being:

Flint	Radnor
Denbigh	Monmouth
Montgomery	Glamorgan
Brecon	
Pembroke	

- introduced English laws to Wales which were administered by Justices of the Peace in each county, with English as the official language of the courts;

- established representation for Wales in Parliament.

The subsequent Act of Union in 1543 further refined the process of integration, establishing:

- the Court of the Great Sessions – a court system based on four circuits each of three counties:

Anglesey, Caernarfon and Merioneth
Flint, Denbigh and Montgomery
Cardigan, Carmarthen and Pembroke
Radnor, Brecon and Glamorgan;

- the Council of Wales at Ludlow, which was to have extensive legal and administrative powers in Wales for more than a century until its abolition in 1689.

The legal systems set in place by the Acts of Union would be well-used by the Welsh gentry over the coming decades, and none were more litigious than the Nanneys of Nannau who embraced the new powers of the magistrates bench and increased their standing in the community in the process.

Gruffudd Wyn was the first member of the family to use the surname Nanney consistently, along with his half-brother Richard who also styled himself Nanney. This adoption, no doubt in line with moves to embrace the English style of fixed surname, would have aided their acceptance into the Tudor gentry.

Grufudd Wyn has the distinction of being the first of the family to experience the effects of the newly introduced legal system as he was

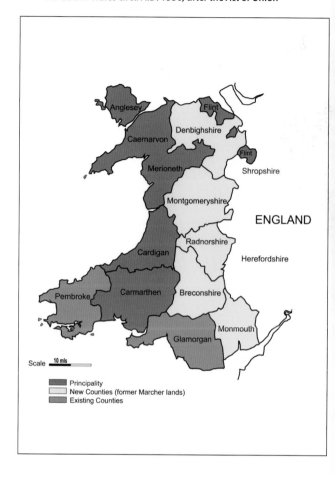

76. below: **Wales circa A.D. 1536, after the Act of Union**

accused of wrongfully entering into ten acres of close pasture called 'Yrallt Llwyd' and fifty acres in Trawsfynydd, land previously owned by Cymer Abbey but now in the possession of a certain John Powys. Gruffudd made further court appearances, but all these pale into insignificance when compared to the legal manoeuvres of his son Huw Nanney I.

Gruffudd Wyn, now styled Nanney, died in 1573, leaving his son and heir Huw Nanney I in charge of an extensive landholding.

77. right: **Valle Crucis Abbey, near Llangollen - a Cistercian abbey built three years after Cymer Abbey**

5

1574-1623

HUW NANNEY HÊN

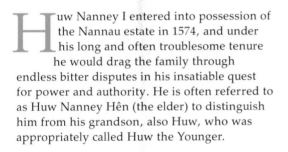

uw Nanney I entered into possession of the Nannau estate in 1574, and under his long and often troublesome tenure he would drag the family through endless bitter disputes in his insatiable quest for power and authority. He is often referred to as Huw Nanney Hên (the elder) to distinguish him from his grandson, also Huw, who was appropriately called Huw the Younger.

Huw Nanney Hên had inherited an extensive estate, and through shrewd business ventures, many of a dubious character, the ancient Nannau estate would rise to the upper echelons of Welsh society. The Nannau family had now become established Tudor gentry, a part of society described as

those who can live idly without manual labour.

(De Republica Anglorum by Sir Thomas Smith, 1586)

Resting on his laurels and idling away the days was the last thing on Huw Nanney's mind as he

planned and schemed the family's continued expansion. It seemed that he would countenance any action necessary to achieve his desired goals.

The 1543 Act of Union had seen the office of Justice of the Peace introduced to Wales and this highly regarded position was considered the domain of the 'chiefest gentlemen in the Shire'. Initially eight magistrates were chosen from the shire gentry with a brief to preserve law and order in their localities. They were to meet quarterly in 'Sessions of the Peace' and deal with a range of judicial and administrative tasks from matters concerning breaches of the peace to repairs to the highways, weights and measures, regulation of alehouses and Poor Law administration to mention just a few. Further responsibilities were added to the justices' brief over time, making it entirely appropriate for them to be referred to as 'maids of all work'.

Justices of the Peace were regarded as essential for the smooth running of county government. The State did not possess a standing army,

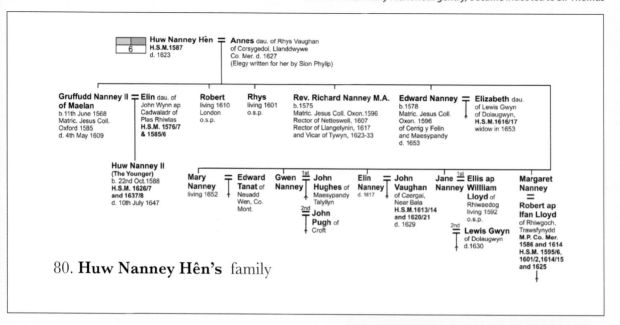

Huw Nanney Hên = **Annes** dau. of Rhys Vaughan
6 H.S.M.1587 of Corsygedol, Llanddwywe
d. 1823 Co. Mer. d. 1627
(Elegy written for her by Sion Phylip)

Gruffudd Nanney II = **Elin** dau. of **Robert** **Rhys** **Rev. Richard Nanney M.A.** **Edward Nanney** = **Elizabeth** dau.
of Maelan John Wynn ap living 1610 living 1601 b.1575 b.1578 of Lewis Gwyn
b.11th June 1568 Cadwaladr of London o.s.p. Matric. Jesus Coll. Oxon.1596 Matric. Jesus Coll. of Dolaugwyn,
Matric. Jesus Coll. Plas Rhiwlas o.s.p. Rector of Netteswell, 1607 Oxon. 1596 H.S.M.1616/17
Oxford 1585 H.S.M. 1576/7 Rector of Llangelynin, 1617 of Cerrig y Felin widow in 1653
d. 4th May 1609 & 1585/6 and Vicar of Tywyn, 1623-33 and Maesypandy
d. 1653

Huw Nanney II
(The Younger)
b. 22nd Oct.1588 **Mary** = **Edward** **Gwen** 1st **John** **Elin** = **John** **Jane** 1st **Ellis ap** **Margaret**
H.S.M. 1626/7 **Nanney** **Tanat** of **Nanney** **Hughes** of **Nanney** **Vaughan** **Nanney** **William** **Nanney**
and 1637/8 living 1652 Neuadd Maesypandy d. 1617 of Caergai, **Lloyd** of
d. 10th July 1647 Wen, Co. Talyllyn Near Bala Rhiwaedog =
Mont. 2nd H.S.M.1613/14 living 1592 **Robert ap**
John and 1620/21 o.s.p. **Ifan Lloyd**
Pugh of d. 1629 of Rhiwgoch,
Croft 2nd **Lewis Gwyn** Trawsfynydd
of Dolaugwyn M.P. Co. Mer.
d.1630 1586 and 1614
H.S.M. 1595/6,
1601/2,1614/15
and 1625

80. **Huw Nanney Hên's** family

therefore it relied upon the gentry to combat rebellion and other subversive activities. The Acts of Union had provided the gentry with the means of consolidating their power in their localities through their positions as justices, and, in return, they were expected to demonstrate loyalty to the State. As previously mentioned, it was widely recognised that the Tudor gentry, through their various official positions, often misused their powers for their own benefit. In this respect Huw Nanney was to be no different to many of his fellow justices when he took up his post as Justice of the Peace for Merioneth in 1584 at the age of forty.

On the land front, estate expansion was progressing apace, and the conditions for estate builders had never been better. The obstacles to procurement of tribal lands had disappeared and monastic lands were increasingly finding their way onto the open market after initially passing through the hands of English speculators. Huw Nanney's estate at this time amounted to 45 holdings, 38 of which

were in the Llanfachreth parish, whilst records show that at least half of the parish was still owned by other families.

Economically times were tough, and the severe inflation of the time must have hit the small freeholders of the area hard, making it difficult for them to hold on to their lands. Losing them to the expanding estates such as Nannau was inevitable. Huw Nanney is also known to have aggressively encroached on waste lands in the locality on no less than six occasions, adding nearly 400 acres of land to his bulging estate. Nanney account books of the period reveal how meticulous they were with their estate management. Clearly Huw Nanney was an enlightened businessman.

Huw Nanney's ambitions were not confined to estate development. He obviously had plans for his sons as he provided a fashionable university education for Gruffudd, Edward and Richard. Poets of the era made much of the need for the gentry to be well-educated to enable them to deal with public life and their role in the

82. *top:* **The ruins of Edward Nanney's house, Cerrig y Felin, Llanfihangel y Pennant, overlooking the Dysynni Valley**

83. *above:* **Cerrig y Felin fireplace, still in situ, an indicator of a high-status gentry house of the 16th century**

community as leaders. All three sons entered Jesus College, Oxford, a favourite destination for the sons of the Welsh gentry. Richard followed an ecclesiastical career taking up the Rectorship of Netteswell in Essex in 1607. Gruffudd and Edward probably spent time in the Inns of Court, at the time considered a 'finishing school' for the sons of gentry, allowing them to gain an understanding of the law to fulfil their roles in estate management and participate more effectively as magistrates. The youngest son Robert turned to trade, becoming a grocer in London.

Edward Nanney married Elizabeth, the daughter of Lewis Gwyn of Dolaugwyn, High Sheriff of Merioneth in 1617, and is known to have lived at Cerrig-y-Felin in the parish of Llanfihangel y Pennant. Edward is credited as being the head of the Maesypandy cadet branch of Nannau, the ancestor of the Nanneys of Llanfendigaid near Tywyn, and the Nanneys of Llwyn at Dolgellau. Cadet branches were considered important at this period in Welsh history and Huw Nanney's descendants were to branch out and form important estates of their own, achieving this primarily through fortuitous marriages to heiresses.

By 1586 Huw Nanney was appointed to the office of sheriff, the first in the family to hold the post, continuing the Nannau trend of office holding that stretched back nearly three centuries. Huw's achievements were heralded by the poets, particularly Richard Phylip the family bard of Nannau. Such was the regard for the family bard that on building his 'magnificent mansion' Huw Nanney is known to have made special provision to accommodate the illustrious poets in a specially constructed window space. An indicator of Huw Nanney's hospitality towards the bards is evident by the large number who wrote elegies to him on his death in 1623, with no fewer than 17 different bards rising to the challenge. On the death of Huw's widow Annes in 1627, Richard Phylip noted that she and Huw had feasted the bards together at Nannau for sixty years.

In the eyes of the bards Huw had achieved the pinnacle of his class, a respected justice of the peace and sheriff of his county, but none were to mention his extra-marital misdemeanours!

In 1588, a verdict was given in the Court of the Marches against Huw Nanney Hên, who had been accused of incontinence (adultery) at Bewdley, Worcestershire. The case concerned

the severall supposed incontinent living of the defendant with Mary verch Hugh, Katharine verch John and Ellen verch Meirike.' Whereas Hugh Nanney 'hath confessed that he about xiii yeres last past offended incontinently with the sayd Katharine verch John and begate one Child upon her body' and 'ys not as yet ponished'.

The court ordered Huw to pay a forty-shilling fine and forty-shillings costs for the first charge. The supposed offences with the said Ellen and Mary were dismissed out of court. To further publically highlight his extra-marital

indiscretions, in 1594 the Bishop of Bangor ordered Huw to do penance in the churches of Llanfachreth, Dolgellau, Trawsfynydd, Maentwrog, Beddgelert and Bangor for his adultery. However adulterous he may have been, he was meticulous in the attention he paid to the future of his legitimate family. In particular, poets commended his diligence in marrying all of his five daughters to good families.

In 1586, with a perceived increased threat from abroad, the Crown introduced the prestigious office of Deputy Lieutenant in Wales. Two deputies were allocated to Merioneth, entrusted with the role of commanding and training the local militia, organising coastal defence and supplying men to fight in actions abroad. It was a period when corruption was commonplace amongst office holders, with many examples of deputy lieutenants and justices of the peace being reprimanded and sometimes dismissed for corrupt practices.

Huw Nanney was no different - a justice of the peace and sheriff, but also a law-breaker of considerable proportions. Such was his contempt for the law that in 1588, he took it upon himself to cut down a forest of trees (30,000 oaks) that were growing on Crown land on the Penrhos Common in the Ganllwyd Valley near Dolgellau. It was an outrageous act and one that would come back to haunt him with a vengeance, but at the time he probably thought he was above the law.

THE PENRHOS Common Travesty

The story unfolds in 1588 when two English speculators, John Smith of Newcastle-under-Lyme and William Dale, a London grocer, were invited by Huw Nanney to set up an iron smelting works in the Ganllwyd Valley on the probable promise of a plentiful supply of timber. It is known that Huw Nanney regularly visited the Midlands at this time, and Bewdley

in particular, as witnessed by his noted indiscretions. Bewdley at this time was a centre for charcoal burning and it is likely he was looking for an outlet for the timber he intended to illegally harvest on the Penrhos Common. During the many visits he made to the Midlands he would have made contact with potential speculators. The demand for timber as fuel for blast furnaces had caused huge amounts of deforestation in England, forcing ironmasters to migrate to more remote areas. Between 1588 and 1594 Huw Nanney Hên and his son Gruffudd Nanney sold all the trees on the common to Smith and Dale for charcoal production to be used in the blast furnaces.

Rowland Lee, Lord President of the Council of the Marches in Ludlow, who had responsibility for Wales, made no bones of his distrust of the gentry of Merioneth and Cardigan.

He considered both counties lawless and unstable and that appointing magistrates in Wales would

mean setting thieves to catch thieves.

Bearing in mind the actions of Huw Nanney Hên and many of his fellow gentry at this

unruly time, Lee had assessed the situation accurately.

In Huw Nanney Hên's time, despite the growth of estates, it was the Crown that still owned most of the land in the shire and the Welsh gentry, through official positions, sought to control this and profit from this valuable resource. Clashes between rival gentry families would ultimately occur as they strove for lucrative administrative offices and battled to compete for leases of Crown lands.

The Nanneys became embroiled in such a struggle in 1593 when they came head to head with the Owen family of the Llwyn. It turned into a bitter feud for the control of the Dolgellau area and would run for nearly two decades, sharply dividing the community in the process.

86. left: **Date stone on Corsygedol Gatehouse** *(1630)*

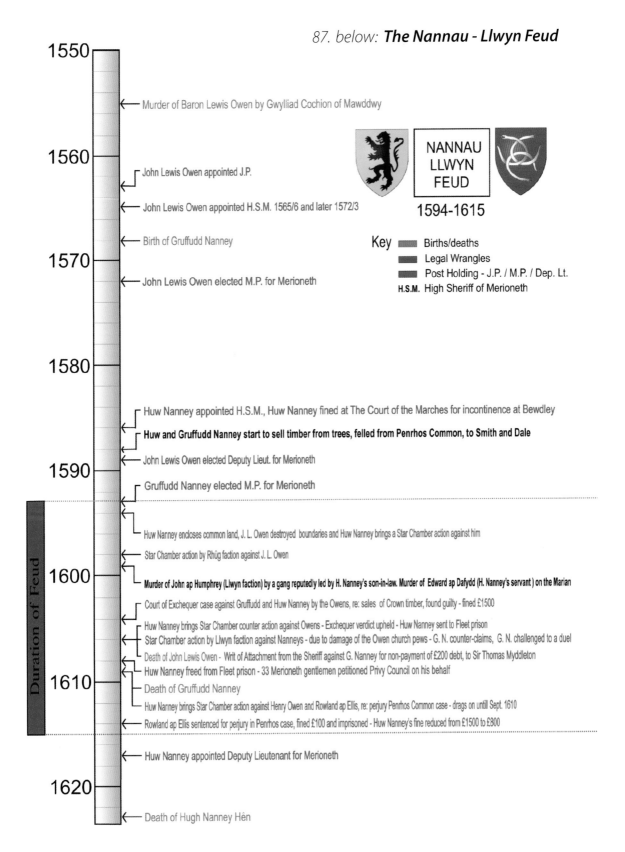

1550

← Murder of Baron Lewis Owen by Gwylliad Cochion of Mawddwy

1560

← John Lewis Owen appointed J.P.

← John Lewis Owen appointed H.S.M. 1565/6 and later 1572/3

← Birth of Gruffudd Nanney

1570

← John Lewis Owen elected M.P. for Merioneth

NANNAU
LLWYN
FEUD

1594-1615

Key — Births/deaths
— Legal Wrangles
— Post Holding - J.P. / M.P. / Dep. Lt.
H.S.M. High Sheriff of Merioneth

1580

← Huw Nanney appointed H.S.M., Huw Nanney fined at The Court of the Marches for incontinence at Bewdley

← **Huw and Gruffudd Nanney start to sell timber from trees, felled from Penrhos Common, to Smith and Dale**

← John Lewis Owen elected Deputy Lieut. for Merioneth

1590

← Gruffudd Nanney elected M.P. for Merioneth

← Huw Nanney encloses common land, J. L. Owen destroyed boundaries and Huw Nanney brings a Star Chamber action against him

← Star Chamber action by Rhûg faction against J. L. Owen

1600

← **Murder of John ap Humphrey (Llwyn faction) by a gang reputedly led by H. Nanney's son-in-law. Murder of Edward ap Dafydd (H. Nanney's servant) on the Marian**

← Court of Exchequer case against Gruffudd and Huw Nanney by the Owens, re: sales of Crown timber, found guilty - fined £1500

← Huw Nanney brings Star Chamber counter action against Owens - Exchequer verdict upheld - Huw Nanney sent to Fleet prison

← Star Chamber action by Llwyn faction against Nanneys - due to damage of the Owen church pews - G. N. counter-claims, G. N. challenged to a duel

← Death of John Lewis Owen - Writ of Attachment from the Sheriff against G. Nanney for non-payment of £200 debt, to Sir Thomas Myddleton

← Huw Nanney freed from Fleet prison - 33 Merioneth gentlemen petitioned Privy Council on his behalf

1610

← Death of Gruffudd Nanney

← Huw Nanney brings Star Chamber action against Henry Owen and Rowland ap Ellis, re: perjury Penrhos Common case - drags on untill Sept. 1610

← Rowland ap Ellis sentenced for perjury in Penrhos case, fined £100 and imprisoned - Huw Nanney's fine reduced from £1500 to £800

← Huw Nanney appointed Deputy Lieutenant for Merioneth

1620

← Death of Hugh Nanney Hên

Duration of Feud

THE NANNAU – Llwyn Feud

The origins of the feud is difficult to ascertain. Local traditions tell of a distrust between the Nanneys and Owens stretching back many generations, but the catalyst for the 1593 outbreak seems to stem from the fact that Gruffudd Nanney had ousted John Lewis Owen of the Llwyn from his seat as M.P. of the County of Merioneth. Politics at this time revolved around a complex web of family allegiances. Gruffudd Nanney's selection by local gentry had challenged and beaten the powerful Plas Iolyn-Rhiwlas-Llwyn confederation that had dominated Merioneth

politics for many years. John Lewis Owen bitterly resented the fact that the Nannau family had deprived him of this coveted position.

By 1596 Gruffudd Nanney was living in Doluwcheogryd, near Dolgellau, a recently constructed house and more appropriate to his status as M.P. of Merioneth. An indicator of the enmity between Gruffudd Nanney and John Lewis Owen is aptly demonstrated in an account presented to the President of the Council of the Marches of Wales on behalf of Gruffudd Nanney. It charges Lewis Owen and Harri Owen, sons of John Lewis Owen of

88. below: **Dol'rhyd, an 18th-century house on the site of Gruffudd Nanney's 1596 home with inscribed stones from his original house on the east wall**

89. **TABLETS ON EAST WALL OF DOL'RHYD** (1596)

G.N.	**ROYAL ARMS**	**E.N.**
Gruffudd Nanney	Viva Diva Elizabetha	Ellen Nanney
Eldest son of Huw Nanney I	Long live the Goddess Elizabeth	Daughter of John Wynn ap
of Nannau		Cadwaladr of Rhiwlas

Non domus dominum sed domines domum
It is not the house that makes the master, but the master the house

**Mellis aer ferrum lapides mens ignis Olympus
Omnia Transibunt sed mea verba manent**
The soft air, iron, stones and volcano. The Heavens,
All things will pass away, but my words remain

Llwyn, with assault in the town of Dolgellau at Christmas 1603, the charge stating:

That Lewis Owen and Harri Owen with others were laying in waite in small houses in the town of Dolgelley with weapons and shorte swords and dagars ready to assault Griffith Nanney on his visiting the towne for service of his maj's being a Justice of the Peace, and he dareth not come to the church aforesaid to heare divine service, & c.

It was during these troubled times that Gruffudd Nanney built Doluwcheogryd, now shortened to 'Dol'rhyd'. According to Edward Griffith, Antiquarian of Dolgellau (1898):

There was at Doluwcheogryd strong and high walls surrounding the extensive court in front of the mansion, and according to the tradition in the neighbourhood, it was within these walls the members used to meet their constituency to give account of their doings in the House of Commons, and when we consider the attitude of the county at that time, it required high walls to defend them from their enemies.

The Dol'rhyd of today is essentially a mid-18th-century house, but remnants of Gruffudd Nanney's 1596 house survive in the form of incredible inscribed stones, now rebuilt into the east elevation.

From the onset of the troubles a number of rival factions joined the vendetta, as illustrated in image number 94. Matters came to a head in 1594 when Huw Nanney enclosed a tenement called Tyddyn Bach in the Township of Garthmaelan. John Lewis Owen, outraged by this, broke down the boundary enclosures with an unruly band of followers. Huw Nanney responded by seeking justice in the Court of the Star Chamber.

Through endless actions and counter actions, the feud escalated to the point where the aggression culminated in the murder of a Nanney servant, Edward ap Dafydd, on the Marian (The Green of Dolgellau) in 1599 while playing bowls with Edward Nanney. The perpetrators (a large contingent of the Owen faction) were brought to justice by Huw Nanney at two separate trials in the Great Sessions at Bala, only to be found not guilty by a biased jury. It seems that the main instigators who had struck the fatal blows, the sons of John ap Humphrey, had fled the country and were still outlawed in 1609.

In 1604 the Attorney General, at the instigation of the Llwyn faction, began an action against Huw Nanney Hên and the two English speculators Dale and Smith for cutting down the Penrhos Common oaks. Huw Nanney was found guilty by a jury who clearly owed their allegiance to the Owen camp. He was fined £1500, the perceived value of the 30,000 oak trees. Refusing, or unable to pay, he was eventually imprisoned in the Fleet Prison in London in 1606.

With Huw Nanney safely interned in prison, the Llwyn faction began an action against the Nanneys for damaging their pews in Dolgelley church and inciting a mob to hatred and malice. Gruffudd Nanney responded with a counter action, claiming that the Llwyn faction had also destroyed Nanney pews. It was at this point in the proceedings that Gruffudd Nanney was challenged to a duel by Lewis Owen, son of John Lewis Owen of Llwyn. No record exists of this duel actually taking place, but Gruffudd's letter replying to the challenge has miraculously survived. It states:

Mr lewes owen, I receaved a lettere subscribed with yor name, as yt should seeme intendinge a challenge to me and my Cozen Edmond lloyd. The maner of yor sendinge, fyrst I utterly dislike, That soe base a messenger should be sent between gent in a matter of that nature, and with all the letters to be delivered me in the open market, and all the towne to knowe the contents befor yt come to my handes, therfor in my judgement, yt was yll handled. I might justly take exceptions to the contents also, beinge in every sentence imperfect; for you make mencion of a little jarr between us, which you doe not recite. And agayne you make Edmond Lloyd and yor brother John owen partakers in the accion, which I doe not allowe: if there be eny dislike between them lett them answer on an other, as they will. I doe not doubt but my Cozen Edmond will performe the part of a gent. To my accions in this matter noe body shall be party nor pryvy but we both, althoughe your letter be blazed over the country allready; and wher you make mencion of an oath, yt is never used, for the credyte of a gent. ys sufficient in that case, because the woords and the

honor are the grounds whereupon poynts of armes doe depend, whereof I greatly marvayle that you are ignorant; and for the secrecy do not think that Gruff Nanney's shyrt shall knowe of our meeting. And in yor post scriptum you name three kyndes of fyght, the last whereof is generally condemmed for a gent to use. And judginge which is fyttest, you seeme to direct me being defft but I am not so rawe but that I knowe I am to appoint the weapons, the tyme, the place, and the maner cosonant to the rules of armes. To answere therfor yor challenge (althoughe I might take many exceptions thereunto, neverthelesse to avoyd the generall judgement of men) I doe promise by the fayth of a gent. to be at the sea shore within full sea marke, about half waye between barmouth and harlech, directly under the chuch of llanddwyy, upon Friday nexte by viii of the clock in the morning, and there to stay an houre at the lest: the weapons that I will bringe wth me shall be only a rapier and dager, the company myself alone, for I will have noe person lyvinge partaker of such an accion in my behalf. the length of my rapier blad I doe send by the berer, what yt meaneth he doth not knowe. I will not fayle to performe what I have written, by the help of the just god to whome I comend my defence, and in whome I only trust. G.N.

P.S. Because you dyd send yor man wth yor letter I do send my man, which I knowe is unseemly.

(Gruffudd Nanney's challenge to Lewis Owen, undated)

92. below: **Corsygedol - 1596 elevation on the right**
93. inset: **Detail of Corsygedol doorway**

92. below: **Corsygedol - 1596 elevation on the right**
93. inset: **Detail of Corsygedol doorway**

The death of John Lewis Owen in 1606 did not end the malice and hatred. On his release from the Fleet Prison in 1608, after a petition signed by thirty-three Merioneth gentlemen, Huw continued unrelentingly to pursue the Owens through the courts for perjury. The whole unsavoury episode continued even with the premature death of Gruffudd Nanney in 1609, whose widow Ellen spent the remainder of her life in the service of God and did not remarry.

Huw Nanney's dogged persistence was 'rewarded' when Rowland ap Ellis of the Llwyn faction was imprisoned for perjury in the Penrhos Common case and Huw Nanney's fine was reduced to £800. The feud finally came to a

94. **Nannau/Llwyn Feud** (1594-1615) Litigations

Owen Faction ■ Main instigators

John Lewis Owen of Llwyn (J.L.O.)
Lewis Owen (son)
John Owen (son)
Henry Owen (son)
Edward Owen of Hengwrt (brother of J.L.O)
Robert Simon Owen (nephew of J.L.O.)
Lewis Simon Owen (nephew of J.L.O.)
Robert Owen (son of Edward Owen)
John ap Humphrey (brother-in-law to Ed.Owen)
Robert (son of John Humphreys)
Edward (son of John Humphreys)
Rowland ap Elisse of Rhiwaedog (Mayor of Bala)
Rich. Nanney (g.son of Rich. Nanney, Cefndeuddwr)
Henry ap Ieuan Lloyd of Hafodunos

Nanney Faction

Hugh Nanney Hên (H.N.H.)
Gruffudd Nanney (son)
Edward Nanney (son)
Edward ap David (H.N.H.'s servant)
Robert Lloyd of Rhiwgoch (son-in-law)

■ Court of the Exchequer
■ Court of the Marches
■ Court of the Star Chamber
☐ Court of the Common Pleas
■ Court of the Great Sessions

Criminal records pre-Feud

■ John Lewis Owen -1597/8 accused of misdemeanours in the office of Deputy Lieutenant and J.P. including the embezzlement of £1,000 worth of armour from Harlech Castle

☐ Rowland ap Elisse -1592/3 as Mayor of Bala, accused of forcing the town's burgesses to re-elect him, thereby gaining great wealth

■ Rowland ap Elisse - 1600/1 accused of forcible entry and stealing evidence. Richard Nanney accused of murdering
and Richard Nanney   David ap John Llewelyn ap Rees at Mawddwy

■ Hugh Nanney Hên - 1590 accused with Robert Lloyd of Rhiwgoch, of forcibly preventing the execution of a Commission of Survey out of the Exchequer

Key Lawsuits of the Feud

■ 1st May, 1594 - Gruffudd Nanney instituted proceedings against John Lewis Owen for breaking down the walls of his tenement of Tyddyn Bach in the township of Garthmaelan - causing a riot - instigators - John Lewis Owen, his 3 sons and nephew

■ Sept.   1601 - Murder of Edward ap David (H.N.H's servant) on the Bowling Green, Dolgellau, 24th June - H.N.H. as J.P. issued warrants for the arrest of the perpetrators - two were indicted - Robert Owen of Hengwrt and David Robert to appear at two trials at the Great Sessions at Bala.The prisoners were found not guilty even though clear evidence to convict was presented

■ 1602 - Gruffudd Nanney opened a case against John Lewis Owen and Lewis Owen regarding Tyddyn Bach - the case revolved around the ownership of Tyddyn Bach - Gruffudd claimed to have bought it legally - J.L.O. claimed he illegally enclosed common land

■ 9th June, 1602 - H.N.H. presented a Bill of Complaint against two of the jurors at the 1601 Great Sessions for perjury, these being, Henry ap Ieuan Lloyd J.P. of Hafodunos, and Ellis David ap Thomas, gent. and four jurors on a charge of bribery

■ 1604 - The Attorney General, at the instigation of the Llwyn faction, began an action against H.N.H., Gruffudd Nanney and two Englishmen. (William Dale and John Smith) charging them with cutting down thirty thousand oak trees on Penrhos Common

■ 1606 - H.N.H. brought a writ of Error, on the grounds that action had been brought forward by old enemies with a grudge

■ 29th May, 1606 - H.N.H. opened an action in the Court in defence of the Penrhos action

■ 1606 - Henry Owen of Llwyn presented a Bill of Complaint, claiming that in Dec.1603, the Nanneys had destroyed the Owen family pew in Dolgellau Church

■ 1606 - Bill of Complaint brought by Nanneys of Cefndeuddwr against H.N.H. and Gruffudd Nanney, for misconduct as J.P.s

■ Feb.   1609 - H.N.H. opened an action, attempting to show that Rowland ap Elisse and Henry Owen had committed perjury by giving false evidence in the 1604 Exchequer trial.

97. *below:* *Detail of the elaborate plaster decoration at Plas Mawr*

close in 1615, after more than 21 years of hatred, violence and bloodshed.

Interestingly, Huw Nanney Hên, a one time convicted felon, was rewarded with the prestigious office of Deputy Lieutenant in 1617, and a status in the community second to none. Along with his increased standing in the community, Huw Nanney Hên, in common with a number of successful gentry families, turned their attention to improving their houses.

In 1592, records show that Huw Nanney was living at Tyddyn Cefn Llanfair, most likely a modest abode, but he had a grander vision in mind and a new mansion at Nannau became a reality.

The bards waxed lyrical over Huw's new house. They were bowled over by the scale and extravagance of the mansion. It is likely that he built this 'magnificent palace' in or about 1612-1615. The poets were amazed by the quality of the building, bearing in mind the huge legal costs incurred in all his numerous litigations.

Poetic descriptions can be exaggerated, to say the least, but whenever a poet described tangible items that could be observed by his audience, it is likely that the descriptions would have stood up to careful scrutiny. Details such

98. above: *Cefndeuddwr, Trawsfynydd - the home of a cadet branch of Nannau who descend from Hywel, 12th Lord of Nannau*

as saddle pommels on the roof and the whitewashed tower could have been accurate descriptions of the building. Such details as a hundred lofts were less easily discernable and could well have been an elaboration.

The main features of the house that impressed the bards most were:

- its chimneys – an indicator of status
- its height – the highest place under the stars!
- the angular roofs with saddle pommels on the ridges
- its long staircase
- its one hundred lofts and sixty doors
- the whitewashed clock-tower with three hundred steps
- the oak roof covered with slates and lead

- the huge expanse of glass overlooking Cader Idris
- the hall, parlours, chambers and of course the most important room for some Nannau household bards – the cellar!

Huw Nanney Hên must have incurred huge expenditure on erecting his palatial domain, but the stately structure stood for less than thirty years, as it was probably burnt to the ground in the Civil War around 1645. No house is recorded at Nannau according to the Hearth Tax of 1662, with the family living in Dol'rhyd in the late 17th century.

Careful analysis of the poetic descriptions reveal a house that is similar in many ways to Plas Mawr in Conway, a house built for a scion of the Wynn family between 1576 and 1585.

Huw Nanney Hên would certainly have known this house: his father-in-law, Richard Vaughan of Corsygedol, was inspired by Plas Mawr to emulate features of this unique house during the construction of Corsygedol in 1576. Plas Mawr's unique lookout tower was possibly copied in Huw Nanney's 'palace', giving weight to the idea that Plas Mawr was the likely architectural influence.

Huw Nanney's daughter Jane's second marriage had been to Lewis Gwyn of Dolaugwyn near Tywyn. Dolaugwyn is a magnificent stepped gabled house that was of the same era, circa 1575. It also displays many features in common with Plas Mawr.

The fact that Huw Nanney Hên built his new house at a time of financial stringency is puzzling. The early years of the 17th century were difficult times for the Welsh gentry owing to bad weather conditions which resulted in successive harvest failures and famine. Sir John Wynn of Gwydir referred to the dire conditions, that resulted in a fall in rents in 1613, as those

which hath burnt up the greater part of our corn and grass and hath brought down the

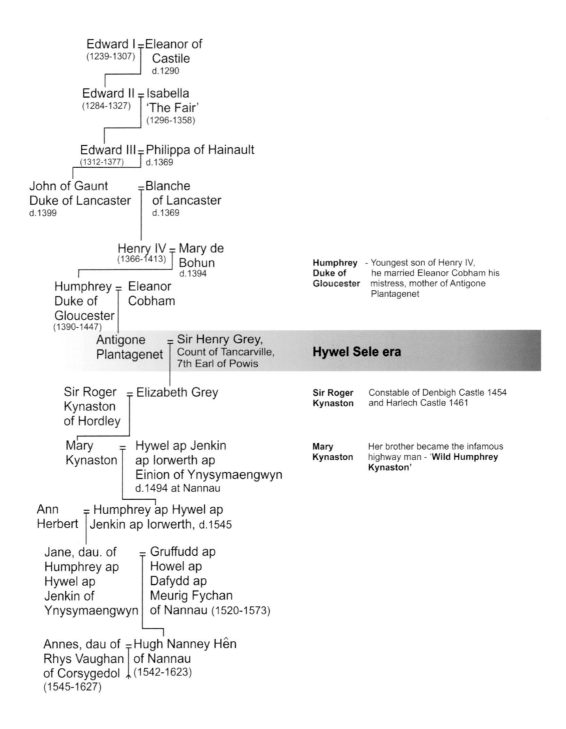

Edward I ═ Eleanor of
(1239-1307)   Castile
            d.1290

Edward II ═ Isabella
(1284-1327)   'The Fair'
            (1296-1358)

Edward III ═ Philippa of Hainault
(1312-1377)   d.1369

John of Gaunt   ═ Blanche
Duke of Lancaster   of Lancaster
d.1399   d.1369

Henry IV ═ Mary de
(1366-1413)   Bohun
           d.1394

Humphrey ═ Eleanor
Duke of   Cobham
Gloucester
(1390-1447)

Antigone   ═ Sir Henry Grey,
Plantagenet   Count of Tancarville,
            7th Earl of Powis

Humphrey - Youngest son of Henry IV,
Duke of   he married Eleanor Cobham his
Gloucester mistress, mother of Antigone
             Plantagenet

Hywel Sele era

Sir Roger ═ Elizabeth Grey
Kynaston
of Hordley

Sir Roger   Constable of Denbigh Castle 1454
Kynaston   and Harlech Castle 1461

Mary   ═ Hywel ap Jenkin
Kynaston   ap Iorwerth ap
          Einion of Ynysymaengwyn
          d.1494 at Nannau

Mary   Her brother became the infamous
Kynaston highway man - '**Wild Humphrey**
             Kynaston'

Ann   ═ Humphrey ap Hywel ap
Herbert   Jenkin ap Iorwerth, d.1545

Jane, dau. of   ═ Gruffudd ap
Humphrey ap   Howel ap
Hywel ap   Dafydd ap
Jenkin of   Meurig Fychan
Ynysymaengwyn of Nannau (1520-1573)

Annes, dau of ═ Hugh Nanney Hên
Rhys Vaughan   of Nannau
of Corsygedol   (1542-1623)
(1545-1627)

102. *above:* **Gatehouse at Corsygedol**

sale of any cattle being the only means my tenants have to live on and to raise my rents hath made them fail payment to me and I to his majesty.

It is highly likely that Huw Nanney Hên funded his extravagant house from the proceeds of the sale of the 30,000 oak trees cut down on Penrhos Common some years previously. Did he also supplement his building costs by borrowing from moneylenders such as Sir Thomas Myddleton of Chirk Castle, to whom it is known Huw Nanney was indebted in this period?

Huw Nanney Hên died in 1623, leaving his grandson Huw Nanney II (Huw the Younger) a magnificent new mansion, an annual income of £300 and debts that amounted to £1,022-19s-10d.

The words of the bard Siôn Phylip, written in 1616 for another patron, partly ring true for Huw Nanney Hên:

For our sustenance it is good for us to see you in your place. You extended and led your estate over two ages at your own expense. You spent many chests full (of silver) on your building.

The numerous elegies written to Huw Nanney Hên on his death praise his achievements and status within the community as a leader of distinction and a worthy patron of Welsh culture.

He is in many ways an enigma, playing an important part in county affairs for nearly four decades, yet ever willing to be utterly lawless, with little or no respect for the property of his neighbours or the Crown. This controversial Nanney has certainly left an indelible mark on the history of his ancient lineage.

103. *Dolgellau Church, built in 1716 on the site of the old church*

104. NANNAU'S
STONE TABLETS

Arms of Huw Nanney Hên & Ann
Nanney daughter of Corsygedol

Royal Arms - Elizabeth I

Englyn written by
bard Siôn Phylip
for the house of
Nannau in Huw
Nanney Hên's time.

Translation
The house of the faithful
is pleasant, where dear
ones tarry. Wealth will be
there. It will always be
full of plenty and
goodness.

The 1581 date stone was probably incorporated into a wall
of Huw Nanney Hên's earlier house.

Explanation
Linked to Psalm 112
His seed shall be mighty upon the earth:
The generation of the upright
shall be blessed.
Wealth and riches are in his house:
And his righteousness endureth for ever.

Adam and Eve stone, once built into the
back wall of Nannau, now lost.

HUGHE NANNE

ANES N

ÆTAT 4

WEIL DUW NA DIM

6

1624-1701

THE TURBULENT 17TH CENTURY

Huw Nanney II (The Younger) inherited a magnificent mansion and a legacy of debt accrued from the multitude of lawsuits the family had so obsessively pursued. It is evident that the Nanneys, in the face of such furious litigation, turned to mortgages to fund their costly suits. The first major lawsuit of 1594 was swiftly followed by a mortgage from Sir Thomas Myddleton of Chirk in 1595. The Nanneys at this troubled time were typical of their class, their capital tied up in their estate and lawyers' fees taking a hefty toll on their limited resources.

Prior to the flurry of litigations the Nanneys had been cautious in the extreme, only entering into mortgages occasionally to fund land acquisitions. Borrowing money to fund litigations, however, was to prove reckless. It is clear that on balance the Nanneys came off the worst when the dust settled in the wake of the Llwyn/Nannau feud, with Huw the Younger having to deal with the aftermath.

Like his grandfather before him, Huw looked to Corsygedol for a wife. He married Anne, the daughter of Gruffudd Vaughan, making this the third union between Nannau and Corsygedol since the era of Hywel Sele. Many more such arrangements were to follow as they strived to keep their wealth within the family. Huw the Younger's sister married Robert Vaughan of Hengwrt, the famous antiquarian. Vaughan's priceless collection of books and manuscripts were to descend to Peniarth and subsequently form the Peniarth Manuscripts, now housed in the National Library of Wales at Aberystwyth.

Huw the Younger was Sheriff of Merioneth on two occasions, 1626/7 and 1637/8. His role as Justice of the Peace and Custos Rotulorum, was eulogised by the bards of the time, who recognised Huw as the chief governor in the county.

The post of Custos Rotulorum was the chief Justice of the Peace and keeper of the court rolls, and as such was singled out for high praise by the bards. Greater familiarity with the law was required of the Custos Rotulorum and Huw the Younger was to follow in the footsteps of his grandfather by taking on the most prestigious law office in the shire.

As Sheriff of Merioneth in 1637/8 Huw would have been embroiled in the problems that befell the county regarding the unpopular 'Ship Money'. This unpopular tax had its basis in the ancient power which allowed kings to levy money from coastal towns in order to build ships to protect the land from foreign invasion. King Charles, facing a financial crisis in 1635, sent a letter to all sheriffs instructing them to collect Ship Money, supposedly for use in boosting the Navy. Encouraged by the receipts, the King demanded more the following year. The abuse of the ancient law to bolster the King's coffers caused much discontent. The burden of collecting the now yearly unfair tax fell on sheriffs such as Huw the Younger, many of whom wrote to the King complaining that their counties were being asked to pay too much. It is unlikely that Huw Nanney complained thus, as he, in common with most of the Merioneth gentry, was staunchly Royalist, but it is likely that he encountered resistance from the population.

At the height of his power in 1632, aged 44, Huw the Younger commissioned a portrait, the earliest known Nanney portrait in existence. No portrait exists of Huw Nanney Hên or his son Gruffudd. Miles Wynn Cato, an authority on early Welsh portraiture, believes that neither were ever painted, as even the wealthy and vain Sir John Wynn of Gwydir did not commission his portrait until the second decade of the 17th century, by which time both Huw Nanney Hên and Gruffudd had died. No artist has been identified with Huw the Younger's portrait, but it gives us an intriguing glimpse of the beginnings of Nannau portraiture, which were aimed at promoting status and ancestry.

In 1625, Huw the Younger's son Gruffudd Nanney III married Anne, the daughter and heiress of Lewis Gwyn of Dolaugwyn, near Tywyn. Lewis Gwyn had been High Sheriff of Merioneth in 1617 and had married Jane, a daughter of Huw Nanney Hên.

In 1642, when the Civil War broke out, Huw the Younger's family would have been in turmoil. His son Gruffudd Nanney III, on the eve of the war, had been declared a delinquent by Parliament and was targeted as a fervent Royalist supporter and a candidate to have his lands sequestrated. Parliamentary retribution was swift and decisive and saw Nannau burnt to the ground around 1645 by the Cromwellian Army. Dolaugwyn was not attacked, but nearby Ynysymaengwyn suffered self-inflicted destruction to stop it falling into Parliamentary hands. Huw the Younger would have witnessed the wilful destruction of his grandfather's palatial house, and from this time on the family based themselves at Dol'rhyd. Nannau would remain abandoned until Colonel Huw Nanney, Huw the Younger's grandson, modestly rebuilt the house around 1693, nearly fifty years later.

Huw the Younger died in 1647 aged 59 years, and a description of his funeral is contained in a letter to his nephew Howel Vaughan of Hengwrt. It was by Randle Holme, a well-known heraldic artist from Chester, who described Huw's armorial bearings and detailed his funeral thus:

> *For the funeral order, first the poore, 2 and 2, then the servants of the house in Clokes, then the banner carried by a kinsman of blood: the helm and crest by another, then the cote of armes by another, then the preacher, then the Corpes carried by the gentry of kindred, then his sonne and heyre along, then his bretheren 2 and 2 (and so all wch have blacks according to nearness of blood), then the women in black, in like maner, then the Knights, Esquires etc...*

Holme's letter contained a sketch of the hearse, which consisted of a piece of wood on the bier above the coffin where the pall was draped. The funeral was certainly indicative of the status achieved by the family, although by now one of their family mansions smouldered in

ruins. Huw's son Gruffudd Nanney III, Sheriff of Merioneth 1640 to 1642, now branded a delinquent, was left to lead the Nanneys through these challenging times. Huw's widow Anne outlived her husband by some 21 years, dying in 1668 aged 84.

It is somewhat surprising to find that Huw the Younger's nephew attended to the arrangements for his uncle's funeral rather than Huw's own son Gruffudd. The reason might lie in the fact that Gruffudd, having been labelled a delinquent, was keeping a low profile, or even more likely that Howell used his 'connections' to elicit the services of the celebrated heraldic artist, Randle Holme of Chester. Howel Vaughan of Hengwrt was well versed in heraldry and genealogy, as his father was the noted antiquarian Robert Vaughan of Hengwrt who had cooperated with Randle Holme on many projects.

ROBERT VAUGHAN - The Antiquarian

Huw the Younger's sister, Catherine, had married Robert Vaughan, then of Gwengraig near Dolgellau, around 1625. It was not until 1626 that mention is made of Robert Vaughan living at Hengwrt, the family home of his mother Margaret. Robert Vaughan's lineage is well documented, with direct descent from

Ynyr Fychan, 6th Lord of Nannau, through his son Howel, a nephew of Bishop Anian II. The marriage of Robert Vaughan and Catherine represented a union of two branches of the Nannau family, reunited after three hundred years.

Robert Vaughan had entered Oriel College, Oxford, as a commoner in 1612 at the age of twenty. He pursued a regular course of studies that was popular at the time of Logic and Philosophy, but left Oxford without taking his degree, returning to his native county. Perhaps he realised that his true vocation lay in studying his ancient Welsh culture and maybe this had caused him to abandon his studies. His lifelong friendship with Rhys and Siôn Cain of Oswestry might have influenced his career path - they came from a centuries old bardic family and were totally immersed in ancient Welsh literature.

The late Tudor and early Stuart period saw a re-awakening of interest in all things Welsh, and this naturally led some of the gentry to reassess their literary heritage. Robert Vaughan was one of a small band of enthusiasts who took on the task of preserving old Welsh manuscripts. On

the dissolution of the monasteries, the repositories of such valuable scripts had been destroyed and their contents had fallen into many other hands. Uniquely, he saw the need to bring together all these important cultural documents and preserve them for posterity. As he lived at a time when printing had not yet become commonplace, Robert was reduced to copying anything he could not procure outright, a laboriously painstaking task which he carried out for most of his life. He is known to have spent his early years in the family home at Gwengraig, an ancient farmstead lying on the north-east slope of Cader Idris. He later relocated to Hengwrt near Dolgellau, his home for the next fifty years, and a safe location to house his growing antiquarian collection. Robert Vaughan's father had provided Robert Owen of Hengwrt with a number of mortgages in the early years of the 17th century, and it is not surprising to find that in 1626, Robert Vaughan and his own father were in total ownership of the Hengwrt estate.

At Hengwrt (Old Court), Robert Vaughan would have enjoyed the advantages of a good estate. By now probably a holding of several thousand acres, and with a landed income, he was free to cultivate his interests, corresponding with many of the recognised antiquaries of the period, and always vigilant of manuscripts that could be purchased or copied.

A quote attributed to him aptly outlines his motives, in that it was

love of my country and our ancestors that drives me.

This drive and determination resulted in the preservation of priceless manuscripts that could so easily have been lost forever. Through his network of like-minded enthusiasts he was kept informed of manuscripts that came on the market or could be copied. Significantly, he considered the preservation of his collection beyond his own lifetime, and he is known to have made an arrangement with a fellow antiquarian, a Mr Jones of Gelli Lyfdy, that the survivor of them should benefit from each other's labours. Robert Vaughan, surviving his friend, was to inherit his important collection.

This strategy employed in future generations would ensure that the collection would not become dispersed, as occurred with many other libraries. His efforts resulted in the finest set of early Welsh manuscripts ever to have been collected by an individual, but this was not the end of his talents. He was also an accomplished genealogist and was often the first port of call for gentry seeking to 'unearth' their ancestry. The late 17th century was fertile ground for the Welsh genealogist, as outlined in a contemporary quote:

and then doe they (the Welsh) rip upp (i.e. open up) their pedigrees at length how eche of them is discended from those theire ould princes.

(A Catalogue of Manuscripts Relating to Wales in the British Museum, Edward Owen, ed.)

Robert Vaughan's only published work, *British Antiquities Revived* (Oxford, 1662), outlining the supremacy of the North Wales princes, as opposed to the South Wales dynasties, does not singularly acknowledge his academic achievements. However, various unpublished scripts that he left behind, such as his massive book of pedigrees, reveal a far more accomplished individual.

In 1643 the bitter Civil War entered Wales, with Major-General Thomas Myddleton, M.P. for Denbighshire, given command of the Parliamentary forces campaign in North Wales. Myddleton's home of Chirk Castle had been overrun and captured by Royalist forces in January the same year. Whilst most of the gentry in North Wales supported the King, Thomas Myddleton, the owner of a large estate, was a devout Puritan who, with other denominations such as the Quakers and Baptists, threw in their lot with Parliament. The gentry, being Anglicans and Catholics, implicitly aligned themselves with the King.

Robert Vaughan's allegiances are more difficult to assess; he seems to have been politically neutral and for the most part managed to hold the confidence of both sides during the conflict. In less than a year after the death of Charles I, Robert Vaughan compiled an elaborate pedigree roll for Colonel John Jones the Regicide, a copy of which still survives in the National Library of Wales, Pedigree Roll 250. He later carried out geneaolgical research for General Mytton, a prominent Parliamentary officer, perhaps on the recommendation of Colonel John Jones. His leanings towards Puritanism are clearly demonstrated by copies he made of sermons by several Puritan preachers of the time, and corroborated by the fact that his daughter Jane had married Robert Owen of Dolserau, a prominent Quaker actively involved on the side of Parliament. Robert Owen and his wife later emigrated to Pennsylvania with Rowland Elis in 1686 to avoid religious persecution.

Robert Vaughan was an active Justice of the Peace, a post he held from 1618, and unlike many of his fellow gentry he continued to serve on the bench throughout the period of the Commonwealth. Although evidently 'cooperating' with the new regime, he managed to survive the Civil War and its aftermath, emerging unscathed at the restoration of Charles II in 1660. He continued his antiquarian quest until nearly seventy years of age, and with failing eyesight he painstakingly copied *The Book of Llandaff*. He died in his beloved Hengwrt on Ascension Day, the 16th May 1667. He is most probably buried in Dolgellau Church, according to his expressed wishes.

His son and heir Howel Vaughan inherited both the manuscripts and estate, which was by now heavily in debt. The family possibly thought of selling the entire manuscript collection as a note survives of a valuation in the region of £1000, but fortunately this did not happen as Howel had inherited his father's love of antiquities. Howel died in 1676 and the manuscripts remained in family hands for the next 200 years. Robert Vaughan's book collection however was less fortunate as it is known that some of his library of printed books was sold for as little as 'a penny a pound'!

The manuscripts continued to lie in tranquil neglect for over a century until they were mentioned in 1778 by Richard Thomas, a visitor to Hengwrt, who commented that they had been

damaged by rats, rain and negligence.

By this time the unfortunate owner of Hengwrt was Hugh Vaughan, the great, great-grandson of Robert Vaughan, and an inveterate spendthrift who had inherited the estate from his father in 1750, only to end up a bankrupt in 1778. Fortunately, family members under the cover of darkness had carried the manuscripts away to Nannau under the noses of the prowling baliffs. On the death of Hugh Vaughan in 1783, his brother Robert, later Sir Robert Howel Vaughan, inherited the estate, and on his death his son Griffith Vaughan became custodian of Hengwrt and its priceless collection. Griffith was also to inherit the Rhûg estate at Corwen from his brother Edward, who had so extravagantly refurbished the house in 1799. Griffith relocated the collection and housed it in bookcases manufactured by the famous cabinet-maker Gillows of Lancaster.

Sir Robert Howel Vaughan's grandson, Sir Robert Williames Vaughan 3rd Bart, inherited the Rhûg estate in 1843 and became the proud owner of the manuscripts until his death in 1859. Fortunately, the 3rd Bart had emulated his famous ancestor and entered into an agreement with a friend of his, W.W.E. Wynne of the Peniarth estate near Tywyn, that the survivor would inherit the other's manuscripts. Hence, on the death of Sir Robert in 1859, the Hengwrt manuscripts were transferred to Peniarth, to be housed in a specially constructed oak bookcase made from timber grown on the Peniarth estate, and recatalogued as the 'Peniarth Manuscripts'.

The collection remained in Peniarth for exactly fifty years, until the reversion of the manuscripts was purchased by Sir John

Williams, an avid collector. On the death of W. W.E. Wynne's son, W.R.M. Wynne in 1909, the manuscripts reverted to Sir John Williams. Now having secured the finest collection of Welsh books and manuscripts, Sir John needed to find a permanent home for his precious documents. To this end he worked tirelessly to secure the establishment of the National Library of Wales at Aberystwyth and gifted his collection to the fledgling National Library in January 1909. Robert Vaughan's collection became the principal foundation of the National Library of Wales Manuscript Department. Sir John's bequest had amounted to some 1200 items in three separate groups. Group 1 contained some 500 items directly passed down from the Hengwrt/Peniarth collection.

115. above: **Bookcase made from timber grown on the Peniarth estate, designed by W. W. E. Wynne to house the Hengwrt and Peniarth Manuscripts in 1859**

116. above: **W. W. E. Wynne of Peniarth (1801–1880)**

Robert Vaughan's mansion of Hengwrt was replaced in the mid 18th century by a grand Georgian design and it stood proudly until 1962, when parts of it were damaged by fire. Most of the house was demolished, but fortunately the present owner has managed to rescue part of this historic building for posterity, a wonderful reminder of Robert Vaughan the Antiquarian, recognised as

one of the foremost antiquaries of his time, taking the keenest delight in the literature, the history, the genealogy, and the heraldry of Wales ... he rendered a service to his country and to its literature for which successive generations owe him an everlasting debt of gratitude.

(Daniel Huws, 2000)

GRUFFUDD NANNEY III

Gruffudd Nanney III was High Sheriff of Merioneth on the eve of the Civil War, his peaceful existence severely challenged as a result of being branded a 'delinquent' by Parliament. Such a term was reserved for adherents to the Royalist cause and the House of Nannau certainly qualified in this respect. Gruffudd's father, Huw the Younger, had sat on the Royalist Commission of Array whose brief was to assist with organising royalist campaigns and enlisting troops. Gruffudd's wife Anne was a daughter and heiress of Lewis Gwyn of Dolaugwyn, a cadet branch of the fervent royalist family of Ynysymaengwyn. To further implicate Gruffudd in Parliament's eyes, his uncle Sir John Owen of Clenennau was the Royalist Colonel who headed the main opposition to the Parliamentary Army in North Wales.

The War eventually came to an end in 1646, although Harlech Castle held out under siege until March 1647 and pockets of rebellion continued even though the King had been captured. As previously mentioned, Nannau lay in ruins by 1645, together with other Royalist seats in Merioneth. Ynysymaengwyn had been destroyed by its owner Robert Corbet, a son of the house of Moreton Corbet, whose impressive family home in Shropshire was also a casualty of the war.

The formation of Sequestration Committees heralded the end of the war; now the defeated Royalists would be made to pay for their actions through 'sequestration' and 'compounding', which were crippling fines for having served the King. Sequestration involved officials holding the delinquent's estate in trust for Parliament, during which time they collected the rents and forwarded them to London. Such officials were allowed to hold ten per cent of the rental revenue collected, a recipe for unfair extraction of money from the delinquents. It is no wonder that the Sequestration Committees were commonly referred to as the 'Committee feast.'

The Ynysymaengwyn estate suffered sequestration at the end of the war, but was later returned to family ownership. Records of the fines for delinquency are sparse and incomplete, with only four Merioneth gentry fined: Humphrey Hughes of Gwerclas, William Price of Rhiwlas, William Salesbury of Rhûg

and Robert Anwyl of Parc. The latter got the stiffest fine amounting to £1,200. The records show no evidence that Gruffudd Nanney paid a fine or had his estate sequestered: quite the contrary, he survived the Interregnum apparently unscathed with his estate intact.

Gruffudd Nanney III was a survivor and part of a group of Merioneth gentry who were ready to sink their political differences and cooperate with the new regime; no doubt his views were closely aligned with his contemporary, Howell Gwynne, who stated,

> *Heigh god, heigh devil I will be for the strongest side.*

Gruffudd's level of complicity was aptly demonstrated by the speed with which he joined the county committees formed at the end of the war, whose main work was to assess and collect taxes. Their first task was to raise £3,000 to pay the fine imposed on the county

118. *Moreton Corbet Castle, Shropshire - a casualty of the English Civil War*

Gruffudd Nanney's name foremost on the writ which returned John Jones as Knight of the Shire.

Gruffudd Nanney's first cousin Jane, the daughter of Robert Vaughan the Antiquarian, had married Robert Owen of Dolserau, who was County Commissioner for the Militia since 1651 and a cousin to Colonel John Jones. Owen sat on many committees for the Parliamentarians, but was clearly distrusted by the upright and highly principled Colonel. Writing to Morgan Llwyd about his cousin Robert Owen, then a sequestration committeeman, he comments on his

lack of discretion and Xitan prudence and hoping that he was free from having the country's monies sticking in his fingers.

Having two parliamentary officers (one highly principled and the other possibly open to corruption) at the highest level of county administration was an asset that Gruffudd Nanney used to advantage.

When Gruffudd Nanney III died in 1656, his widow, after thirty years of marriage, continued to live at Dolaugwyn and erected an over mantle in one room with armorial bearings to honour her husband who had skilfully steered the family through the bitter years of Civil War.

Colonel John Jones was to have a much less salubrious ending. His second marriage was to a sister of Oliver Cromwell, and signicantly he was a signatory to the death warrant of Charles I. For perpetuity, he has become known as 'John Jones the Regicide'. On the accession of Charles II, retribution was swift and brutal. Colonel John Jones, along with others, was tried as a regicide. He was found guilty of treason and was hanged, drawn and quartered in London on the 17th October 1660.

by the Parliamentary regime. Later Gruffudd circumspectly reappeared on the magistrates' bench, all indicators of his complete change in allegiance. Foremost in his mind would have been the fate of his famous Royalist uncle, Sir John Owen of Clenennau, Major-General and Vice-Admiral of North Wales, who said:

I have bin a very great sufferer in these times to the uter ruine of my estate.

(N. L. W. Brogyntyn MS 713)

By showing deference to the new ruling party, Gruffudd was able to avoid crippling fines on his estate. He also had possible 'allies' in the Parliamentary camp that could well have assisted his path from delinquent to 'upright parliamentary citizen'. The noted Parliamentary Commander Colonel John Jones probably aided Gruffudd's return to favour: being a native of Ardudwy and the son of a minor gentry family, he was a natural candidate to head the newly formed county committee in Merioneth. With the county almost devoid of Roundhead candidates, John Jones was inevitably selected. In 1647, the enterprising Colonel was elected Member of Parliament for Merioneth with

...nenney: Kn...
Admiral of
...Wales
...66...

Gruffudd Nanney's heir Huw, still a minor on his father's death in 1656, is often referred to as Huw Nanney III or more distinctively as Huw of Dol'rhyd.

HUW OF DOL'RHYD

Huw received a good education, as was the norm for his family at this time, attending Jesus College, Oxford, and Lincoln's Inn in 1663. This was closely followed by his marriage to Jonet, the daughter of Owen Salesbury of Rhûg in 1664. He administered the will of his grandmother in October 1668, at which time he probably relocated to Dol'rhyd near Dolgellau, the Nannau dower house that had been occupied by Hugh the Younger's widow on the destruction of Nannau. Although Merioneth does not seem to have been badly affected by the Civil War, some families were seriously compromised, such as the Anwyls of Parc, who having borne the greatest fine in the county, found themselves a much diminished force in later years.

The Nanneys had seemingly survived the war with minimal damage to their estate and stature, but I believe the reality was somewhat different. Their finances must have been considerably curtailed, aptly demonstrated by the fact that the family mansion at Nannau was not rebuilt for more than thirty years and only then on a more modest scale.

Huw's formative years would have witnessed the Restoration and the beginnings of the persecution of the Puritans and Quakers. Robert Owen of Dolserau, the one-time Militia Commissioner for the Parliamentarians, was arrested and thrown into prison in Caernarfon and later Dolgellau, where he languished for five and a half years, before sailing to America to escape persecution on the 17th September 1684.

It was not only a period of retribution, it was a time of stringent and punitive taxation, manifested in the form of Land Tax, Tithes and the hated Hearth Tax. The Hearth Tax was introduced in 1662. Designed to make up the shortfall in the King's revenue, it was a tax of two shillings per annum (paid half yearly) on all hearths and stoves in all houses, lodgings and chambers in the land, with the exception of the very poorest individuals. The collection of this derisive tax was initially carried out by constables, later to be farmed out to individuals, aptly nicknamed 'chimney men', who were given powers to enter homes and 'search out' chimneys. The population was quick to seize on ways to circumvent this unpopular tax, with 'chimney men' commenting in returns that households had 'damb'd up chimneys', or even pulled them down to avoid the dreaded tax. Conclusive proof of Nannau's destruction in the Civil War is demonstrated by the fact that no house existed at Nannau during the time of the

122. *above:* **Huw Nanney III, of Dol'rhyd (1643 - 1676)**
Oil on canvas. 30 x 25 inches

123. left: **Gruffudd Nanney IV (1667 - 1689), aged 8**
Oil on canvas. 33 x 26 inches. (His high chair inscribed 'G. N. 1669' is in the Welsh Folk Museum, St. Fagans)

Hearth Tax from 1662 until its repeal in 1688, when it was replaced by the Window Tax!

During such periods of financial stringency the gentry's economic status declined and fewer strove to enter Parliament. Many gentry deprived the bards of their patronage, the family bard becoming an almost extinct breed. Nannau somehow maintained its bardic patronage until the beginning of the 18th century, where it ended under Huw of Dol'rhyd's son, Colonel Huw Nanney.

Huw of Dol'rhyd had three sons. The eldest William died young, while the other two were to succeed to the Nannau estate in turn, Gruffudd in 1676, and Huw in 1690. Each son had his portrait painted on succession to the estate, as was the family tradition. Gruffudd's portrait is interesting as he succeeded to the estate at the age of eight when his father died prematurely in 1676. Gruffudd was well-educated, commensurate with his role as heir: Eton followed by St. John's College, Cambridge, and the gentry 'finishing school' of Lincoln's Inn in 1685. By the age of 21 Gruffudd was High Sheriff of Merioneth, but tragically died at the age of 23 in 1690, unmarried. He left his brother Huw, who had matriculated at Jesus College Oxford in 1687, to take up the reins at the age of 21.

THE LAST OF THE NANNEYS
of NANNAU

Colonel Huw Nanney took control of the Nannau estate at a low ebb in the family's history, their status and authority considerably weakened by the course of history. Under his leadership, however, the family would be destined once more to become a dynasty to be reckoned with, both at county and national level.

In his short but illustrious career he held many prestigious posts including:

1691 - High Sheriff of Merioneth at the age of 22
1695 - Member of Parliament for Merioneth
1697 - Colonel of the Merioneth Militia
1697 - Deputy Lieutenant of Merioneth
1701 - Vice-Admiral of North Wales

In 1695, at the age of 26, he appeared an exemplary candidate for Member of Parliament. His education at Jesus College, Oxford, and at Lincoln's Inn, certainly gave him credibility and, with his family connections, carried him to Parliament. He arrived in Parliament at a period of considerable upheaval in North Wales and of disquiet regarding the actions of King William. In 1696 there was a failed assassination attempt on the King, which ironically had bolstered his popularity. In order to strengthen support for the King, M.P.s were asked to voluntarily sign up to an Association for the protection of the Monarch. Later it was suggested by

124. above: **Catherine Vaughan, daughter of William Vaughan of Corsygedol. (Her second husband was Colonel Huw Nanney).**
Oval Oil on Canvas. 30 x 25 inches

125. left: **Colonel Huw Nanney, M.P. (1669 - 1701)**
Oil on Canvas. 30 x 25 inches. Randle Willcocke.
Signed and dated 1695

126. above: **'Old Nannau'** sketched by Moses Griffith, circa 1805

Parliament that all persons in public office throughout the country should likewise sign. Consequently, Colonel Huw Nanney found eliciting signatures from Merioneth's public servants very difficult. The response was poor to say the least, with many leading gentry seemingly ignoring the request. Whether or not this apathy affected Colonel Huw Nanney's political aspirations is not known, but he does seem to have been a serial absentee as far as Parliamentary business was concerned.

In the Parliament of 1698, Colonel Huw Nanney was returned unopposed, probably because no other candidate was forthcoming. The elections that the Colonel fought were low key to the extreme, being carried out at Harlech within the course of a day and decided by an assembly of gentry.

In his role as Vice-Admiral of North Wales, Colonel Huw Nanney was charged with important duties connected with the defence of the area, such as the impress of seamen. It is likely that he farmed out much of his responsibilities to his deputies.

A relic of Huw Nanney's time as Colonel of the Militia exists in the form of a regimental drum. The drum, measuring $21^1/_4$ x 16 inches, proudly bears the Nanney arms. It was probably only ever used for ceremonial purposes, but in theatres of war it would have been used to transform the officer's commands into signals that could be heard above the noise of battle.

Colonel Huw Nanney's home was Dol'rhyd near Dolgellau, but sometime between 1693-7 he busily rebuilt his ancestral home at Nannau,

as 1694 is provided by comments on the poet Siôn Dafydd Las, the last live-in bard of Nannau, who died that year

as a result of spending too much time between the kitchen and cellars at Nannau. (E.D. Jones, 1953-1956)

In February 1701 Colonel Huw Nanney was elected to Parliament for the third time, but this was to be his last, as he tragically died that winter, catching a severe cold on his journey to London. It was the end of the male line of Nannau, one that had continued for six hundred years. He left behind a widow, Catherine, and four daughters. The tenure of Nanneys at Nannau was at an end. The Colonel's parliamentary seat was filled by his brother-in-law, Richard Vaughan of Corsygedol, and would remain safely in Nannau/Corsygedol hands for the next 140 years.

Colonel Huw Nanney is known to have spent more time on his family estate in the latter years of his life and Nannau apparently flourished under his stewardship, but it is quite likely that improvements to the estate were in part due to the influence of his wife, the incredibly astute and formidable Catherine Nanney. Under her direction the estate was run in a meticulous business-like manner.

Colonel Huw Nanney left a complicated will, with a complex mass of acquired and inherited lands that were to prove difficult to disentangle in the interest of providing for his daughters. The fate of Nannau would eventually be decided by the 'chosen' spouses of the Colonel's daughters, with more than a helping hand from his termagant widow, Catherine Nanney.

which had been destroyed some fifty years earlier. Fortunately we can glimpse the Colonel's rebuilt Nannau through the eyes of Moses Griffith, who in his role as artist to Thomas Pennant, sketched 'Old Nannau' when he was asked to sketch the Georgian Nannau of 1797. Presumably the artist was informed by Sir Robert Williames Vaughan, 2nd Bart of Nannau, of the design of the former house, which had been replaced by the time Pennant visited in connection with his book, *A Tour in Wales*. It is likely that the Nannau 'rebuild' took a number of years to complete and that it stood as a much-reduced house in comparison with Huw Nanney Hên's palatial edifice. Moses Griffith's version of 'Old Nannau' stands tall, with one lateral chimney and a profusion of windows. Further evidence of a house at Nannau as early

128. Catherine Nanney, widow of Colonel Huw Nanney
Oil on canvas. 28 x 24 inches

129. *Hengwrt - near Dolgellau* (2014)

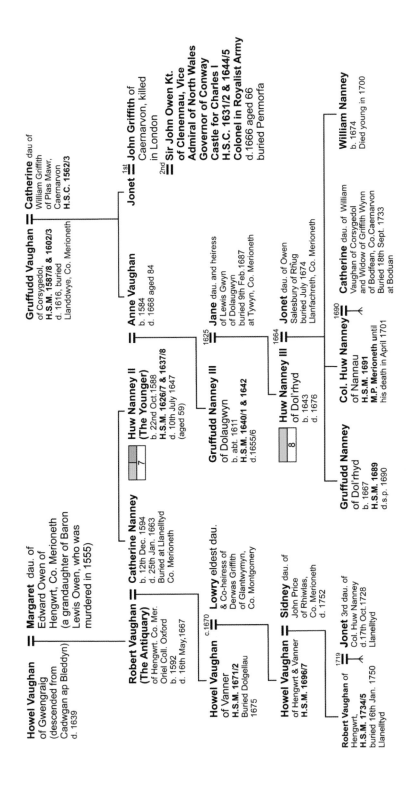

7

1702-1783

VAUGHANS OF NANNAU

Colonel Huw Nanney's marriage to the widow Catherine Wynn had produced four daughters; the elusive male heir to perpetuate the dynasty did not materialise. A portrait of their eldest daughter Anne, aged 6, by Sir John Medina in 1697, interestingly depicts the hoped for male child who never appeared.

On his death in 1701, all of the Colonel's children were minors; Anne the heiress was only ten. Within six months of the Colonel's death a petition was drawn up by the guardians of Anne Nanney, an infant, to the Lord Keeper of the Great Seals – it was a complaint against her mother for concealment of her father's will. The guardians were supposedly working on behalf of the child heir to protect her interests, no doubt after clashes with the termagant widow Catherine Nanney. This would be the first of many such encounters that they would have with the formidable dowager.

The Colonel's contentious will was proved on the 20th August 1702, and evidently, by now, the Nanney widow was very much in the driving seat, a position she would enjoy until her death in 1733 aged 74. In the meantime, she was launching into an entrepreneurial career that would thoroughly transform the ancient Nannau estate into a highly profitable enterprise. Her telling annotations on a Nannau rent roll, such as 'this is worth more', leaves us in no doubt of her future intentions. During the next thirty years the Nanney widow left no stone unturned in her quest for greater profits for the estate.

The 18th century saw a remarkable growth in estate expansion, with many gentry families striving to acquire more and more land, aptly demonstrated by the fact that

> *every field upon sale too often passes into the hands of the rich landowner of adjacent land.*
> (Arthur Young, *Annals of Agriculture*, 1803)

Catherine Nanney certainly 'acquired' some of her neighbours' lands, accomplishing this in a very mercenary manner. The wealthy 18th century squires quickly perceived that it was potentially

131. left: **William Vaughan of Corsygedol (circa1707 - 1775)**
by James Fellowes. Oil on canvas

115

133. left: **Anne Nanney (1691 - 1729), eldest daughter of Colonel Huw Nanney (the little boy represents the hoped for heir, of whom Siôn Dafydd Las wrote in 1691)** Oil on canvas. 48 x 45 inches. Medina. 1696

Kelsale agreed to

buy all trees, underwoods, brushes, &c. excepting such Oak, Ash and Elms as are already marked and appointed ... to stand and be preserved in Coed y Cae Du, Hengae, and Tir Rhys Davies; bark included, also rights of ingress, egress and regress, for agents and workmen; liberty to dig pits and cut turf necessary for making charcoal (doing, in all this, as little damage as possible on the premises). All trees, cordwood, bark and charcoal to be cleared on or before 1 April, 1733; for all the above privileges Kelsale and the Paytons to pay £147 at or upon 24 June, 1733.

(Nannau Manuscripts, 536)

more profitable to lend money to their neighbours than to purchase land outright, but with the proviso that the mortgaged lands would be used as security. The enterprising widow shrewdly realised the potential rewards, and was known to have granted no less than eight mortgages to owners of small estates in the Dolgellau area between 1705 and 1717. When the mortgagors inevitably failed to repay the advances, Madam Nanney, with little apparent sympathy, foreclosed on the ill-fated landowners. By 1719 she had absorbed £1,807 worth of land into the Nannau estate, and effectively turned the borrowers into landless tenants.

Madam Nanney's business aspirations knew no bounds. She is known to have speculated in the South Sea Company along with other securities. Her early entry into the domain of mining leases made her a pioneer in this potentially profitable activity. As early as 1713 she was involved in granting mining leases on Nannau lands, and by 1724 her daughter Anne was also signatory to new leases. Through the diaries of John Kelsale, who ran a forge in Dolgun near Dolgellau in the 1730s, we catch fleeting glimpses of the Nanney widow as she bargained for the best prices.

She was a formidable business woman but also, without doubt, a scheming mother who skilfully engineered the marriages of her daughters with varying degrees of success. Evidently she hoped her eldest daughter Anne would 'tow the line' and marry her first cousin, William Vaughan of Corsygedol, to preserve the family wealth. The headstrong Anne had other ideas, relocating to London and dying unmarried in 1729. Undeterred, Catherine Nanney forged ahead, arranging the marriage of the eldest of her twin daughters Catherine, who on the 8th September 1732 married the said

134. above: **The Nanney Twins, Catherine and Jonet - twin daughters of Colonel Huw Nanney.** Oil on copper. Circa 1710

135. above: **The Iron forge between Dolgelle and Barmouth in Merionethshire** *P. Sandby, 1776*

William Vaughan of Corsygedol. Jonet, the younger of the twins, had previously married Robert Vaughan of Hengwrt (a great grandson of Robert Vaughan the Antiquarian) on the 9th November 1719.

Catherine, being the eldest, inherited the family estates, and on her marriage to William Vaughan he became the owner of no less than six major estates: Corsygedol, Plas Hên, Llwynduryus, Nannau, Dol'rhyd and Dolaugwyn. The fifth union between the family of Corsygedol and Nannau had resulted in an immense landholding.

On 14th September 1733, Catherine Nanney, widow extraordinaire, died at her son's home in Bodfean, Caernarfonshire. She was still

wheeling and dealing with Kelsale, who noted a business visit to the 'old Lady Nanney' shortly before her death. In her will she left £100 to the poor of Dolgellau and Llanfachreth and a well-ordered and profitable Nannau estate.

WILLIAM VAUGHAN OF NANNAU AND CORSYGEDOL

William Vaughan of Corsygedol was a son of Ardudwy's most prominent family, with direct descent from Osbwrn Wyddel (Osborn the Irishman, fl.1292-3). Osbwrn, the dynastic founder of the Corsygedol family, is said to have come from Ireland in the 13th century and settled in the Commote of Ardudwy in north west Merioneth.

136. *Corsygedol Hall, Dyffryn Ardudwy, near Barmouth*

wooden screen, dated 1620, bearing the initials W.V.: A.V. for William and Ann Vaughan.

As the great grandson of the above, William was the first in his family to receive a University education, one that would prepare him for public life and the management of his estates. He attended St. John's College, Cambridge, but left after only one year. He held many prestigious posts at county level, Custos Rotulorum and Deputy Lieutenant, and followed his father into politics as M.P. for Merioneth in 1734, a post he held through six parliaments, finally retiring in 1768.

His marriage to Catherine Nanney was a happy one, even though William was some thirteen years younger than his wife. On the 16th February 1733, there was great rejoicing upon the birth of their daughter Anne, with family members bringing presents before and after her christening. In her youth Anne contracted smallpox but fortunately recovered, and as heiress to her father's vast estates went on to marry David Jones Gwynne of Taliaris, Carmarthenshire.

William Vaughan was a cultured man who actively supported the Welsh Literary revival at a time when many of his class had turned their backs on the native language and culture. He was nominated as the first Chief President of the Honourable Society of Cymmrodorion in London, and in his poetic guise took on the appropriate bardic name of 'Y Brawd Du o Nannau.' It was during this creative period that William Vaughan occupied Dol'rhyd and built the 'Apollo' in the grounds. This small but intriguing building stands neatly adjacent to the house and is thought to have been a meeting place for the local members of the Cymmrodorian Society and William Vaughan's poetic friends.

Corsygedol is magnificently situated in an elevated position, commanding spectacular views of Cardigan Bay and the Lleyn Peninsular. It is approached by an avenued drive of lime trees, stretching from Llanddwywe Church to the mansion, a distance of approximately one mile. This large and prestigious gentry house was first constructed by Richard Vaughan in 1576, and was extended by his son in 1592/5. In 1630 it was furnished with an impressive gatehouse, reputedly designed by the great architect Inigo Jones. The family church at Llanddwywe, although much restored in the 19th century, still contains the Vaughan Chapel with its remarkable

William's retirement from politics in 1768 had been precipitated by the death of his daughter Anne in 1767, tragically followed by his wife's death in 1768. It was a bitter blow for William

138. above: **The 'Apollo' meeting room adjacent to Dol'rhyd house, built by William Vaughan for his learned circle to meet, circa 1770**

139. left: **Detail of the Apollo's spectacular semi-domed ceiling, exuberantly decorated with a range of Adamesque motifs**

who seemingly withdrew to Corsygedol. He embarked on writing the history of his family, assured of the sad fact that there would be no heir to inherit his estates. His wife Catherine had ensured that he would be appointed as tenant-for-life of her estates during his lifetime and only then would they descend to her sister Jonet's son, Hugh Vaughan, an inveterate spendthrift!

In 1775 William Vaughan, one of the last of the 'Old Welsh Noblemen' died, and Nannau became the property of Hugh Vaughan. Under his tenure the Hengwrt and Nannau estates would plummet to an all-time low. In the meantime, Nannau would remain unoccupied, with Hugh Vaughan choosing to spend his inheritance on making Hengwrt the outlet for his wild extravagances.

RICHES ARE FOR SPENDING

In 1750, on his father's death, Hugh Vaughan succeeded to a heavily encumbered Hengwrt estate, and seemingly launched into an unfettered spending spree. He began with the rebuilding of the family's ancient edifice between 1750/4. He possibly considered the old mansion inappropriate for the entertaining of his guests in this 'age of extravagance', and Hugh was not averse to funding such indulgences by debt, in this case mortgage

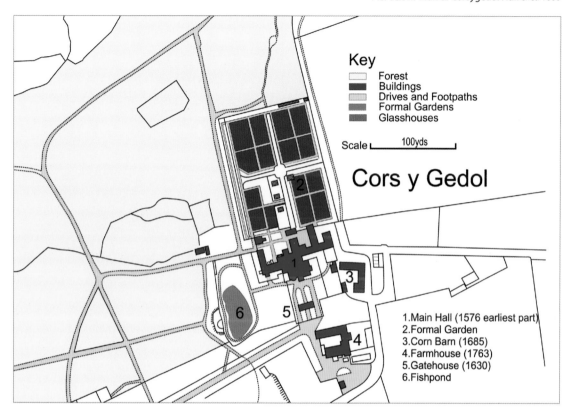

Key
- Forest
- Buildings
- Drives and Footpaths
- Formal Gardens
- Glasshouses

Scale ⊢──── 100yds ────⊣

Cors y Gedol

1. Main Hall (1576 earliest part)
2. Formal Garden
3. Corn Barn (1685)
4. Farmhouse (1763)
5. Gatehouse (1630)
6. Fishpond

debt. His father Robert Vaughan had entered into a mortgage with a certain William Powell of Gyngrog near Welshpool for £600 in April 1749. This fateful transaction would have terrifying repercussions in the next decade as the debts compounded with Hugh seemingly oblivious to the dire financial situation that was unfolding.

The 'Prodigal son' was whittling away the family's wealth with little regard for future generations, a stance diametrically opposed to advice given by many fathers to their sons. He could well have benefitted from Edward Lloyd of Rhagatt's counsel:

know exactly the state of your affairs and keep regular and intelligible accounts.

Hugh Vaughan clearly did not have his finger on the financial pulse of his estate. His reckless behaviour was evident in the cavalier manner in which he signed documents, often without even reading them or taking legal advice. Such irresponsible attitudes inevitably made him an easy target for any unscrupulous person who came along. His father's initial mortgage of 1749 set Hugh on a crash course to meet his nemesis, the unprincipled lawyer, Robert Lloyd of Oswestry.

The ensuing mortgages clearly chronicle Hugh's downfall, beginning with:

1749 – William Powell - £600
1761 – William Owen   - £2,400
1762 – William Owen   - £1,740

1763 – William Owen is owed £4,203-00 @ 4.5%

1763 – (December) – William Owen's mortgage was in the possession of Rev. H. Pryce, and worth £3,240-15s-6d. Rev. Pryce transferred the mortgage to a widow of Oswestry, one Sinai Lloyd, and Hugh Vaughan borrowed a further £6,435-4s-6d. The mortgage climbed to £10,000.

1765 – William Powell's initial mortgage had been added to, and with interest charges, amounted to £5,350-0s-0d. This mortgage was transferred to his son Robert Powell, whose daughter and heiress, married Robert Lloyd, son of Sinai Lloyd!

By a series of unfortunate connections, the principal mortgages on the Hengwrt estate passed to the Oswestry lawyer Robert Lloyd by inheritance and marriage. He had acquired mortgages to the value of £15,350 secured against the estate.

To fund his lifestyle, Hugh Vaughan also borrowed lesser amounts from certain individuals, primarily in the Dolgellau area. Robert Lloyd made it his business to track down many of these creditors and purchase their debts. It was a calculated attempt at owning as much of the debt of the estate as possible, with the ultimate intention of foreclosing, which he did on the 7th October 1766. He then arranged the sale of the Hengwrt demesne, to be held at the Golden Lion, Dolgellau. In a gesture of solidarity, a number of the local gentry came to Hugh's rescue and bought in some £400 of effects from the house, but the sale of the mansion and estate seems to have been averted. Later that year Robert Lloyd was jointly managing the Hengwrt estate with Hugh Vaughan, having now a 'legal hold' on the rental and effectively reducing Hugh to a meagre pension.

The Hengwrt estate was now mired in debt but Hugh Vaughan continued his reckless spending, in 1775 buying a coach for £19-10s-0d, two pairs of coach horses (one pair valued at £84, the other at £75-10s-0d), and a lottery ticket for £16!

Fortuitously, on the 22nd of April 1775, Hugh's affairs took a turn for the better when he succeeded to the Nannau estate as his uncle, William Vaughan, the tenant for life, died. As heir of his mother Jonet, Hugh inherited an estate with a rental totalling £2,310 p.a. and an annual mortgage charge of £1,268 p.a. It is reasonable to assume that he would have attempted to pay down some of the debt. Nothing was further from the truth. The spending continued, interest payments went unpaid, and the estate got deeper and deeper into debt.

With the debts mounting, the inevitable happened in the summer of 1778, when Hugh was declared bankrupt. He fled his creditors, running to Plas Hên, then Chester and on to London, leaving two rather indifferent solicitors to fight the action. Even on the eve of

bankruptcy, Hugh's improvidence had continued apace, and

with a margin of solvency of £1-8s-3d a day he kept an establishment of 50 servants, not fewer horses, dogs and fighting cocks, tradesmen of every sort besides the heavy taxes, yearly increasing which must be paid when they become due.

(Peter R. Roberts, *The landed gentry in Merioneth circa 1660 - 1832*)

Being 'banished' from his ancestral home did not preclude him from attending to the training of his prized fighting cocks, in preparation for the annual match between Hengwrt and Ynysymaengwyn. This match was a major event in Merioneth's sporting calendar and was held at the Cockpit of the Golden Lion in Dolgellau.

Plans were again made to bring Hengwrt under the hammer. It looked bleak for Hugh, but he was not entirely bereft of friends.

A formidable lady rose to his salvation in the unlikely form of Mrs Elizabeth Baker. Elizabeth lodged at Hengwrt from 1777-8. Having been greatly disillusioned by a failed mining venture in the locality, she established herself at Hengwrt as secretary to Hugh who was floundering hopelessly in a sea of debt and ineptitude. Miraculously her diaries have

survived the centuries and give us a unique insight into the events that unfolded. Elizabeth Baker's diaries open around the 6th December 1778, when the Deputy Sheriff, a Mr Lever, took possession of Hengwrt. Elizabeth was evicted and took refuge in nearby Dol'rhyd. Her diaries reveal a stoical character, who held out against numerous assaults from the bailiffs and undersheriffs as they strove to take possession of Dol'rhyd. Her drive to assist the hapless squire is commendable, as she worked tirelessly to get a 'true' account of Hugh's debts with Robert Lloyd.

By the end of 1778, two new lawyers were appointed to fight Hugh's case, John Maddocks and John Lloyd of Oswestry. In conjunction with Mrs Baker, they worked diligently to unearth the truth behind a morass of mortgages, sales, payments and rents, searching for evidence of double charging and much non-cancelling of paid debt. Mrs Baker became convinced that Robert Lloyd had vastly inflated Hugh Vaughan's debts, and, with John Lloyd, pressurised Robert Lloyd for a breakdown of the £30,000 debt he now asserted was due. The estate was practically in Robert Lloyd's possession, with many household effects having already been sold. Robert Lloyd then mercilessly set his sights on extending his rights to the proceeds of the Nannau estate - there seemed no end to his grasping. Things

143. above: **Hugh Vaughan of Hengwrt**

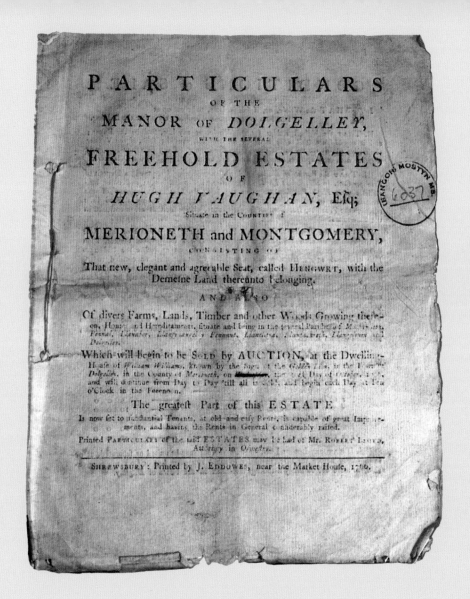

144. above: **Sale catologue drawn up by Robert Lloyd, for the foreclosure sale of Hengwrt in 1766**

looked extremely bleak and the locality was in turmoil. Parson Owen of Dolgellau aptly expressed the situation when he said:

O! Nanney – One of the last instances of British Hospitality – where Rich & Poor found Peace and Plenty.

Under the cover of darkness many items had been removed from Hengwrt in an attempt to salvage something; a prized stallion, cattle and hounds, and, significantly, many priceless manuscripts and books were relocated to Nannau.

When the sale of the estate was advertised, John Lloyd placed notices in the newspaper disputing the legality of the sale, and by now the many tenants were becoming confused and agitated. The determined John Lloyd sought an injunction to stop the sale, but this came too

145. above: **Hengwrt, the home of Robert Vaughan as it appeared in 1793** by John Ingleby

late for Hugh Vaughan, who died in January 1783, at the home of his brother Robert Howel Vaughan of Rhûg.

Robert Howel Vaughan had been a surgeon at Chester before inheriting the Rhûg estate, and could now add Hengwrt and Nannau to his possession. He evidently had the collateral to fight for his brother's legacy. Robert Lloyd sought arbitration, but the determined Robert Howel Vaughan, now convinced of the likelihood of winning, backed John Lloyd to

the hilt. They succeeded in gaining a Commission of Enquiry into the case, headed by the influential Councillor Richard Richards of Caerynwch (an eminent barrister-at-law), which sat at the Golden Lion in July, August and September of 1786. The outcome of the enquiry was decisive; the Hengwrt estate was restored to the family with Robert Lloyd having to pay £12,000 in compensation to Robert Howel Vaughan. John Lloyd's persistence and hard work had been rewarded. He received £3,000 fees and an annuity of £50 a

146. **Dolgellau** circa 1820, a tourist's illustration

147. above:
Ynysymaengwyn, seat of the Corbets, near Tywyn

148. left: **A painting showing cockfighting**
J. Hill & Harraden
(Aquatint engravers)
Circa 1805

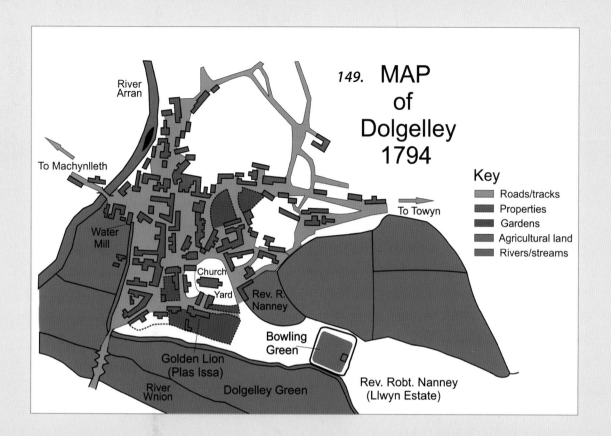

149. MAP of Dolgelley 1794

River Arran

To Machynlleth

To Towyn

Key
- Roads/tracks
- Properties
- Gardens
- Agricultural land
- Rivers/streams

Water Mill

Church Yard

Rev. R. Nanney

Bowling Green

Golden Lion (Plas Issa)

River Wnion

Dolgelley Green

Rev. Robt. Nanney (Llwyn Estate)

year, increased to £150 by Robert Howel Vaughan's son. Elizabeth Baker, whose diligence and intellect had unearthed the fraud, was given nothing and died in 1788, buried in a pauper's grave in Dolgellau.

It had been a long and arduous struggle between two ambitious lawyers. Robert Lloyd had failed to eject the Vaughans from their patrimony; John Lloyd, however, went on to successfully establish an estate of his own in Corwen

Robert Howel Vaughan entered into full possession of the Hengwrt estate on the 10th September 1788, amid huge celebrations in the locality. The family were now in the ascendancy with six estates (Hengwrt, Dol'rhyd, Nannau, Rhûg, Meillionydd and Ystum Colwyn), unified under a single head and looking to the future with renewed optimism.

8

1723-1859

THE BARONETS
OF NANNAU

As a younger son, Robert Howel Vaughan had not expected to inherit the family estates, his elder brother Hugh Vaughan being the rightful heir to the Nannau and Hengwrt estates. Robert, as was the lot of a younger son, sought his own way in life, not through the usual route of law or the Church, but through medicine, becoming a physician-apothecary at Chester. He must have served an apprenticeship to qualify, as the laying down of prescribed courses for doctors was yet to be established by the Royal College of Physicians and Surgeons.

Living in Chester, he would have lost touch with his family's estate, and was perhaps oblivious to the developing financial gloom that was enveloping the Hengwrt estate under his brother's tenure. In 1765, at the age of 43, Robert married Anne Williames, heiress of the Ystum Colwyn and Meillionydd estates. From 1768 to 1776 the couple took up residence at Erbistock Hall in Denbighshire, a mansion owned by her uncle, Robert Williams, brother to Sir Watkin Williams Wynn, 3rd Baronet (Bart) of Wynnstay. Anne's aunt, Meriel Williames,

had married Robert Williams who was M.P. for Montgomeryshire throughout most of the 1740s. After the death of her aunt and uncle, the family continued to live at Erbistock, baptising each of their three boys in the local church, Robert in 1768, Edward in 1769 and Griffith in 1770.

On the 1st July 1776 Robert Howel Vaughan and family relocated to Dee Bank, Chester, to be not only amidst the fashionable society of the day but also closer to his place of work, the Chester Infirmary. His wife's estates were far from settled, with trustees administering on her behalf. The news of Hugh Vaughan's financial troubles loomed ever large and caused the trustees, who were aware of potential claims that could emanate from the Hengwrt creditors, to keep a firm grip on Anne's inheritance.

At this crucial time in his family's history it is surprising to find Robert Howel Vaughan taking an active role in 'The Cycle of the White Rose', a Denbighshire Jacobite club. Presumably he had been recruited by the then

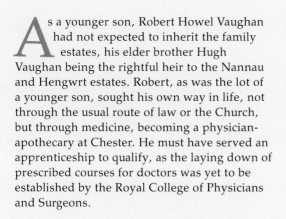

leader of the Cycle, Sir Watkin Williams Wynn, 4th Bart of Wynnstay. His involvement in this 'subversive' society however went deeper than family ties and stretched back into Robert Howel Vaughan's early adulthood.

The Cycle of the **WHITE ROSE**

The 'Cycle' had been the creation of Watkin Williams (later the 3rd Bart of Wynnstay), formed in 1710 when he was only 18 years of age. Membership of this secretive society was confined to the most powerful Tory squires in Denbighshire, Flint and Cheshire, all within an easy travelling distance of Wynnstay, their spiritual headquarters. Cycle members were united in their hatred for the Hanovarian Dynasty. They were adherents to the exiled James Francis Edward, son of King James II, who had died exiled in France in 1701 after his inglorious defeat at the Battle of the Boyne in Ireland some ten years previously.

By 1770 the Cycle's numbers had doubled, and it was now under the control of Sir W. W. Wynn, 4th Bart of Wynnstay. Cycle members met at monthly meetings, rotating between the members' private houses to avoid any one member being seen as the principal organiser. In order to 'publicise' the meetings and their venues, the members were issued with a printed form which contained names and dates of when the Cycle would meet and in whose house. The names radiated out from a central point like spokes on a wheel and was considered the derivation of the society's name – the Cycle, with the White Rose being the Jacobite symbol. Meetings were held behind closed doors, with toasts symbolically taken over bowls of water for the Jacobite family exiled over the water in France, with rousing songs adding to the occasion. It was amongst such meetings that Robert Howel Vaughan and his fellow magnates met to discuss their plans and make preparations for the next occasion to recover the Crown for the exiled grandson of James II, Charles Edward Stuart, 'The Young Pretender', also known as 'Bonnie Prince Charlie'.

Two serious attempts were made to restore the Stuarts to the throne: the Jacobite Rebellion of 1715, which had proved a disaster, and the second rebellion of 1745, which although more successful ended brutally on the field of Culloden in April 1746, prompting the flight of Bonnie Prince Charlie into exile aided by the young Flora Macdonald.

156. *left:* **Prince Charles Edward Stuart - Bonnie Prince Charlie (1720-1788)** *by William Mosman*

157. *bottom:* **Flora Macdonald** *by Allan Ramsay*

that Bonnie Prince Charlie's lack of support from Wales was one of the deciding factors in his decision to withdraw back to Scotland. Certainly the quote reputedly attributed to him rings true:

> *I will do as much for my Welsh friends as they have done for me; I will drink to their health.*

(Prince Charles Edward Stuart)

Robert Howel Vaughan, however, stood out from other Cycle members in that he is known to have actually participated in the 1745 Rebellion. Presumably, as a younger son with no estate to forfeit, he rode to join the Prince and held a Commission in the invading army. According to Cycle records, he was captured with the Royal Stuart Commission in his pocket, but fortunately, after his arrest he was able to slip the incriminating document unnoticed into a fire, which undoubtedly saved him from a traitor's execution.

When Sir W. W. Wynn, 3rd Bart of Wynnstay, died in a hunting accident on the 26th September 1749, with him died the true spirit of Welsh Jacobitism. From then on the Cycle would exist, to all intents and purposes, as merely a high class drinking club. Robert Howel Vaughan was to play his part and host two meetings of the Cycle: one at his home at Erbistock in 1773, and the other at his home in Dee Bank, Chester, on the 21st October 1776, which roughly coincided with the four yearly interval of playing host as proposed by the Cycle.

No rising ever took place in Wales, nor did any Welsh force march to join Bonnie Prince Charlie; it seems that the Cycle was more an expression of sentiment rather than action. Sir W. W. Wynn, 3rd Bart of Wynnstay, never concealed his Jacobite leanings and promised Charles Stuart (Bonnie Prince Charlie) assistance on the proviso that he would be accompanied by a French Army, but evidently this never materialised. The 3rd Bart astutely hedged his bets, and at the height of the 1745 Rebellion was known to have subscribed troops to oppose the Stuart Prince, whilst simultaneously offering him promises of support!

In reality the gentry of North Wales provided little or no actual support in the 1745 Rebellion; all their rhetoric came to nothing. It is thought

158. *right:* **Robert Howel Vaughan.** *Black and white chalks on laid paper. 13 x 10 inches. William Parry. 1770*

160. *right:* **Griffith Howel Vaughan of Hengwrt (1770-1848) in a red coat**
Coloured chalks. 14 x 11 inches. William Parry
161. *below right:* **Edward Salesbury Vaughan, of Rhûg (1769-1807) in a black suit and Vandyke collar**
Coloured chalks. 14 x 11 inches. William Parry

Robert Howell Vaughan was not the only one to destroy incriminating evidence in the wake of the failed 1745 Rebellion. Frances Shackerley, the wife of Sir W. W. Wynn, 3rd Bart, and personal friend of Flora Macdonald, is said to have spent the night following her husband's death in September 1749 burning all the compromising evidence at Wynnstay, and is quoted to have said that

there was enough in the manuscripts to hang half the county.

In the wake of the Culloden defeat, Jacobitism as a political force faded into a romantic ideal, and the Cycle into a dining club with no real meaning. The cherished mementoes, in the form of Cycle glasses, were proudly displayed in cabinets at Nannau for more than two centuries and are a tangible reminder of long lost aspirations and distant toasts:

Send him victorious,
Happy and glorious,
Soon to region over us,
God save the King.

(A Jacobite toast that ironically inspired our present National Anthem)

SIR ROBERT HOWEL VAUGHAN, 1st Bart

In 1780, Robert Howel Vaughan came into the first of his many inheritances, when Maria Charlotte Lloyd left the Rhûg estate near Corwen to him and his heirs. Accounts detail that she left it to his son, Edward, who was only eleven years of age at the time. Elizabeth Baker of Dolgellau entered in her diary on Monday 28th August:

Mrs Lloyd of Rug is Dead and buried and she has left that estate to Robt Vaughan and his heirs, to Mr Hugh Vaughan only a legacy of £500!

159. *left:* **Robert Williames Vaughan, of Nannau (1768-1843) in a blue suit with Vandyke collar**
Coloured chalks. 14 x 11 inches. William Parry

With an income of £3,000 a year from the rental of the Rhûg estate, Robert Howell Vaughan was quick to relinquish his medical career and install his family at Rhûg. Events unfolded tragically, with Hugh Vaughan's demise on the 20th January 1783 at Rhûg, although it was to be a further five years before the Hengwrt estate was restored to the family. Robert Howel Vaughan was no doubt content to move to Nannau, now in his possession and closer to the action. It was probably at this time that Robert Howel Vaughan commissioned William Parry to draw the portraits of his three young sons. Even though he had many more years of tedious litigation ahead, Robert would have contented himself with the belief that the Vaughan family fortunes were emerging from the stranglehold of debt. Elizabeth Baker was at the Christmas and New Year celebrations of 1782/3 at Rhûg and noted that, apart from the natural anxiety of the family over Hugh Vaughan's illness, *'never was the season merrier or the parties gayer'*. Under an entry on the 4th January 1783, she enthusiastically described the evening's entertainment:

The younger part of the family have been busily employed in preparing for the evenings diversion: which was a Masqued Ball, and very well sustained – Mr Vaughan of Hengwrt was pleas'd with the minuets, particularly those of Mastr. Grif. Vaughan and Miss

Davies – Mr Parry the Limner, in the dress of a lady of the last Century, afforded much mirth; and the Spaniard whom she adopted for the scene kept up the ridicule by dancing a hornpipe in his cloak and Mustachoes – the under gardiner enter'd as a servt. from the Wynstay and delivered letters as from thence, deceived the whole assembly.

Robert Howel Vaughan was appointed High Sheriff of Merioneth in 1784, and as part of the festivities held when the Assizes visited Dolgellau, Elizabeth Baker described the occasion:

I walked to see the Sheriff's entry which I exulted at – it far surpassed any one ever seen at Dolgelley before: his Coach and Chaise, Horses and servants liveries made a fine appearance: The uniform of the horseman was a striped cloth manufactured (I think) by the Sheriff's tenants; that many disapproved; in number I am not included as I am certain the Sheriff meant it a right step ... my stand was upon the steps near Mrs Jones Curate where I received the bows of the Sheriff – from the Chaise, and then an equal compliment from his Lady and those with her in the Coach, which stopt. Mrs Vaughan honoured me with a kiss in the street a distinction indelible and the recollection will for ever be attended with Envy by the Dolgellians.

162. *left:* **Robert Howel Vaughan in costume for a masquerade**
Oil on canvas. 30 x 25 inches. William Parry

163. *below:* **Arms of Vaughan impaling Williames of Ystum Colwyn - a stained glass armorial shield**

The Vaughans of Nannau had regained their standing within the county and were poised to once more assert the family's grip on the locality.

By the restitution of the Hengwrt estate in 1788, Robert Howel Vaughan had accrued a considerable income from no less than six major estates: Hengwrt, Nannau, Dol'rhyd, Rhûg, Meillionydd and Ystum Colwyn, and it was time to build a mansion commensurate with his status. He consequently embarked on rebuilding Nannau around 1787/8. No building records survive, but tangible proof of the completion of the mansion exists in the form of 'house warming glasses', inscribed 1797 - they are an accurate indicator of the occupation of the newly rebuilt Nannau.

Neither Robert Howel Vaughan nor his wife lived long enough to enjoy their new mansion, Robert dying in 1792, a year after being created a Baronet for political services, and his wife dying in early 1791, deprived of the title of Lady Vaughan.

Sir Robert's sons completed the rebuilding, with the heir, Sir Robert Williames Vaughan, 2nd Bart, adding the pavilion wings in 1805. Sir Robert Howel Vaughan's vast estates were amicably distributed amongst his sons. The heir, Sir

164. *above:* **Drawing of 'Old Rhûg', prior to being rebuilt by Edward Salesbury Vaughan**

165. above: ***Llanelltyd Church*** *by H. Gastineau (early 19th century)*

Robert, was given Nannau, Ystum Colwyn and Meillionydd; Griffith Howel Vaughan inherited Hengwrt, and Edward Williames Vaughan, Rhûg. Edward, on succeeding to the Rhûg estate, took on the name of Salesbury, and in 1800 embarked on a lavish rebuild of the mansion. He pursued a military career, rising to Colonel of the 1st Regiment of Foot Guards, dying bravely whilst leading his troops in an action at Syracuse in 1807. Griffith Howel Vaughan, his younger brother, inherited the Rhûg estate and took up residence.

Sir Robert Howel Vaughan was buried in Llanelltyd Church, as the weather was too severe for him to be conveyed through the snow to the Nannau family church at Llanfachreth. His wife Anne had been buried in Erbistock Church the previous year. Numerous reminders of the 1st Bart and his wife exist scattered around Nannau, in the form of tablets on estate houses bearing their initials. A public house at Bontnewydd was renamed in his honour, known as 'Hywel Dda', but the most tangible reminder of his tenure must be the magnificent Georgian Nannau that exists today high up in the hills above Dolgellau.

Sir **ROBERT WILLIAMES VAUGHAN** - 2nd Bart

The Nannau family 'ruled' the Llanfachreth area for more than eight hundred years, but during that long tenure, no one individual did so much to alter and improve the locality as Sir Robert Williames Vaughan, 2nd Bart, whose legacy stands today in the myriad of buildings and structures that still grace the countryside.

The Remarkable **ESTATE BUILDER**

The closing years of the 18th century witnessed a great revival in estate building, manifested in landlords replacing or upgrading their substandard cottages and farmhouses. Nannau estate, under Sir Robert Williames Vaughan, 2nd Bart, was at the vanguard of this progressive movement. The vast sums of money he spent on his estate produced one of the most unique and distinctive architectural landscapes in North Wales.

This period is often referred to as the 'Golden age of Nannau' and represented a level of investment unequalled in the family's history, all indicators of the increased prosperity which the family were experiencing after the earlier retrenchments. The 2nd Bart also expanded the estate through major purchases in 1805 and 1815, selling off the Lovesgrove estate (a legacy from Maria Charlotte Lloyd of Rhûg) near Aberystwyth, for £6,000 in 1811, preferring to invest in his own locality. Rental incomes are known to have fluctuated considerably at this time, but the general trend was upwards, driven up sharply by the Napoleonic Wars.

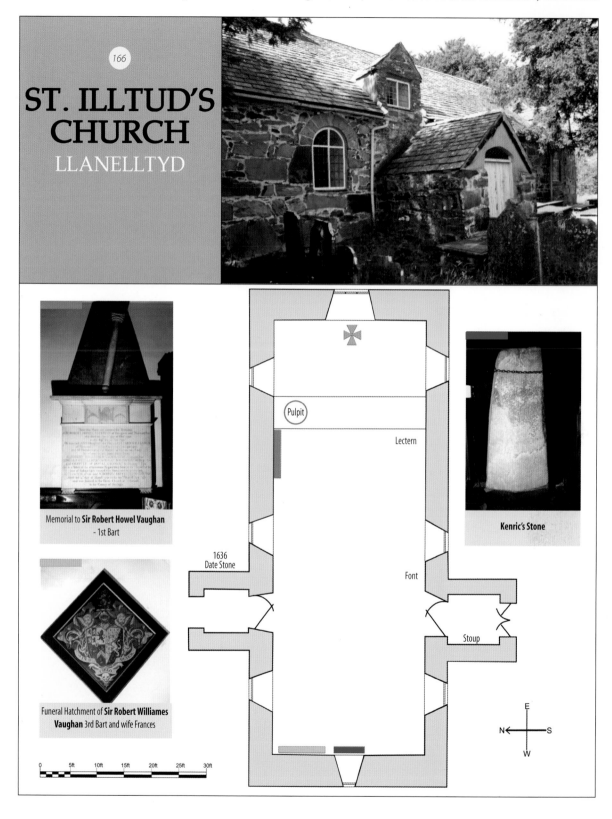

166

ST. ILLTUD'S CHURCH
LLANELLTYD

Memorial to **Sir Robert Howel Vaughan** - 1st Bart

Funeral Hatchment of **Sir Robert Williames Vaughan** 3rd Bart and wife Frances

Pulpit

Lectern

1636 Date Stone

Font

Stoup

Kenric's Stone

0   5ft   10ft   15ft   20ft   25ft   30ft

Sir Robert Williams Vaughan's Estate Building Period - 1810 - 1840

CAE CRWTH — 1810

TY CANOL — 1812

TAI NEWYDDION — 1812

A Former Nannau Estate Cottage — 1820

HYWEL SELE LODGE — 1820

COED Y MOCH LODGE — 1830

GARTH BLEIDDYN — 1831

NANT Y CNYDYW — 1832

NANNAU HOME FARM — 1834

Former Nannau Barn — 1842

Sir Robert embarked on a lifelong journey of design and build, constructing lodges, gates, arches and eyecatchers to which he supplemented huge quantities of trees, expressing his unique design flair on a massive scale.

In common with many other estate owners, he could well have employed the services of an architect to undertake all the work, but seemingly preferred to oversee the building work for himself, adapting designs from a book by the architect P.F. Robinson. Close scrutiny of these layouts reveal that Sir Robert was indeed inspired by Robinson's work, but uniquely added his own subtle adaptations, resulting in no two cottages being the same. Sir Robert's creations are architectural gems containing a number of recurring features, such as a preponderance of

curved walls and the classical shaped chimneys that so elegantly grace his cottages and lodges. Sir Robert unusually introduced porticos to many of his cottages, a feature not typically associated with cottage design, but one that works beautifully in the Nannau Alms houses (Tai Newyddion) at Llanfachreth, built in 1812 to house the widows of Sir Robert's tenants.

Many of Sir Robert's cottages incorporate Tudor elements, such as the Coed y Moch Lodge built in 1830. It spans the entrance to the main carriage drive to Nannau. The lodge contains a totally unique feature in the form of a painted clock on the gable, with the fingers denoting six minutes to five. The rationale behind this frozen moment in time was the brain-child of the 2nd Bart. He was neurotic about his guests being late for supper and thought that this would aid their punctuality. Coed y Moch Lodge, formerly

171. *Tai Newyddion, Llanfachreth (Nannau Alms Houses)*

ARCH 1 - Entrance to Deer Park

ARCH 2 - Hen Ardd Arch

ARCH 3 - Y Garreg Fawr

ARCH 4 - George III Arch Maesybrynner

ARCH 5 - Coed y Moch Lodge

173. above: **Nannau Home Farm, with the initials of Robert Williames Vaughan and his wife Anna Maria picked out in port bottles**

known unsurprisingly as 'Clock Lodge', stood six minutes ride from Nannau, giving guests an uncompromising order to be on time, precisely 5 pm! Many late arrivals would have ridden at 'break-neck speed' up the drive to arrive at the prescribed time, knowing that late-comers would be banished to a side table, and suffer the wrath of the 2nd Bart.

Nannau's antiquity is often revealed in the place names associated with the many estate holdings and in the field names around Nannau Deer Park. Coed-y-Moch is a good example, stretching back to medieval times when it was customary for herds of swine to be turned into ancient oak woods to feed on the acorns on the 24th June, the Festival of St. John the Baptist. A field name near to Coed y Moch Lodge, Cae Garth Bleiddyn, harks back to a long-gone time when wolves roamed the land.

Sir Robert's motives for rebuilding many of his estate farmhouses and cottages could not be considered financial. Rental values in the region of only £2 a year meant that

> *Cottages were expensive to build and you got nothing for it.*

(Owen Slaney Wynne, Land Agent for the Wynnstay estate in the late 19th century)

It is likely that the 2nd Bart was driven by altruism, wishing to improve the lot of his tenant farmers. A contemporary quote of 1818 reveals a typical peasant cottage of the era:

> *The house had only one small window in it so that we could hardly distinguish from one end of it to the other. The floor was bare earth, & the walls had no plastering or whitewash, but merely the rough stone of which the cottage was built. A few sticks were blazing in the hearth or rather mud floor over which was suspended a large saucepan, full of potatoes. There was a large open chimney to let out the smoke. The candle which the woman lighted to fetch the milk from a dark corner, was a rush twisted and dipt in grease.*

(Liz Pitman, Llanrwst, 2009)

About a mile south of the village of Llanfachreth stands Sir Robert's impressive monolithic arch, spanning the highway.

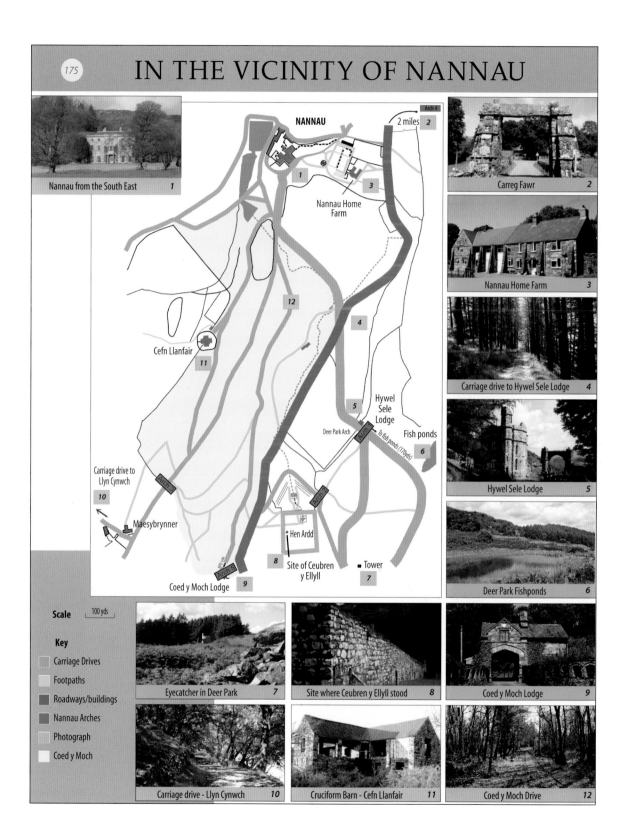

IN THE VICINITY OF NANNAU

NANNAU

2 miles

Arch 4

Nannau from the South East   1

Carreg Fawr   2

Nannau Home Farm

Nannau Home Farm   3

Carriage drive to Hywel Sele Lodge   4

Cefn Llanfair

Hywel Sele Lodge   5

Hywel Sele Lodge

Deer Park Arch

To fish ponds (170yds)

Fish ponds

Deer Park Fishponds   6

Carriage drive to Llyn Cynwch

Maesybrynner

Hen Ardd

Site of Ceubren y Ellyll

Tower

7

8

Coed y Moch Lodge   9

Scale   100 yds

Key

- Carriage Drives
- Footpaths
- Roadways/buildings
- Nannau Arches
- Photograph
- Coed y Moch

Eyecatcher in Deer Park   7

Site where Ceubren y Ellyll stood   8

Coed y Moch Lodge   9

Carriage drive - Llyn Cynwch   10

Cruciform Barn - Cefn Llanfair   11

Coed y Moch Drive   12

This large rubble-built arch is more familiarly called Y Garreg Fawr (The Large Stone), so named because of the huge stone that surmounts it.

Its construction in 1820 was to celebrate the completion of walling the 10,164 acres which Sir Robert had been awarded by the Enclosure Acts. Another arch near Maesybrynner was said to have been completed on the very day King George III breathed his last breath on the 20th January 1820.

Sir Robert's fascination for arches led to the construction of a further three, all constructed between 1820-30, and spanning different carriage drives that converge on Nannau. Sir Robert enjoyed driving his guests around the deer park, with each arch revealing an impressive vista, and allowing the 2nd Bart to recount the intricate legends associated with Hywel Sele and other ancestors. Sir Robert sometimes took his guests further afield on his estate, and to this end devised imaginative means of identifying his properties. One such way was to build bottle ends into the gables of his buildings, spelling out his hallmark signature of R.W.V. and A.M. for himself and his wife Anna Maria. Such hallmark signatures were really unnecessary as Sir Robert's buildings were so unique and easily identifiable.

Not content with improving his estate, Sir Robert turned his attention to Dolgellau town. In the 1830s he set about rebuilding the town centre, most notably Eldon Square, the only formal terrace in Dolgellau, named after a friend, Lord Eldon, who he held in high regard. Sir Robert went on to facilitate the building of a new market hall in the town and was instrumental in acquiring a new courthouse, and a replacement county gaol. He was also founder of the National School. His influence on the architecture of Dolgellau cannot be overstated. Other building ventures in Dolgellau included the rebuilding of the Golden Lion Hotel in 1839. Further afield, he

constructed The Blue Lion Coaching Inn at Harlech, a prestigious undertaking that was completed in 1830.

Sir Robert was M.P. for Merioneth for over 40 years, his tenure coinciding with the Napoleonic Wars and its aftermath of unemployment and poverty. He is known to have constructed 55 miles of walling in the parish of Llanfachreth and many new roads around Nannau, which provided much needed employment for many ex-service men.

Sir Robert Williames Vaughan was clearly a man of vision and was fortunate enough to have the means to make it a reality. The fruits of his work are clearly visible to us today in the magnificent legacy of buildings and structures in the landscape that he so carefully nurtured.

THE AGRICULTURAL Improver

The end of the 18th century heralded many changes in the predominantly agricultural landscape of Merioneth, once described by Professor A.H. Dodds as the most economically backward county in Wales. Changes in animal husbandry and cultivation were desperately needed, and many were brought about as a result of innovations broadcast by Sir Robert and other Merioneth landowners.

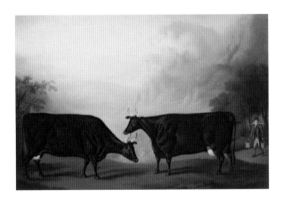

177. above: **Nant y Cnydyw, a former Nannau estate farmhouse, with 1832 clearly visible on the gable in port bottles**

Sir Robert obviously kept abreast of new developments, consulting with the foremost agricultural experts of his day, using this knowledge to great effect by acting as a role model for others to follow.

Rev. Walter Davies (Gwallter Mechain), as early as 1810, noted that:

Sir Robert's ideas were very progressive and that no detail of his estate management, however small escaped his attention.

He further described Nannau farm as being:

well contrived, for soiling and accumulating manure…. Gates, properly so called are framed either of sawed, or of cleft oak: and are hung to strong posts of the same wood, by means of iron hinges. The gates about Nannau are made upon a similar plan. The span ten feet clear between the posts: - the top and bottom rails are of oak, the intermediate ones of foreign deal, all taper in towards the fore-post in order to lessen the pressure on the hinges.

Such descriptions convey a very innovative, modern and efficient farming venture, destined to impress and inspire.

When the Merioneth Agricultural Society was founded in 1801, it is not surprising to hear that they elected Sir Robert as their first President. The Society was part of the agricultual improvement movement sweeping the country. With Sir Robert at its helm, we see awards being issued for such diverse activities as 'bee keeping', 'rearing stallions' and building 'neat fences and stone walls'. The latter skills would be eminently useful to Sir Robert's stone-walling projects. In order to build over fifty miles of walls in the parish of Llanfachreth, Sir Robert kept a special team of eighteen horses and mules, together with nine carters. Rev. Walter Davies described some of the early Nannau walling in 1810, stating that:

they are 5ft 6 inches high under the coping, which projects 4 inches each side; 3 foot thick at the base, and 20 inches at the top; masons' wage 2/6 per rood. The greater part of the stones were collected and some of them blasted, in the fields which the walls now enclose.

So well built were these walls that many still stand today two hundred years after their initial construction, a testament to the skill of Sir Robert's dry stone wallers, who toiled on those

bleak, windswept slopes in the age of enclosure, when the gentry of Wales 'carved up the hills between themselves'.

Most of Nannau's farms before enclosure were on average less than 50 acres in size. Sir Robert would have to wait until after the Napoleonic Wars to expand the size of his holdings significantly, and, together with land improvements, see his rent roll increase to a healthy £20,000 by the 1840s.

Sir Robert was very proud of his stock, his sheep and cattle being singled out for preferential treatment. Regarding the former he stated:

they will not taste a Norfolk turnip, as long as a Swedish one remains in the field…

So that he could view his sheep as he travelled around his estate, Sir Robert ordered that the carriage-ways should be gated, allowing the sheep to graze the verges. A boy was employed to run in front of the carriage and open the gates ahead of the carriage's arrival, and indicative of the timeless character of the Nannau estate, the drives were to remain gated until well after the First World War!

The Welsh Black cattle must have been prized possessions, particularly 'Benthal and Brân' who were painted by the renowned sporting artist Daniel Clowes of Chester in 1824. It was noted that these prize livestock had small brass finials at the tips of their horns, and ear clips in the form of a 'V' to denote their owners, the Vaughans. The Nannau Ox was also highly prized, although not treated quite so kindly!

Sir Robert also kept a pack of harriers and foxhounds, which his son would follow on foot, Sir Robert trailing the action in his 'Crogan', a small carriage in the shape of a snail's shell. He travelled for miles around his estate, often accompanied by a companion or house guest, liking nothing better than showing off his agrarian improvements. On the rare occasion when he was bereft of a companion, he was not averse to picking up a hapless traveller to keep him company, whether they wanted the 'tour' or not!

Sir Robert's fame in the county and beyond spawned numerous stories, many of which contributed to the folk-lore about this idiosyncratic individual, a larger than life character with a kindly heart, who became affectionately known as 'Yr Hen Syr Robert', (Old Sir Robert).

A Picture of **Welsh Hospitality**

Sir Robert was famous for the indiscriminate hospitality he offered. Emulating the stance taken by his ancient ancestors, he truly kept an open house for literally anyone in the neighbourhood to attend meal times without any special invitation.

*179. above: **Sir Robert Williames Vaughan, 2nd Bart** Oil on canvas by Sir M. A. Shee (1769-1850)*

'The Golden Calf of Dolgellau', as Sir Robert was often called, was a true 18th century gentleman whose hospitality was renowned. Sir Robert's table was famed for its cuisine and for the quality and quantity of wine on offer. Guests refusing to partake could invoke the 2nd Bart's wrath as he regarded such refusals as an insult. One poor unsuspecting guest at a dinner party recalls such a 'celebration' in 1824:

We sat down to dinner, about forty in number, occupying two tables placed parallel to each other, in the spacious dining-room of the mansion. Choice fish of every kind; venison from Nannau Park, celebrated for the delicious flavour of its fat bucks; mountain-mutton, from the fertile pastures of Llanfachreth; the noble sirloin, and, in fact, every substantial delicacy that wealth could procure, pressed even to groaning the broad tables of our host; while the harper in the hall twanged his instrument with a force and a fury, that plainly showed his previous intimacy with the good cheer of the place. But noble and magnificent as the entertainment was in the eating department, it was infinitely surpassed by that which was devoted to the orgies of Bacchus. No sooner was the brief and scarcely audible grace pronounced by the chaplain, than in marched old Pearson, the gray-headed butler, bearing in each hand a goblet, in form like an acorn, and fashioned of dark polished oak of the far-

famed Spirits-Blasted Tree, richly ornamented with appropriate silver emblems. One of these was placed reversed by the side of the president and croupier of each table, and presently afterwards flanked by a huge silver tankard of foaming ale, strong enough almost to blow into the air a first-rate man-of-war. Filling this goblet, which held very nearly a pint, the president made his speech to the health and happiness of the young 'squire, and draining it dry, passed it on to his left-hand neighbour ... so the acorn of Nannau started to make its rounds ... Unfortunate for me, I sat between two determined and well-seasoned toppers, who took especial care that I should not only fill to each toast, but drain the cup to the very bottom; so that, novice as I was in this sort of hilarity, I found myself, in a very short time, lying down under a laburnum tree on the lawn, and composing myself not very comfortably ... to sleep . I had my sleep, however; and when I awoke and re-entered the house, a merry group of guests had surrounded the harper in the hall, and were singing Penillion at full stretch, to the now unsteady and somewhat discordant accompaniment of the minstrel; the laugh was of course against me, but good-nature, rather than contempt, characterised the bantering, and I bore it all in good part. The party broke up about eleven, and before midnight I was at home, after a magnificent

walk of three miles, over the mountain, in the moonlight.

(*The Inspector*. 'The Mirror of Literature, Amusement, and Instruction.' Vol. X, No. 271. Saturday, September 1st, 1827)

It was the custom at Nannau to fill 12 great casks of 120 gallons with strong ale. Each cask was kept for 12 years before it was tapped and replaced with a newly brewed replacement, so ensuring that there was always a full complement of 12 casks available for consumption.

Mr Hugh John Reveley of Brynygwin, Dolgellau, writing in his journal regarding the hospitality given by Sir Robert and his brother Colonel Vaughan of Rhûg, noted:

My father would have much oftener accepted the Colonel's hospitable invitations had he not dreaded the set which was always made upon so sober an individual. After tasting lots of different bottles of wine, port etc. he would wisely walk home leading his horse, and on arrival at his home, he would hold out the reigns to his groom only to find that the animal had slipped his head out and escaped.

Considering its remote setting, it is not surprising that Sir Robert and his family welcomed guests so readily, no doubt eager to dine with them and elicit gossip from the 'outside world'. One family is even known to have sent daily compliments to hotel guests in Dolgellau, openly inviting them to dine, a ploy that the Nannau family could well have embraced.

The beginning of the 19th century saw a great up-surge in the number of travellers to North Wales and the Dolgellau area in particular, drawn by the yearning for the Picturesque, their appetite whetted by Pennant's *Tours in Wales* and other publications. The increase in tourism was also a direct result of the French Revolution, as travelling through Europe as part of the Grand Tour had lost its appeal with the barbarous acts of the revolutionaries foremost in travellers' minds.

Pennant had visited Nannau on several occasions and had experienced the 2nd Bart's hospitality at first hand. The subsequent account of Nannau, and in particular the story of the 'Ceubren yr Ellyll' and Hywel Sele's demise, would have placed Nannau as one of the 'must see' locations on any self-respecting tour of North Wales. Pennant is known to have dined at Nannau with Sir Robert, who no doubt presented himself favourably to welcome his important guest, complete with wig and pig-tails, especially powdered for the occasion. If this scenario is accurate, the 2nd Bart might well consider himself fortunate to have survived the evening unscathed, given this report in *Byegones* of January 1874, which alludes to a disturbance in Chester:

Mr Pennant is a most ingenious and pleasing writer, his tours display a great variety of knowledge, expressed in an engaging way. In private life I am told that he had some peculiarities and even eccentricities. Among the latter may be classed his antipathy to a wig!, which however, he can supress till reason yields to a little wine. But when this is the case, off goes the wig next to him and into the fire! During once at Chester with an officer who wore a wig, Mr Pennant became half seas over and another friend that was in company carefully placed himself between Mr Pennant and the wig to prevent any mischief. After much patience and many a wistful look, Pennant started up and seized the wig and threw it in the fire. It was in flames in a

183. *Coed y Moch Lodge (2014)*

moment, and so was the officer, who ran to his sword. Downstairs runs Pennant and the officer after him, through the streets of Chester. But Pennant escaped from superior knowledge of the topography, a wag called this 'Pennant's Tour in Chester!'

It is to be hoped that the 2nd Bart's wig survived Pennant's visit intact!

Perhaps the most interesting and informative account of the 2nd Bart's hospitality is to be found in the reminiscences of Mrs Frances Stackhouse, who in 1824 visited Nannau with her husband as part of a carriage tour of North Wales. After being 'press-ganged' into visiting Sir Robert, on the recommendation of the 2nd Bart's brother, Colonel Vaughan of Rhûg, they arrived at Coed-y-Moch Lodge:

So it ended one morning, in our arriving at the Lodge gate of Nannau, feeling very ashamed of ourselves, and before we had accomplished the drive of nearly five miles from the Lodge to the house, we had repented that we had yielded. When we arrived and asked if Sir Robert and Lady Vaughan were at home, the butler said that they were out walking and again we

hesitated; but the butler said we were expected, so we took possession of the house. Presently our hosts came in and gave us a most hearty welcome, the shake of the hand almost dislocated my shoulders. We made our apologies which they did not at all understand, and it only seemed a natural thing to them that five human beings, a pair of horses and a dog should inflict themselves upon strangers to them, and from whom they had not received an invitation. However nothing could exceed their kindness and we all settled down very comfortably ... Sir Robert Vaughan was about six feet high and rather portly. He was dressed in a suit of home made grey cloth, the waistcoat with flaps which reached nearly to the knees, and partly covered the other articles of his dress which ended below the knees where blue woollen stockings completed the costume. Lady Vaughan had been a handsome woman, and of a good Welsh family, having been a Miss Mostyn, but her education was not what we should call first class in England. The next day Sir Robert took us on a drive about his grounds in his private carriage which was exactly like a small wild beast's van, he sitting in front under the projecting roof... there was a regular dinner of five dishes in each course every day, to

which all the neighbourhood came without any special invitation, and, in consequence, the company was not of the most select kind. One day a lady sat by me, who, I found, was not very polished, she soon told me the rats were very troublesome in her Father's malt house at Dolgelley and I then found that she was the maltster's daughter.

(Elizabeth Inglis-Jones, 1961-4)

From Nannau the Stackhouses hoped to visit Barmouth and hence to make for their home in Shropshire. Sir Robert clearly had other ideas and drove the beleaguered pair to Barmouth himself. Later that night the convivial baronet reluctantly bade them goodbye and wished them a safe journey the following day. Rising early the next morning, the Stackhouses awaited their carriage at the front of the hotel when

an upstairs window was thrown open and Sir Robert appeared, just as he had turned out of bed, in a tall white night-cap and his shirt collar open, displaying a wonderful expanse of chest. In a fashion he repeated his adieux of the night before.

(Elizabeth Inglis-Jones, 1961-4)

Overwhelmed, the couple boarded their carriage and headed homewards, no doubt with Sir Robert's pleadings ringing in their ears:

You must visit again … again … again!

Mrs Stackhouse never forgot the hospitality she had experienced at Nannau with Sir Robert. Writing her recollections down when a very old woman, it is clear that the experience had been vividly etched on her mind. She commented in the prelude that:

The Welsh hospitality that was at that time dying out, has now become a thing of the past.

The **GEORGIAN NANNAU**

The Nannau of today stands in a truly dramatic setting, under the west flank of towering 'Moel Offrwm', against a rugged backdrop of mountain and forest. Standing over 700 feet above sea level, it was aptly described by Thomas Pennant in 1784 as

perhaps the highest situation of any gentleman's house in Great Britain.

As mentioned previously the core of the present house was the brain-child of Sir Robert Howel Vaughan, 1st Bart, but it was left to the 2nd Bart to complete the design process, which he accomplished in 1795. The surviving lead rain-water hoppers record that important milestone, complete with the statutory Nannau Lions! The house stood as a square block, beautifully faced with granite slabs, on the basic

footprint of Colonel Huw Nanney's former mansion. In 1805 Sir Robert, 2nd Bart, added the perfectly proportioned pavilion wings, making it a classic example of the best period of Georgian architecture, the Adams period.

Sir Robert had shrewdly employed the Shrewsbury architect Joseph Bromfield to design and oversee the 1805 project. He was responsible for the wings and many of the internal decorative features. A fire is known to have destroyed part of Nannau in 1808, and at that particular time Bromfield exchanged designs for rebuilding the stairs and banisters with the 2nd Bart.

Joseph Bromfield's attention to detail and design flair was in great demand in North Wales and the Border counties, and having worked on Sir Robert's brother's house at Rhûg he was unsurprisingly recommended for the Nannau extensions. The 2nd Bart would, no doubt, have been extremely pleased with his creation. Bromfield had initially been a plasterer before becoming an architect in his own right around 1791, and this initial skill enabled him to complete some incredible plasterwork for his

distinguished clients. Nannau's ornate plaster details were a testament to the master's skill.

Having completed his mansion, Sir Robert would have turned his attention to the ancillary buildings, most notably the stable block behind the house, built of the same roughly dressed stone as the new mansion. Ever the innovator, and wanting to keep up with new developments, Sir Robert installed a 'carriage-washing pit' in the stable yard, although remnants of this 'modernistic' feature have long since vanished.

A classic Georgian building requires an appropriate setting, and Nannau's position in the landscape does not disappoint, being located in a truly magnificent parkland, the core of which is likely to have been laid out in the 17th century. Under Sir Robert's auspices, Nannau park developed into a romantic, designed landscape, complete with an extensive Deer Park and all the other 'essential' ingredients: the lodges, arches, gates, eyecatchers, all complemented by the magnificent

189. *left: Keeper's cottage, and Hen Ardd (Old Gardens)* (1956)
190. *below right:* ***Llanfachreth Church - showing the Vaughan private chapel adjacent to the front porch*** *by H. Gastineau (early 19th century)*

fruit trees and manicured Lady Vaughan's Knot Garden, set out in the form of her initials. Nearby, the 2nd Bart also built the kennels for his fox hounds, just far enough from Nannau that their howlings could not be heard!

A glimpse of the opulence of the garden can be gleaned through the eyes of Richard Fenton, who viewed them with his colleague Sir Richard Colt Hoare in 1813:

> *The Gardens are at a good distance from the house, in a sheltered hollow to the South East of the house, and abound with vegetables of all sorts, and at the time we visited it, with all fruits then in season, viz., Strawberries, Raspberries, Gooseberries, Currants, &c., Cherries.*

Another more formal garden existed near the mansion, with formal walks and flowerbeds in profusion, and a compliment of heated greenhouses to assist with plant propagation. Sir Robert was no doubt self-sufficient in most respects and well-placed to capitalise on fresh fruit in the growing season, but for 'exotic delicacies' he would have needed to ship them in by coach from London.

ECCLESIASTICAL Matters

Sir Robert, like so many of his Nannau ancestors, was a great supporter of the Church, his

Precipice Walk. The walk is a scenic, three-and-a-half-mile footpath, revealing panoramic views of the Mawddach Estuary, and is still much in use today.

The main Deer Park stands some distance to the south east of the house, next to 'Hen Ardd' (Old Garden) and Hywel Sele Lodge. Its high stone walls, designed to prevent the deer from escaping, still stand today but are devoid of the splendid iron gates that once barred their openings. 'Hen Ardd' is particularly interesting, being a 3.5 metre high walled garden, built by the 2nd Bart in a noted sheltered position on the estate in 1828, with a date plaque commemorating its completion.

A carriage drive once passed through woodlands adjacent to the walled garden, accessed by an impressive Tudor-styled arch which is still in existence, although the driveways are now, with the passage of time, overgrown. Sir Robert, in true idiosyncratic style, cleverly incorporated a cottage into the very walls of the garden. The 'Keepers Cottage', as it was known in its heyday, became the home of the gardener who tended the

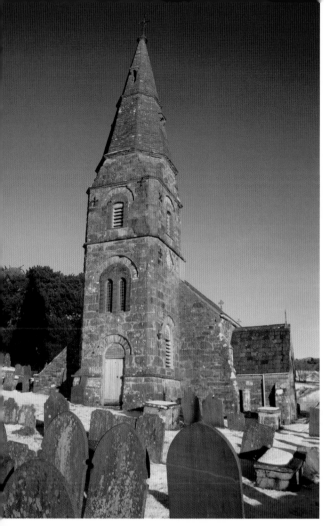

A.D. 1820, To the Memory of George III, King of Great Britain and Ireland. This structure (together with that of the South Side) intended to preserve the religion which he loved and practiced, and to preserve which in its purity was the constant object of his endeavours, through a reign of unexampled length, were erected in the same year which deprived his people of their Father and Friend, by his dutiful and attached subject, Robert Williames Vaughan.

In Sir Robert's rebuilt church, it seems that the congregation was allocated the main body of the church whilst the south transept was the private domain of the Nannau family and their retainers, making it a type of private family chapel. To further reinforce the family's territorial claims, Sir Robert had installed specially constructed oak pews with his name inscribed on the back of each. One such pew still exists in the porch of the church. Sir Robert further claimed that an extended church was needed to cope with the increased attendance. An early etching of the church clearly shows the Nannau Family private chapel in place circa 1840.

Sir Robert must have felt secure in the belief that the whole parish were happy to attend the church he had built for them, blissfully unaware of the growth of Nonconformity that would soon shatter his peaceful existence.

In common with many landed gentry, Sir Robert treated the Methodist Revival that came to the area with hostility. As early as 1785 the Methodists held their first service in the parish, near Pwllgela Lake, Llanfachreth. It was held in the open air as no one dared to evoke the wrath of Sir Robert by holding the service in their own house. The local church bell-ringer foolishly opened his doors to a Methodist Quarter Session and soon paid for his action, as once Sir Robert and the vicar caught wind of his 'transgression' he was immediately sacked!

For the next 15 years Sir Robert was involved in a bitter struggle to stave off the inevitable building

patronage extending to numerous churches in the area, but the Nannau family church at Llanfachreth was singled out for preferential treatment. The family's involvement with Llanfachreth Church reached far back into medieval times, when Dafydd ap Meurig, the 11th Lord of Nannau, bequeathed the sum of six shillings and eight pence towards the construction of the church in 1494. More than three hundred years later, the 2nd Bart embarked on a series of improvements that would span three decades, beginning in 1800 when he re-roofed, re-seated and thoroughly repaired the small parish church.

Twenty years later Sir Robert added a chancel and south transept to the church, dedicating the work to the memory of George III. He also installed two large slate slabs on either side of the lychgate, commemorating his late Majesty, one in Welsh, and the other in English, which reads:

of a chapel in the Parish, he being determined that they should not get a foothold anywhere on the Nannau estate. Sir Robert's fierce intolerance of the Methodist cause resulted in many parishioners turning their back on the Church and joining the Methodists.

During these troubled times, the Methodists met to worship in one of the few properties in the parish not owned by the Nannau estate, but when the brave owner was taken ill and decided to sell it, a struggle ensued between the rival factions to purchase the place. The Methodist faction won by paying an exorbitant price to secure possession. No doubt fearing the imminent building of a chapel, the 2nd Bart made it known that he would punish anyone who contributed in any way to the building or worshipped in it. He then set about ensuring that no one would provide them with building materials locally. Despite all of Sir Robert's protestations, a new chapel was built in Llanfachreth in 1804, measuring 8 yards by 8 yards. Sir Robert had to come to terms with the fact that the power of the gentry to control their localities was waning.

A BIRTHDAY PARTY to remember!

On Friday 25th June 1824, Sir Robert's only son and heir Robert came of age, and the celebrations that followed in its wake reverberated throughout much of North Wales.

Coming-of-age celebrations had increased in popularity and opulence since the outrageously lavish affair of Sir Watkin Williams Wynn of Wynnstay in 1770, when the bill of fare at the entertainment, consisted of:

30 bullocks, one roasted whole; 50 hogs,50 calves, 80 sheep, 18 lambs, 70 pies, 51 guinea fowls, 37 turkeys, 12 turkey-poults, 84 capons, 24 pie-fowls, 300 chickens, 360 fowls, 96 ducklings, 48 rabbits, 15 snipes, 1 leveret, 5 bucks, 242 pounds of salmon, 50 brace of tench, 40 brace of carp, 36 pike, 60 dozen of trout, 108 flounders, 109 lobster, 96 crabs, 10 quarts of shrimps, 200 crawfish, 60 barrels of pickled oysters, 1 hogs-head of rock oysters, 20 quarts of oysters for sauce, 166 hams, 100 tongues, 125 plum-puddings, 34 rice-puddings, 7 venison pies, 60 raised pies, 80 tarts, 30 pieces of cut pastry, 24 pound cakes, 60 Savoy cakes, 30 sweet-meat cakes, 12 backs of bacon, 144 ice-creams, 18,000 eggs, 150 gallons of milk, 60 quarts of cream, 30 bushels of potatoes, 6,000 asparagus, 200 French beans, 3 dishes of green peas, 12 cucumbers, 70 hogs-heads of ale, 120 dozen of wine, brandy, rum and shrub rock-work shapes, landscapes in jellies, 1 large cask of ale which held 26 hogsheads.

Such events, whilst remarkable in their ostentation, performed a more mundane role, signalling the young heir's coming to power, akin to the 'royal succession to the throne' but at a local level. The celebrations that followed served to formally introduce the heir and enhance his status in the community.

Preparations for the feasting to be held at Nannau went on for some time. A new kitchen wing had been built to the rear of Nannau to cater for the large number of guests that would descend on the house over the celebratory period, and the meticulous planning would ensure that nothing was left to chance. As the entertaining rooms at Nannau were much too small to accommodate the hundreds of invited guests, a large temporary building, 120 feet long and 30 feet wide, was erected in front of the house. It was the marquee of its day, covered with brown canvas and a

193. above: Detail of the rear of Nannau, circa 1950. The building on the right was a specially built kitchen for the 3rd Bart's coming-of-age celebrations in 1824

thatched roof, and to facilitate the culinary logistics, it was linked to the house through the front portico. Tables ran the full length of the room, and on the right and the left were side tables to assist the servants with serving. An observer at the time, commented:

A better place suited for the purpose could not have been contrived.

Over the chairs of the Presidents were placed the young heirs initials, R.W.V., and the date June 25th 1824, and six banners with the following mottos:

1. Long life and health, to live in fear of God. Obey the King, and for the good of the country.

2. Where the acorn is rooted, the oak succeeds.

3. The prime laws of the nation's leader, respect the best. Help the weak, and be respectful to all.

4. Whilst the sun's rays shine on Cadair Idris, there will be a welcome at Nannau, and a Vaughan to organise.

5. Success to Meirion and all who love it.

6. It's better to live and able.
   Under his acknowledgement.
   Than to walk emptily away from belief.
   From the vivacity of the journey to new land.

To coincide with the party at Nannau, simultaneous festivities were planned at Bala, Barmouth, Corwen, Conway, Ystum Colwyn, Llanfyllin, Meifod, Meillionydd, Dolgellau and Chester, which prompted one observer to state:

With celebrations everywhere it seemed that most of North Wales was engaged in celebrating the event.

High on Moel Offrwm the break of the momentous day was heralded by a discharge of 20 rock cannon that echoed around the encircling hillside. Another battery of cannon on majestic Cader Idris answered with deafening effect and as if to end the tumultuous explosions, the heights of Barmouth rallied with a grand reply that reverberated through the Mawddach Estuary.

The two batteries of rock cannon on Moel Offrwm and Moel Cynwch nearby would be fired many

194. *below:* **Detail from one of the Ceubren Cups used in the 1824 coming-of-age celebrations**
195. *right & inset:* **Rock cannon on Moel Offrwm, overlooking Nannau**

times during the day adding immensely to the occasion. They were often fired to celebrate all manner of public events, such as royal coronations, weddings and of course the coming-of-age celebrations of local gentry. The rock cannons were formed by hand boring a series of holes into boulders high up on the mountainside which were then charged with gunpowder. The whole process was very dangerous and required skilled operators to carry it out safely. Night time detonations, in addition to loud explosions, produced large orange flashes, adding to the effect.

Later in the morning, amid the pealing of church bells, a procession formed in Dolgellau and made its way to Nannau. At the head was an elaborate new coach, the 'Lady Stanley', sumptuously decorated with laurels and drawn by four beautiful bay horses.

About 4 o'clock in the afternoon, dinner was announced by the buglers who played the 'Roast Beef of Old England', summoning the 200 guests to partake of the magnificent banquet that awaited them:

> *The tables literally bent beneath the weight of the good things, and amongst other substantial's was an immense BARON OF BEEF, roasted to a turn ... venison for which Nannau has for centuries been famed was delicious, six fine fat bucks ... the wines were varied and beautiful and enormous jugs of CWRW-DA was placed at proper distances on the table.*

(*The Chester Chronicle*, 6th July, 1824)

After the usual toasts to the Church and King and the statutory God Save the King, Sir Robert addressed the company with these words:

> *Gentlemen, I have the happiness of proposing to you the health of my son; may he fear God and honour the King; show reverence to his superiors and respect his inferiors. Heddwch dedwyddwch a Chym'dogaeth dda!*

No sooner had he uttered the last word of his speech, when a 21 gun salute echoed from the lofty summit of Moel Offrwm, followed by a volley of replies from the Mawddach and beyond. The harps struck up with a range of airs, the bugles outside played 'God Save the King', with

> *the roar of the guns echoing amongst the hills from Moel Offrwm, round by Nannau, to the stupendous heights of Cader Idris, the shouts of the multitude forming a pleasing response, and the soft sound of the bugles dying away amid the valleys. We must confess we never witnessed a scene so peculiarly grand and imposing.*

(*The Chester Chronicle*, 6th July 1824)

196. **The White Ox of Nannau** by Daniel Clowes (1774-1829)
The famous Nanney Ox, the last of the white herd of Nannau, was
slaughtered for the 1824 coming-of-age celebrations of the Vaughan heir

197. above: **The White Ox Candelabra. The horns and hooves mounted in silver, raised on a wooden plinth. The horns were detachable and used as drinking vessels in the 1824 coming-of-age celebrations**

After a number of poetic renditions in honour of the young heir, he arose to return a note of thanks, but was so overwhelmed with emotion that he was not able to utter a word. After a period of expressive silence, the whole company burst into spontaneous and repeated cheers.

After the speeches, an elegant set of six cups were brought into the pavilion and placed in front of the Presidents, each inscribed with one of the mottos set about the walls on banners. Each cup was of beautifully turned oak in the form of an acorn, richly mounted in silver and crafted from the wood of the celebrated old tree, 'Ceubren yr Ellyll', the famed tree in which Hywel Sele was buried by his cousin Owain Glyndŵr. The tree had been blown down in 1813, only eleven years before the celebrations, and had been fabricated into many wooden items: tables, picture frames,

candlesticks and of course the acorn cups. Having charged the Ceubren Cups, the toasting began and in due course huge punch bowls appeared, and the guests joyfully partook of the contents. The day's festivities came to a close with a massive bonfire lit on the summit of Moel Offrwm, significantly the site of the start of the proceedings many hours before.

On the following day over 200 Nannau tenants were entertained to a dinner in the pavilion in front of Nannau, while Sir Robert's brother, Colonel Vaughan,

198. right: **A seal used by the Vaughans depicting the Nannau Ox**

CELEBRATING THE COMING OF AGE OF ROBERT WILLIAMES VAUGHAN, 3RD BART 25TH JUNE, 1824

BARMOUTH The morning was ushered in by a tremendous discharge of cannon, the whole town filled with joy and hilarity. Ships in the harbour proudly flew their flags - 7am signalled a well-contested boat race. An excellent Ox was roasted and together with bread and potatoes distributed to the poor, 16lbs for each family. At 3pm a dinner was held at Corsygedol Arms Hotel. Sports were held & a large bonfire was lit in the street. In the night every house lit candles in their windows.

CONWAY Friends of the House of Nannau dined at the White Lion, then sang Welsh songs.

CORWEN The celebrations began with the ringing of the church bells and at 4pm a large party sat down to a dinner at the Glyndŵr Head. Four fine sheep were roasted and a noble ox given to the public with bread.

BALA A subscription of £70 was collected and a fine ox was cut into 4lbs pieces and with 500 shilling loaves and distributed to the poor. An immense bonfire was lit in the centre of the town for roasting sheep. About 4 pm, 150 gentlemen, tradesmen and farmers sat down to an excellent dinner in the elegantly decorated Assembly rooms. At 9.30 pm town bells rang to signal the lighting of candles in the windows of the town.

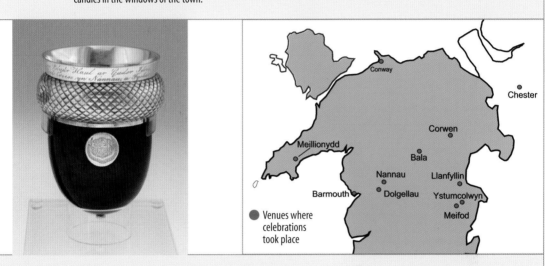

Venues where celebrations took place

MEILLIONYDD 250 tenants and guests gathered together at 2pm at Meillionydd for a dinner. John Evans, Sir Robert's Agent, was in charge of the proceedings, toasts were made for the young heir from silver acorn cups. Drinking went on until the early hours and a barrel of pitch was burnt on the hill above Meillionydd mansion.

YSTUM COLWYN Canon fire was heard from different parts of the estate. A fine ox had been provided by the tenants and distributed to the poor with a plentiful supply of Cwrw Da and bread. A hundred of the tenantry assembled at the mansion house of Ystumcolwyn for dinner at 4pm. Mr Walter Jones, the land agent, gave a short speech and drank the health of the young heir from an elegant silver cup, shaped like an acorn.

DOLGELLAU The church bells pealed and the town band played music. A large hot air balloon was launched, but due to being poorly inflated rose very little and sank into the hillside. Due to the programme of events that went on in Dolgellau the rest of the week, the town drifted into darkness with every window lit by candle light and an eerie glow was cast over the town from a huge bonfire on Moel Offrwm. A story circulated about an old woman in the town who lived in a hovel and did not have a window to light, but was keen to enter into the spirit of things. She took out a table and set it outside and lit her celebratory candle propped up with clay. One witness stated., 'The corners of the lanes were lighted up, and a more gratifying scene has seldom been witnessed'.

CHESTER A dinner of the Friends of the House of Nannau was held at Blossoms Inn, Chester.

dined his tenants at Hengwrt. In recognition of the sterling work they had done, Nannau's hardworking servants were rewarded with gifts: the male servants were each given a silver watch, the female servants gowns and six silver teaspoons each, whilst the upper female servants were presented with elegant silk dresses.

To commemorate the event, Sir Robert commissioned the celebrated sporting artist Daniel Clowes to paint the Nannau White Ox, a magnificent beast that was consumed during the celebration dinner – 'THE BARON OF BEEF'. Prints were made of this beautiful painting and distributed to guests. As a further memento of the occasion, a London silversmith was commissioned to mount the horns and forefeet of the Nannau White Ox and set these into a silver candelabra, complete with a walnut base. While at Nannau, Daniel Clowes was engaged to produce another five pictures: Sir Robert's black cattle, Benthal and Brân, his foxhounds, Lictor and Sancho, and his carriage horses, Butcher and Trimmer. Clowes's painting of the Nannau White Ox was to hang above the dining table at Nannau until the house was sold in 1965.

Celebrations continued all the following week in Dolgellau, with further dinners and balls, ending what had been a truly unforgettable event, surely the high point of the social calendar of 1824. The Vaughan's of Nannau had many treasured mementos to remind them of one of Wales's grandest 21st Birthday celebrations.

THE KNIGHT of the Shire

Sir Robert Williames Vaughan, 2nd Bart, had been elected to represent Merioneth in Parliament in the by-election of January 1792. He was carried to Westminster on the wave of support that had

previously sustained his great-uncle Evan Lloyd Vaughan of Corsygedol, who had died in 1791. The young member was already well-schooled in politics when he took up his seat, and well qualified to follow generations of Vaughan ancestors to Westminster. Seeing his son installed unopposed would have been a satisfying occasion for Sir Robert Howel Vaughan, 1st Bart, the tangible result of years of political manoeuvres. Actively eliciting the support of different gentry factions possibly took a toll on the first Bart's health, as at the end of October 1792 he died at the age of sixty-nine.

Within a few months of taking his seat, Britain was at war with France, and Sir Robert's

199. top: A door head detail from 'Meillionydd' marked AW (Arthur Williams) 1616, with the clear addition of 1824, commemorating the 3rd Bart's coming-of-age
200. above: Sir Robert Williames Vaughan, 2nd Bart's election chair, used to carry him around in the celebrations that followed his parliamentary election successes

IB . Sketches Nᵒ 266

AN
M.P.

Published by Thoˢ Mᶜ Lean 26 Haymarket June 8ᵗʰ 1833.

J Doyle lithog. 71 Martins Lane.

202. above: **Hen Ardd arch, where Sir Robert installed the old doors from Westminster. The arch is clearly dated 1828**

parliamentary initiation was driven by preparations for war. He was appointed to a committee looking at Naval matters, but appears to have taken a back seat in the proceedings. This political detachment seems to have been the hallmark of his four decades of representation. His parliamentary career was typical of most of the squires who represented their county: they had little in the way of political ambition, rarely spoke in parliament and attended only sporadically. Sir Robert's one and only reported parliamentary speech was made on the 27th May 1830, when a Justice Bill was being debated in the House. The debate involved the assimilation of the Welsh Court of the Great Sessions into the English Assize Court system, and he commented:

As the representative of a county, which feels strongly on this subject and the majority of whose constituents are strongly opposed to this measure, I feel bound to give it my opposition; and I oppose it on the ground of its abolishing the ancient jurisdiction of the country, and one to which the people are with justice attached. The charges which (the home secretary Peel) has brought against the opponents of this measure shall not prevent me from pursuing this course; and, aware of the ultimate object of this bill, I should betray my duty to those who send me here did I not endeavour, by every means in my power, to prevent its passing into law.

Sir Robert held his seat unopposed for 44 years, through a total of 12 elections, which saw the Vaughan grip on the Merioneth seat amount to an astounding 135 years! Such political domination by county families was not uncommon at a time when M.P.s were unpaid and therefore only the gentry had the means to attend Westminster. The political representation of the time was aptly demonstrated by Christopher Hill, who noted:

This island is governed by the influence of a sort of people that live plentifully and at ease upon their rents, extracted from the toil of their tenants and servants, each of whom within the bounds of his own estate acts the prince ... They sit at the helm in the supreme council, they command in chief at sea and land; they impose taxes and levy it by commissions of the same quality. Out of this rank select we the sheriffs, Justices of Peace and all that execute the authority of a judge; by the influence of which powers they do so order all elections, to Parliament or otherwise, that the whole counties follow their respective factions, and all the commonalty in the votes are managed by them as the horse by his rider.

(Christopher Hill, London, 1961)

Sir Robert's re-elections were celebrated in style at Corsygedol, now in the possession of his brother-in-law, Sir Thomas Mostyn. Being close to Harlech, where the voting took place, Corsygedol had been the focus of celebrations for all the Vaughan's successes, and this was maintained although the seat was now held by the 'Nannau Vaughans'. As part of the celebrations, Sir Robert was carried around the town on a specially constructed sedan chair with the dates of his election successes inscribed on the back. Sir Robert continued with the same political independence shown by his uncles, although he was an ardent supporter of William Pitt the Younger.

He was also a great supporter of King George III, and, on the death of his beloved monarch, he immediately called a county meeting on the 28th February 1820 to express his condolences and 'extol the blessing of his reign.' A number of tributes are to be found scattered around the Llanfachreth area to commemorate the King. One such tablet is to be found against the wall of Llanfachreth Church tower in the form of a bilingual tribute to George III.

The 2nd Bart enthusiastically promoted many new turnpikes, realising their importance to the viability of the county, and built so many private roads on his Nannau estate that a friend of his, Mr Reveley of Brynygwin, appropriately referred to him as 'The Colossus of Roads'.

He is known to have been a fervent opponent of the Abolition of Slavery, actively impeding the Anti-Slavery Society's distribution of literature in his home county. As mentioned previously he attempted to supress the rise of Methodism by denying them land on his estate to build chapels, although he did mellow in his outlook in later years with regards to the latter. Although Sir Robert did not achieve much celebrity on the political scene, he made an impact in other ways. *The Times* wrote of him:

In this gentleman there remains the finest specimen of the old County Tory School, the race is nearly extinguished.

A drawing of him, described as 'A Welsh M.P.' was circulated around London and displayed in many shop windows as a representative of times past:

He is a gentleman quite of the old school, wears a pigtail and dresses in every way conforming with an old fashioned style, so that he walks about London, where he goes every Spring in worsted stockings... a reference to the fact that these may have been knitted near Dolgellau.

(Peter Howell Williams, 2002-5)

On returning to London in May 1836, Sir Robert was taken ill and was forced to return to Nannau, where later that year, with failing health and after a remarkable 44 years in Parliament, he applied for the Chiltern Hundreds and retired his seat. Claiming the right to appoint his successor, he put Richard Richards of Caerynwch forward. Richard was the son of Councillor Richard Richards, the formidable barrister who had helped to save the debt ridden Hengwrt estate, and who in 1792, was the main promoter of Sir Robert's initial foray into politics. Richard Richards, a Baron of the Court of the Exchequer and Sir Robert's nominee, was challenged by Sir William Wynn of Maesyneuadd, but Wynn was defeated at the polls.

To commemorate Sir Robert's unique service to the county, a subscription was set up to fund a Scholarship to assist the sons of Merioneth to attend Oxford University, appropriately named the Vaughan Scholarship. As a memento of his time in Westminster, Sir Robert proudly displayed a pair of gates on one of his carriage drive arches

*203. below: **The vault of the 2nd and 3rd Baronets of Nannau and their wives***
*204. right: **Sir Robert Williames Vaughan, 3rd Bart, depicted at Balliol College,**
***Oxford** Oil on canvas. 37 x 45 inches by S. Drummond*

mile in length. The 'Offrwm' (money collected for the priest officiating in the service) amounted to a significant £42!

His son and heir, Sir Robert Williames Vaughan, 3rd Bart, was bequeathed all his possessions, and his wife, Dowager Lady Vaughan, was left the sum of £500 and continued to live at Nannau until her death in May 1858, aged 80, having survived her husband by 15 years. In Sir Robert's detailed will, he made very generous annuities to many of his servants who had so faithfully served him for many long years.

It was truly the end of an era, and many wondered what would become of Nannau. An old man re-roofing one of the Nannau barns went into shock when he heard of Sir Robert's death, and was heard stuttering:

This is the end of Nannau.

that had been rescued from the old Palace of Westminster after a fire.

THE END OF AN ERA

The retirement of Sir Robert signalled the end of an era, and Westminster would not see his like again. Sir Robert's only son and heir, the 3rd Bart, showed no interest in following his father into politics. It is not surprising, knowing his father's larger than life reputation, that he declined the challenge!

After a long and distinguished career, Sir Robert Williames Vaughan, 2nd Bart, died at Nannau on the 22nd of April 1843, aged 75 years. The Principality had lost one of its most worthy and unique characters. The tenants of his estate had lost a patriarch of the highest order. Much of his large income had been utilised to improve his estate, and, in the process, it had given much-needed work to many unemployed men in his locality.

Sir Robert was interred in the family vault in Llanfachreth churchyard near to the church tower on Saturday 29th April. His funeral was the largest ever seen in the area with three thousand in attendance, and a procession that stretched all the way from Nannau to Llanfachreth, more than a

The next few years would prove how accurately the slater had interpreted the situation. Whilst not the end of Nannau, Sir Robert Williames Vaughan, 3rd Bart, did not take much interest in the Nannau mansion.

SIR ROBERT WILLIAMES VAUGHAN - 3rd Bart

Having had such an illustrious father proved to be daunting for the young heir, and one gets the impression that he shunned the limelight, a stance diametrically opposite to his father.

Events that unfolded during the young heir's wedding celebrations hardly endeared him to the locality and probably upset and annoyed his parents. The story begins in the run up to the wedding of young Robert to Margaret Frances Lloyd of Rhagatt. It was customary in such a high profile wedding for the community to descend on the house armed with offerings for the young couple, which could be anything from poultry, pigs, calves, eggs, tea, in fact anything edible! In return for the offerings, the doners

206. above: **Hengwrt, near Dolgellau, as rebuilt by Griffith Howel Vaughan**

expected to be hospitably entertained. The busy household quickly ground to a halt, unable to cope with the deluge of uninvited guests. Orders were reluctantly given that no more offerings could be received, a break with tradition that was known to have caused considerable consternation in the locality, but things would go from bad to worse.

On the morning of the wedding a large crowd had gathered by the bridge in Dolgellau, eagerly awaiting the arrival of the happy couple. The intention was to intercept the couple's carriage and un-hitch the horses, then manually pull the matrimonial carriage up the steep road to Nannau. This procedure was commonplace at such events, and often, as in this case, the participants were in varying stages of intoxication, Sir Robert having kindly provided them with as much strong beer as they could drink. The bridegroom, on seeing the heaving mass of drunken revellers, ordered the coachman to drive on. With the screams of the disappointed rabble in their ears, they sped for home and safety. So disappointed were the crowd that they demolished the specially constructed floral arches that had been erected. A week later it appeared the crowd were still hostile, as the young couple

were pelted with mud as they attended the Sunday church service!

On his marriage young Robert took up residence at Hengwrt, now owned by his uncle Griffith Howel Vaughan, and lived there until 1848. Although not living at Nannau, he clearly took a great interest in the estate itself and the parish of Llanfachreth. Surviving records show that he was actively involved in setting up the village school, offering the land to build it and a contribution of £50, together with the proviso that he could be a trustee and have a say in the appointment of a schoolmaster. Similarly, he made generous contributions towards the building of a parsonage in Llanfachreth, contributing land and money.

Sir Robert's inheritances brought with them considerable worries; his uncle's finances were in tatters, with debts of £275,000 on the Rhûg estate, and an income of only £10,000 a year. The fact that Sir Robert's father had acted as guarantor for his reckless brother came back to haunt the 3rd Bart, who was drawn into his uncle's quagmire of debt. Drastic action was needed to avert a financial tragedy, and to this end, the 3rd Bart set in motion the sale of his Caernarfonshire estate of Meillionydd to Colonel Pennant in 1843, and his Ystum Colwyn estate to James France France of

205. left: **Frances Margaret, Lady Vaughan, wife of Sir Robert Williames Vaughan 3rd Bart.** *Oil on canvas*

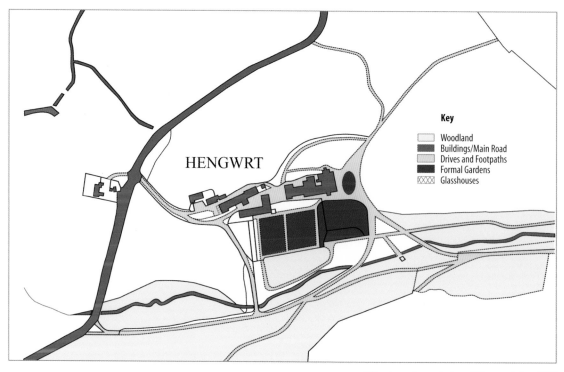

HENGWRT

Key
- Woodland
- Buildings/Main Road
- Drives and Footpaths
- Formal Gardens
- Glasshouses

207. above: ***Layout plan of Hengwrt*** *circa 1900*

Bostock in 1847. Sir Robert and the trustees of the Rhûg estate maintained a vigilant eye on his uncle's affairs until his death in 1848, when the Rhûg estate devolved to the 3rd Bart. Henceforth Sir Robert Williames Vaughan, 3rd Bart, decided to live at Rhûg, it becoming his home until his death in 1859.

Sir Robert was a significant benefactor to the Church, as had been his father. In 1860 he promised a £500 contribution and land on which to build a new church at Llangar near Rhûg. It was very much seen as the moral responsibility of the premier landholder in the parish to provide most of the finance for such projects, and it is acknowledged that most of the church refurbishments in 19th century Merioneth were indeed gentry funded.

When Sir Robert's mother, Dowager Lady Vaughan, died on the 30th of May 1858, he continued to reside at Rhûg. Shortly after the Dowager's demise, Sir Robert's wife Frances was known to have trampled the Dowager's knot garden at Nannau, kicking it and ordering its destruction, an action no doubt signifying that there had existed some kind of animosity

between the 'Ladies'! Tragically, within four months of burying his mother, the 3rd Bart also buried his wife Frances, who passed away at Rhûg on the 16th of September, aged only 47 years, and was interred in the family vault in Llanfachreth churchyard.

The loss of his life's companion bore heavily on him, and in just over a year he died at Dover Street, Piccadilly, leaving no issue. It is thought that his mother Anna Maria had persuaded her son to split the family estates between family members and distant relations, knowing that no issue would be forthcoming. Consequently, according to Sir Robert's will, his estate was distributed thus:

- Rhûg estate to the Hon. C.H. Wynn (godson of Sir Robert)
- Hengwrt estate to the Hon. Misses Lloyd for life (sisters of Frances, Lady Vaughan)
- Nannau estate to the Hon. Thomas Pryce Lloyd for life (Frances, Lady Vaughan's nephew)
- Both the Nannau and Hengwrt estates were to pass to Mr John Vaughan of Chilton

Grove, Atcham (A fifth cousin of Sir Robert) after the life interests ceased.

In 1859, a huge sale was held at Rhûg, and many of its treasures were dispersed. Included in the inventory was a dagger, reportedly once owned by Owain Glyndŵr, and, as mentioned previously, the Hengwrt Manuscripts passed to W.W.E. Wynne of Peniarth, an action that no doubt indirectly preserved them for the Nation.

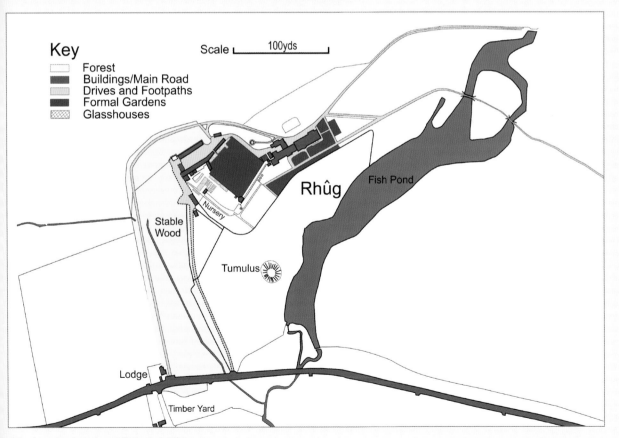

Key
- Forest
- Buildings/Main Road
- Drives and Footpaths
- Formal Gardens
- Glasshouses

Scale |———— 100yds ————|

Rhûg

Fish Pond

Nursery

Stable Wood

Tumulus

Lodge

Timber Yard

*209. above: **Layout plan of Rhûg** circa 1900*

210. below: ***Rhûg Sale Catalogue 1859***

RE THE LATE SIR ROBERT WILLIAMES VAUGHAN, BART.,
DECEASED.

RHUG, MERIONETHSHIRE.

CATALOGUE

OF THE

MAGNIFICENT ASSEMBLAGE OF PROPERTY,

WHICH WILL BE

SOLD BY AUCTION,

BY ORDER OF THE TRUSTEES,

BY MR. WILLIAM DEW,

(OF BANGOR,)

ON MONDAY, TUESDAY, AND WEDNESDAY, AUGUST 1, 2, & 3, 1859,

(COMMENCING AT ELEVEN O'CLOCK EACH MORNING PRECISELY),

Comprising a FINE COLLECTION of valuable

GALLERY & CABINET PICTURES & PORTRAITS,

INCLUDING

FIVE SPLENDID LANDSCAPES,

BY R. WILSON,

PORTFOLIOS OF ENGRAVINGS, &c.,

UPWARDS OF

8000 OUNCES OF ANTIQUE AND MODERN SILVER PLATE,

JEWELLERY,

CURIOUS AND INTERESTING RELICS, COINS, &c.,

A LIBRARY COMPOSED OF TWO THOUSAND VOLUMES,

MANY OF THE WORKS EXCEEDINGLY SCARCE,

A CELLAR OF 200 DOZ. OF CHOICE OLD WINES,

&c., &c.

May be viewed between the hours of Eleven and Four, on FRIDAY and SATURDAY, the 29th and 30th of July, by Catalogues only, admitting three.

THE SALE WILL BE CONDUCTED UNDER A SPACIOUS MARQUEE.

Refreshments will be supplied on the spot, by Mr. MALTBY, of the Owain Glyndwr Hotel, Corwen

PRICE SIXPENCE.

A. R. MARTIN, PRINTER, BOOKSELLER AND STATIONER, BANGOR.

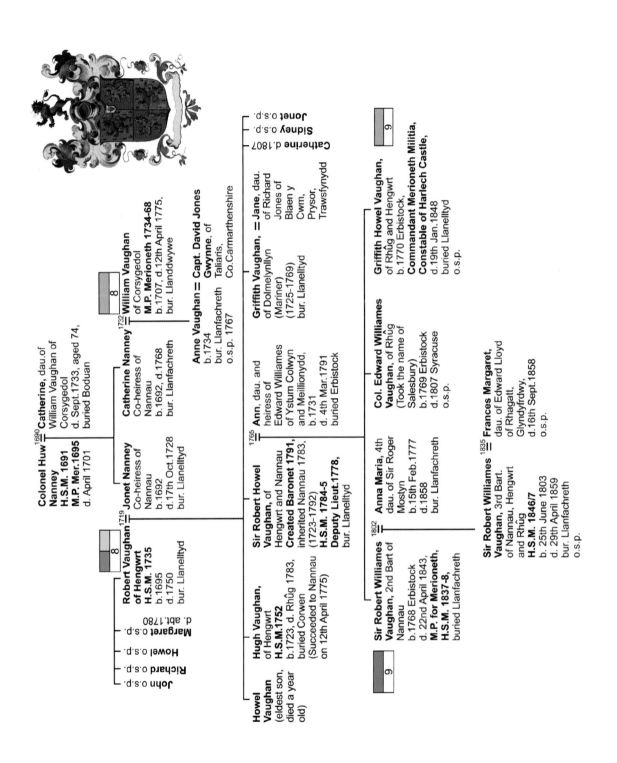

Colonel Huw ⁱ⁶⁹⁰ **Catherine**, dau.of
Nanney William Vaughan of
H.S.M. 1691 Corsygedol
M.P. Mer.1695 d. Sept.1733, aged 74,
d. April 1701 buried Boduan

Jonet Nanney ¹⁷¹⁹
Co-heiress of
Nannau
b.1692
d.17th Oct.1728
bur. Llanelltyd

Robert Vaughan ⁱ
of Hengwrt
H.S.M. 1735
b.1695
d.1750
bur. Llanelltyd

John o.s.p.
Richard o.s.p.
Howel o.s.p.
Margaret o.s.p.
d. abt.1780

Howel
Vaughan
(eldest son,
died a year
old)

Hugh Vaughan,
of Hengwrt
H.S.M.1752
b.1723, d. Rhûg 1783,
buried Corwen
(Succeeded to Nannau
on 12th April 1775)

Sir Robert Howel
Vaughan, of
Hengwrt and Nannau
Created Baronet 1791,
inherited Nannau 1783,
(1723-1792)
H.S.M. 1784-5
Deputy Lieut.1778,
bur. Llanelltyd

Catherine Nanney ¹⁷³²
Co-heiress of
Nannau
b.1692, d.1768
bur. Llanfachreth

William Vaughan ⁱ
of Corsygedol
M.P. Merioneth 1734-68
b.1707, d.12th April 1775,
bur. Llanddwywe

Catherine d.1807
Sidney o.s.p.
Jonet o.s.p.

Anne Vaughan = **Capt. David Jones**
b.1734 **Gwynne,** of
bur. Llanfachreth Taliaris,
o.s.p. 1767 Co.Carmarthenshire

Ann, dau. of ¹⁷⁶⁵
heiress of
Edward Williames
of Ystum Colwyn
and Meillionydd,
b.1731
d. 4th Mar.1791
buried Erbistock

Griffith Vaughan, = **Jane,** dau.
of Dolmelynllyn of Richard
(Mariner) Jones of
(1725-1769) Blaen y
bur. Llanelltyd Cwm,
Prysor,
Trawsfynydd

Col. Edward Williames
Vaughan, of Rhûg
(Took the name of
Salesbury)
b.1769 Erbistock
d.1807 Syracuse
o.s.p.

Griffith Howel Vaughan,
of Rhûg and Hengwrt
b.1770 Erbistock,
Commandant Merioneth Militia,
Constable of Harlech Castle,
d.19th Jan.1848
buried Llanelltyd
o.s.p.

Sir Robert Williames ¹⁸⁰²
Vaughan, 2nd Bart of
Nannau
b.1768 Erbistock
d. 22nd April 1843,
M.P. for Merioneth,
H.S.M. 1837-8,
buried Llanfachreth

Anna Maria, 4th
dau. of Sir Roger
Mostyn
b.15th Feb.1777
d.1858
bur. Llanfachreth

Sir Robert Williames ¹⁸³⁵ **Frances Margaret,**
Vaughan, 3rd Bart. dau. of Edward Lloyd
of Nannau, Hengwrt of Rhagatt,
and Rhûg Glyndyfrdwy,
H.S.M. 1846/7 d.16th Sept.1858
b. 25th June 1803 o.s.p.
d. 29th April 1859
bur. Llanfachreth
o.s.p.

213. Precipice Walk - A magnificent scenic walk with views over
the beautiful Mawddach estuary, originally set out
by Sir Robert Williames Vaughan, 2nd Bart

9

1863-1917

THE VICTORIAN AND EDWARDIAN ERA

JOHN VAUGHAN of Chilton Grove

With the death of Sir Robert Williames Vaughan in 1859, the baronetcy became extinct as he left no issue. His vast estates were systematically redistributed in accordance with his will. Nannau was left to Sir Robert's cousin, Thomas Pryce Lloyd of Pengwern, in Flintshire, as a 'life tenant': a legal tenure that meant Thomas Pryce Lloyd could draw income from the estate and even raise mortgages on it, but was precluded from selling land or property. Such arrangements safeguarded the reversion of the estate for future generations.

A suitable candidate to inherit the Nannau estate on the death of Thomas Pryce Lloyd was found in the form of a very distant relation of Sir Robert, namely John Vaughan of Chilton Grove, near Shrewsbury. Sir Robert had also ensured that the Hengwrt estate would devolve to his wife's sisters and ultimately to John Vaughan. In the meantime, the 'heir in waiting' had benefited from the proceeds of the sale of the contents of Rhûg in 1859, and had contented himself with the knowledge that he

would eventually inherit. Nannau would devolve to him in 1874, but he never realised the Hengwrt estate, as he died some ten years before the last Lloyd sister, when the estate passed to his son.

John Vaughan's family were well known to the Nannau Baronets. The old Sir Robert, 2nd Bart, when on his travels to London in connection with his parliamentary business, would break his journey by staying with his Vaughan relations at Chilton Grove in Shropshire. Both families were bound together by their mutual descent from Robert Vaughan the Antiquarian, Sir Robert descending from the Antiquarian's first son and John Vaughan from the third.

John Vaughan's father, the son of a successful linen draper of Shrewsbury, had at the tender age of 15 in 1793, set sail to India working as a cadet in the Civil Service of the East India Company. He rapidly achieved promotion; his facility with the native languages and his application enabled him to rise to the position of First Judge in the Madras Circuit. His marriage to Catherine Maitland Babington in

216. below: **Chilton Grove, Atcham, Shropshire**

217. right: **John Vaughan (1793-1842)** painted in India by August Theodor Schoefft 1838.

Oil on canvas. 104 x34 inches

1828 produced four children, John being the eldest. Tragically, Catherine died in 1833 aged only 23. John Vaughan senior remained in India, whilst his children were sent back to England to be educated. The overwhelming grief of losing his wife never left him and in hope of dispelling this affliction, he returned to England hoping to find solace amongst his relations. The whole sad affair came to a tragic end when, on the 4th October 1842, John Vaughan senior took his own life at the family home, leaving his children orphans to be raised by their grandfather. A well-educated John Vaughan junior joined his grandfather's flourishing Shropshire business, full in the knowledge that he was the heir apparent to the Nannau estate.

Nannau mansion under the 3rd Bart's tenure had been somewhat neglected, and under the control of the absentee Thomas Pryce Lloyd it was destined to further decline, but fortunately Lloyd is known to have allowed John Vaughan to take up residence at Nannau in 1863, some ten years before the estate would be devolved to him in its entirety.

With a prestigious house to reside at in his adopted locality, John Vaughan wasted no time in finding a suitable bride, marrying Ellinor Anne Owen, a daughter of Edward Owen of Garthangharad near Dolgellau, a successful lawyer and landowner. This was a beneficial marriage for John Vaughan in many ways, without doubt a good match, but also the 'passport' to local gentry circles, as family traditions recount that prior to this union he initially found difficulty in being accepted by the county set. On the day of the wedding the community of Dolgellau were determined to show their support for the happy couple, in scenes reminiscent of the celebratory occasions for the 3rd Bart:

... the day was ushered in with the most terrible sound of cannons and the sweet merry peals of St. Mary's Church Bells, in celebration of the marriage of John Vaughan Esq. of Nannau with Miss Owen of Garthangharad which took place on that day in London. The inhabitants of Dolgelley and Llanfachreth were most anxious to manifest their esteem and respect to the married pair.

Upwards of 50 gentlemen sat down to a sumptuous dinner of all the delicacies of the season at the Lion Hotel. The children of the National and Infants schools were treated to an abundance of oranges and buns in their respective schoolrooms, called together by their able and efficient master Mr R.O. Williams. The Rev. E.C. Owen of Bryn y Gwin reminded the children of what had called them together on that occasion, and hoped that the union that morning contracted in Paddington would be a happy one and that never would there be wanting plenty of the olive branches to enliven the ancient walls of Nannau and proposed three cheers for the Mr & Mrs Vaughan which was responded to in the most deafening applauses which lasted many minutes. Fireworks of first rate order appeared on the Green and bonfires from the tops of the adjacent mountains illuminated the valley below... (and in Llanfachreth) when the shades of evening closed around the village, all the

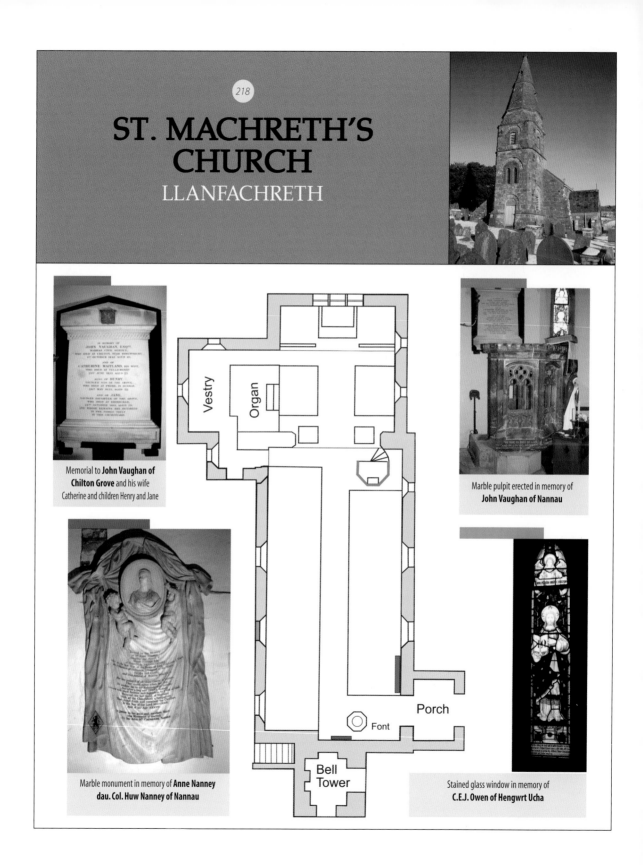

ST. MACHRETH'S CHURCH
LLANFACHRETH

218

Memorial to **John Vaughan of Chilton Grove** and his wife Catherine and children Henry and Jane

Marble pulpit erected in memory of **John Vaughan of Nannau**

Marble monument in memory of **Anne Nanney** dau. Col. Huw Nanney of Nannau

Vestry

Organ

Porch

Font

Bell Tower

Stained glass window in memory of **C.E.J. Owen of Hengwrt Ucha**

IN MEMORY OF
JOHN VAUGHAN, ESQRE,
MADRAS CIVIL SERVICE,
WHO DIED AT CHILTON, NEAR SHREWSBURY,
4TH OCTOBER 1842, AGED 49.

AND OF
CATHERINE MAITLAND, HIS WIFE,
WHO DIED AT TELLICHERRY
23RD JUNE 1833, AGED 23.

ALSO OF HENRY,
YOUNGER SON OF THE ABOVE,
WHO DIED AT PROME, IN BURMAH,
28TH MAY 1853, AGED 22.

AND OF JANE,
YOUNGER DAUGHTER OF THE ABOVE,
WHO DIED AT EDINBURGH,
25TH OCTOBER 1861, AGED 29;
AND WHOSE REMAINS ARE INTERRED
IN THE FAMILY VAULT
IN THIS CHURCHYARD.

*houses as well as the neighbouring
farmhouses were illuminated.*

(*North Wales Chronicle*. Saturday 18th
April, 1863)

For John Vaughan, living at the heart of the
Nannau estate with little real authority must
have been a frustrating experience. In an
attempt to put his mark on the community he
launched into rebuilding Llanfachreth Church
in 1872, promising £500 and building materials
to accomplish the task. The Hon. Thomas Pryce
Lloyd matched John Vaughan's donation. The
whole of the 2nd Bart's old church of 1824 was
reduced to rubble, with the exception of the
tower, which was saved and incorporated into
a design by architect Benjamin Ferry.

It took a year to accomplish the rebuild and
John Vaughan's eldest son, Robert Vaughan,
was charged with the task of laying the
foundation stone, no doubt with a degree of
assistance.

The reopening of the Llanfachreth Church on
the 30th April 1873 was deliberately selected to
coincide with the 30th anniversary of the death
of the great and beloved Sir Robert Williames
Vaughan, 2nd Bart. Although the weather was
atrocious there was a large congregation
present. At 11 o'clock a sermon was given in
Welsh, conducted by the Bishop of Bangor, and
later in the afternoon preached in English. The
Bishop also consecrated additional land given
by the Hon.T.Pryce Lloyd and John Vaughan
for an enlargement of the churchyard. The
evening was rounded off by John Vaughan
entertaining the Bishop and a large company at
Nannau. The following Thursday the workmen
who had been involved in the restoration were
treated to dinner at Nannau, as witnessed by a
reporter from the *North Wales Chronicle*:

*The restoration has been complete and
thorough, and the unsightly old structure,
which was built in direct violation of
every recognised principle of architecture
and was simply an eyesore, is now
replaced by a handsome modern edifice, a
fitting monument of the liberality which
has been displayed by Mr and Mrs
Vaughan of Nannau, who were the
principal subscribers to the restoration
fund, and the energy and perseverance of
the vicar, the Rev. R. Roberts.
The renovated church, which is dedicated
to St. Machreth, stands on the site which
was occupied by the old building. The old
tower at the west end has been left
untouched and contrasts singularly with
the restored work, which is new from the
foundations. It consists of a single nave
and chancel with an entrance porch at the
west end, and a vestry room on the north
side of the building. The length is seventy
feet by twenty seven, and the internal
elevation is fifteen feet to the eaves.*

(*North Wales Chronicle*. Saturday 3rd
May, 1873)

220. above: **Servants outside Nannau**
221. left: **Trespassing notice**

NOTICE.

Trespassing on the NANNAU ESTATE having become excessive, all persons are requested to keep to the Roads and Paths, and to abstain from picking Nuts, gathering Ferns, or otherwise injuring Trees and Plants.

Fishing in the Lakes and Streams not allowed without leave.

Any person infringing the above Notice will be prosecuted.

NANNAU, *August 4, 1874.*

OWEN REES, PRINTER, DOLGELLEY.

Further accounts noted that the building material had been provided by the Nannau estate and similarly the altar of polished oak was from trees grown on the estate. The only tangible record of the Nanneys and earlier Vaughans that remained in situ was the magnificent monument to Anne Nanney, eldest daughter of Colonel Huw Nanney, affixed to the west wall ajoining the tower, which presumably had not been altered.

The rebuilt church was the embodiment of the new regime soon to take over the management of the Nannau estate, and with the son and heir laying the foundation stone the dynasty was clearly here to stay! Within a year the Hon. Thomas Pryce Lloyd died, and John Vaughan was installed as the new squire of Nannau in the remaining years of Queen Victoria's reign.

John Vaughan in many ways emulated his great kinsman old Sir Robert, in that from the onset of his tenure he seems to have done his best to maintain the estate, building many new farm cottages and genuinely taking an interest in the welfare of his tenants. The farms on the estate were so numerous that it took two days to carry out the Rent Audit, followed by the traditional hearty dinner held for tenants in the servant's hall. In one such gathering in 1884, John Vaughan announced to the jubilant tenants that he would be returning ten percent of all rents paid that year!

Nannau had once more become the entertainment hub of the district, and under its convivial hosts, one long calendar of parties, dinners and social events ensued. Towards the end of the summer, just before the onset of the shooting season, the Vaughans seized the opportunity to take a holiday. A number of staff accompanied the family on such occasions, leaving the rest of the household behind to thoroughly clean the extensive mansion. On completion of the frenzy of cleaning, the Vaughans traditionally provided a treat for the servants. The treat took the form of an expedition up to the wilds of Llanfachreth, to an isolated farmhouse where a sumptuous tea was provided.

*222. oval: **John Vaughan (1829-1900)** - Miniature on ivory by M. G. B. Hall. 4.25 x 3.25 inches*
*223. below: **Nannau servants preparing to travel to their annual***
'treat' in the wilds of Llanfachreth

The incumbent Vaughans had become well-respected members of their community, and the Nannau dynasty seemed safe and secure in their hands. In reality, the heir apparent's behaviour caused the family many sleepless nights. Robert Vaughan, or 'Robbie' as he was known, was an eccentric rebel who challenged the family's strict social rules. Early indicators of Robbie's rebellious nature surfaced in 1884, when John Vaughan received a telegram from Robbie's school master informing him that his son had run away from school, seemingly after failing test papers. After a flurry of damage limitation exercises, Robbie was installed at another school in Rhyl, under the watchful eye of B. Hayward Brown, a teacher who was better able to deal with Robbie's outbursts of temper. Further placements and an expulsion did little to allay the parent's fears regarding the suitability of their eldest son, as heir for taking on the family estate.

In marked contrast to Robbie's delinquent behaviour, their second son John, a pupil at Eton, was receiving glowing accolades. Despite the many set-backs, the family seemed to have rallied round and Robbie's coming-of-age celebrations saw the family emerge as a unified force, expressing great public optimism for the future. Preparations for the day had been going on for some two months,

224. above: **Internal view of the marquee erected to house the celebration of the coming-of-age of Robbie Vaughan in 1887**

with the whole locality buzzing in anticipation, as described in the local paper:

Local celebrations for Nannau heir

It is likely that Dolgelley has never witnessed such euphoria as experienced over the last few days. The preparations have been in place for many weeks. Last Saturday Mr Vaughan presented two oxen to feed the poor, this was distributed to over three hundred individuals.
On Monday the town committee was invited to Nannau for lunch, travelling there by carriages. Mr Robert Vaughan, the heir, was presented with a greeting on an old oak frame constructed from the wood of Owain Glyndwr's Parliament House. The greeting was presented by Mr C. E. J. Owen of Hengwrt Ucha.

A magnificent lunch followed with Llanfachreth Brass Band providing the musical entertainment. Later the committee and Nannau family were photographed by Mr Whitehouse the Photographer.

After an enjoyable three hours the participants began to make for the town, where a procession formed from the

multitude of onlookers who had gathered to witness the joyful occasion. Sadly I have to report that an inhabitant of the town accidentally broke his leg during the processing.

Sports were held on the Marian and later that evening a dinner was prepared for a hundred guests in the Lion Hotel. The streets and the houses of the town were handsomely lit.

Fireworks were lit on the Marian (Town Green) by Mr Fellows of Stafford. A large number of townsfolk had prepared arches and flags to show their respect for the young gentleman. The inhabitants of Eldon Row, all Nannau tenants, had decorated their houses beautifully with evergreen foliage. The Ship Hotel was impressively glowing with glass lanterns and the shops were splendidly presented.

Many arches decorated the town, especially commendable being Mr H. Owen's arch on Bont Fawr.
On Tuesday night an excellent ball was held in the Lion Hotel, which was greatly enjoyed by all in attendance.

225. *right:* **Commemorative transfer-printed tea set produced
for the coming-of-age of Robbie Vaughan**
226. *below:* **Festive decorations in Eldon Square, Dolgellau,
celebrating the coming-of-age of the heir of Nannau**

*On Wednesday, Llanfachreth Parish had
the opportunity to show their respect for
the young heir. A feast was provided for
the tenants and the school children and a
bonfire was lit on Moel Offrwm late in the
evening. Earlier in the day Robert Vaughan
received a splendid reception in Dolgelley
Market Hall.*

*Throughout the festivities all preparations
have exceeded expectations.*

(*Y Dydd*. 23rd September, 1887)

During the celebrations the young heir had to
endure the unhitching of his carriage horses and
the statutory hauling around town. It is pleasing
to note that both Robert and his father
wholeheartedly entered into the spirit of the
proceedings, having learnt from the experience
of the 3rd Bart, who on that fateful day in 1824
had rebuked the human haulage. The statutory
right of passage passed over with great mirth
and excitement; there were few indicators of the

turbulent times that were ahead for the young
heir and his beleaguered family.

John Vaughan senior was elected High Sheriff of
Merioneth in 1880, and in 1886 he stood for the
Conservative party in the General Election, but
was ignominiously defeated by T. E. Ellis, the
able son of a tenant farmer from Bala. His forays
into public office henceforth were confined to
his work on the Magistrates' bench.

In 1889, together with Mr Owen-Jones of
Hengwrt Ucha, John Vaughan established the
Llanfachreth Horticultural and Agricultural
Show, with the aim of, 'improving farm and
cottage culture', and in common with other
landlords, became

*the main patron of his local agricultural
society, paying the highest subscription*

227. *Guests at the wedding of Miss Mary Vaughan of Nannau and Mr Charles Edward Jones Owen of Hengwrt Ucha, 11th July 1889*
(Image reveals details of the Nannau stone tablets installed above each arched window)

228. above: **Mr & Mrs C. E. J. Owen with best man and bridesmaids**
229. below: **Letter from Sir Henry Ponsonby, Equerry to Queen Victoria, detailing arrangements for the Queen's visit to Merioneth**

230. *below:* **Nannau coach on tour in Beaumaris with Owen Slaney Wynne at the helm**
231. *insert:* **A whip inscribed 'W. Williams, Groom, Nannau 1880'**

and undertaking all the organisational work.

(L. A. Rees, 2009)

The marriage of his second daughter Mary, on the 11th July 1889, was described as a 'truly modern' wedding. Modern maybe, but it was certainly not lacking in prestige and opulence. Although it took place in the local family church, it was attended by no less than three bishops, and was enthusiastically celebrated in the Dolgellau area.

With the wedding festivities over, the family braced themselves for the most prestigious event to be held in Merioneth for some considerable time, namely, Queen Victoria's visit to the county.

It was only the fourth time the Queen had visited the Principality and she stayed five days, based in the mansion of Palé in the beautiful Dee valley, near the village of Llandderfel.

Mrs E.A. Vaughan's brother-in-law, Owen Slaney Wynne, the 2nd son of W. W.E. Wynne of Peniarth, in his position as Land Agent for the mighty Wynnstay estate, had been fundamentally involved in many of the preparations for the momentous visit. His communications with Osborne House prior to the event reveal much of the etiquette observed on Royal occasions.

QUEEN VICTORIA'S
VISIT TO MERIONETH
1889

Blaenau Ffestiniog

Maentwrog

Llandderfel

Bala
PENLLYN

14
13

ARDUDWY

Harlech

15
16

17

18

19
20
Corwen
EDERNION

12

5

4

1

3

2

6

7

Dolgellau
TALYBONT

MAWDDWY

Mallwyd

Barmouth

Corris

8

9

11

10

YSTUMANER

Towyn

Aberdovey

PRINCIPA

1	Nannau
2	Llwyn
3	Hengwrt
4	Dolmelynllyn
5	Caegoronwy
6	Bryn y Gwin
7	Caerynwch
8	Maesypandy
9	Peniarth
10	Ynysymaengwyn

1. Queen Victoria leaving the Railway Station at Llandderfel

2. Presentation of an address to the Queen at Bala by W.R.M. Wynne

3. Queen Victoria's carriage passing near Rhiwlas

4. Palé Hall, used by the Queen during her visit

5. Queen Victoria's carriage entering Bala

ERIONETH ESTATES

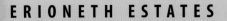

QUEEN VICTORIA'S
visit to Merioneth, 1889

Friday, 23rd August - The Royal Train, amounting to no less than 14 carriages, pulled into Llandderfel railway station having travelled via Shrewsbury. Earlier in the day some 200 people had gathered at Gobowen station, some arriving before 5 am, with the desired aim of catching a glimpse of their Monarch. They were to be disappointed as at precisely 6.21 am the Royal Train passed through, leaving:

> *those who wished for sight of her Majesty disappointed as the blinds of the Royal saloons were closely drawn, as were also, for the most part, those in the other cars. Directly after the train had passed the gathering of sightseers dispersed.*

(A complete record of the Royal Visit to Wales, 1889)

A red carpet had been laid along the platform and the Lord-Lieutenant, Mr R.D. Pryce, resplendent in his brilliant uniform, with sash, cocked hat, and plume of red and white feathers, headed the welcoming party with his wife. Other dignitaries joined the High Sheriff, Deputy-Lieutenants and military officials:

> *The first of the royal party to be seen was H. R. H. the Princess Beatrice, who sat with her face to the platform, and sitting*

near her in a chair upholstered in blue and gold, and with her back to the platform, was her Majesty herself. While the final arrangements were being made, her Majesty stood up while a shawl was thrown over her and resumed her seat to await the completion of the arrangements. Prince Henry of Battenburg and the Princess Alice of Hesse were in the other royal saloon. The train, having been adjusted, remained stationary; a moment or two was spent while her Majesty's two Highland servants made arrangements for her to leave the saloon. She came out in a few seconds looking very well, and smiling as the Lord-Lieutenant was introduced to her. Her Majesty remarked to the Lord-Lieutenant that there appeared to have been a good deal of rain, and he replied saying he hoped the weather would not mar her Majesty's pleasure ... (after the floral presentation) ... her Majesty took her seat on the right of the waiting carriage, while the Princess Beatrice took the left, the Princess Alice and Prince Henry of Battenburg occupying the seats immediately opposite. The Highland attendants at once took their seats, and the carriage drove away amidst the subdued but none the less loyal cheers of those who lined the two hundred yards or so, which divide the railway station from the entrance to Palé. The

second carriage to leave the station contained one of the turbaned Indian attendants.
(A complete record of the Royal Visit to Wales, 1889)

Queen Victoria had arrived in Merioneth, fifty-seven years since her last fleeting journey through the county, when she stopped at Llangollen whilst the horses were changed on the Royal carriage.

Later that afternoon the Queen set out from Palé in her carriage bound for Bala, taking with her a walking stick made of hazel and crafted by Mr Hugh Ellis, a joiner on the Palé estate. It was adorned with a gold band and inscribed 'Llandderfel, to H. M. Victoria, R. I., 1889'. In the numerous etchings of her visit, Victoria is seen using the walking stick, expressing her thanks with the words:

Diolch yn fawr i chwi.

Approaching the Rhiwlas estate, Victoria was greeted with an inscription over the archway leading to the mansion which read, 'Rhiwlas greets you, Rhiwlas greets you' complete with the Royal Arms above. At the entrance to the town a similar sentiment, 'Welcome to Bala', and a mass of bunting and streamers had been suspended across the street at intervals of 20 yards, the carriageway narrowed to a point where it was covered by an awning of blue and white canvas, with stands on either side which

accommodated nearly 400 people. The stand in front of the White Lion Hotel was occupied by the main officials.

Visitors had been pouring into Bala throughout the day, with between four and five thousand people thronging the streets. By three o'clock the spectators began taking up their positions. At approximately half past three the 800 school pupils assembled wearing the commemorative medals designed and supplied by Mr A.C. Minshall. A few moments later the Penllyn United Choir marched up the High Street and took their place in front of the White Lion, followed by the Oakeley Silver Band who marched through the street playing rousing music, taking their position opposite the choir. The guard of honour provided by the 2nd Battalion, Royal Welsh Fusiliers, took up their position in single file facing the Lord-Lieutenant and other dignitaries on the podium, amongst whom were John Vaughan of Nannau, Mr H.J. Reveley of Bryn y Gwin and other magistrates and their families. The Queen was expected at half past four, but it took another fifteen minutes before the Royal cavalcade appeared in the distance, travelling at a 'good pace', slowing as it moved up the High Street to tumultuous cheering and waving. The Queen's carriage was drawn by four greys, the near horses mounted by postilions. Her Majesty occupied the seat on the right, dressed in her usual black, and sitting behind her were the gillies in their Highland costume and plaid. As the Queen drew up, the guard of honour presented arms and the band struck up the National Anthem.

237. below left: **Sir Henry Ponsonby's letter outlining the royal etiquette regarding the Queen's visit to Glanllyn**
238. right: **Princess Beatrice detonates an explosion at the Wynnstay Colliery**

Unfortunately not everything went to plan, with the Royal carriage stopping a few yards short of the desired spot. The error was noted and the carriage moved on … and on … moving beyond the podium! The Queen was heard to shout, 'STOP!' and rescued the situation and saved the possible embarrassments!

After the compulsory receiving of bouquets, the Lord-Lieutenant presented the Queen with the address, embossed on a parchment. The Queen's reply was likewise presented on parchment, and the dignitaries, John Vaughan and W.R.M. Wynne among them, were presented to her Majesty. In less than five minutes the Queen was speeding alongside Bala Lake to a reception at Glanllyn, the picturesque summer residence of Sir Watkin Williams Wynn, some four miles distant from Bala. The welcoming party at Glanllyn were alerted to her Majesty's departure from the town by the thunderous cheering that reverberated down the lakeside. Sir Watkin and Lady Williams Wynn received the Royal party, and among the honoured guests was Owen Slaney Wynne, Sir Watkin's recently retired chief-agent, who had been intimately involved in the planning of many aspects of the visit. Amongst the Nannau family archives is a letter addressed to Owen Slaney Wynne from Sir Henry Ponsonby, the Queen's equerry, informing him that:

I would suggest the shooting party receive the Queen outside the house (Glanllyn) and then go into the Dining Room with us. As to the number, many people make her think there is a crowd. There will be no objection to the tenantry lining the road to the house.
Sir Watkin and Lady Wynn would receive the Queen at the door. We will help the Queen – I should not put out liveried servants, white breeches, black evening dress-trousers, would do very well for them… and I should say 2 servants would be quite enough for the Queen, indeed one could do it all as Lady Wynn would probably make the tea and Sir Watkin help to hand it to the Queen … should put the footmen in dress livery. If Sir Watkin and Lady Wynn meet her Majesty by the door – leave plenty of room for her to get out… I should advise him to simply bow and say how glad he is to receive the Queen at his house and lead the way to the Dining Room. I don't think her Majesty will offer to shake hands – she never does. But if she does so offer, the right thing is to bow and kiss the hand.

It is to be hoped that the appropriate etiquette was observed and that the forty-five minute visit passed without issue. Queen Victoria returned to Palé to be entertained in the evening by the Llandderfel Choir.

Saturday, 24th August – The Queen visited Wrexham, travelling by train to Ruabon, then by carriage to Wrexham, escorted by the Lancers and Hussars, where she received a tumultuous welcome with a rich profusion of decorations along the entire length of the Royal route.

239. **Queen Victoria** *by Heinrich Von Angeli. 1899*

Monday, 26th August – The Queen visited Llangollen by train and the Royal Prince and Princess adventurously descended to the coal face at the Wynnstay Colliery. The Royal couple ceremonially cut a piece of coal from the coal face and under instruction fired a detonation.

Tuesday, 27th August – Princess Beatrice and Prince Henry travelled by train to Barmouth to lay the foundation stone of St. John's Church. John Vaughan was amongst the dignitaries who welcomed the Royal couple, with great celebrations in the town during the day and subsequent evening. The Queen and her entourage left Llandderfel Station at four minutes past ten. About five hundred people assembled to witness the departure:

> The Queen bowed her acknowledgements to the assembled crowd before leaving, and expressed the greatest pleasure at the loyalty of her Welsh subjects.

(A complete record of the Royal Visit to Wales, 1889)

The gentry of North Wales had risen to the occasion and had provided an unsurpassed welcome for their Monarch which left an indelible mark on the Queen, as it is rumoured that she later made enquiries regarding the purchase of the Palé estate. So enchanted was she with the beauty of the surrounding countryside that she is said to have declared:

> If Heaven is as beautiful as this, I shall be very satisfied.

THE LAND QUESTION

John Vaughan's humiliating election defeat had not affected the family's status within the community, but undeniably such a defeat heralded the decay of landed power. The rise of Methodism and the growth of the Liberal party would help to give voice to a movement that would shake the landed interests to their very core, and become embodied in the strongly held grievances commonly referred to as the 'The Land Question'.

The tenant farmers had many valid grievances: lack of security of tenure, the payment of tithes, extortionate rents and 'pressure' to vote for the landlord's candidate were sited as many legitimate reasons for an inquiry. It eventually came in the form of a Royal Commission on Land which sat from 1893 to 1895.

Political campaigns leading up to the Commission had become ever more bitter and openly blamed the landlords for all the tenant's ills. One such vitriolic attack, made by Thomas Gee in his newspaper in 1887, clearly demonstrated the contempt in which landlords were held, stating:

> It is almost as difficult to get hold of a white rook in Wales, or a white elephant in Bengal, as it is to find a kind landlord. It is necessary for a man to walk scores of miles over hills and vales, through the wilderness and the forests, past many a village and hamlet, before he will see the cheerful face of one of these characters ... The common idea of a landlord is a man who has the mouth of a hog, the teeth of a lion, the nails of a bear, the hoofs of an ass, the sting of a serpent, and the greed of the grave ... The landowners of our country are, in general, cruel, unreasonable, unfeeling and unpitying men ... Many of them have been about the

Baner ac Amseran Cymru.

TAIR PRIF DDYLEDSWYDD;—
YMGYFARCHWEL A DUW,
LLESAU DYN,
A GWELLHAU GWYBODAU.

Y GWIR YN ERBYN Y BYD,
GWELL DYSG NA GOLUD,
GWELL AWEN NA DYSG,
GWELL DUW NA DIM.

CYF. XXX.—Rhif. 1601).   DINBYCH: DYDD MERCHER, TACHWEDD 2, 1887.   PRIS | Wedi ei Stamio, 2g. / Heb ei Stamio, 1½c.

most presumptuous (arrogant) thieves that have ever breathed ...

(*Banner ac Amserau Cymru.* 2nd November, 1887)

Feelings did not run to this fever pitch in Merioneth until 1899, when notices to quit were served on three prominent tenants of the Nannau estate, one of whom was 94 years of age, and whose connection with the estate went back to the 2nd Bart's tenure. The condemnation of John Vaughan's actions was swift and decisive, and, as a result, a public meeting was held in Llanfachreth to protest against the notices.

Reports in the *Cambrian News* and *Welsh Farmers' Gazette* of 31st March 1899 noted that one of the tenants who had been given notice to quit regularly withheld a proportion of her rent to express her condemnation of the condition of the buildings and the uneconomic rent. It appeared that the Nannau estate had a policy of issuing notices to quit when rents were in arrears, later withdrawing the notice when the tenant paid the rent up to date. After many such protests the tenant eventually decided to vacate the premises and put her stock up for sale. Another tenant on the estate received notice to quit because he allegedly refused to contribute towards the repair of his house as required by the District Council.

An open air meeting was held after the sale, presided over by Mr Howell Gee of Denbigh and addressed by Mr William Jones, M.P. for North Caernarfonshire. After condemning the state of some of the farm buildings and the plight of the poor tenant farmer in such inhospitable terrain, he noted that:

Good landlords prided themselves, not in big rentals but in a prosperous tenantry and an estate of happy homes ... for the landlord to reduce the number of tenant famers by not repairing their houses and their out-buildings was a waste, but to reduce them by turning them from their homes, especially old tenants, was disgraceful and offensive ... he hoped that from that meeting at Llanfachreth a torch would be taken to light the beacon fires upon all the hills of Wales to rouse the people to say that the legislation must be conceded. Let them be faithful to one another, and let no true Nonconformist or true Liberal take a farm from which a farmer has been turned. Let them act in the spirit of the hymn that was sung. The whole of Wales has something to say to the land question, and for the sake of Wales and the world, let them be united in their action in the matter.

Another speaker interjected,

Are the rents of Llanfachreth fair rents?

242. above: **The Charge of the 21st Lancers at Omdurman** *by Richard C. Woodville*

Mr Jones continued, further commenting that:

> He had no hesitation in saying that they were not. In the interval between the death of Sir Robert Vaughan and the coming to Nannau of the present Mr Vaughan the rents were raised. At that time agriculture was very prosperous and high prices were obtained for sheep and cattle. But when times got worse and lambs were selling for 3s 6d and 4s and ewes from 7s 6d to 8s 6d, Mr Vaughan refused to make a permanent reduction and it was clear to everyman of common sense that it was impossible to say that fair rents were the rule in Llanfachreth. Another matter was that relating to compensation for improvements. Mr Robert Hughes would leave Felinnewydd after being there for sixty-five years without a penny of compensation. His (the speaker's) mother had been at Tyissa for thirty-five years and had paid £2,000 in rent, and now for a whim she was turned away... (her farm amalgamated with another larger local one) ... he appealed to the meeting to say,
>
> One farm for one family and let everyone have a chance to live.

Reverend Eiddon Jones added his reflections, stating that:

> There was a time when the farmers of the neighbourhood did not feel at liberty to attend chapel. Some of them, however, went to the chapel house adjoining and

listened through a hole in the wall to the preaching of the Gospel. On one occasion a child in the chapel recognised her father so listening and called out, " There is Dada." With the result that her father had notice to quit and was compelled to leave his home ... his wife knew that things would probably have been different if she went to church, worked for the Conservatives and had brought up her sons to work on the farm ...

The speaker then moved the following proposition:

This meeting of farmers and inhabitants of Llanfachreth and district deeply sympathise with the families who are compelled to leave their homes and totally condemns the insolent system which allows such injustice; and emphatically urges union and cooperation with a view to facilitating legislation which will secure a land court for Wales to meet out justice and fairness between landlord and tenant.

The meeting terminated with the singing of 'Hen Wlad fy Nhadau.'

While this volatile gathering was being held, John Vaughan senior was confined to his room with an illness, as were Mrs and Miss Vaughan with two trained nurses in attendance. Nannau estate, under the 2nd Bart, was noted for its benevolence and consideration towards its tenants, but now it had become the very embodiment of the injustice exercised by landlords, and its actions were emblazoned on newspapers throughout the land.

John Vaughan and his family had little to celebrate with the ever-looming agricultural unrest that had violently erupted at his own back door, and a son and heir whose behaviour was becoming ever more eccentric, all this

compounding the concerns for the survival of the estate.

John Vaughan junior, however, was excelling in his chosen military career, gaining the highest mark in the Cavalry cadetship training of 1890, in stark contrast to his brother Robert, who was now causing the extended family much concern. In a letter dated 11th January 1890, the vicar of Llanfachreth, Francis Parry Davies, nephew to Mrs E. A. Vaughan of Nannau, wrote:

My Dearest Aunt,

At last I have got the time to write you a line of most sincere and hearty congratulation upon Jack's capital performance. It is needless for me to paint in glowing words how thankful I am – I know your troubles and I hope you feel that in me you have one who truly sympathises with you. I need add no more here.

I am afraid Robbie must have his way and the 'prickliness' of that way can alone open his eyes to see his folly. Poor boy I have told him as forcibly as I can and now we can only be still and wait.

I must shut up!

*Your loving nephew
Francis*

245. *left:* **Pulpit erected in memory of John Vaughan of Nannau**
246. *right:* **Nannau servants,** *circa 1890*
247. *below right:* **Eleanor Catherine Vaughan of Dol'rhyd, later the wife of Colonel Percy Henry Enthoven**

On a sadder note, John Vaughan senior died on the 29th June 1900 and left the Nannau estate, valued at £63,476-5-9, absolutely to his wife, Ellinor Anne Vaughan, and the reversion of the Hengwrt estate to his younger son John. The choice of the Nannau heir had troubled him greatly, and he is known to have changed his will more than once in an attempt to do the right thing. It proved to be a 'poisoned chalice' as the widow likewise deliberated hard and fast over the inheritance, changing her will many times over the coming years.

A number of the tenants of the Nannau estate collected money to provide a memorial for John Vaughan, sending a letter to his widow on the 8th January 1901 stating:

To Mrs Vaughan,

Dear Madam,

A wish has been expressed by the tenants of the Nannau Estate to erect a memorial in Llanfachreth Parish Church in respectful affectionate memory of the late Mr Vaughan, whose kindness and goodness will always be remembered.

A sum of money has been subscribed and we would like to suggest that a window shall be placed in the Church if this would meet with your approval.

Signed,

Owen Thomas	*Evan Thomas*
Robert Roberts	*Evan Pugh*
Howell Pugh	*Edward Jones*

Mrs Ellinor Anne Vaughan's response, a few weeks later, was clearly emotional:

There had, however, been some occasions for celebration. One such joyous event marked the return of Lt. John Vaughan from the Sudan, having taken part in the Battle of Omdurman in 1898. A school holiday was announced to celebrate his return and an enthusiastic welcome awaited the young soldier at Dolgellau station. He later described the event:

When I arrived at my home town, Dolgelley, I was welcomed as a hero. People were not so used to Wars in those days. The carriage was man-handled from the station to the steps of the Market Hall, where the well-known local bard Llew Meirion (The Lion of Merioneth) much to my embarrassment, declaimed an Ode in Welsh which he translated subsequently into English prose.

(*Cavalry and Sporting Memories*, Major-General John Vaughan, 1954, p.61)

My dear Friends,

*Thank you sincerely for your most kind
letter expressing your wish to place a
memorial to my dear husband in
Llanfachreth Church. It is of great
comfort to me in my sad bereavement that
you sympathise so fully in the loss we
have sustained and I value most highly the
affection and appreciation you are now
showing for Mr Vaughan's memory. I
believe a window in the church as a
memorial from you to be the most lasting
proof of your affection for him, and you
well know how great his regard was for
you at all times.
Assuring you how greatly I, with my sons
and daughters value your great kindness
and sympathy, and with most heartfelt
thanks,*

*Believe me always
Yours very sincerely,*

Ellinor A. Vaughan.

The window was duly installed with the
following transcription beneath:

*To the Glory of God and in respectful and
affectionate memory of John Vaughan of
Nannau Esq: who died June 29th, 1900.*

*This window is erected by the tenants and
employees on the estate.*

Ellinor continued to live at Nannau with her
eldest daughter Eleanor Catherine Vaughan,
and together, with a large contingent of
servants, the house and garden was maintained
at its usual impeccable standard. Nannau,
under the widow's direction, took on an almost
'feudal' state as she ruled the estate and its

*248. above: **Nannau,** circa 1890*

servants with a veritable rod of iron. Every evening without fail, all the servants, dressed in the livery of the family, were expected to file into the great dining room to witness the widow of the house reading prayers.

Attendance at church was statutory for the servants, who walked down to Llanfachreth whilst Mrs Vaughan rode resplendent in her carriage, in a manner reminiscent of Queen Victoria. She was a fervent upholder of the established Church, having no time at all for Nonconformism. Clearly uncompromising in her beliefs, she was not averse to 'persuading' tenants who had strayed to Nonconformity to return to the fold by less than subtle means. When a certain Nannau tenant farmer changed from Chapel to Church, Mrs Vaughan immediately sent in the estate carpenters, who set about repairing his long neglected cow house!

The family's peaceful existence was shattered once again on the 2nd April 1902 when they received an alarming telegram from the War Office in London:

To Mrs Vaughan, Nannau, Dolgelly,

*249. above: **Ellinor Anne (1832-1917) - wife of John Vaughan***
Miniature on ivory by M. G. B. Hall. 4.25 x 3.25 inches

NANNAU
DOLGELLEY
FLOOR PLAN

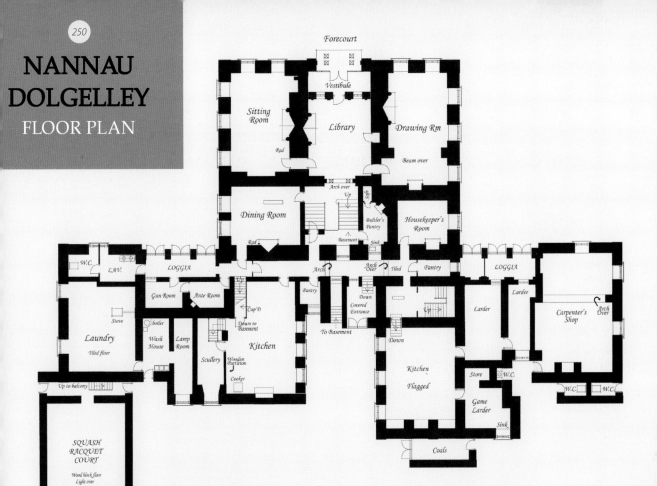

Forecourt

Vestibule

Sitting Room

Library

Drawing Rm

Beam over

Dining Room

Arch over

Up

Safe

Butler's Pantry

Basement

Sink

Housekeeper's Room

Rad

W.C.

LAV.

LOGGIA

Arch Over

Arch Over

Tiled

Pantry

LOGGIA

Gun Room

Ante Room

Pantry

Down Covered Entrance

Larder

Larder

Carpenter's Shop

Arch Over

boiler

Cup'D

Down to Basement

To Basement

Up

Stove

Laundry

Tiled floor

Wash House

Lamp Room

Kitchen

Down

Kitchen

Flagged

Store

W.C.

Scullery

Wooden Partition

Cooker

Game Larder

W.C.

W.C.

Up to balcony

Sink

SQUASH RACQUET COURT

Wood block floor
Light over

Coals

251. below: **Drawing room at Nannau,** circa 1950

Regret to inform you that telegram from Lord Kitchener reports your son Brevet Major J. Vaughan 7th Hussars wounded on 1st April near Boschmans Kop no further particulars.

Military Secretary

The next day, Major John Vaughan telegrammed his mother, playing down the wound, saying,

Have a very slight flesh wound in the calf of leg do not worry.

On the 4th of April a further telegram arrived informing them that Major Vaughan was severely wounded in the left knee, and on the 7th of April, more details emerged in the newspaper, describing John Vaughan as wounded below the knee, not serious, thought bone not injured – two horses shot from under him.

By 1904 Ellinor Anne Vaughan could quite reasonably hope that her eldest son was losing his wayward ways when he settled down and married Patricia, the daughter of Sir Fredrick John Goldsmid. Sir Frederick had earned his knighthood for his work installing the telegraph system across Asia.

Her youngest son John, by now thoroughly recovered from his injuries, was revelling in his life in the Army. In a letter to his mother on 23rd November 1905, while on active service in India, he outlined aspects of his tour of duty and made his case for not wanting to be squire of Nannau. He deemed that it would seem too parochial to him after his action-packed life, and he further looked forward to promotion and a command as his professional target.

With her preferred son verbally relinquishing the chance to be heir, she might well have considered that her eldest son could now be a contender to inherit the family estate, but family dissent militated against this ever

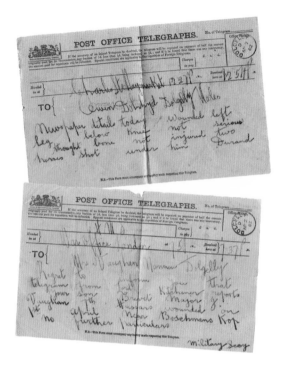

becoming a reality. In a last ditch attempt to convince her eldest son to 'tow the line', it is rumoured that Ellinor sent for Robert and told him that she would leave him the estate if he would work with the trustees to run it, and also to alter his way of living to become more appropriate to his 'class'. He blatantly refused to compromise his way of life and stormed out, and so relinquished his birthright.

As head of the household, Ellinor was not an easy mistress to get along with. She would regularly root around the kitchens, and was on many occasions observed stirring the bucket of pig's swill, to ensure that no food was needlessly consigned to the bucket! She had a glass eye as a result of an illness and would often wake up in a foul temper, and in her haste place the eye in back to front. Whilst this was a cause for sniggering amongst the ranks, it alerted the servants to be vigilant, and not to cross their mistress. Her interfering knew no bounds, she even concerned herself with the sexual morality of her servants and tenantry. Woe-betide any family if their unmarried daughter became pregnant; they could well be

given notice to quit if the offending daughter was not turned out.

She was uncompromising in her dealings with trades people and professionals alike. In reply to a local doctor's plea for the payment of his long awaited account, she unashamedly stated:

I am not willing to pay a guinea for a quack visit! ... [reiterating] ... that 10/6d would be more acceptable!

Although Ellinor Anne Vaughan in many ways was a tyrannical and overpowering figure, the household servants demonstrated unwavering loyalty to their mistress, often approaching the now ageing widow for advice and support. Unfortunately for the family, not all the servants were equally as loyal!

BUTLER CAUGHT red-handed

One dreadful day in July 1911, the peace and tranquillity of Nannau mansion was shattered by news of a burglary. Servants were alerted to a break-in when they discovered a broken window in the dining room and the family were quickly notified.

Close scrutiny of the crime scene revealed that brown paper and treacle had been applied to the glass, a well-known burglar's technique to prevent the noise of broken glass. Crucially the police deduced that this was an inside job due to the position of the applied 'sound proofer'. When inventory checks revealed that a large amount of silver was missing, immediate suspicion fell upon the butler who was

responsible for its care. Miss Eleanor Vaughan flew into a rage on hearing the Chief Constable accuse her favourite servant, and immediately ordered the perplexed officer out of the room, furiously exclaiming,

Do you really imagine that we keep thieves at Nannau?

Not unsurprisingly, after the space of a few weeks, the butler left his employ and returned to his home in Brackley, Northamptonshire. The ever-vigilant constabulary kept up a presence in the area, secure in the knowledge that some of the stolen silver had probably been hidden nearby, and would be collected at a later date. Their suspicions were rewarded when, on the 30th August, Nannau's ex-butler reappeared in the Dolgellau area accompanied by a stranger. The following day the two suspects boarded the train to Barmouth and

255. *Guests at the wedding of Mr & Mrs Percy H. Enthoven, 1913*

there hired a pony and trap to return back along the Dolgellau road. They were observed walking up a narrow track to the Precipice Walk, just behind Nannau. On their return to Llanelltyd bridge to meet their transport, they were apprehended by undercover police and caught with several bags of the stolen silver in their possession.

It was later revealed that the ex-butler's accomplice was no less a person than his own brother, a jeweller from Leicester. During the trial both pleaded guilty to the charges, the ex-butler receiving nine months hard labour and his brother six.

In total, silver to the value of £716-7-0 was recovered. Amongst the items were:

- One silver teapot, dated 1782
- Four round entrée dishes, 1789
- Two fluted silver sugar basins, 1680
- A James II fruit dish, 1764
- Eight silver gilt desert plates, 1764

The remarkable undercover operation had been a total success, returning the prized silver to their grateful owners. No doubt the Vaughan household took great care in appointing their replacement butler!

Within a year, Miss Eleanor Vaughan would be hiring her own butler as she married Colonel Percy Henry Enthoven and set up home in Dol'rhyd, near Dolgellau, closely followed in 1913 by her youngest brother John's marriage to Mrs Wardell which was celebrated in style. *The Farmer's Gazette* of October 24th reported:

MARRIAGE OF COL. VAUGHAN

Prince and Princess Alexander of Teck sent a set of twelve coffee cups and saucers as a wedding present to Mrs Wardell, whose marriage to Colonel John Vaughan. D.S.O., (son of the late John Vaughan J.P., D.L. and of Mrs Vaughan of Nannau), Commandant of the Cavalry School, Salisbury, took place on Wednesday, at St. Peter's, Eaton Square, London. The bride is the widow of Mr Harold P. Wardell of Brynywern, Newbridge-on-Wye, and daughter of the late Captain Stewart of Alltyrodyn, Cardiganshire. The ceremony was performed by the Rev. and Hon. C. Lawley. Major W. Stewart D.S.O. gave away his sister, who wore a gown of pale grey charmeuse and lace, with a smart black velvet hat plumed with grey feathers. She was attended by her daughter, who wore pale champagne charmeuse, with heron plumage on a black velvet hat, her bouquet of yellow roses being given by Sir Owen Philipps, who also gave the bride a sheaf of pink carnations. Major the Hon. W. Cadogan, M.V.O., 10th Hussars attended Colonel Vaughan as best man. The reception was held at 76 Eaton Square and was largely attended. The bells of Dolgelley Church were rung in honour of the occasion.

In later life Ellinor Anne Vaughan's eyesight diminished to such an extent that, by 1915, she became quite blind. The housekeeper and other servants had to read her communications for her, and likewise, she dictated letters. She partly relinquished control of the estate by appointing her daughter Eleanor to deputise on her behalf.

In a moving letter to her son on the 24th July 1914, after dealing with the arrangements for a shoot held locally for him, she went on to say:

I am not at all well myself, and I feel it presumptuous to look forward to October... whether it is phlebitis or gout or both! I cannot go on bearing the pain, which comes on at times. I cannot walk up or down stairs and now it is beginning to tell on me. I am afraid Mary is still suffering very much and we cannot meet,

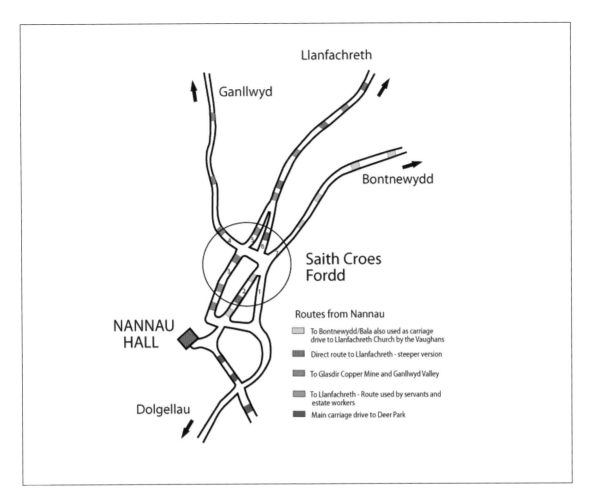

Llanfachreth

Ganllwyd

Bontnewydd

Saith Croes
Fordd

Routes from Nannau

To Bontnewydd/Bala also used as carriage drive to Llanfachreth Church by the Vaughans

Direct route to Llanfachreth - steeper version

To Glasdir Copper Mine and Ganllwyd Valley

To Llanfachreth - Route used by servants and estate workers

Main carriage drive to Deer Park

NANNAU
HALL

Dolgellau

I cannot get as far as Hengwrt Ucha as I cannot stand these rough roads. I am afraid Harry is very poorly with a kind of feverish cold, so Nellie has her hands full, and as I never see Robbie and Patricia you can imagine I feel a bit lonely in my blindness.

Eleanor was a great support to her mother in these difficult times, but the pressure of running the estate took a toll on her already frail health. She battled on, evidently caring passionately for Nannau and its extensive holdings.

Ellinor Anne Vaughan died on the 16th October 1917, aged 86. She left her eldest son Robert: certain farms near Dolgellau, houses in Eldon Row, Dolgellau, and a number of farms in Cwm. Her daughter Eleanor received an annuity of £500 charged on the Nannau estate, and her daughter Mary a lesser sum. Her youngest son John, however, inherited the entire Nannau estate.

Ellinor was buried with utmost pomp and ceremony at Llanfachreth Church with huge crowds in attendance. The funeral was described by locals as 'a very dry one' as no apparent tears were shed. Her death saw the end of an era at Nannau, a way of life that would now be gone forever. The old house stood forlorn, devoid of its army of busy servants scurrying about their daily toil.

John Vaughan and his wife Louisa, however, had other ideas for the old house. As early as 1918, plans were made to turn Nannau into a hospital for shell-shocked army officers, with Louisa Vaughan as its Commandant.

257. **Vaughan Family** of **Nannau** 1863-1958

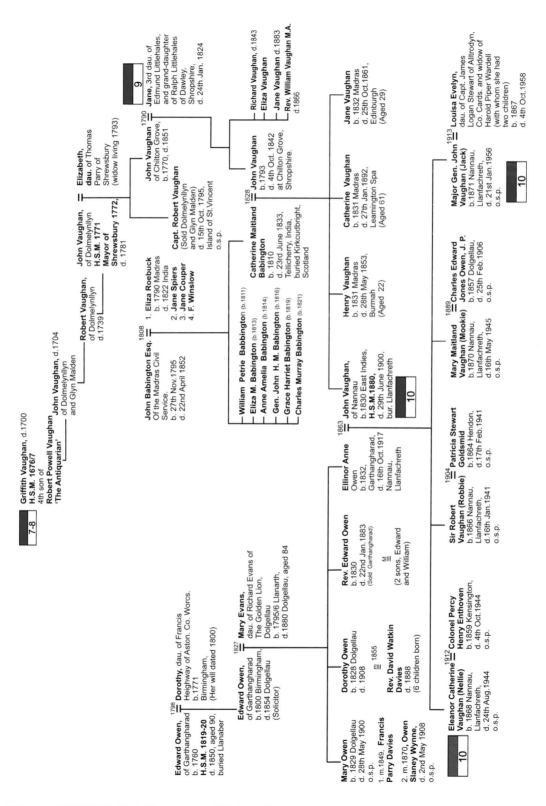

258. *Nannau with detail of one of the pavilion wings*

259. left: *Major General John Vaughan*
Oil on canvas. Charles H. Wilson. 1936. 24.75 x 21 inches
260. right: **Insignia of the 10th Royal Hussars**

10

1871-1956

MAJOR-GENERAL JOHN VAUGHAN

John Vaughan was born on the 31st July 1871, the second son of John Vaughan of Nannau. His early childhood must have been idyllic: endless days following his outdoor pursuits, first and foremost amongst which was riding. Under the ever-watchful eye of Nannau's coachman, Hugh Rowlands, John's riding prowess flourished. Hugh, a one-time farrier of the Crimean War, no doubt transferred his knowledge and love of horses to the eager pupil.

Charming drawings preserved in the family archive, made by John aged 11 whilst at boarding school at Chalfont St. Giles, are early indicators of his affinity with horses and hunting. Although John's mother prized his artistic endeavours, she discouraged him from spending too much time at the stables. As early as 1880, when John was only 8 years of age, she wrote to her daughter Eleanor from a Parisian Hotel, whilst on a visit to an exhibition, stating:

> *... I hope that Jack (John) is a good boy and not often in the stable yard!*

No amount of discouragement, however, would have deterred the young rider, destined to become one of the best horsemen of his generation.

John progressed to Eton and then to the Royal Military College at Sandhurst, where he passed out top of the list of the Cavalry Cadetship and started his military career as a 2nd Lieutenant in the 7th Hussars in 1891. He saw active service in Matabeleland and Mashonaland, and in Sudan took part in the charge of the 21st Lancers at the Battle of Omdurman. As a seasoned cavalry officer he was propelled into active service in the Boer War, where he distinguished himself by winning the D.S.O. for gallantry at Boschmans Kop on the 31st March 1902.

Action at **BOSCHMANS KOP**

Brevet Major John Vaughan, the 7th Hussars Intelligence officer, had spent six nights observing the Veldt with the help of a Boer guide and a native tracker when he observed twenty-five Boers establishing themselves in a derelict farm. At 1am, he led a column

261. *left*: **Colonel Douglas Haigh and Major John Vaughan** (October 1900)
262. *below*: **Kadir Cup trophies 1907 : Major John Vaughan on Vedette, with silver mounted boars' tusk trophies**

the happiest years of my soldiering life.

In the winter of 1906, the 10th Hussars and the R.H.A. Battery from Mhow, along with the Indian Cavalry Regiment, were ordered to Bombay to provide the escort for Their Royal Highnesses the Prince and Princess of Wales, later to become King George V and Queen Mary, who were taking a cold-weather tour of India.

In 1907 he led the 10th to victory in the Inter-Regiment polo match at Meerut, closely followed by victory in the Kadir Cup, taking part on his pony 'Vedette'. The spear that he had used in the competition, and a photograph of Vedette, hung for many years on the wall at Nannau. Of Vedette, John Vaughan wrote:

he could jump like a cat, gallop like a racehorse and yet with the temperament to calm a child

Before winning the Kadir Cup, John Vaughan and his faithful Vedette had won the 10th Hussars Regimental point-to-point and the Divisional Sword v. Sword competition.

containing the Queen's Bays and scattered the Boer horse lines. Astutely, Major Vaughan heard the sound of a cart moving away from the farm and galloped off alone capturing the local Boer leader, General Pretorious, single-handedly. When he rejoined the Bays at dawn a fierce battle ensued, where Major Vaughan was wounded in the knee. Outflanked by a stronger force of Boers, he ordered his men to charge, but fortunately was relieved at the last moment by the 7th Hussars who quickly put the Boers to flight. As Major Vaughan rode to report back to the commanding officer a third horse was shot from under him!

In 1904 he was invited by the War Office to exchange to the 10th Hussars and promoted to Major and within two months he was second-in-command of the regiment. He had joined the 10th at Mhow in India and soon became chairman of the polo committee, guiding the regiment to many victories.

In 1905 the regiment was transferred from Mhow to Rawal Pindi where they were to spend six years. Through endless training, hunting, polo matches and socialising, it is of no surprise to learn in John Vaughan's book that his time in the 10th Hussars was:

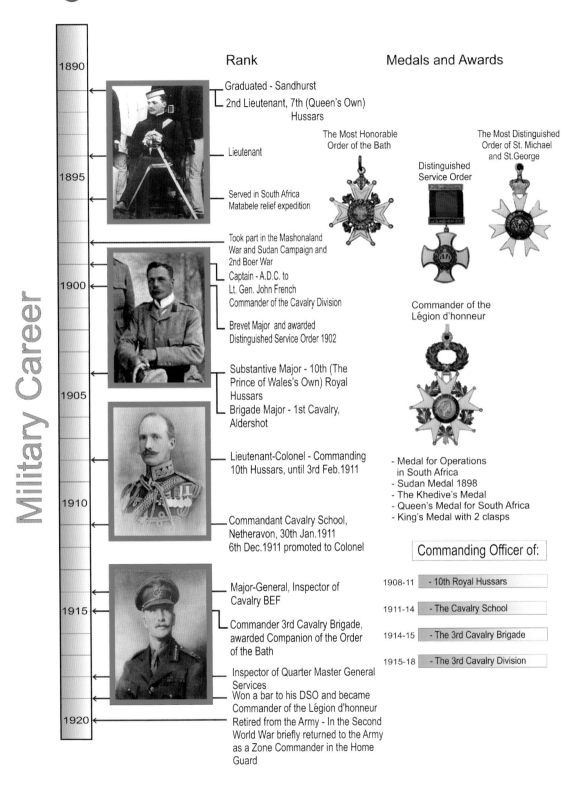

Military Career

Rank

1890

Graduated - Sandhurst

2nd Lieutenant, 7th (Queen's Own) Hussars

Lieutenant

1895

Served in South Africa Matabele relief expedition

Took part in the Mashonaland War and Sudan Campaign and 2nd Boer War

1900

Captain - A.D.C. to Lt. Gen. John French Commander of the Cavalry Division

Brevet Major and awarded Distinguished Service Order 1902

Substantive Major - 10th (The Prince of Wales's Own) Royal Hussars

1905

Brigade Major - 1st Cavalry, Aldershot

Lieutenant-Colonel - Commanding 10th Hussars, until 3rd Feb.1911

1910

Commandant Cavalry School, Netheravon, 30th Jan.1911 6th Dec.1911 promoted to Colonel

Major-General, Inspector of Cavalry BEF

1915

Commander 3rd Cavalry Brigade, awarded Companion of the Order of the Bath

Inspector of Quarter Master General Services

Won a bar to his DSO and became Commander of the Légion d'honneur

1920

Retired from the Army - In the Second World War briefly returned to the Army as a Zone Commander in the Home Guard

Medals and Awards

The Most Honorable Order of the Bath

The Most Distinguished Order of St. Michael and St.George

Distinguished Service Order

Commander of the Légion d'honneur

- Medal for Operations in South Africa
- Sudan Medal 1898
- The Khedive's Medal
- Queen's Medal for South Africa
- King's Medal with 2 clasps

Commanding Officer of:

1908-11	- 10th Royal Hussars
1911-14	- The Cavalry School
1914-15	- The 3rd Cavalry Brigade
1915-18	- The 3rd Cavalry Division

264. *left:* **Lieutenant Colonel John Vaughan, D.S.O.**
(Commanding Officer, 10th Royal Hussars, 1908-11)
265. *below:* **The Officers of the 10th Royal Hussars, Rawal**
Pindi, India, 1906 - (Lt. Col. John Vaughan – seated centre)

... from the first time he donned the uniform of a Hussar, he has extracted the admiration of all, the implicit confidence that whatever he does is the right thing to do, and much better, the love of his comrades of all ranks. Of him it can be asserted without fear of contradiction, he is nothing if not a soldier. Those who believe the doctrine of re-incarnation will declare that the martial instincts, displayed from his earliest days, must be the outcome of previous accumulations, and could we trace back through his genealogical tree, it would be surprising if we did not find among its branches an Owen Glyndŵr, a Cadwaladyr, a Llywelyn, or others of the renowned warrior Kings, who abound in the pages of history of the Principality which gave him birth ... Colonel Vaughan is a dominant and strenuous personality. He possesses in a marked degree that curious intangible quality of popularity, that power which attracts, draws men to him and inclines them to do his bidding without question,

On the 7th May 1908 John Vaughan was promoted to Lieutenant Colonel and given command of the 10th Hussars, a command he held until 3rd February 1911 when he travelled back to England to become Commandant of the Cavalry School at Netheravon in Wiltshire.

A fellow officer in the 10th Hussars wrote a biography of Colonel Vaughan:

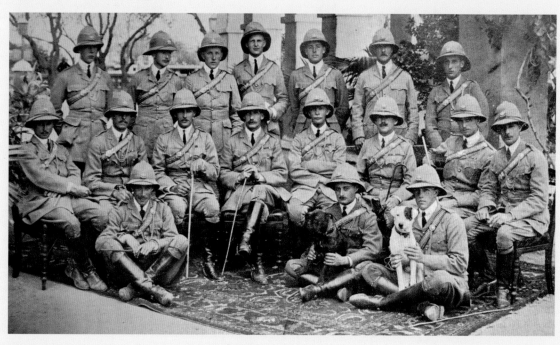

266. above: **10th Royal Hussars, Rawal Pindi, circa 1906. (Lt. Col. John Vaughan, centre)**

feeling that whatever he decides is the outcome of sound judgement and ripe experience.

(Major Roland Pillinger, from the pages of *The 10th Hussars Regimental Gazette*, April 1911)

Whilst en route to take up his post at Netheravon, John was ordered to detour to Europe to visit the Cavalry Schools in Tor di Quinto and Pinerolo in Italy, Saumur in France and Ypres in Belgium to assess the best practices employed in these institutions.

NETHERAVON CAVALRY School

The idea of establishing a Cavalry School in Britain was the brainchild of Lieutenant-General Robert Baden-Powell (1857-1941), the later founder of the Scout movement. His vast experience as a cavalry officer was put to good use when he was appointed Inspector-General of the Cavalry in 1903, with the aim of transforming existing cavalry training.

Baden-Powell's experiences in India and South Africa, particularly during the Second Boer War, had awakened him to the fact that the development and

availability of modern weaponry had greatly diminished the traditional role of the cavalry. To reverse this trend, cavalrymen needed to recreate themselves by acquiring new skills in scouting, re-connaissance, tracking, signalling, despatch riding and the use of rifles.

(University of Limerick, http://longwaytotipperary.ul.ie)

To achieve these aims, the Cavalry School had been established at Netheravon in 1904, built in the grounds of Netheravon House, on Salisbury Plain. John Vaughan spent three and a half years at Netheravon and from the onset he was determined to employ the most humane methods of horse training available, the welfare of his 'charges' being foremost in his mind. As an enthusiastic supporter of fox hunting he included the sport in the school's syllabus under the pretext of 'memory training'!

Baden-Powell was an old friend of John Vaughan from the Boer War days, and supported his former colleague by giving lectures. Baden-Powell was also a regular visitor to Nannau as witnessed by the numerous letters of thanks he sent to Ellinor Anne Vaughan thanking her for the hospitality. It is

well known that Baden-Powell often visited
various gentry houses, bringing his own tent
and erecting it on their lawns, stating that he
found it a most agreeable form of
accommodation. No photograph exists of his
tent erected in front of Nannau, but he may
well have pitched one on the mansion's
manicured lawns!

In addition to Commandant of the Cavalry
School, John Vaughan was Staff Officer to
General Allenby, the then Inspector of Cavalry.

In 1912, John Vaughan inherited the Hengwrt
estate on the death of the last Miss Lloyd (sister
to the deceased Frances Lady Vaughan) who
had been bequeathed a life interest in Hengwrt,
after which it then descended to John Vaughan
and his heirs. In possession of a fine house,
with good fishing, he now thought it
appropriate to get married, marrying Louisa
(Louey) in 1913, widow of Harold Piper
Wardell, and a sister of John's friend Captain
James Stewart from his time in the 7th Hussars.
In John's own words:

> ... everything was couleur de rose for nine
> months or so when I had to go to the 1914
> War.

Whilst John Vaughan was fighting in the war,
Louey occupied herself with sterling work,
establishing hospitals for officers in Ablington
House and Bulford Manor and later setting her
sights on establishing one in John's family
home. Nannau hospital came into being on the
death of Ellinor Anne Vaughan in 1917, in the
form of the 'Nannau Red Cross Auxiliary
Officers Hospital, Dolgelley', a hospital
established to treat shell-shocked officers.

The **FIRST WORLD WAR**

As the dark clouds of war spread over Europe,
John Vaughan was ready and raring for action
although still Commandant at Netheravon. As
news filtered through that the British
Government had decided not to fight, a
conversation was overheard between John
Vaughan and General Allenby, Commander of
the 1st Cavalry Division:

> It is a disgrace, John I shall send in my
> papers!
>
> So shall I! replied John Vaughan.

268. above: **Netheravon Cavalry School stables**

(Michael Wardell, John Vaughan's stepson, in *The 10ᵗʰ Royal Hussars Gazette*)

Fortunately, the wholesale resignations were avoided as, within a few days, Britain was at war with Germany and John went out with Allenby's 1ˢᵗ Cavalry Division as GSO1 (Chief of Staff). On the 16ᵗʰ September 1914, he took over from Hubert Gough as Commander of the 3ʳᵈ Cavalry Brigade with the rank of temporary Brigadier-General.

The 3ʳᵈ Cavalry Brigade consisted of:

4ᵗʰ (Queen's Own) Hussars (Curragh)
5ᵗʰ (Royal Irish) Lancers (Dublin)
16ᵗʰ (Queen's) Lancers (Currah)
3ʳᵈ Signal Troop, Royal Engineers (Currah)

together with a number of attached units comprising:

III Brigade, RHA (D and E Batteries) (Newbridge)
4ᵗʰ Field Troop, Royal Engineers (Currah)

South Irish Horse of the Special Reserve (Dublin)
3ʳᵈ Cavalry Brigade Field Ambulance

Under his command the 3ʳᵈ Cavalry Brigade took part in the First and Second Battle of Ypres and the Battle of Neuve Chapelle.

On the 7ᵗʰ April 1915, John wrote to his sister Eleanor Enthoven, outlining his frustration with the lack of action and general stalemate that had developed:

... The war is at a standstill here at present but when we get plenty of ammunition and more men I expect we shall wake up the Bosches again. The Army out here is visibly swelling every day and the Russians appear to be doing well also. Personally I haven't seen any fighting for a long time but I daresay we shall get some more before long ... the trenches are often

269. left: **Programme of the Cavalry School Spring Tournament**

NOTHING is to be written on this side except the
date and signature of the sender. Sentences
not required may be erased. If anything
else is added the post card will be destroyed.

I am quite well. + wish you a happy _____

I have been admitted into hospital
{ sick } and am going on well.
{ wounded } and hope to be discharged soon.

I am being sent down to the base.

I have received your { letter dated_____
{ telegram ,, _____
{ parcel ,, _____

Letters follows at first opportunity.

I have received no letter from you
{ lately.
{ for a long time.

Signature }
only. } J. Vaughan

Date 18. XII. 14

[Postage must be prepaid on any letter or post card
addressed to the sender of this card.]

(6464) Wt. W2197-293 1,000m. 11.14 F. T. & Co., Ltd.

270. left: **Field Service Post Card sent by John Vaughan
to his sister Eleanor, Christmas 1914**
271. below: **Major-General John Vaughan
C.M.G., D.S.O., D.L.**

Later, on the 8th June 1915, John wrote a long
letter to his sister on the pretext of 'having
nothing to do'. In the detailed letter that
follows he vividly conveys his view on the war:

*The most annoying thing is that we are
held up for want of ammunition though I
am always being told that this will be put
right very soon, in fact I was told that last
Xmas, but it isn't right yet... we are
sitting still doing nothing. We have lost a
good deal of ground near YPRES owing to
the gas but I hope that the worst of that is
now over as we have all got respirators
which are effective and will prove more so
when the men have confidence in them. I
hope that between the French attacks and
the necessity of sending men against the
Italians the German line will soon begin to
wear thin, but it is very annoying being
able to do nothing to help at present ... of
course it is entirely an artillery war and I
don't see any chance of the Cavalry being*

*so close that it is necessary for our snipers
to put khaki handkerchiefs over their faces
and not expose themselves at all or they
get done in.*
*It is very dull here as you can imagine. We
do our best to train our new officers and
men but we are not allowed off the roads
on account of the crops. They cultivate
right up to the trenches at least to the
regularly shelled area.*
*We are going to have a big cock fight on
Sunday, they charge one franc each... cock
fighting is the one sport of the country.
The old ironmonger at whose house I live
keeps six good fighting cocks.*

Yours ever John

272. above: **Cavalry regiment, Royal Scots Greys resting their horses by a roadside in France**

any more use… the infantry work is very murderous owing to the number of machine guns that the Germans have … we did 26 days in the trenches last month.

When the 2nd Army Staff get things into a proper mess and their infantry exhausted, G.H.Q. chucks the cavalry in and then they all go to bed happy. I would rather like to have a section of my own trenches to run permanently but last month I was thrown into 5 different muddles in different spots and that is about the limit. It's pretty boring being a reserve doing nothing but these are our alternatives, doing nothing or mending muddles. I am happy in having a top hole general in Charlie Kavanagh and a good brigade. The infantry divisional commanders who I have lately been associated with appear to me never to go to the trenches to see how things are themselves. They sit in chateaux miles back and try to make war off maps, which most of them can't read,

and by telephones which are usually broken when there is a scrap on.

In his memoirs John Vaughan spoke about his time in command of the Brigade:

I was of course more than sorry to leave the 3rd Cavalry Brigade with whom I had been for the toughest part of the war with very few men, very few shells and no reserves. I had however absolute confidence in every unit and they had proved themselves absolutely reliable and versatile in everything they were asked to do.

In October 1915, John Vaughan was promoted to temporary Major-General and given command of the 3rd Cavalry Division, commanding the 6th, 7th and 8th Cavalry Brigades. As the 10th Hussars were part of the 8th Brigade, it meant that they once more served under their popular commander.

273. above: **Cavalry and tanks at Arras, 1918** by Lieutenant Alfred Bastien

Under his command the 3rd Cavalry Division were not involved in any major battles until 1917, when they took part in the Battle of Arras and subsequent offensives:

9th-12th April - The first Battle of the Scarpe
10th -11th April - The attack at Monchy-le-Preux

His command ended abruptly on the 14th March 1918 when he became the Inspector of Quarter Master General Services, entrusted by General Sir Douglas Haig to deal with the imminent and potentially disastrous shortages of forage for the wartime horses owing to U-Boat attacks on shipping.

Leaving his Division at such a crucial time had a marked effect on John who recalled in his memoirs:

This was the worst blow I ever received, or am likely to receive, to leave my beloved Division and take on a non-fighting administrative job. However there was nothing to do except buckle in on it.

With his usual drive and determination he set about addressing the forage problem by cutting waste and improvising, ever vigilant of the course of the war and frustrated that he was not in the thick of the action.

During the war John was mentioned in despatches, and in 1915 honoured as Companion of the Order of the Bath. In 1919 he received a Bar to his D.S.O. and became a Commander of the Légion d'honneur.

By the end of the war, Louey, contemplating his impending retirement, wrote to him stating:

now the war is over you need do nothing but hunt and play polo for the rest of your life.

274. *left: Mrs John Vaughan, Commandant of Nannau Hospital*
275. *below: Captain A. B. Howitt, R.A.M.C, M.O.I.C Nannau Aux. Hospital, Dolgellau*

mental breakdown, making it impossible for them to return to front-line duty.

Some doctors argued that the bursting of shells on the battlefield created a vacuum in the ear drum, and air rushing in to fill this vacuum disturbed the cerebro-spinal fluid, upsetting the working of the brain.

In the four years of war, the British Army identified 80,000 men as suffering from shell-shock, some 2% of all those on active service. Tragically, many were sent back to the front, classified as malingerers. When some broke down under pressure and were unable to take orders, disastrous consequences followed.

Corporal Henry Gregory, who served with the 119th Machine Gun Company, recalled seeing his first case of shell-shock:

> *It was while I was in this Field Hospital that I saw the first case of shell-shock. The enemy opened fire about dinnertime, as usual, with his big guns. As soon as the first shell came over, the shell-shock case nearly went mad. He screamed and raved, and it took eight men to hold him down on the stretcher. With every shell he would go into a fit of screaming and fight to get away. It is heart breaking to watch a shell-shock case. The terror is indescribable. The flesh on their faces shakes in fear, and their teeth continually chatter. Shell-shock was brought about in many ways, loss of sleep, continually being under heavy shell fire, the torment of lice, irregular meals,*

The War Office, however, had other plans for John, replying to his request to resign his commission thus:

> *We are still at war with Turkey, and you will proceed to Aldershot and take the appointment of Cavalry Brigadier there.*

John Vaughan would have to wait until 1920 to retire from the Army, while his wife Louey enthusiastically threw herself into running the Nannau Hospital for shell-shocked officers.

Nannau Red Cross Aux. Officers Hospital

Nannau Red Cross Auxiliary Hospital, to give it its full title, officially opened on the 11th February 1918 with five patients, these being the first contingent of shell-shocked officers to be expertly treated by one of the leading authorities on the condition in Britain, namely Dr. A.B. Howitt.

The term 'shell-shock' had been coined to describe the reaction of some WW1 soldiers to the trauma they experienced in battle. Early symptoms of the condition included tiredness, giddiness, irritability, lack of concentration and headaches, which could eventually result in a

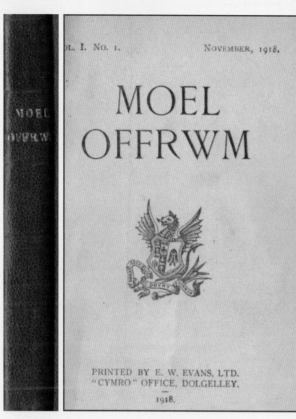

276. above: **First edition of 'Moel Offrwm', Joural of the Nannau Aux. Hospital**

nerves always on end, and the thought is always in the man's mind that the next minute was going to be his last.
(www.spartacus-educational.com)

Robert Graves (later renowned poet and author) joined the Royal Welch Fusiliers in 1914 and wrote of the condition of shell-shock (neurasthenia) from the perspective of the serving officer,

Having now been in the trenches for five months, I had passed my prime. For the first three weeks, an officer was of little use in the front line; he did not know his way about, had not learned the rules of health and safety, or grown accustomed to recognising degrees of danger. Between three weeks and four weeks he was at his best, unless he happened to have any particular bad shock or sequence of shocks. Then his usefulness gradually declined as neurasthenia developed. At six months he was still more or less right; but

by nine or ten months, unless he had been given a few weeks' rest on a technical course, or in hospital, he was usually worse than useless. Dr. W.H.R. Rivers told me later that the action of one of the ductless glands – I think the thyroid – caused this slow general decline in military usefulness, by failing at a certain point to pump its sedative chemical into the blood. Without its continued assistance the man went about his tasks in an apathetic and doped condition, cheated into further endurance. It has taken some ten years for my blood to recover.

Officers had a less laborious but more nervous time than the men. There were proportionately twice as many neurasthenic cases among officers as among men, though a man's average expectancy of trench service before getting killed or wounded was twice as long as an officers. Officers between the ages of twenty-three and thirty-three

could count on a longer useful life than those older or younger. I was too young. Men over forty, though not suffering from want of sleep so much as those under twenty had less resistance to sudden alarms and shocks. The unfortunates were the officers who had endured two years or more continuous trench service. In many cases they became dipsomaniacs. I knew three or four who had worked up to the point of two bottles of whiskey a day before being lucky enough to get wounded or sent home in some other way. A two-bottle company commander of one of our line battalions is still alive, in three shows running, got his company needlessly destroyed because he was no longer capable of taking clear decisions.

(Robert Graves, 1929)

The reaction of some Generals on first hearing of shell-shocked soldiers was to consider them cowards and dismiss the condition as nonsense, as they had not witnessed the effects first hand. It is evident that Major General John Vaughan was sympathetic to the plight of all who suffered from this debilitating condition. Having operated at the front line, he was well aware that both weak and strong suffered alike, and as early as 1917, he offered Nannau as a neurasthenia hospital for officers, with Louey his wife as Commandant.

Fortunately, we can catch a fleeting glimpse of the life of the recovering officers in the Nannau Hospital through the pages of a rare journal entitled *Moel Offrwm*, a publication started on the 30th November 1918, nine months after the

official opening of the facility. It took its name from the hill in front of Nannau, namely Moel Offrwm (Hill of Sacrifice).

We must turn to Dr. A.B. Howitt to discover the motives for this innovative journal:

The chief object of this magazine is to interest and amuse, but perhaps another purpose which may not be quite so obvious is to bring into greater prominence that communal spirit which, I am glad to say, is one of Nannau's best characteristics. We have it in our games, concerts, debates and photography, sport and amusement in which all join, and I hope that in these pages will be emphasised again and again that spirit which knows neither clique nor party, but which works for the common happiness and for the common good.

(Captain A.B. Howitt – Medical Officer)

Dr. Howitt had a very clear strategy for treating neurasthenia, firmly believing that sleep was an important dimension to any cure. In order to induce sleep he believed that hard physical work was necessary and as a result every patient had to perform outdoor work on the golf course, sawing wood, and even raking Nannau's drive, humorously referred to by patients as 'gravel-scratching'.

Most of the articles in 'Moel Offrwm' were written by the young officers themselves, with occasional contributions by staff. The journal takes the form of a public school magazine with jokes and much literal sending up of colleagues with a dash of local interest thrown in for good measure.

Through its lively pages we discover long-lost memories of once traumatised heroes, who set about rekindling their appetite for life after experiencing the dark days of war.

On Friday 14th November 1918, the following article appeared:

A State banquet, followed by a pyrotechnical fete on the Southern Spur of Moel Offrwm was given on Friday the 14th ult. in honour of the Armistice. A telegram confirming the good news was very opportunely received during the dinner and announced by the Presence to the cheering 'convives' causing scenes of indescribable enthusiasm. The fete included a torch light procession to the summit of the Druid's Cairn. There, a monstrous funeral pyre, tended with frenzied fury by Lieutenant Phillips, reduced to ashes an effigy.

It is impossible to imagine how beneficial it was to the young officers to know that the war had come to an end. Psychologically they could proceed with their recovery in a blissfully beautiful part of the country, in perfect peace and tranquillity interspersed by the odd 'fling' in a dance at Nannau's squash court!

The forthcoming Christmas was joyful indeed for Nannau's residents, with the return of General Vaughan from four years active service in France,

Monday, 23rd December 1918

The General, who was accompanied from the gate at Nannau by a torch-light procession, was given a cordial reception.

Christmas Day, 1918

The Holy Communion was celebrated in 'A' Ward at 7.30 a.m. and 8.30 a.m. by

Padré Gardner-Brown. At 11.30 a.m. Matins were sung at Llanfachreth by the Vicar. Unfortunately the organ broke down early in the Service, and this was irritating. However, Mr Best came to the rescue, and we sang our Christmas Carols in full force. At 5 o'clock Mrs Vaughan distributed presents from under the Christmas tree in the Squash Court.

At 7.30 p.m., dinner was served by a goodly number of volunteer waiters – led by the gallant Major Morgan … the toast of the King was proposed by General Vaughan; that of General and Mrs Vaughan by Captain Donaldson D.S.O., and replied to by the General; that of Captain and Mrs Howitt by Captain Hughes and replied by the Doctor. All toasts were drunk with great gusto, particularly the spontaneous toasts to the waiters.

After dinner, which was attended by most in fancy-dress, the Camouflage evening continued, and 'A' Ward very beautifully decorated, did duty as a ball room. During the evening Mr. McMillan sang to us. A very enjoyable Christmas Day terminated about 11 o'clock.

280. *above left:* **John Vaughan riding 'Merrie England' in an open race, 1924**

281. *above centre:* **Major General John Vaughan's horse 'Merrie England'** Oil on canvas. Nia Colmore (1889 - 1973)

282. *above right:* **John Vaughan riding his hunter, 'Brock'**

December 31ˢᵗ, 1918

The old year went out trailing glory in its wake. Of 1918, as of a certain other great reprobate, may it be truly said, that 'nothing in life so became him as the leaving of it'... But at Nannau there was joy aloft, as much at the burying of the last grim year of the war, as at the dawn of Peace.

A whist drive kept patients busy till 10.30. Then a dance in the Squash Court gave a just interpretation to the feeling of the community. A number of guests were present. At half past eleven all adjourned to the Dining-room where cake and claret kept body and soul together until a gong boomed out the midnight hour. Then General Vaughan proposed the toast of the New Year, and linking hands, Staff Patients and Guests welcomed young 1919 to the tune of Auld Lang Syne.

Afterwards the mistletoe in the hall put in some hectic moments, and Mrs Myles informs us that she lost a comb. We wonder how?

January 2ⁿᵈ, 1919

General and Mrs Vaughan departed for London, the General en route for France.

With Nannau still a hospital and Hengwrt let, John Vaughan, on his retirement from the Army, took a seven year lease on a house in Rugby, with a view to setting up a training facility for polo ponies and hunters. He 'recruited' some of his old colleagues from the 10ᵗʰ Hussars to assist him with the venture. Finding the area unsuited for his initial purposes, he soon relocated to Craven Lodge near Melton Mowbray, Leicestershire and set up the 'Craven Lodge Club' with his stepson Mike Wardell. Both enjoyed great success in the venture, one season attracting the Prince of Wales, the Duke of York, the Duke of Gloucester and the Duke of Kent. To accommodate the Prince of Wales's many visits a new wing was added to the club. Throughout the next ten years John Vaughan spent his winters hunting from Craven Lodge with little regard for his advancing years. He won the Open Army Point-to-Point three times on 'Merrie England', a remarkable achievement considering that he was well into his fifties.

The Nannau Red Cross Auxiliary Hospital continued to support its deserving patients, as did the local community, until May 1921 when it closed its doors and was handed back to the family.

General Vaughan chose not to live at Nannau at this time, preferring to take up residence at nearby Maesybrynner and Craven Lodge. Nannau was let out to a succession of high-profile tenants who utilised the incredible opportunities for shooting and fishing that were on offer.

bound for Rio de Janerio. The sea air and the extended tropical voyage worked wonders, as within days of reaching his destination, the now irrepressible old 'warrior' was galloping recklessly around a polo field.

Although seemingly leading an extravagant lifestyle, the reality was somewhat different, as the reminiscences of his stepson, Michael Wardell, outlined:

> *He liked a good horse, a glass of port and a good cigar; but rarely paid a lot of money for them. He had acquired frugal habits as a young subaltern on £400 a year – though £400 in the nineties was the equivalent of quite a fortune in the present day fifties. An appetite for good sport forbade indulgence, and he never changed his habits.*
>
> *As with his habits so with his dress. He never believed in spending money on tailors, and he had a rare assortment of old clothes when he died, which since he was lean as a young man, dated back over half a century. This characteristic of his was a loveable one, and one that appealed to those who were fondest of him. He had tremendous pride, pride of race, pride of Regiment, pride of home. But none of the pride of the dandy.*

(A tribute to John Vaughan in *The 10th Royal Hussars Gazette*, by Brigadier John Michael Stewart Wardell M.B.E.)

Throughout the early 1920s John took a greater interest in the Nannau estate, and although managed by an agent, he kept a close eye on proceedings. During this period many farms were sold as he strove to 'get credit on the estate account'. However, there is little doubt that country pursuits took up most of his time and interested him most.

In 1924, whilst hunting with the Quorn Hunt in Leicestershire, John had a serious fall, breaking seven ribs and puncturing both lungs. He returned to Maesybrynner to recover, but found himself breathless after walking even a short distance. A stint in the sun was prescribed by Doctor Heath of Barmouth and John immediately embarked on R.M.S.S. Almanzora

The onset of the Second World War put pay to hunting at the Craven Lodge Club and John returned to Dolgellau to take up residence at Maesybrynner, his home near Nannau, to continue his work as President of the Welsh British Legion. Also during the war he commanded the Home Guard of Merioneth and Montgomeryshire. Under his direction seven battalions of the Home Guard were formed amounting to an incredible 7,200 men! With remarkable gusto he set about preparing his men for the ultimate defence of the area,

equipping and training the volunteers in the Home Guard School which he established at the Trawsfynydd Artillery Camp in 1940.

Nannau in the meantime had been occupied by the Bedgebury Park School for Girls from Kent, who had evacuated to the area on the 24th May 1940, and were to remain there for the duration of the war.

On the 16th January 1941, John Vaughan's elder brother Robbie died. Although he had not inherited the estate, he had maintained good relations with his younger brother. Despite his eccentricities, he had forged a name for himself in the area, through years of committed public service, being awarded a knighthood for services to the county. Robbie had lived at Garthmaelan, close to Nannau, where he farmed all his life. His wife, however, was never completely happy in Wales, so he had purchased a farm for her in England. Every year the couple spent two months on their English holding and literally took all their livestock with them by train. This included the cattle, sheep, goats and dogs, not forgetting their 30 cats! He was also a director of the Great Western Railway and had a great interest in trains. At the time of a railway strike he is known to have seized the controls of a train and crashed through a level-crossing that had been barred deliberately as part of the strike action.

Not having issue to pass his estate on to, John Vaughan deliberated hard on his successor. Due in no small part to his sister Eleanor's pleadings, he decided on his second cousin, Charles Hilary Vaughan Pritchard, who was a Brigadier in the Second World War, and in command of the 2nd Independent Parachute Brigade.

John's eldest sister Eleanor died on the 24th August 1944, leaving the Dol'rhyd estate to Brigadier Charles Hilary Vaughan Pritchard. Throughout her life she had suffered from ill health at one time or another. She had battled hard against what she saw as selling off parts of the Nannau estate far too cheaply. She cared passionately about the plight of the family mansion, but was powerless to intervene as her brother John, the 'tenant for life', had the power to dispose of property when necessary. In the latter part of her life she threw herself into fund-raising for the Dolgellau Hospital, and with her husband Col. Percy Enthoven, raised large sums of money to bring the project to completion.

In a letter to Hilary on the 6th January 1946, John Vaughan gave him clear advice on succession duty and discussed the income of the Nannau estate. He recommended that he continue serving in the army for as long as he was interested, stating:

> *There is very little for an active man to do in this county now. Landowners might as well be non-existent because the Agricultural Committees butt in without consulting them and give orders to the tenant farmers direct. There is no shooting of any kind now and I am not getting a moor keeper, though I may later, but it would take at least 5 years to get anything of a stock of grouse back. Then if the Forestry Commission buy the Glanllyn estate and become my Eastern neighbours I shall have forests on my East as well as on the South and West.*

 285 **John Vaughan's Sporting Pursuits (1940-41)**
© Christopher Quail

1. Maesybrynner, John Vaughan's residence near Nannau
2. Game Keeper Eames in front of Maesybrynner
3. Maesybrynner

4. John Vaughan
5. Major General John Vaughan D.S.O., Home Guard Zone Commander
6. John Vaughan fishing at Llyn Cynwch, near Nannau
7. 'Roy'

286. below: *Her Royal Highness, The Princess Elizabeth at Dolgellau, Friday 29th April 1949*

COUNTY OF MERIONETH

PROGRAMME

of the tour of

THEIR ROYAL HIGHNESSESS
THE PRINCESS ELIZABETH
and
THE DUKE OF EDINBURGH
(Earl of Merioneth)

through

MERIONETHSHIRE

Thursday 28th April
and
Friday 29th April
1949

HARLECH
Lord Lieutenant

A ROYAL VISIT to Nannau

Friday 29th April 1949 was a landmark day in Nannau's history and the culmination of weeks of preparation by Major-General John Vaughan. It was the day that Princess Elizabeth and the Duke of Edinburgh (Earl of Merioneth) visited Nannau on the second day of their visit to Merioneth.

Overnight the Princess and the Duke had stayed at 'Glyn', the Welsh seat of Lord Harlech, and it was at another historic mansion, 'Nannau', that the Royal couple took their lunch.

On leaving Harlech Castle on Friday morning, the Royal couple's progress passed through Llanfair, Llanbedr, Dyffryn, Barmouth, Bontddu and Llanelltyd arriving at Dolgellau at 12 noon.

289. below: **Awaiting the Royal Guests in Dolgellau**

© Christopher Quail

The Programme of the Tour at this point was as follows,

The Bells of St. Mary's Church, Dolgelley, will be rung as
Their Royal Highnesses drive into Dolgelley.

12 Noon. **THEIR ROYAL HIGHNESSES**

will be received by
The Lord Lieutenant and Lady Harlech, accompanied by the High Sheriff, Chairman of the County Council, the Member of Parliament, and The Clerk to the Lieutenancy.

The Lord Lieutenant will present :-

The Chairman of the Quarter Session
(The Honourable Sir Wintringham Norton Stable, M.C.)

The Chairman of the Dolgelley Urban District Council
(D. R. Meredith, Esq., J.P.)

The Clerk of the Dolgelley Urban District Council
(E. J. Pugh, Esq.)

The Chairman of the County Reception Committee
(County Councillor John Evans)

Major General John Vaughan, C.B. C.M.G., D.S.O., D.L., J.P.

Brigadier E. O. Skaife, O.B.E.
(Bi-County Cadet Commandant of Merioneth and Montgomeryshire)

12.05 p.m. **THEIR ROYAL HIGHNESSES**

will inspect the Guard of Honour provided by the 10th Cadet Battalion The Royal Welch Fusiliers under the command of Lieutenant W. J. Jones.

Units of the following contingents will assemble :-

"R" Battery 636 L.A.A. Regt. R.A. (R.W.F.) T.A. under the command of Lieut.- Colonel The Hon. R. E. B. Beaumont, T.D.

R. A. Garrison, Tonfannau.

No. 20 Squadron R.A.F. Station, Llanbedr.

THEIR ROYAL HIGHNESSES will proceed to the Dias.

12.10 p.m. The Dolgelley Section of the Welsh National Eisteddfod Choir under the Conductorship of John Hughes, Esq., Mus. Bac., County Music Organiser, will render the following :-

Welsh Hymn Tunes - (a) "Hyfrydol" (R.H.Pritchard) and (b) "Aberystwyth" (Dr.Joseph Parry)

12.17 p.m. An Address will be presented to **THEIR ROYAL HIGHNESSES** on behalf of the Merioneth County Council by Frank Owen Esq. (Chairman of the County Council) and Hugh J. Owen Esq. (Clerk of the County Council).

ADDRESS

12.22 p.m. **THEIR ROYAL HIGHNESSES** will leave the Dias.

The Lord Lieutenant will present to **THEIR ROYAL HIGHNESSES**:
Various dignitaries and Council Officials.

THEIR ROYAL HIGHNESSES will inspect the following contingents assembled in the square :-

British Legion
British Legion (Women's Section)
British Red Cross
Merioneth Girl Guides
Women's Voluntary Services
Women's Institutes
Young Farmer's clubs
2058 Squadron Air Training Corps
1st Towyn Troop Boy Scouts
National Savings Voluntary Workers

The Assembly, accompanied by the Band of the Welch Regiment, will sing "Hen Wlad fy Nhadau".

12.50 p.m. **THEIR ROYAL HIGHNESSES** will leave Dolgellau Square for Nannau.

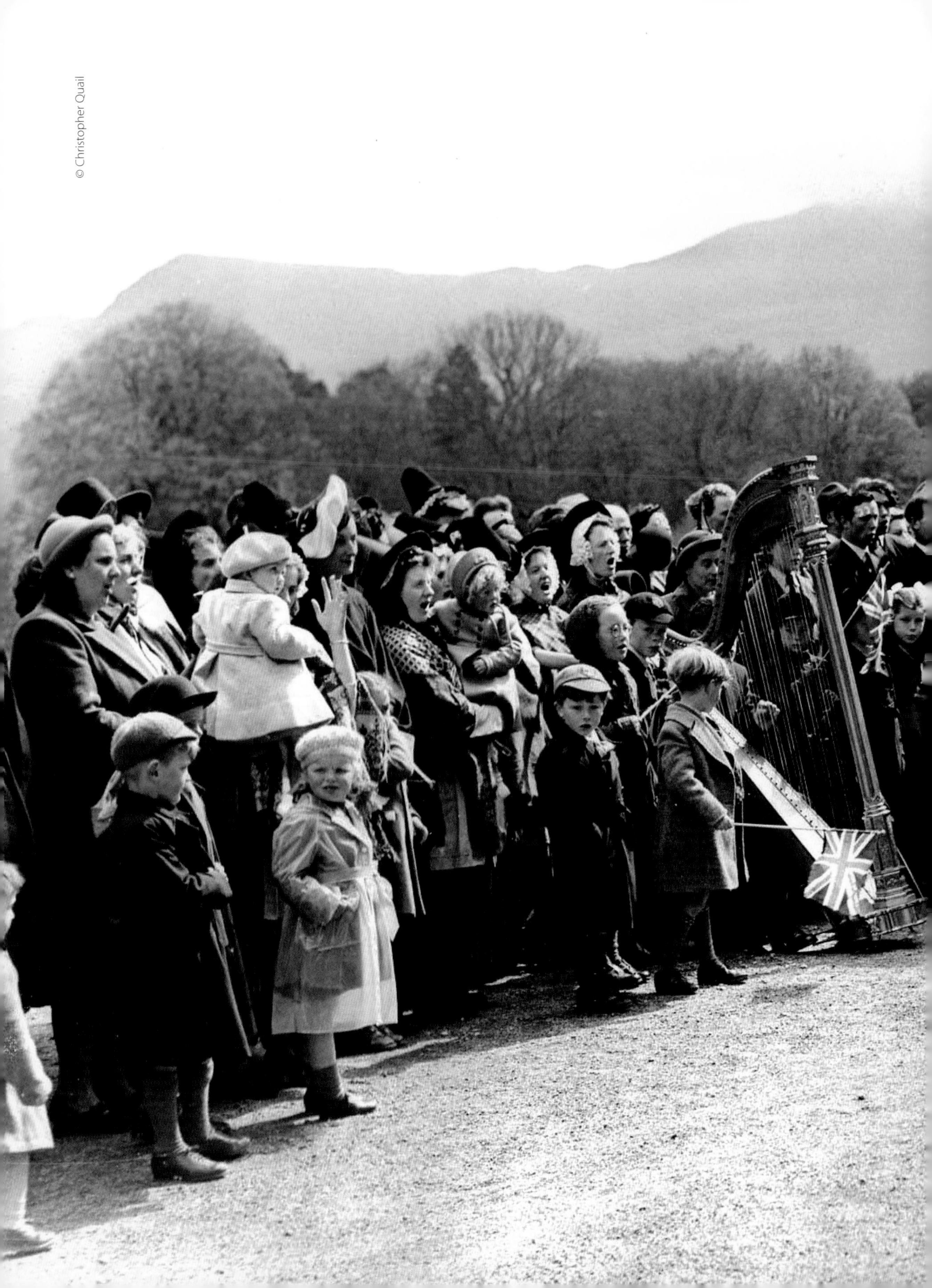

291. left: **Invitation cards given to locals to witness the arrival of the Royal couple at Nannau**

292. bottom left: **Handwritten seating plan for the Royal Lunch**

293. below right: **The Nannau Bucket**

THE **NANNAU BUCKET**

With the excitement of the successful Royal Tour behind him, the General settled down to a quieter life, his riding punctuated by the occasional dinner party. The repercussions of one such social event was to have far-reaching consequences in the field of archaeology.

The intrigue began at a luncheon party hosted at Nannau in 1951, when Major-General John Vaughan revealed a bronze urn to one of his guests. The urn had been used for many decades as a receptacle for cigar ash and waste paper.

He recalled to his guests the excitement of its discovery in 1881 by his two younger sisters, Eleanor and Mary.

The Royal couple arrived at Nannau at 1 pm to a rousing welcome by invited local residents complete with musical accompaniment.
The Royal couple and guests sat down to a relaxed lunch in the mansion, with background musical accompaniment by the harp, as General Vaughan had noted that such accompaniment was the tradition in ancient times in the halls of the Welsh nobles, and Nannau was pre-eminent in this respect.

A handwritten seating plan has been preserved in the family archive showing the General and Mrs Vaughan occupying the head of the table in the dining room. During the lunch break, the Duke borrowed one of the guest's cars, and, accompanied by the General, enjoyed a thrilling thirty minute drive in the mountains above Nannau. Later the Royal couple were shown the sundial that marked the spot where Hywel Sele, Lord of Nannau, was killed and subsequently thrust into the hollow oak tree.

At 3 pm the Royal couple left Nannau to the accompaniment of Welsh songs and travelled the 35-mile-journey to Corwen to meet the Royal Train.

They had both awoken early on a Saturday morning, eagerly awaiting the faithful old coachman Rowlands who had arranged to accompany the girls on their treasure hunt. They, well aware of the antiquity of Nannau, were expecting to make the find of a lifetime! Eventually old Rowlands appeared and the quest was underway. Rowlands was devoted to the Vaughan children and they to him. When young John Vaughan ran short of money at private school it was to Hugh Rowlands that he wrote for a 'sub', not to his father!

Later that eventful day the girls were to uncover a battered bronze urn hidden buried behind Hywel Sele Lodge, in a hollow at the foot of a buried flight of steps that they had miraculously excavated. Conveniently, Hywel Sele Lodge happened to be the home of the retired family retainer, Rowlands! We can only but imagine the

NANNAU,
DOLGELLEY,
NORTH WALES.
DOLGELLEY 72.
MRS JOHN VAUGHAN

LORD HARLECH
LADY STABLE
BRIGADIER SKAIFE
MISS ROSEMARY PRYSE-RICE
CHIEF CONSTABLE
MISS ISAAC
HUGH J. OWEN ESQ
SIR U. STABLE
MRS WYNNE JONES.
BRIGADIE PRITCHARD.
LADY HARLECH.

H.R.H. THE DUKE OF EDINBURGH
THE HON. MRS. PRITCHARD.
LIEUTENANT PARKER
MRS WARDELL
MAJOR WYNNE JONES
THE HON. MRS ORMSBY-GORE
BRIGADIER WARDELL
LADY MARGARET HAY
THE HON. D. ORMSBY-GORE
H.R.H. THE PRINCESS ELIZABETH

MAJOR-GENERAL JOHN VAUGHAN.

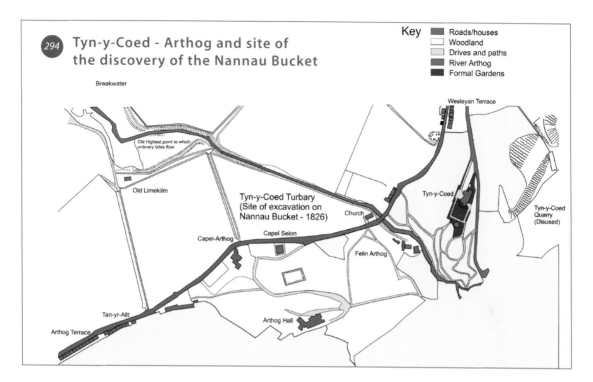

294 Tyn-y-Coed - Arthog and site of the discovery of the Nannau Bucket

Key
- Roads/houses
- Woodland
- Drives and paths
- River Arthog
- Formal Gardens

Breakwater

Old Highest point to which ordinary tides flow

Old Limekilm

Tyn-y-Coed Turbary (Site of excavation on Nannau Bucket - 1826)

Church

Capel-Arthog

Capel Seion

Felin Arthog

Wesleyan Terrace

Tyn-y-Coed

Tyn-y-Coed Quarry (Disused)

Tan-yr-Allt

Arthog Terrace

Arthog Hall

---

excitement of the young treasure hunters as they carried their ancient relic wearily back to Nannau and fame.

The urn was presumably given pride of place in the family mansion for seventy years or so and probably became a talking point after many dinners, right up to 1951, when a luncheon guest was to persuade the elderly General to allow his family urn to be taken to the British Museum.

On close scrutiny of the urn, Professor C.F.C. Hawkes and the museum staff concluded that they were dealing with an item of great antiquity, belonging to the first half of the 1st Millenium B.C. within the Late Bronze Age, approximately 750-700 B.C.

What a find the Vaughan girls had uncovered, a 2,700-year-old artefact!

The Nannau bucket, as it was to become known, was the sole example of its kind to be discovered in Britain, a remarkable find of great significance. Experts concluded that it resembled one discovery found in Hungary. Close examination of the condition of the Nannau relic revealed that for most of its existence it would have been set in the vertical position and not in soil, the top few inches

being exposed to the air at some time in its burial phase.

We must therefore cast doubts on the validity of the Vaughan children's lucky find, and conclude that in an attempt to please his young charges, Hugh Rowlands planted the urn and engineered the discovery.

If this was the case, where did the infamous urn come from?

A find is recorded in 1826 at Arthog, five miles from Dolgellau, of a bronze urn of almost identical size, buried in the peat with only the top few inches exposed to the atmosphere. The fact that it was buried in peat accounted for its remarkable state of preservation.

The site of the 1826 find was the Tyn-y-Coed Turbary, on the south side of the Mawddach Estuary, roughly opposite Barmouth.

It is conceivable that the Arthog find found its way to Nannau, as Sir Robert Williames Vaughan 2nd Bart showed great interest in all forms of antiquities and it is likely such finds would have gravitated to him. The urn probably spent the next 70 years at Nannau, perhaps lurking in an attic

295. *John Vaughan on 'Merrylegs', a sturdy Welsh pony which he rode regularly into his eighties*

room or outdoor store until the resourceful Rowlands hit on the cunning plan. It could not have had a prominent place in Nannau prior to its discovery, otherwise the plot would have been noticed and thus foiled.

The use of the urn can only be speculated on. Was it buried as part of a ritual burial? Clearly many barrows dot this ancient landscape.

This remarkable story aptly demonstrates the bond between a servant and a gentry family, and the lengths taken to entertain his young charges.

In 1952, a year after the urn was sent to the British Museum, John Vaughan wrote a short letter:

Nannau
Dolgelley
N.Wales.
19.3.52

Dear Wilfred,

Thanks for your P.C.

Will you and your wife come to lunch 1 p.m. Saturday or Sunday and bring the bucket home. I have a wicker substitute but it will not last long.

Yours ever,
John Vaughan

Tragically, John Vaughan died in 1956 as a result of a riding accident, aged 84.

His stepson later wrote:

It was the end he would have chosen. He was carried home, shaken, bleeding, and put to bed, conscious but in no pain. Within a week he died peacefully.

He had always loved a horse, and many was the fall he had had from first to last over eighty years of his riding life. Shortly before his final one, his mare, never reluctant to kick up her heels and not at all a suitable ride for an old man with a weak heart, was frightened by a farm dog and Fly jumped like a goat. The General was pitched off and landed on a bank in a sitting position, hands on his lap. The groom was startled, jumped off, ran to him,

'Don't be silly.' the General said with a broad grin.
'It isn't my first fall, nor, I hope my last, and don't say anything about it.'

The old warrior was brave to the end,

as hard as nails, Spartan in his disregard of luxury, danger or death ... he was a man absolutely without fear...

(John Michael Stewart Wardell)

Despite his immense achievements and contacts at the highest levels of society, perhaps the greatest compliment we can pay him was uttered by his butler the day after he died:

He was a very plain man, without adornment of any kind. He wore an old leather watch strap and his clothes were never new.

But the faithful butler worshipped him, as did many who were fortunate to make his acquaintance.

The Bishop of Bangor said of him at his funeral:

John Vaughan represented a great tradition, whose two pillars were to do one's duty and to fear God. His death is like the passing of an age. I marvel at his quiet serenity and the utter peace he enjoyed.

The running of the Nannau estate had never been a priority for John Vaughan, who only took up residence at Nannau at the end of his long life. Years of neglect had taken its toll on the estate, as did the policies of successive governments towards landowners, making it difficult for estates to survive. As early as 1937, John Vaughan wrote to the Nannau estate solicitor, Wilding Jones:

It is fitting to let his stepson have the final tribute:

The little grey church was filled to overflowing, the coffin draped with a Union Jack and resting in a mass of poppies, fronted with his many medals and the wreaths of the Tenth Hussars.

The choir was a composite one consisting of men and women from the hills for many miles around who had voluntarily joined together and had practiced to perfection each evening since the General's death. The core of these were Eisteddfod winners, and the burst of sound that came from them as they sang in Welsh their tribute to their friend was something never to be forgotten. Chests expanded, mouths wide as opera singers, tears glistening in their eyes, they sang with an emotion that is only Welsh and with the musical genius bred of generations. Probably they could never quite reproduce that anthem as it sounded that day. They loved the old General, and he was one of themselves, theirs through the ages.
His death to them was the passing of an era, and they knew they would not live to see his like again.

(John Stewart Michael Wardell, 1956)

During the 20 years that I have dealt with the estate I have rather overspent the revenue in repairs and modernisation and have personally received nothing from it ... my experience as a landowner leads me to think that having a surplus is largely illusionary in these Welsh estates, because the number of buildings to be maintained on low rented farms and cottages is out of proportion to the income received from them ... [and later talking of succession duty] ... of course all landed estates will be wiped out by these duties in 2 or 3 generations, all I want to do is to postpone the date as long as possible.

Nevertheless, he did what he could, rebuilding a number of cottages in Llanfachreth and others on the estate. His second cousin Brigadier Pritchard, as heir, inherited a formidable task when he enthusiastically took on the running of a much reduced and run down Nannau estate in 1956.

11

1905-1976

CHARLES HILARY VAUGHAN PRITCHARD

EARLY LIFE

Hilary was born in London in 1905, the son of Lieutenant-Colonel Charles Hamerton Pritchard and his wife Katharine (née Vaughan). When Hilary's mother Katharine died prematurely in India, her husband Charles ensured that his two young children were taken care of back in England.

Nesta and Hilary, then only 5 and 3 years respectively, were sent to live with their maternal grandmother, Edith Priscilla Elizabeth Vaughan, herself already a widow, living at The Old Rectory at Beckington near Bath. The children also spent time at Dol'rhyd, with their 'Aunt' Mrs E.C. Enthoven, where they would have become familiar with the family seat of Nannau and its dramatic landscape.

HILARY VAUGHAN PRITCHARD'S
military career

Hilary's military aspirations were evident at an early age. Whilst attending Sherborne School in Dorset he joined the Army Training Corps

301. *above:* **Hilary and his sister Nesta,** *circa 1910*

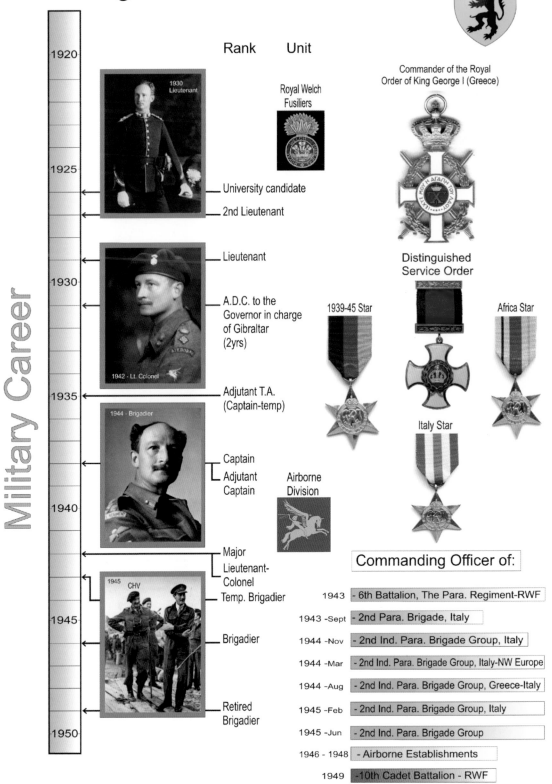

302 Brigadier C.H.V. PRITCHARD

Military Career

Year	Rank
1920	
1925	University candidate
	2nd Lieutenant
	Lieutenant
1930	A.D.C. to the Governor in charge of Gibraltar (2yrs)
1935	Adjutant T.A. (Captain-temp)
	Captain
	Adjutant Captain
1940	Major
	Lieutenant-Colonel
	Temp. Brigadier
1945	Brigadier
	Retired Brigadier
1950	

1930 Lieutenant

1942 - Lt. Colonel

1944 - Brigadier

1945 CHV

Rank   Unit

Royal Welch Fusiliers

Airborne Division

Commander of the Royal Order of King George I (Greece)

Distinguished Service Order

1939-45 Star

Africa Star

Italy Star

Commanding Officer of:

1943	- 6th Battalion, The Para. Regiment-RWF
1943 -Sept	- 2nd Para. Brigade, Italy
1944 -Nov	- 2nd Ind. Para. Brigade Group, Italy
1944 -Mar	- 2nd Ind. Para. Brigade Group, Italy-NW Europe
1944 -Aug	- 2nd Ind. Para. Brigade Group, Greece-Italy
1945 -Feb	- 2nd Ind. Para. Brigade Group, Italy
1945 -Jun	- 2nd Ind. Para. Brigade Group
1946 - 1948	- Airborne Establishments
1949	-10th Cadet Battalion - RWF

as a cadet, progressing to a senior entrant. He was following closely in the army traditions set by his father Lt.Col.Hamerton Pritchard.

In 1924 he attended Cambridge University, studying Military Studies and French, and satisfying his military leanings by serving with credit in the Cambridge University Officer Training Corps. Whilst still a Cambridge student Hilary was commissioned as 2nd Lieutenant in the Territorial Army. He was well-placed to receive a parallel experience to trainee officers at Sandhurst. No doubt his tutors would have seen glimpses of the student whose meticulous attention to detail would prove fundamental in his future role as Airborne Commander. His bravery and concern for soldiers under his command was evident even at this early age.

 In 1927 he received a commission in The Royal Welch Fusiliers (RWF) and was posted to the 2nd Battalion RWF, serving in the Rhine. From 1931 to 1932, he was aide-de-camp to General Sir Alexander Godley, the Governor of Gibraltar. As personal assistant to the General he would have experienced high society events and occasions.

1933 saw Hilary serving as Adjutant of the RWF Depot, being an administrative assistant to a senior officer. By 1935 he was appointed Adjutant 5th Battalion Territorial Army (RWF) with a temporary rank of Captain. With five years administrative experience under his belt, Hilary was selected to attend Staff College at Camberley.

MARGARET'S CHURCH
WESTMINSTER

Thursday, November 28th, 1935
at 2.15 p.m.

MARY   HILARY

Entry for this prestigious institution was by examination and confidential reports. By implication, only a small minority were fortunate enough to attend. The course would have concentrated on war studies, leadership and higher-level tactics. Hilary's outstanding levels of ability and leadership were being recognised.

On the 28th November 1935, Hilary married the Hon. Mary Patricia Monck, daughter of the Hon. Charles Henry Stanley Monck and the Hon. Mary Florence, daughter of Sir William Wyndham Portal, 2nd Bart at St. Margaret's Church, Westminster. On the 10th December 1936 their first child Susan was born, the first of four daughters.

Early 1940 saw him serving in the War Office as General Staff Officer GSO grade III (Military Operations), giving him further valuable operational insights. On the 18th January 1941 their twin daughters, Molly Cecilia and Patricia Nesta, were born, and the family relocated to Diplands, St. Mary Bourne in Hampshire. Hilary was promoted to BDE Major (Brigade Major) and by February 1942 he was posted to the 10th Battalion RWF as 2nd in command on the rank of Temporary Colonel, and by July of that year was in command with the rank of Lieutenant-Colonel.

305. Mary Vaughan and Susan with twins Molly and Patricia, 1941

Under the command of Lt. Col. Charles Hilary Vaughan Pritchard, the 10th Battalion RWF was converted to the 6th (Royal Welch) Parachute Battalion (6th Para.) in August 1942 and was assigned to the newly raised 2nd Parachute Brigade Group (2nd Para.Bde.).

Life was destined to become challenging to say the least, as he was shortly to command this elite brigade through some of the most daring parachute operations of World War Two.

Winston Churchill, the then Prime Minister, had first originated the idea of creating an elite corps of parachute troops. He had been impressed by the success of German parachute troops who had secured key objectives ahead of the armoured 'Blitzkrieg' of Western Europe.

In June 1940, Churchill, writing to the Head of the Military in the War Cabinet, stated:

> *We ought to have a corps of at least 5,000 parachute troops .... I hear something is being done already to form such a corps but only, I believe, on a very small scale. Advantage must be taken of the summer to train these forces who can none the less play their part meanwhile as shock troops in home defence.*

(Winston Churchill)

Churchill's concept of an airborne assault force was to achieve much success in numerous operations of WW2. One such operation occurred in February 1942 when a company of the British 2nd Parachute Battalion dropped into Bruneval, France, and under the enemies' noses captured a new type of German Wurzburg radar installation, bringing the equipment back home in an audaciously daring raid.

The planned training for the 2nd Para.Bde. was exceedingly demanding. All the troops were volunteers; no members of the converted battalions were in any way co-opted.

Volunteers were left in no doubt as to the associated dangers of their chosen course of action.

All members of Hilary's battalion (6th Para.) undertook a twelve-day parachute training course at No: 1, parachute Training School, RAF Ringway (now Manchester Airport). The whole battalion, together with officers, started their jumps from a converted barrage balloon and ended with five jumps from an aircraft. Anyone failing to jump was sent back to their old unit, but the successful parachutists were awarded their maroon beret and parachute wings.

Hilary's battalion was one of the three parachute battalions in the 2nd Para.Bde., consisting of:

• 4th Parachute Battalion transferred from 1st Parachute Brigade

308. left: **Lieutenant Colonel C. H. V. Pritchard, Commander 10th Battalion, Royal Welch Fusiliers** *(1942)*

309. below left: **Brigadier C. H. V. Pritchard, Commander 2nd Independent Parachute Brigade** *(1943)*

What manner of men are these who wear the maroon beret? ... They have shown themselves to be as tenacious and determined in defence, as they are courageous in attack. They are in fact men apart. Every man an Emperor.

Their nickname was – 'The Red Devils'

Their Motto was – 'Ultrinque Paratus' – Ready for anything!

In a letter to his daughter Susan in 1950, Hilary talked about the men in his battalion (6th Para.), evoking clearly his feelings at the time:

the Parachutists were just normal fellows such as quarry men from Blaenau Ffestiniog, small hill farmers from Merioneth and coal miners, all facing fear, suffering and loneliness in the fight for the preservation of a Christian World.

• 5th (Scottish) Parachute Battalion converted from 7th Batt. Queen's Own Cameron Highlanders

• 6th (Royal Welch) Parachute Battalion converted from 10th Batt. (RWF) commanded by Lt.Col. C.H.V.Pritchard.

Field-Marshall Montgomery of Alamein said of the 2nd Para.Bde:

The 2nd Ind.Para.Bde. was commanded by Brigadier E. E. Down who was a highly focussed commander, ruthless and uncompromising. Initially unpopular, within six months every man in the brigade 'would have gone to the ends of the earth for him', such was the level of respect and loyalty.

During April 1943, the 6th Para, under Hilary's command, arrived in North Africa to join the 2nd Ind.Para.Bde. in preparation for seaborne operations against Italy. By May of that year, now a full Colonel, Hilary was promoted to Deputy Commander of the 2nd Ind.Para.Bde. having relinquished command of 6th Para.

In addition to the 3 battalions, the 2nd Ind.Para.Bde., had the following attached units:

• 300th Air landing Anti-Tank Battery R. A.
• 64th Air landing Battery
• 2nd Parachute Squadron
• 2nd Ind.Para.Brigade Group Signals

- 1st Ind.Glider Squadron
- 23rd Ind.Platoon Para.Regiment
- 751st Para.Brigade Company
- 12th Para.Field Ambulance
- 2nd Ind.Para.Brigade Group Workshop REME

In June 1943, Mussolini resigned and Italy's new Prime Minister immediately opened secret talks with the Allies. On the 8th September the 2nd Ind.Para.Bde. sailed from Bizerta in Tunisia to land in the great harbour of Taranto in Italy, as part of **'Operation Slapstick.'**

On the voyage they had been informed of Italy's unconditional surrender and were not

310. *left:* **Major Richard S. Hargreaves MC, Commander of B Company, 4th Parachute Battalion, who led the attack on German forces holding Laterza Bridge, Italy (1943)**

311. *below left:* **Brigadier Pritchard with General Down near Monte Cassino (the Brigadier having just suffered shrapnel injuries)**

expecting much, if any, resistance. On reaching the port, the flotilla sought an Italian pilot to navigate the harbour minefield.

However, disaster struck *HMS Abdiel*. The fast minelaying ship carrying the 6th Para. hit a magnetic mine which had lain on the harbour floor until the ship passed over and attracted it. This in turn detonated mines stored on board the ship, resulting in it being blown in half. Fifty-eight men of the battalion and four officers were drowned. About one hundred and fifty men were taken to hospital with injuries. Despite this major setback, within six hours the battalion was ready for action again!

Amongst the fatalities was Lt.Col. J.A. Goodwin, Hilary's replacement as C.O. of 6th Para. It is difficult to imagine how Hilary took the news of the loss of so many of his fellow officers and men.

Taranto was successfully occupied and forward reconnaissance carried out. During one such operation, the Divisional Commander Major-General Hopkinson was tragically killed by a sniper. He had been observing the fierce fighting of his men with a German rear-guard patrolling the town and airfield of Gioia del Colle. Brigadier E.E. Down, Commander of the 2nd Ind.Para.Bde, was promoted to Major-General and took over the command of the Division. In the theatre of war, changes occur rapidly and by the 11th of September, Hilary, now a Brigadier, was in command of the 2nd Ind.Para.Bde. and propelled into the thick of the action.

C.H.V. PRITCHARD
as Airborne Commander

In common with other inspirational military leaders of the 20th century, Hilary managed to foster a deep unwavering loyalty in his men.

312. **Action at Laterza Bridge** by Stuart Brown, Skipper Press
   (Major Hargreaves centre, pointing at machine gun placements)

Tel. No.: Liverpool Wavertree 4000.

Any further communication on this subject
should be addressed to:—

The Under Secretary of State,
The War Office,
    Blue Coat School,
        Church Road, Wavertree,
            Liverpool 15.

and the following number quoted:

Our Ref./ OS. 3272.P.

Your Ref./

THE WAR OFFICE,
BLUE COAT SCHOOL,
CHURCH ROAD,
WAVERTREE,
LIVERPOOL 15.

1st June, 1944.

Madam,

    I am directed to inform you that a report has been
received from the Military Authorities in the Central
Mediterranean, that your husband, Brigadier C.H.V. Pritchard,
was wounded on the 10th April, 1944. The report adds that
he remained at duty.

    It is probable that you are already aware of this
information, but it is thought that you would like to
receive official confirmation.

    The delay in the receipt of this report is much
regretted, but the information was only recently received
at the General Headquarters from your husband's unit.

            I am, Madam,
                Your obedient Servant,

                A.Williams

The Honourable Mrs. M.P. Pritchard,
    Diplands,
        St. Mary Bourne,
            Hampshire.

They were comrades fighting together against adversity. This leading from the front was aptly demonstrated in a story told of Hilary's reaction on hearing of the tragic death of one of his officers as a result of a non-functioning parachute. He immediately picked up a parachute from the same batch and ordered an aeroplane. He took off and jumped with his men, landing safely to ground amongst the battalion, thus proving with his own life the safety of the parachutes!

Throughout the winter of 1943 the 2nd Ind.Para.Bde., greatly hampered by lack of reinforcement, were attached to the 2nd New Zealand Division under the command of General Freyburg.

On the night of the 15th/16th September, The 4th Battalion, The Parachute Regiment, fought its first significant action of the war. The action was carried out by the men of B Company, 4 Para., commanded by Major Dick Hargreaves. The objective was the heavily defended Laterza Bridge which was vital to the 2nd Ind.Para.Bde's advance from Taranto. After a long night's march over difficult terrain they carried out an uphill assault on strongly defended German positions. Despite heavy mortar and machine gun fire, B Company forged forward hampered by the hidden tripwires releasing flares. The enemy, however, suffered considerable casualties and were driven from their positions, leaving their heavy weapons behind.

Although four men of B Company were tragically killed in the action, it was a significant strategic advance, and for his inspirational and gallant leadership Major Hargreaves was awarded the Military Cross. Hilary, always concerned for the safety of his men, observed the action from a nearby hillside.

The 2nd Ind.Para.Bde. formed the left flank of the 8th Army, fighting for four months as

infantry soldiers on the Adriatic front. The hard winter of 1943 saw little movement, and so hampered were they by the conditions that they sought the assistance of an Indian company to provide mule transport!

The fighting pattern they adopted was to send out detachments aimed at seeking out and ambushing German patrols. Through the harsh winter they became adept at this mode of action. By the end of March 1944, the brigade moved to Cassino. On one occasion, whilst General Down was on a visit, he was 'greeted' with salvoes of phosphorous shells which partially ignited the General and wounded Hilary in the head. Needless to say the following day Hilary was back in action, head bandaged, and making light of his injury!

By the end of May 1944, the brigade was withdrawn from action for a rest to later take part in 'Operation Hasty,' the last deployment they would see in Italy.

OPERATION HASTY

In June 1944, a small detachment of sixty men commanded by Captain Fitzroy-Smith took part in 'Operation Hasty'. The operation was carried out by the 6th Para. and involved a parachute landing behind German lines near Torricella. Its objective was to harass the Germans who were withdrawing to the Gothic Line and to prevent them from carrying out demolitions in the wake of their retreat. Hilary's orders to Captain Fitzroy-Smith, the mission commander, was to

*occupy the dominating heights by day
and descend into the valleys and wreak
havoc by night*

The mission, which was a success, diverted the Germans into hunting for the British. This action weakened the German frontline force and supply lines, rendering them less able to challenge the heavily engaged 8th Army. Hilary had also cunningly employed the use of decoy

314. left: 'Rupert' Decoy Dummy Paratrooper as used during
'Operation Hasty'
315. below left: Copy of a leaflet dropped to recall
'Operation Hasty', June 1944
316. right: Message to Brigadier Pritchard from The 8th Army,
wishing him luck with 'Operation Hasty'

When all lines of 'Operation Hasty's'
communications to Fitzroy-Smith suddenly
failed, Hilary intuitively hatched a plan to
recall Fitzroy-Smith's detachment by dropping
leaflets in the area, which read,

Proceed Awdry forthwith

The detachment, knowing that this message
referred to one of their officers at Brigade
Head Quarters, realised that it was a 'cloaked'
message to recall. Slowly but surely, less than
half of the incredibly brave detachment was to
return to base.

A coded top secret message had been sent to
Hilary by the 8th Army wishing them luck on
their difficult task ahead with 'Operation
Hasty'.

For Hilary, the stress of command was clearly
visible in a letter to his wife on the 9th July
1944, in which he stated:

> *Yes pray that I make the right decisions
> and am given good advice and leadership
> from God. The worst part of the whole
> thing is the liability of making wrong
> decisions or being slack in thought that
> could cost many lives. Above all, most of
> the lives are decent ones that are lost and
> only the self-reckless, which I am afraid I
> feel there are a lot of at home, get spared.
> I am writing this letter outside my
> caravan and in the shade of Muscatel
> vines; in other circumstances it would be
> very pleasant.*

dummy paratroopers (nicknamed Ruperts) to
trick the enemy into believing he had a larger
force than he actually had. This tactic worked
beautifully.

(Jokingly, the soldiers nicknamed their officers
'Ruperts'!)

During the rest of June the brigade was
stationed at Salerno undertaking strenuous
training in preparation for 'Operation
Dragoon', the code name given to the Allied
Invasion of the South of France.

PROCEED AWDRY FORTHWITH

TO 2 Para Bde

(ABOVE THIS LINE IS FOR SIGNALS USE ONLY)

FROM 8 Army | Originator's Number **AC 027** | Date **312310** | In Reply to Number

Personal and Top-Secret to Brigadier PRITCHARD from General LEESE ○ I wish you luck and success in your venture tomorrow ○ your task is difficult but I have watched your fine ○ fighting qualities during the Winter ○ undertaking and am confident that are you will overcome every difficulty ○ it be will be an important contribution to the advance of the 8th Army ○ I am grateful for your speedy and willing response to my call for airborne action ○ Good Luck to end one of you.

This Message may be sent AS WRITTEN by any means

If liable to be intercepted or fall into enemy hands, this Message must be sent IN CIPHER. SIGNED

Originator's Instructions / Degree of Priority — **Immediate**

Time of Origin **0830**

(BELOW THIS LINE IS FOR SIGNALS USE ONLY.)

System In	Time In	Reader	Sender	System Out	Time Out	Reader	Sender	System Out	Time Out	Reader	Sender

T.I.I.

T.O.R.

OPERATION DRAGOON
(earlier called 'Anvil')

As a result of the success of the Normandy airborne landings, the Allies were eager to use airborne troops to support the parallel invasion of the South of France by the American 7th Army and the Free French 1st Army.

'Operation Dragoon' involved the capture of the port of Marseilles as its main objective, to be followed by a sweep up the Rhone valley, to join up with the Normandy invasion force.

The Allies assembled an airborne division, the 1st Airborne Task Force (1st ABT), comprising 9,732 men, 535 US Army Air Force C47's and 465 British and American gliders. The 2nd Ind.Para.Bde. was the only British element, paired up with five battalions of American parachutists. The 2nd Ind.Para.Bde. was to be involved in the airborne operations, the code name being 'Operation Rugby'. Just prior to the operation the brigade had been in Rome with a contingent visiting Pope Pius XII, as Hilary had revealed to his wife in a letter:

I had a great day with the Pope last week. I haven't turned R.C. but had a long talk with him.

The overall objective was to land in the River Argens Valley, between Le Muy and Le Luc, to block any German reinforcements from

317. below: **Brigadier Pritchard welcomes Major-General Crawford, Deputy Commander US Army Air Forces Services (Mediterranean) to 2nd Ind. Para. Bde.**

318. below: **Brigadier Pritchard and Brigade Officers with Major-General Crawford, prior to 'Operation Dragoon'**

reaching the beaches and compromising the landings.

After weeks of preparation D-day dawned on 15th August 1944. Early in the morning the 2nd Ind.Para.Bde. left Rome, which Hilary aptly described as

beautiful with the lights of the city twinkling below.

They crossed the coast at 0440 hrs and entered France, carried to their Drop Zones (DZ) in 396 Douglas Dakota C-47 transport planes. The Royal Navy had deployed submarines on the surface to initially guide the flight to Corsica and beyond.

A revealing account of the paratroopers 'unwavering belief' in their commanders and fellow soldiers is demonstrated in a contemporary American newspaper article – 'Invasion Chutists Confident'.

'Pritchard's Flying Circus', as Hilary's men routinely called themselves, were airborne and raring to go!

The 4th and 6th Paras all landed on course. Hilary had jumped at 1000 feet, because of visibility issues, but still landed only 15 yards from the Eureka Beacon! The 5th Para. and the battalion HQ of the 4th Para. were dropped 20 miles off course due to an electrical fault in the lead aircraft which had prevented the pilot from establishing the DZ accurately. Despite this they made their way to the rallying point, causing much damage to the enemy en route with the assistance of the French resistance fighters, the Maquis. A wave of British Horsa gliders later landed in the planned landing zones (LZ) and efficiently unloaded the back-up artillery.

The main bridge leading to the town of Le Muy was captured ahead of schedule, and with the assistance of the American 550th Glider Battalion, the town and the objective was achieved on D+1.

By the end of the first day of 'Operation Dragoon', more than 94,000 troops and 11,000 vehicles had come ashore ready to extend the successes of the airborne operations with the beach-head successfully established.

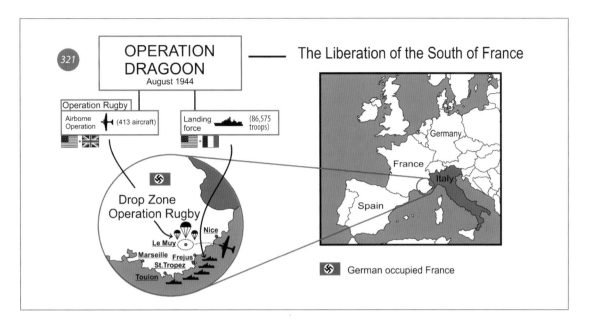

Cannes was being liberated on the 25th August, when the 2nd Ind.Para.Bde. sailed to Naples to take part in 'Operation Manna', the airborne landings in Greece, their next challenge. During 'Operation Rugby' the 2nd Ind.Para.Bde. had recorded: 362 casualties, 51 dead, 130 wounded and 181 missing.

On the 1st September, Hilary's letter home reflects the pride he had in his brigade and on the 5th September, he was able to communicate the magnitude of what had been achieved.

Invasion Chutists Confident

British Sing and Sleep on Way to Battle

By Newbold Noyes Jr.

Rome, Italy – I have just returned from the southern France beach area now under attack by Allied forces. I flew in one of hundreds of planes of a troop carrier command, carrying thousands of American and British parachutists who were dropped in a hamlet some miles inland just before dawn Tuesday.

The delivery portion of the airborne operation was flawlessly executed. Carriers were able to release their jumpers on schedule over the designated dropping zones. At 6.30 a.m. on the way home, we passed a long column of tow planes and gliders going in with supplies for the men we had dropped. The gliders were scheduled to reach their objectives as the sea borne forces hit the beach at Frejus.

The British paratroopers, with whom I flew, were magnificent. At take-off in Italy as our plane shuddered for a second at the top of the runway before hurtling into the darkness, one pink faced boy, grotesque in his bulky paraphernalia, threw back his head and shouted:

'Look out Jerry, here we come.'

With that battle cry, he caught the spirit of this whole invasion.

Absolute Confidence

The most amazing single thing about what is going on here is that from the beginning and everywhere there seems to have been a feeling of complete and absolute confidence. I told a fusilier who sat next to me in the carrier that I couldn't understand why nobody in the plane seemed worried.

'The only thing we are worried about,' he said, *'is the fact that two of our blokes are new to this. They've made practice jumps, but this jumping with full equipment is something else.'*

'Not to mention,' I said, *'the presence of the enemy.'*

He blew the ash off his cigarette, *'Jerry,'* he said, *'I should very much dislike being Jerry this morning.'*

The other members of the platoon were just as wonderful and just as British. As our plane took off from a field teeming with the lights of scores of other planes, they sang a song to the tune, 'Red River Valley.' Which ended with the words,

'but remember the poor parachutist and the job he is trying to do?'

As the planes headed over the Mediterranean they sang the songs of another simpler war: 'Tipperary.' , 'Pack Up Your Troubles,' and Hinky Dinky Parlez Vous.' Just then the American radio operator stuck his head out of the forward cabin and shouted;

'Hey, you guys are going to wear yourselves out if you keep that up all the way to France.'

They Count on Yanks

'Good bloke,' said the fusilier, *'that's one reason why we are not worried. We know these Yanks and we know they will get us where we are supposed to be. That's the big thing about parachuting. It's a bad show if you do not know where you are when you come down.'*

Then a remarkable thing happened. About half of them appeared to go to sleep. They half lay down on the benches – no mean feat when you have about 100 pounds of equipment tied to your body. They put their heads in each other's laps and closed their eyes, and in the light of a match I lit, their faces looked peaceful.

These men, with few exceptions, had been together in the war almost two years, but there was something special in their attitude towards one another. I remember that when we were waiting for take-off, these – the toughest soldiers of the war – were gentle, almost tender, as they helped each other on with their equipment, offered each other what remained of a cup of tea and passed around precious cigarettes.

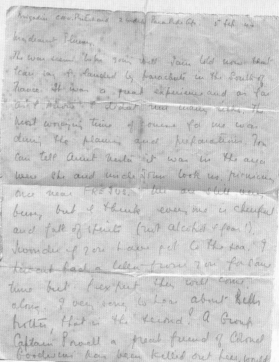

Hilary and his HQ could rightly be proud of their involvement in one of the best planned and well-executed invasion operations of WW2, referred to by many as 'The Forgotten D-Day.'

OPERATION MANNA

It was known that the Germans were about to withdraw from Greece. It was considered vital that British troops should occupy Athens as soon as possible to assist with food distribution and to prevent Greek guerrillas from establishing a foothold in the city, and provoking a Civil War. Fortunately, the German evacuation took longer than expected, allowing the Allies time to properly plan 'Operation Manna.'

Imminently, the 2nd Ind.Para.Bde., under Hilary's command, would be propelled into the middle of a bloody Civil War and action very different to anything they had experienced thus far.

An initial company of the 2nd Ind.Para.Bde. dropped into Megara, 15 miles from Athens, on the 12th October 1944.

323. above: **Letter written by Brigadier Pritchard to his wife after 'Operation Dragoon'**
324. right: **Lt. General Scobie, Commander of British Forces in Greece, visiting the 2nd Ind. Para. Bde.**

Due to adverse weather conditions the bulk of the brigade followed on 2 days later, entering Athens on the 15th. Over the next few days the brigade received a tumultuous welcome. So furious was the welcome on one occasion that Hilary became concerned for the safety of his men. He immediately summoned the Athens Chief of Police and Greek Commander to a conference, urging the officials to disperse the crowds, but without success. The huge crowd became even more unruly.

2nd Independent Parachute Brigade's Operation in Greece 'Operation Manna'

The presence of Hilary on the balcony was greeted with three deafening cheers, which had hardly died away, when sounds of gunfire alerted him to the dire situation. His troops were completely hemmed in, but fortunately the weather came to the rescue in the form of a cloudburst which dispersed the crowd and allowed the brigade to regroup.

Company B and C of the 4th Battalion were allocated to a special unit under the command of Lord Jellico, and fought the retreating Germans for three months, advancing to Salonika. The remainder of the 2nd Ind.Para.Bde. sailed to Salonika.

Subsequently, the whole brigade returned to Athens and fought the Greek Communists, the National Popular Army of Liberation (ELAS), who attempted to fill the vacuum left by the Germans. The street fighting in Athens was very fierce, with more casualties occurring there than in all of their other conflicts.

The brigade's victory was enhanced with news of Hilary's Distinguished Service Order (D.S.O.). In addition he received one of the highest military honours awarded by the Greek Nation, in the form of the Order of King George with crossed swords, for his service to the Greek people. An indication of the 2nd Ind.Para.Bde's. contribution is aptly demonstrated by the fact that at the height of

327. *left:* **Athenians welcome the 2nd Ind.Para.Bde. October 1944**

328. *centre:* **Greek civilians crowd the streets to welcome British paratroopers**

329. *bottom:* **British paratroopers involved in a firefight on a street corner during 'Operation Manna'**

330. left: Silver plated Parachute Regiment tankard, inscribed 'Presented to Brigadier C.H.V. Pritchard D.S.O.' - also silver napkin ring inscribed with postings of his military career and a Spode commemorative porcelain plate

331. below: Hilary and family at Dol'rhyd, 1946

Hilary's pride in his brigade was clearly evident in a letter he sent to his men, dated 5th January 1945, when he forwarded two messages of congratulations received from Generals Hawkesworth and Arkwright.

The 2nd Ind.Para.Bde. came out of the War with an excellent record and high praise. History, for its part, should record Hilary's contribution in the 'airborne hall of fame'.

The end of the war signalled many changes in the British Armed Forces. Hilary's brigade, the 2nd Ind.Para.Bde., lost its attached units and became the 2nd Para.Bde. attached to the 6th Airborne Division deployed in the Middle East.

The 2nd Para.Bde. disembarked at Haifa on the 22nd October 1945 and were moved by rail to the Gaza region, to a barren camp on the edge of the Sinai Desert. Their role quickly became apparent: to maintain an uneasy peace between Arabs and Jews - essentially to be an internal security task force.

On the 1st April 1946, Hilary left the brigade to take up the post as Commander of the Airborne Establishments in England.

The Airborne Establishments (AE) was essentially concerned with coordinating all the airborne training units in the country. In 1948, along with the reduction of the number of parachute brigades, the Airborne Establishments was disbanded.

During his tenure as commander of the AE, Hilary undertook the task of setting up the first Museum of Airborne Forces, now relocated to the Imperial War Museum at Duxford near Cambridge.

Hilary ended his military career in 1949, retiring as Commanding Officer, 10th Cadet Battalion, The Royal Welsh Fusiliers.

After a distinguished and demanding military career, spanning nearly a quarter of a century, one would imagine that he would yearn for a peaceful and restful retirement. Nothing was further from his mind as he was determined to take on the daunting task of running his family's ancient estates in North Wales, the Nannau and Dol'rhyd estates. Hardly retirement!

the problems they were feeding 20,000 civilians a day, and in one battle killed 170 rebels, wounded 70 and captured 520 prisoners!

By the beginning of February 1945, the brigade was withdrawn from Athens and returned to Italy. From 19th March to 8th May they remained in a constant state of readiness for a supporting role with the 8th Army, but were not mobilised.

Following VE day (8th May 1945), the brigade left for England, with a glowing endorsement from General Alexander, Allied Commander in Chief:

You have a wonderful record of successes... and in every battle you have fought you have shown all the true qualities of good soldiers – high morale, dash and fighting efficiency.

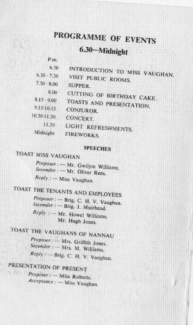

PROGRAMME OF EVENTS
6.30—Midnight

P.m.
6.30   INTRODUCTION TO MISS VAUGHAN.
6.30 - 7.30   VISIT PUBLIC ROOMS.
7.30 - 8.00   SUPPER.
8.00   CUTTING OF BIRTHDAY CAKE.
8.15 - 9.00   TOASTS AND PRESENTATION.
9.15-10.15   CONJUROR.
10.30-11.30 CONCERT.
11.30   LIGHT REFRESHMENTS.
Midnight   FIREWORKS.

SPEECHES

TOAST MISS VAUGHAN
Proposer : — Mr. Gwilym Williams.
Seconder : — Mr. Oliver Rees.
Reply : — Miss Vaughan.

TOAST THE TENANTS AND EMPLOYEES
Proposer : — Brig. C. H. V. Vaughan.
Seconder : — Brig. J. Muirhead.
Reply : — Mr. Howel Williams.
        Mr. Hugh Jones.

TOAST THE VAUGHANS OF NANNAU
Proposer : — Mrs. Griffith Jones.
Seconder : — Mrs. M. Williams.
Reply : — Brig. C. H. V. Vaughan.

PRESENTATION OF PRESENT
Proposer : — Miss Roberts.
Acceptance : — Miss Vaughan.

MISS SUSAN VAUGHAN
10 DECEMBER, 1957

NANNAU
NORTH WALES

THE NANNAU and DOL'RHYD ESTATES

Prior to the death of his second cousin, Major General John Vaughan, Hilary had for twelve years managed the Dol'rhyd estate, left to him by the will of his aunt Eleanor Enthoven. In 1956 he also inherited the Nannau estate, running both estates together.

Although not a pre-requisite to inheriting the estate, Hilary chose to assume his mother's maiden name, changing his name by deed poll in 1956 to Charles Hilary Vaughan Vaughan, thus perpetuating the tenure of Nannau under a Vaughan.

Nannau mansion posed a dilemma for Hilary; years of neglect had left the ancient edifice in a poor state of repair and quite unsuitable for letting out. The fact that its fishing rights had been taken and settled on the Hengwrt estate meant that Nannau was no longer able to attract the sporting tenant it had in previous years. The neglected moorland for shooting likewise added to the problem.

Perceiving no viable use for the old mansion, Hilary relocated his family from Dol'rhyd to Nannau, and set about carrying out essential repairs. The magnitude of the task must have been quite daunting: the roof needed to be completely replaced and the pavilion wings required some attention.

From the outset Hilary adopted a 'hands on' approach to the management of his estates. Preferring not to employ an agent, he oversaw the whole venture personally with a workforce of eight: one secretary, two shepherds, two stockmen and three general workers.

He worked tirelessly with huge determination to refurbish and improve the estates. In 'retirement' he arose at the crack of dawn every day and was a constant presence in the day-to-day running of the farm and estates.

It was with great optimism for the future that the family entered into the coming-of-age celebrations for the Nannau heir, Miss Susan Vaughan, on the 10th December 1957.

In a booklet to commemorate the auspicious event, Brigadier Vaughan announced:

I and my family welcome you to Nannau to celebrate the coming-of-age of my eldest daughter, Susan. It is interesting to note that this is only the third coming-of-age

CHARLES M EVANS

334. *Nannau in the 1950s* by Charles M. Evans. Watercolour. 20 x 25 inches. 2014

Celebrations at Nannau

Coming of age of Miss Susan Vaughan

NANNAU, the historic seat of the Vaughan family, was the scene of rejoicing , yesterday, when 150 tenants and employees of the Nannau and Dolrhyd estates were guests at celebrations to mark the coming-of-age of Miss Susan Vaughan, eldest daughter of Brigadier and the Hon Mrs. C. H. V. Vaughan. Miss Vaughan is the heiress to the estate.

On Saturday she will be married at St. Mary's Church, Dolgelley, to Mr David Muirhead, son of Brigadier and Mrs. James Muirhead, of Boath, Nairn (Scotland).

The coming of age celebrations began when the family, relatives, and friends attended a service at Llanfachreth Parish Church, conducted by the Vicar (the Rev. Boner Jenkins).

Their return to Nannau was greeted by the salute of 21

Miss Vaughan.

guns from Moel Offrwm. Their followed a luncheon party, at which the chief guests were Colonel J. F. Williams - Wynne (Lord Lieutenant of Merioneth) and Major C. L. Wynne Jones (Vice - Lieutenant) together with Brigadier and Mrs Muirhead.

There have been some interesting personalities in this old Welsh family. In 1404 Hywel Sele, the grandson of Meurig, sixth Lord of Nannau, who was a staunch Royalist, was killed by his rebel cousin, Owain Glyndwr. Owain hid the body in a hollow oak tree, and burned down the house. Hywel's skeleton was discovered forty years later, and buried with great ceremony in Cymmer Abbey.

The oak, known as Ceubren yr Ellyll and referred to by Sir Walter Scott in "Marmion" as vived until 1813.

The oak, known as Ceubren yr Ellyll and referred to by Sir Walter Scott in "Marmion" as vived until 1813. "The spirit-blasted tree." survived.

Welcome to tenants and employees

Yesterday the luncheon party went outside to watch Miss Susan Vaughan plant another oak tree on the site of Ceubren yr Ellyll to commemorate her coming of age. Later 150 tenants and employees were welcomed at Nannau by Brigadier and the Hon. Mrs Vaughan and their family

to celebrate the coming of age. Mr David Muirhead and his parents were present.

In his welcome, Brigadier Vaughan, who is High Sheriff of Merioneth, said it was interesting to note that this was only the third coming of age celebration to be held at Nannau as it stood to-day since its completion in 1796. He pointed out that last year Nannau had been classified by the Minister of Works as a Welsh historic home, and he was assisting in its preservation.

During the celebrations a clock in a rosewood case, made in 1820, was presented to Miss Vaughan on behalf of the tenants and employees.

The final programme included a concert by the well-known Welsh harpist, Mrs Frances Mon Jones, and a fireworks display.

Mr Muirhead.

celebration to be held at Nannau, as it stands today, since its completion by Yr Hen Syr Robert in 1796. The last one was the coming-of-age of Sir Robert Vaughan of Garthmaelan on 18th September 1887. Another interesting point is that this is not the first time in the

history of the Nannau family that the heir was a daughter. The previous one to my daughter Susan was Janet, who like her, also had three other sisters. Colonel Huw Nanney, her father, was great, great grandson of Hugh Nanney Hên, to whom the Bards composed their elegies in 1623 ...

There have been some interesting personalities in this old Welsh family. In 1404, Hywel Sele, who was a staunch Royalist, was killed by his rebel cousin Owain Glyndŵr. Owain hid the body in a hollow oak tree and burnt down the house.

Hywel's skeleton was discovered 40 years later and buried with great ceremony at Cymer Abbey. The oak, known as 'Ceubren yr Ellyll.' and referred to by Sir Walter Scott in 'Marmion' as 'The Spirit's Blasted Tree,' survived until 1813. Sir Richard Colt Hoare sketched it the night before it finally fell, and a copy of this sketch can be seen in the hall. The drinking cups and candlesticks in the Dining room were made from its timber.

This afternoon my daughter, Susan, planted another oak tree on the site of 'Ceubren yr Ellyll' in Nannau Old Kitchen Garden to commemorate her coming-of-age ...

I often ask myself where else in the British Isles can such a house be found standing 700 ft. above sea level in some of the finest scenery of Europe. It is indeed a monument to the Welsh Nation. The stone used to build it was Welsh granite probably quarried from Moel Offrwm. The house was designed by a Welsh Country Squire for his Welsh family, using Welsh material and Welsh Craftsmen.

In a few days, my daughter Susan hopes to marry David Muirhead, and Nannau may have as its 27th Lord a Briton from North of the Tweed. With your sympathy and favourable circumstances in this ever changing way of life I know we will do our best to preserve this ancient House, and its treasures for our Principality.

THE MARRIAGE OF MISS VAUGHAN OF NANNAU – 14th December 1957

With the sun shining brightly, St. Mary's Church, Dolgelley, was packed to capacity on Saturday on the occasion of the marriage of Miss Susan Katharine Vaughan, eldest daughter of Brigadier C.H.V.Vaughan, High Sheriff of Merioneth and the Hon. Mrs Mary Vaughan of Nannau, to Mr David Spencer Muirhead, son of Brigadier and Mrs James Muirhead, of Boath, Nairnshire, Scotland.

The ceremony was performed by the Lord Bishop of Bangor, the Rt. Rev. Dr. G. O. Williams assisted by Rev. J. Elwern Thomas, Rev. D. Bonner Jenkins and Rev. Glyn Morgan.

The bride who was given away by her father wore a full-length dress of white brocaded silk, with veil of tulle and a head-dress of orange blossom. She carried a bouquet of white camellias and lily of the valley and wore a diamond spray brooch, a gift from the bridegoom's parents.

Among the 450 guests at the church were a large contingent of tenants and employees of the Nannau and Dol'rhyd estates and friends of the bride and groom from Oxford University. At Oxford the bride was reading Politics and Economics, and the groom had recently obtained a Law degree.

Two hundred and fifty reception guests were later entertained in style at Nannau, which had been flood-lit all week to celebrate the occasion. The guests were welcomed by the Brigadier and Mrs Vaughan, and introduced by them to Brigadier and Mrs Muirhead before passing on to meet the bride and groom and bridesmaids in the large drawing room.

Following refreshments, the bride and groom cut the wedding cake and toasts were offered. A large number of presents were on display in the billiard room at Nannau, and guests had ample time to view them.

After the reception, the young couple left Nannau in the groom's car, only to find that all exits had been blocked by the estate employees. (A local wedding tradition in the Llanfachreth area). Eventually, the happy couple were allowed to leave for their honeymoon, which was spent in the South of France.

Following on from the coming-of-age celebrations earlier that week, it had been a time to remember. The ancient halls of Nannau had for a short time echoed to the sound of revelry and entertainment, as it had so often done in byegone times.

The entertainment over, Hilary once more focussed on the running of his estates, but the warm glow of the recent celebrations could not mask the stark reality facing his estates in the long-term. As early as 1958, it was evident that Hilary had grave concerns regarding the future viability of the Nannau estate. In a letter to a trusted agent he noted:

337. *Marriage of Miss Susan Vaughan and Mr David Muirhead - family wedding portrait in the Drawing room at Nananu*

338. left: **The cutting of the cake in the hall at Nannau**
339. centre: **Hilary and Mary welcoming guests to the Reception - Nannau Drawing room**
340. right: **Wedding guests in the Drawing room at Nannau**

... I would very much like to have your advice over the Estate and its future survey, as I feel certain I could by contracting its acreage to an economic size, turn it into a profitable agricultural unit which will be of far more use to my daughter than a decaying hill estate, yet keeping the traditions of the last 100's of years."

His strategy for long-term survival was to run the two estates together and eliminate non-viable farms, selling the farmhouses and amalgamating the lands under Nannau home farm. The steady progress along the rationalisation of land proceeded, but it was not until 1959 that farm rents were increased substantially from the level they had been in 1870!

On the 28th July 1962, Nannau once more rang to the sounds of joyus celebration when Hilary's second daughter, Miss Molly C.V. Vaughan married Mr I.H. Davies. The local newspaper reported:

Foxglove Arch for Nannau Bride

Tenants of Tyddyn Bach and Penyfridd farms on the Nannau estate, Dolgellau made an arch of foxgloves and bell-heather on Saturday for the bride on her

way from Nannau to St. Machreth's Church, Llanfachreth.
The bride was Miss Molly C.V. Vaughan, second daughter of Brigadier C.H.V. and the Hon. Mrs Vaughan of Nannau. She was married to Mr I.H. Davies, elder son of the Rev. J.R. and Mrs Davies of Birmingham.

The Bishop of Bangor and the Rev. Ifan Williams (vicar) officiated, with Mr D.J. Thomas as organist.

Miss Vaughan, who was given away by her father, was attractively attired in a gown of cream silk, with a fitted bodice and a full skirt, pleated at the back and falling into a train. Her family veil of old Limerick lace was held in place by a tiara of diamonds and pearls. She carried a bouquet of white roses, stephanotis and jasmine.

The bridesmaids were attired in dresses of lime green wild silk and head-dresses of white roses. They carried similar bouquets to the bride's, Misses Patricia Vaughan, Jane Vaughan, Annabelle Dunstan and Rosemary James. Mr Roger Wellesley-Smith was the best man.

*The ushers were, Mr David Muirhead
(bride's brother-in-law), Mr Bryn Davies,
(bridegroom's brother) Mr Christopher
Batt and Mr Chas. Pritchard (bride's
cousins) and Mr Ronald Bartle.*

The honeymoon is being spent in Ireland.

Molly's wedding in 1962 was sadly to be the
last Vaughan marriage celebrated at the family
mansion. It was becoming apparent to Hilary
that his family seat would require greater
expenditure to preserve it than the estate could
sensibly spare, and with this in mind, he
continued relentlessly to pursue the means to
make it viable.

Whilst no doubt reflecting on the preservation
of his own family seat, Hilary would have

received the disturbing news that Hengwrt
mansion had been badly damaged by fire and
the later news that it had been irreparably
damaged.

The scheduling of Nannau as a historic
building back in 1956 should have been an
occasion for jubilation as it could have
unlocked future vital grants to preserve the
ancient buildings. However, an offer of a grant
for £5,000 in 1963 was refused by Hilary,
because it was under the proviso that it was
only to be used for the restoration of the roof
and not for the restoration of the wings. The
authorities had deemed the wings 'not of
sufficient historic or architectural interest to be
restored'. An architect's report commissioned
by Hilary indicated that the roof could be
repaired for about £8,000!

In support of a planning request regarding Nannau in 1963, Hilary's agent noted:

Our Client fully appreciates the interest that the Welsh Nation takes in Nannau and the Vaughan family and he and his family are quite prepared to do their best to preserve this monument for the future, but in its present state it is a millstone to any owner of the Estate. The domestic facilities are very substandard, there is no central heating and the kitchens require complete modernisation and the electric wiring is not fit to be connected to the main supply and the cost of wiring alone would be extremely heavy.

At present Nannau is shown to the public not as a Museum but as a Welsh Family Home but unless a considerable amount is spent on it in the near future it will not be possible to use it as such a home... Our Client feels that you will appreciate the dilemma in which he and his heirs are placed and he feels that the future preservation of Nannau as a historic home must rest on an adequate grant being made for structural repair and the right to have flexibility in its use.

Reluctantly, in 1965 Hilary put Nannau mansion up for sale with ten acres of land, selling it to Mr Edward Morrison, a retired barrister, for £8,000. Edward Morrison had won the Distinguished Flying Cross during WWII, whilst serving in the R.A.F., rising to the rank of Wing Commander.

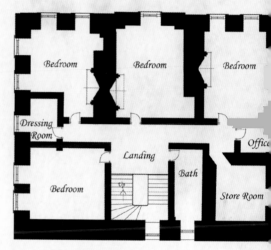

Second Floor Plan

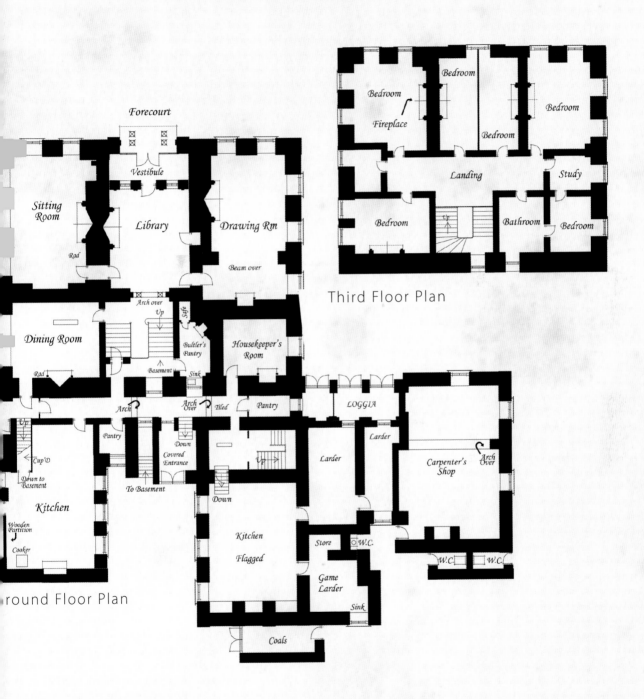

Forecourt

Vestibule

Sitting
Room

Library

Drawing Rm

Rad

Beam over

Bedroom

Bedroom

Fireplace

Bedroom

Bedroom

Landing

Study

Bedroom

Up

Bathroom

Bedroom

Third Floor Plan

Arch over

Up

Soft

Dining Room

Butler's
Pantry

Housekeeper's
Room

Rad

Basement

Sink

Arch

Arch
Over

Tiled

Pantry

LOGGIA

Up

Pantry

Down

Larder

Larder

Carpenter's
Shop

Arch
Over

Cup'D

Covered
Entrance

Kitchen

Down to
Basement

To Basement

Down

Kitchen
Flagged

Store

W.C.

W.C.

W.C.

Wooden
Partition

Cooker

Game
Larder

Sink

round Floor Plan

Coals

Faced with the daunting task of refurbishing the wings, Edward Morrison sought permission to demolish them, on the grounds that they were a much later addition, and was subsequently allowed to remove them in 1968. The rubble produced, amounting to 1,500 tons, was dumped in a gully near the Precipice Walk car park. In recent times it has been shown that the Pavilion Wings were actually an 1805 addition by Joseph Bromfield, erected only ten years after the construction of the main Georgian block!

In 1969, Edward went on to rebuild Nannau's roof. The massive 12" x 12" main beams were replaced with RSJ's and the valley removed, converting it to a single roof space. The brick chimneystacks were lowered completing a sound refurbishment of the previously defective structure.

After the sale of Nannau mansion in 1965, Hilary and his family moved to nearby Maesybrynner, and from the 14th - 16th June a huge sale of 'Valuable Period Furniture and Effects' was held at Nannau as the family had to drastically downsize. All the important Nannau artefacts and portraits were retained in the family's ownership, but the removal of the contents heralded the end of the tenure of the descendants of Cadwgan, after nearly nine centuries!

Parting with the ancient family seat would have been traumatic for Hilary, but with some renewed optimism he launched himself into the management of the Nannau and Dol'rhyd estates, in partnership with his eldest daughter and heiress, Mrs Susan Muirhead.

The partnership, with Hilary very much in the driving seat, had built up a fine herd of Welsh Black Cattle and five flocks of Welsh Mountain Sheep, grazing a much reduced acreage of some 2,392 acres in hand, and some 1,162 acres of tenanted farms. Interesting farm

records reveal that Hilary, with due regard to family history, named some of his home-bred Welsh Black Bulls: Nannau Owain Glyndŵr, Nannau Hywel Sele, Nannau Meurig and Nannau Cynwch!

On the 26th September 1970, Hilary's youngest daughter, Jane Arabella Vaughan, married David Patrick Mark Allen, son of Paddy and Brid Allen of Sutton, Dublin. The marriage took place at Llanelltyd Church and the service was officiated by Archdeacon Wallis Thomas. After a reception at Maesybrynner, the young couple honeymooned in Ireland. They later returned to London, where David was employed in advertising and Jane worked for the Readers' Digest.

By direction of Brigadier C. H. V. Vaughan, D.S.O., D.L., J.P.

NANNAU
Dolgellau-Merioneth

CATALOGUE OF

Valuable Period Furniture and Effects

Comprising 1000 lots

which

Beresford Adams & Son

THE CROSS, CHESTER

will sell by auction on the premises on
MONDAY, TUESDAY and WEDNESDAY
14th, 15th and 16th JUNE, 1965

Illustrated Catalogue four shillings

347. above: **The Wedding of Miss Jane Arabella Vaughan and Mr David Allen,** *September 1970*

Despite much hard work and many improvements, by 1975, now in his 70s, Hilary reluctantly made initial forays into the idea of selling the estates. Years of battling with death duties and poor returns on 'uneconomic land' had led to this inevitable course of action.

With the agonising decision made, Hilary forged ahead with plans to sell the Nannau and Dol'rhyd estates as a whole, so that they would be preserved under one owner and, critically, the tenure of his workforce could be preserved.

J.D. Wood of London and Morris, Marshall & Poole of Mid-Wales were appointed as joint agents for the sale, and a comprehensive press release and advertising scheme was launched to find a suitable buyer. Initially Hilary had insisted that the estate should be offered for private sale as a whole during the summer of 1975, and, only if this was unsuccessful, in 34 lots at a later date. Hilary was well aware of the upheaval that could be caused in a small farming community by the dispersal of an estate in piecemeal fashion, and wanted to avoid this prospect at all costs.

Fortunately, a buyer was found for both the estates - a successful businessman, Mr Vaughan Gaskell from Warrington.

With an offer accepted, the disposal of the family estates, after 900 years of occupation,

Nannau Estate Farm 1963

1. Nannau prior to the demolishing of the wings with Welsh Black cattle grazing in the foreground
2. 'Nannau Cynwch'- one of the home-grown Welsh Black bulls
3. Brigadier braving the elements, 20th January
4. 'Water carrying'-Tom and the Brigadier, 20th January
5. 'Farm Tea at Boetheuog', 26th May
6. Tom and Evan loading silage on the cart under the Brigadier's ever watchful eye, 4th February
7. Lime spreading in the Deer Park,1st May
8. Hughie and the Brigadier inspecting the burst water main at Nannau Home Farm

was imminent. Tragically, whilst driving his
Land Rover from Nannau, Hilary struck a bus
and the Brigadier suffered very serious head
injuries. Whilst in hospital his son-in-law,
David Muirhead, acted with power of
attorney, thus continuing the sale process on
the Brigadier's behalf.

After many weeks in Walton Hospital,
Liverpool, Hilary returned home but spent the
rest of his life as an invalid. The injury had

taken its toll, and on the 28th March 1976 the
indomitable warrior passed away at
Maesybrynner.

A worthy tribute to Hilary in a local newspaper
stated:

> In 1956 he inherited from his cousin
> General John Vaughan the historic
> Nannau Estate at Dolgellau and with the
> same energy and determination that

JOHN D. WOOD

*By Direction of Brigadier C. H. V. Vaughan D.S.O. and of
Mrs. David Muirhead*

SNOWDONIA NATIONAL PARK

Dolgellau 2 miles, Barmouth 12 miles, Shrewsbury 54 miles.

**THE HISTORIC NANNAU AND DOLRHYD ESTATE
DOLGELLAU—GWYNEDD**

Nannau Home Farm of 2,112 ACRES comprising **A Balanced and
Viable Farming Unit** with 7 modernised cottages (2 let),
impressive range of modern stock buildings, 130 acres of dedicated
woodlands and including the noted Precipice Walk.

**Maesybryner House uniquely sited with panoramic views to
Cader Idris.** Lounge hall, 4 reception rooms, 7 bedrooms,
3 bathrooms. Farmbuildings and 38 Acres with Planning Consent
for an agricultural cottage.

**Six Lots of Accommodation-Land, from 1 ACRE to 69 ACRES.
7 Cottages and 3 Historic Lodges for Modernisation.
Penresgynfa Chapel Cottage, with Planning Consent for
Residential Conversion**

All the above with **Vacant Possession** (except for 2 Cottages)

LAKE OF 6 ACRES WITH LAND—17½ ACRES

**Also 5 Let Farms from 23 ACRES to 520 ACRES and 7
Cottages (2 with early possession)**

The let portions producing **£1,402 per annum** (capable of improvement)

The whole extending to about **3,578 ACRES.**
of which the lower ground and woodlands provided a noted
Pheasant Shoot in the inter-war-years

**FREEHOLD FOR SALE PRIVATELY AS A WHOLE OR
IN 34 LOTS OR BY AUCTION LATER AT A DATE TO
BE ANNOUNCED**

Joint Agents:
JOHN D. WOOD & Co., 23 Berkeley Square Office. Tel: 01-629 9050
and
MORRIS MARSHALL & POOLE, Newtown, Powys. Tel: Newtown
26160 25900

By direction of Brigadier C. H. V. Vaughan, D.S.O., and of Mrs. David Muirhead

Bydd yn bleser gan Morris Marshall a Poole

ymdrin ag ymholiadau a thrafodaethau yn yr iaith Gymraeg

Snowdonia National Park

The Historic Nannau and Dolrhyd Estate

DOLGELLAU
GWYNEDD

3578 Acres

FOR SALE - 1975

JOHN D. WOOD & CO.   MORRIS MARSHALL & POOLE

farm at 5.30 every morning and rarely indeed did he spend a day away from his beloved Merioneth hills. He had a great interest in people, real people, and he had an intense concern for their welfare and problems, loathing all humbug and pretention.

As he was loved by those who served with him in the war so he gained the affection and loyalty of his employees and tenants, and they will never forget 'the Brig' as he was universally and affectionately known.

He had indeed worked tirelessly to make a success of the estates and had hoped for their survival for future generations, but considering all the factors militating against this objective, it became an impossible task.

In later years he was asked how he would like to be remembered, as a soldier or as a farmer? His reply gave the questioner the strong impression that his second career had given him the greater satisfaction!

marked his military career. He worked tirelessly to re-furbish and improve the farm and estate and to create the fine herd of Welsh Black Cattle of which he was so proud. At an age when most men would have retired he was around the

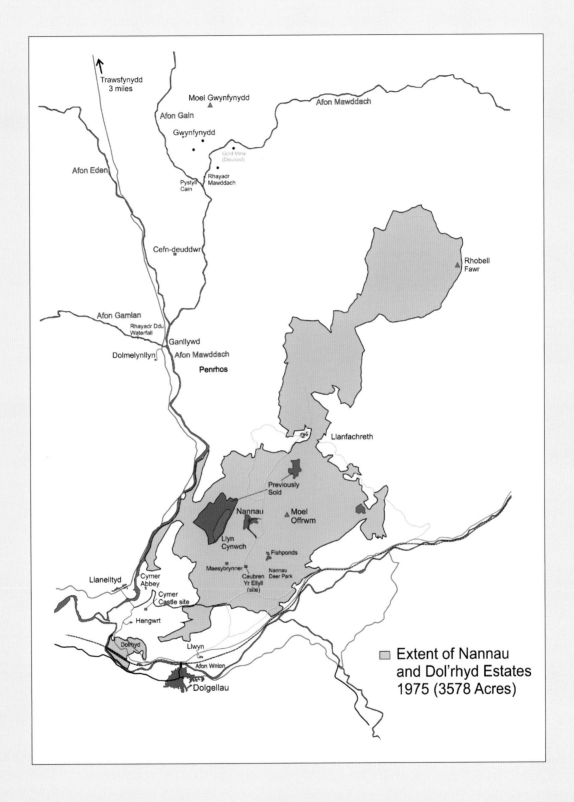

Trawsfynydd
3 miles

Moel Gwynfynydd

Afon Gain

Afon Mawddach

Gwynfynydd

Afon Eden

Gold Mine
(Disused)

Pystyll
Cain

Rhayadr
Mawddach

Cefn-deuddwr

Rhobell
Fawr

Afon Gamlan

Rhayadr Ddu
Waterfall

Ganllywd

Dolmelynllyn

Afon Mawddach

Penrhos

Llanfachreth

Previously
Sold

Nannau

Moel
Offrwm

Llyn
Cynwch

Fishponds

Maesybrynner

Ceubren
Yr Ellyll
(site)

Nannau
Deer Park

Llanelltyd

Cymer
Abbey

Cymer
Castle site

Hengwrt

Dol'rhyd

Llwyn

Afon Wnion

Dolgellau

■ Extent of Nannau
and Dol'rhyd Estates
1975 (3578 Acres)

354. Brigadier C.H.V. VAUGHAN of NANNAU

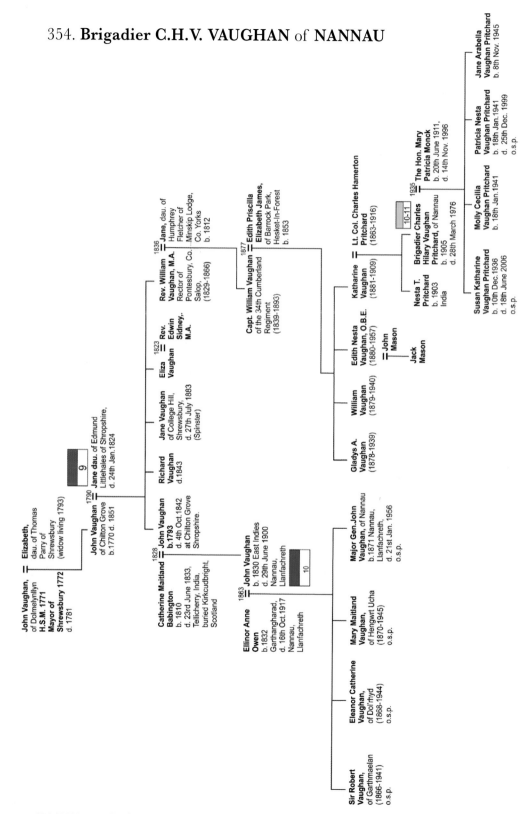

John Vaughan,
of Dolmelynllyn
H.S.M. 1771
Mayor of
Shrewsbury 1772
d. 1781

= Elizabeth,
dau. of Thomas
Parry of
Shrewsbury
(widow living 1793)

1790
John Vaughan
of Chilton Grove
b.1770 d. 1851

= Jane dau. of Edmund
Littlehales of Shropshire,
d. 24th Jan.1824

9

Richard
Vaughan
d.1843

Jane Vaughan
of College Hill,
Shrewsbury,
d. 27th July 1883
(Spinster)

1823
Eliza
Vaughan

= Rev.
Edwin
Sidney,
M.A.

1836
Rev. William
Vaughan, M.A.
Rector of
Pontesbury, Co.
Salop,
(1829-1866)

= Jane, dau. of
Humphrey
Fletcher of
Minskip Lodge,
Co. Yorks
b. 1812

1828
Catherine Maitland
Babington
b. 1810
d. 23rd June 1833,
Tellicherry, India,
buried Kirkcudbright,
Scotland

= John Vaughan
b.1793
d. 4th Oct.1842
at Chilton Grove
Shropshire.

1877
Capt. William Vaughan
of the 34th Cumberland
Regiment
(1839-1893)

= Edith Priscilla
Elizabeth James,
of Barrock Park,
Hesket-In-Forest
b. 1853

1863
Ellinor Anne
Owen
b.1832
Garthangharad,
d. 16th Oct.1917
Nannau,
Llanfachreth

= John Vaughan

10

Gladys A.
Vaughan
(1878-1939)

William
Vaughan
(1879-1940)

Edith Nesta
Vaughan, O.B.E.
(1880-1957)

= John
Mason

Jack
Mason

Katharine
Vaughan
(1881-1909)

= Lt. Col. Charles Hamerton
Pritchard
(1863-1916)

Nesta T.
Pritchard
b. 1903
India

Brigadier Charles
Hilary Vaughan
Pritchard, of Nannau
b. 1905
d. 28th March 1976

10-11

The Hon. Mary
Patricia Monck
b. 20th June 1911,
d. 14th Nov. 1996

1935

Susan Katharine
Vaughan Pritchard
b. 10th Dec. 1936
d. 18th June 2006
o.s.p.

Molly Cecilia
Vaughan Pritchard
b. 18th Jan.1941

Patricia Nesta
Vaughan Pritchard
b. 18th Jan.1941
d. 25th Dec. 1999
o.s.p.

Jane Arabella
Vaughan Pritchard
b. 8th Nov. 1945

Mary Maitland
Vaughan,
of Hengwrt Ucha
(1870-1945)
o.s.p.

Major Gen.John
Vaughan, of Nannau
b.1871 Nannau,
Llanfachreth,
d. 21st Jan. 1956
o.s.p.

Eleanor Catherine
Vaughan,
of Doll'rhyd
(1868-1944)
o.s.p.

Sir Robert
Vaughan,
of Garthmaelan
(1866-1941)
o.s.p.

In the closing words of the newspaper tribute:

Whatever the verdict of history on Brigadier Vaughan, the soldier, the farmer, those who knew him and had the privilege of working with him will always remember with gratitude, respect and affection – the man.

In less than a year, Hilary's son-in-law, David Muirhead, died at his home in Northampton at the young age of 43. David had agreed to help his father-in-law with the estates, and from the day of the Brigadier's accident in August 1975, he had taken over entirely. Travelling weekly from Northamptonshire to Nannau, he acted for the family until the sale was completed. He was buried alongside his father-in-law in Llanfachreth Churchyard on Friday 9th December 1977. David's widow, Mrs Susan Muirhead, continued to live at the family home in Northamptonshire, and built up a thriving equine establishment.

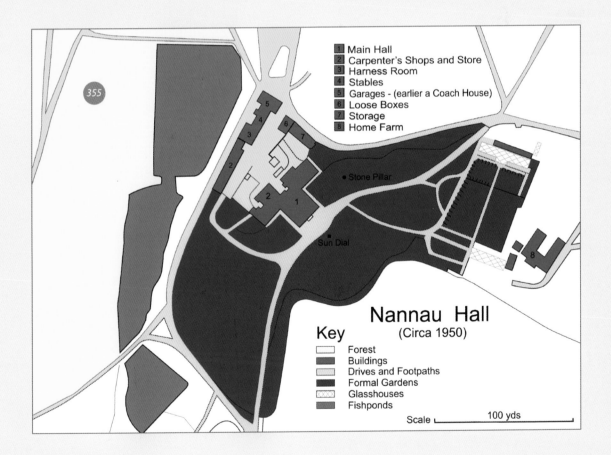

1 Main Hall
2 Carpenter's Shops and Store
3 Harness Room
4 Stables
5 Garages - (earlier a Coach House)
6 Loose Boxes
7 Storage
8 Home Farm

Stone Pillar

Sun Dial

Nannau Hall
(Circa 1950)

Key

Forest
Buildings
Drives and Footpaths
Formal Gardens
Glasshouses
Fishponds

Scale   100 yds

356. *top left:* **Maesyneuadd, near Harlech, initially the principal home of the Wynn family and latterly the Nanney-Wynns**

357. *bottom left:* **Llwyn Hall, Dolgellau, the seat of the Nanney Williams family for over two centuries**

358. *right:* **Detail of a carved heraldic lion found on a Llwyn Hall chair**

12

1579-1941

CADET BRANCHES

Since the introduction of primogeniture the fate of the younger sons of the gentry had been sealed. They were often obliged to seek employment in either the Church, legal profession or the army. Some even resolved to follow a career in trade and commerce.

The more fortunate younger sons married heiresses and set up estates of their own, becoming well-respected leaders in their communities, often maintaining close links with the senior branch, united by a strong kindred solidarity and pride in their ancestry.

The evolution of Nannau's cadet branches' rise to prominence aptly demonstrates how skilfully they capitalised on many fortuitous marriages on their journey up the social ladder. Whilst many sons pursued a career in the Church, one branch developed into a legal dynasty and subsequently diversified by becoming prominent landowners in their own right.

The two main cadet branches of Nannau are represented by the Nanneys of Cefndeuddwr and the Nanneys of Maesypandy, the latter branch becoming sub-divided into the Nanneys of Maesypandy and the Nanneys of Llwyn in the early 18th century.

NANNEYS OF MAESYPANDY

The head of the Maesypandy cadet branch was Edward Nanney, one of the younger sons of

359. *above:* **Cefndeuddwr, Trawsfynydd - once the home of an ancient cadet branch of Nanneys**

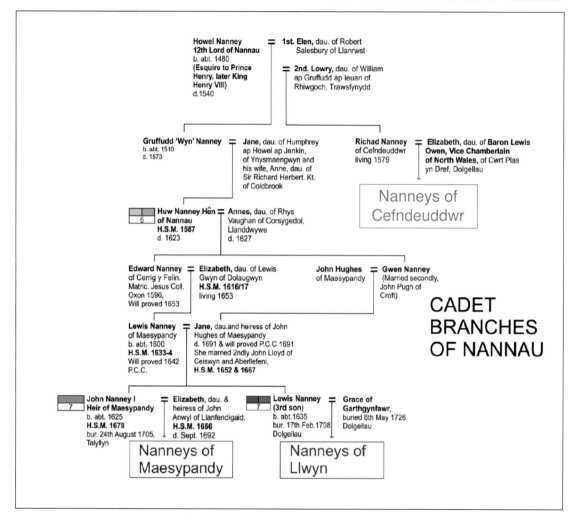

Huw Nanney Hên. Following in the footsteps of his two older brothers, Gruffudd and Richard, he matriculated Jesus College, Oxford, on the 12th November 1596, aged 18.

On returning home after completing his studies at Oxford, Edward was immediately drawn into the increasingly bitter Nannau/Llwyn feud. By 1599, he found himself in the 'thick of the action' whilst playing bowls on the Green at Dolgellau, with the Nannau servant Edward ap David,

upon the last daie of the Faier in dolgelley towne, being midsomer daie.

(Nannau MS 1169)

Members of the Owen faction burst on the scene and brutally murdered the Nannau retainer.

In 1603, in less distressing times, Edward Nanney wrote a jovial letter home from Chancery Lane to his brother Gruffudd,

361. left: **Maesypandy farmhouse, Talyllyn** (2014)
362. below: **Plan of Maesypandy**, circa 1900

recounting all the latest gossip of the day from the scandals of the Court of King James I, stating that:

soe many fleminge ladies dayly in curt (court) commencing now affares out of all reason more than you have in Merionith Shire.

He went on to discuss the political news of the time, *'the great love betwixt us and Spain,'* the defeat of the Spaniards by the Dutch and the increasing rift between England and France. A later passage revealed his motive for visiting London, in that he was in search of a patron at Court. His father, Huw Nanney Hên, had found a patron in Sir James Croft, Lord Deputy of Ireland and Controller of the Royal Household under Elizabeth, and had no doubt instilled in his son the need to foster such beneficial connections. Such 'allies' would become a lifeline to the Nanneys as the full repercussions of the Llwyn/Nannau feud played out in the coming years.

Edward's diligence in the pursuit of a patron was rewarded, as he was later found to be in the

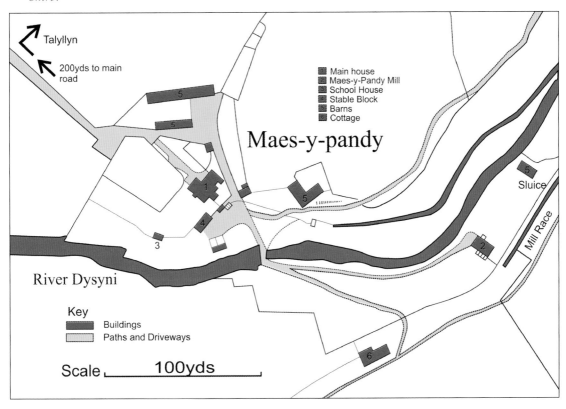

service of the Lord President of Wales, Lord Zouch, and on course to establishing a network of well-connected associates.

By 1606, Huw Nanney Hên was languishing in the Fleet Prison and Edward himself had been committed to jail with five of the Nannau retinue for their part in the Dolgellau Church riots. The relatively inexperienced Gruffudd Nanney was left to fight the Owens' now relentless litigations.

In less than three years Gruffudd, the son and heir of Nannau, was dead and Huw Nanney Hên, after release from prison, was still feverishly pursuing his adversaries through the courts.

Edward in the meantime had settled down to a more peaceful existence, marrying Elizabeth, a daughter of Lewis Gwyn of Dolaugwyn near Tywyn, a well-established local gentry family. Lewis Gwyn, the High Sheriff of Merioneth in 1617, had married twice; his second wife had been Jane, one of Huw Nanney Hên's daughters. Edward and Elizabeth took up residence at Cerrig y Felin, Llanfihangel y Pennant.

Edward and Elizabeth's union produced six children, four boys and two girls. The eldest son and heir Lewis Nanney (born about 1600) married Jane, the daughter and heiress of John Hughes of Maesypandy, a powerful local gentry family with a considerable landed estate.

The Maesypandy estate would be held by Lewis Nanney's descendants for the next three hundred years, merging with other estates through marriages.

Maesypandy is situated in the parish of Talyllyn. Although now a much-reduced farmhouse, it was in its hey-day in the 18th century an imposing mansion with a substantial collection of ancillary buildings.

Through the eyes of an 18th century traveller, John Jackson, we can glimpse a sight of the remnants of old Maesypandy. His account states:

> *This family mansion wears an antique garb; presenting its irregular front through a short avenue of beech and fir, the hall*

wainscoted, in small panels, with native oak embrowned by time, exhibiting at the lower end its buttery hatch, over which was served the cakes and good things to the regaling feasters. A large window looks into a walled garden, darkened with clipped holly and figured yew trees.

The building is roomy, but the apartments rather awkwardly connected, having been erected at different periods, and the fixtures and furnishings, both in fashion and look, wear the features of age...

Later he describes its setting in a vale with enormous hills encircling the mansion:

... the hills are indeed so high and so perpendicular that, sitting in one of the rooms at Maesypandy, I was obliged to stoop very low to see the horizon on either side through the window. A pleasant walk along a footpath from the house to the church and the village of Talyllyn, distant half a mile up some inclosures... brings us to a beautiful sheet of water.

(*Journal of the Merioneth Historical Society*, 1967, Letters from and relating to North Wales)

The Maesypandy we see today is a 19th-century three-bay stone farmhouse with an older rear wing. Its much reduced stature displays little of its ancient origins, but its setting is still recognisable from Jackson's vivid account, being approached through an avenue of trees. An interesting architectural relic survives on the front lawn in the form of a small two-storey hipped structure, dated 1743, the upper floor being once used as a schoolroom. This unique remnant is clearly identifiable on a surviving 1790 estate survey map. Maesypandy (or Meadow of the Fulling Mill) first appeared on the historical record as a fulling mill as early as 1545, making it one of the earliest recorded in the county. It is also acknowledged as the seat of the Hughes family stretching back to Einion Sais and Caradog Freichfras (Caradog Strong Arm), the legendary 6th-century King of Gwent. Records exist of the visitation of Lewis Dwnn, the Deputy Herald, to Maesypandy in 1588, when Rhys Hughes, late sheriff of the county, paid Dwnn ten shillings for his labour in making the family tree and verified his right to bear the arms of Caradog.

Of Lewis Nanney, High Sheriff of Merioneth 1634, little is known, with the exception of a few poetic tributes. In Sion Cain's estimation, Lewis

was godly, wise and contented in his public offices ... he protected the weak and dispensed justice with probity.

Lewis died about 1642 aged about 40, leaving nine children and a young widow. The eldest son John Nanney I (born about 1625) was the heir. The third son, Lewis Nanney (born about 1635) went on to found the Llwyn dynasty of Nanneys, who rose in prominence throughout the 18th and 19th centuries, building an estate founded on the proceeds of legal practices, supplemented by the occasional 'prudent' marriage.

NANNEYS OF LLWYN

When Lewis Nanney of Maesypandy died in 1642, he predeceased his father Edward who died circa 1653. Lewis's widow Jane married secondly John Lloyd of Ceiswyn, an eminent attorney from a nearby estate. Lewis's son and

364. Nanneys of Llwyn, Dolgellau

Lewis Nanney
(3rd son of Lewis
Nanney of Maesypandy)
b. abt. 1635
buried 17th Feb. 1708,
Dolgellau

c. 1675 ═ **Grace of
Garthgynfawr,**
buried 6th May 1726,
Dolgellau

Robert Nanney
c. 18th Dec. 1679
Attorney at Law,
of Llwyn, Dolgellau
buried 29th Nov. 1751
(aged 71) Dolgellau

1712 ═ **Mary,** grand-daughter
and heiress
of Edward Wynne, of
Llangower
She was buried 10th August
1723, Dolgellau

Justice Lewis Nanney
of Llwyn, Dolgellau,
c. 29th Dec. 1716,
Attorney at Law,
**J.P. 1758, Deputy. Lt. 1762,
& H.S.M. 1775-6**
buried 7th September 1779,
Dolgellau

1745 ═ **Anne,** dau. of
Nicodemus Jones,
of Dolgellau and
grand-daughter of Lewis Owen,
of Erwgoed and Weenfach,
buried 25th Dec. 1787,
Dolgellau

Rev. Robert Nanney
of Llwyn, Dolgellau
c. 22nd March 1746
Matric. Jesus Coll. Oxon.
10th April 1764 (aged 18)
Rector of Llanfwrog
Co. Denbigh 1766-91,
Vicar of Llanymawddwy
Co. Mer. 1792-1818,
d. 5th Dec. 1818, buried
St. George's, Hanover Sq.
London

1773 ═ **Jane,** dau. of
Thomas Meredith, a younger
son of Monachdy Gwyn,
Clynnog, and Mary, his wife
of Hendre Eirian, Ardudwy
c. 25th August 1749
Sole heiress of the Hendre Eirian estate,
Llanaber, Co. Mer.
buried 10th Nov. 1784,
Llanaber

Rev. Hugh Nanney M.A.
of Hall Meadows,
Haltwhistle,
Northumberland,
c. 25th May 1747 Dolgellau.
Matric. Jesus Coll. Oxon.
B.A 1767, M.A. 1772,
Vicar of Mitford & Haltwhistle,
buried at Haltwhistle
1st July 1809

1775 ═ **Barbara,** dau. of
Thomas Middleton,
of River Green,
(4th son of Sir John
Middleton 2nd Bart.
of Belsay Castle,
Co. Northumberland)
bur. 11th May 1823

**Capt. Lewis
Nanney**
b. 1748 Dolgellau,
bur. 10th Feb. 1798
Will proved May
1798, P.C.C.

Mary Nanney
c. 26th Oct. 1749,
bur. 26th Dec. 1751
(Infant Death)

William Nanney
c. 19th Mar. 1757
(Mercer)
bur. 24th Sept. 1783,
Dolgellau
Will proved 25th June
1785, P.C.C.

Mary Nanney
b. 1774 Eastbourne,
Sussex
(Heiress of Llwyn and
Hendre Eirian estates)
d. 1st Dec. 1854
(aged 80)
buried Dolgellau

1805 ═ **Thomas Hartley J. P.**
of Llwyn,
c. 1778 Llangelynin,
Co. Mer.
St. John's Coll. Camb. 1796,
H.S.M. 1827, D.L. Co. Mer.
d. 28th Aug. 1850 (aged 71)
buried Dolgellau

Lieut. Lewis Nanney R.N.
c. 6th March 1778, Llanfwrog
(Blundells School, Tiverton
15th Oct. 1792, aged 13)
d. 1817, Belgium

Jane Nanney
b. 1781
d. Feb. 1833,
Aberystwyth, Co. Cards.
(Aged 52)

**Jane Nanney
Hartley**
b. 1807
d. June 1813
(Aged 6)

Anne Hartley
of Llwyn,
b. 10th Oct. 1809,
Dolgellau
d. 24th Feb. 1886
(Spinster)
buried Dolgellau

Griffith Williams
of Llwyn,
c. 21st July 1810,
Dolgellau
B.A. Jesus Coll. Oxon.
1829, Attorney at Law,
bur. 15th June 1860
Dolgellau

1835 ═ **Mary Nanney Hartley**
Heiress of Llwyn,
b. 1812 Dolgellau
d. 16th Jan. 1859,
bur. Dolgellau

Robert Nanney Hartley J.P.
of Llwyn,
c. 4th Feb. 1814, Dolgellau
Matric. St. John's Coll.
Camb. 1836,
Commissioner of the
Turnpike Trust,
d.s.p. 1860, Dolgellau

**Jane Elizabeth
Hartley**
c. 5th Oct. 1815
d. April 1819
(Aged 4)

**Thomas
Meredith
Hartley**
b. 1821
d.s.p. 1847
(Aged 26)

**Margaret
Williams**
b. 1835
Dolgellau,
d. 1919

1869 ═ **Rev. Lewis
Jones**
Queen's Coll.
Camb.
Minor Cannon of
Bangor Cathedral,
d. 1899

**Thomas Humphrey
Williams** of Llwyn
c. 30th July 1836,
Dolgellau,
B.A. Jesus Coll. Oxon.
1856,
d.s.p. 18th March 1891

1869 ═ **Sarah
Watkins**
of Teignmouth,
Devon
d.s.p. 25th Feb. 1897
at Tywyn (aged 72)
bur. Dolgellau

**Robert Nanney
Williams** of Llwyn
c. 10th July 1840
Dolgellau,
d. 2nd April 1896
at Llwyn, aged 56,
bur. Dolgellau

1872 ═ **Elizabeth
Miles**
b. 1843
Dolgellau,
d. 1908
Dolgellau

**Jane
Elizabeth
Williams**
b. 1838
d. 1844
(Aged 6)

**Laura Anne
Williams**
b. 1842
d.s.p. 1924,
bur. Llangollen

**Mary
Meredith
Williams**
b. 1845
d. 1846
(Infant death)

**Dr. Meyrick Meredith
Williams, G.P.**
b. 1847, Dolgellau,
d.s.p. 9th Feb. 1940,
Dalbeattie, Scotland

**Ludovic Nanney
Williams** of Llwyn
b. 1874, Dolgellau
(Coming of age
celebration,
23rd August 1895,
Dolgellau)
d. 22nd June 1947,
buried Llanelltyd

1899 ═ **Mary Emily
Maud,** dau. of
William Simms Bull,
Dep. Mayor of Cheltenham,
Grand dau. of William Adams
of Greenfield Hall, Tunstall,
(Master Potter)
d. 1954
Birmingham,
buried Llanelltyd

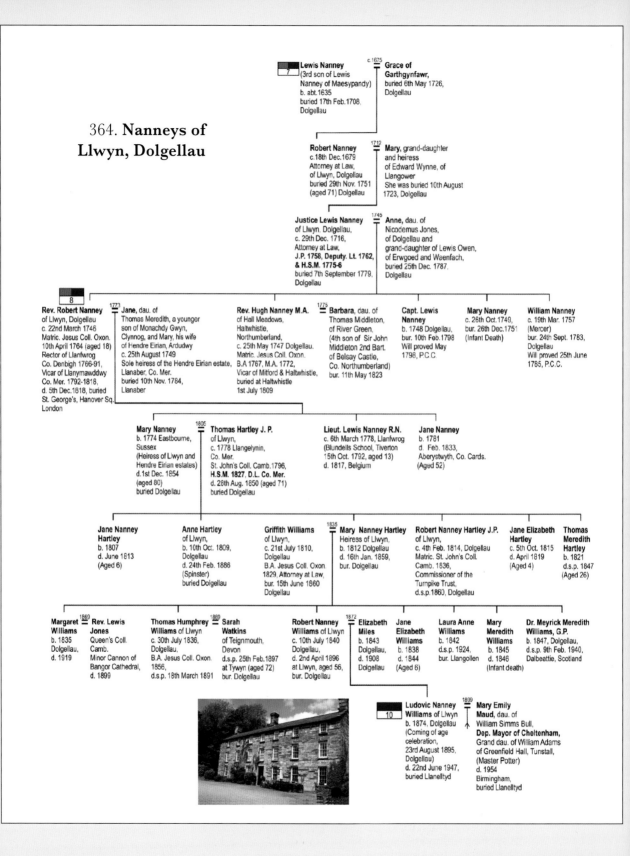

365. left: *Oval oil painting of Lewis Anwyl, son of William Lewis Anwyl who purchased the Llwyn estate from Richard Ireland in 1619*

366. below: **Lead armorial plaque in Dolgellau Church to Lewis Nanney, son of Lewis Nanney of Maesypandy**

income of his inherited property. In the 1662 Hearth Tax record, a Mr Nanney is referred to as 'living in Garthgynfawr with six hearths' (a substantial house); this is most probably our Lewis Nanney.

Archival records show Lewis involving himself with many deeds and documents, possibly alluding to a budding career in law. It is not surprising therefore to see Lewis and Grace's only surviving child, Robert Nanney, emerge as a prominent Merioneth attorney in the early part of the 18th century.

When Lewis Nanney died in Dolgellau in 1708, his son Robert erected an impressive heraldic lead plaque to his father in Dolgellau Church, situated on the south side of the Chancel.

heir John Nanney I, having married the heiress of Llanfendigaid, took up residence there, whilst Lewis's widow continued the occupancy of her family seat at Maesypandy during her lifetime.

The probate of Lewis's will was granted on the 5th December 1642, in which he made his widow Jane Nanney his sole executrix. All of Lewis's children were well provided for, but it is the bequest to his third son, Lewis Nanney junior, that concerns us at this stage, in that he received:

> *full and singular those messuages and heriditaments commonly known by the several names, 'Hendre Wallog' and 'Foel Crug' together with several parcels of lands called and known by the names of 'Tyddyn Nant Hir' and 'Bryn yr Wadda' all in the township of Maestrevnant in the Parish of Llanfihangel y Pennant.*

Lewis Nanney junior married Grace of Garthgynfawr and took up residence in the Dolgellau area, living comfortably off the

LUDOVIC: NANNEY gen: SEPULT: FUIT 17°FEB: A:D:1708

Robert Nanney had close family connections to many of the powerful legal families of the area, such as the Anwyls of Parc, the Lloyds of Ceiswyn and the Wynnes of Llangower, all legal dynasties with large family estates. It was a period when law was regarded as the gentry's main profession and successful attorneys capitalised on their professional careers.

The Anwyls had built up a large estate of some 15,000 acres and were an ancient family, directly descended from Owain Gwynedd through the families of Ystumcegid, Rhiwaedog and Clenenney. During the 17th century, the Anwyls purchased much additional land, and in 1619 they purchased the Llwyn estate in Dolgellau

of Parc or the Lloyds of Ceiswyn, two of the most prominent legal families in North Wales at the time.

Through the diaries of Thomas Kelsale, a Quaker residing in Dolgun Isaf near Dolgellau in the 1730s, it is revealing to note that Robert Nanney, together with another prominent attorney, Edward Owen of Garthangharad, worked regularly for the Quaker Movement. Both attorneys travelled the country on the Quakers' behalf, professionally handling their legal work.

Robert Nanney had inherited his father's property in 1708 and supplemented this with

from Richard Ireland, son of a Shropshire landowning family who had married the heiress of Llwyn. The Llwyn would become one of the Anwyl's main family homes for most of the 17th century.

It is likely that Robert Nanney acquired his legal skills through working with either the Anwyls

other purchases, building up a nucleus of a small estate in the early part of the 18th century. On the 3rd of July 1712 he married Mary, a daughter of Howel Wynne of Plas Newydd, Llangower, near Bala. Mary was an heiress of her grandfather, Edward Wynne of Llangower, by his will proved on the 1st August 1689. Robert's marriage to Mary added some 1,500 acres of

land in Llanuwchllyn, along with a number of dwellings and public houses in Bala, to his already sizeable landholding.

The union of Robert and Mary produced three offspring:

Margaret, baptised on 21st May 1715, Lewis, on 29th December 1716, and Mary, on 6th October 1718.

Sadly both daughters died in their infancy, leaving Lewis Nanney as an only child. His mother Mary died when Lewis was only seven years of age in 1723, and although his father was relatively young, he never remarried.

Lewis was most probably born at Llwyn, Dolgellau, as his father Robert had taken up residence there. The earliest reference to Robert living at the Llwyn occurs in a Quarter Session record of 1716, when Robert Nanney of Llwyn, together with fellow Justices of the Peace, discuss the urgently needed rebuild of the Dolgellau Church which had been costed at upwards of £1,449.

Although initially renting the Llwyn from the Anwyls, it would appear to be the beginnings of the Nanney's occupation of this ancient edifice, a tenure that would extend to two and a quarter centuries.

Robert Nanney, Attorney-at-Law of the Llwyn, died at the age of 71 years in 1751, passing on a substantial estate to his only son Lewis, by this time comprising nearly 6,000 acres and a large number of houses in Dolgellau and Bala, and a rent role of £2,000 a year.

Lewis Nanney erected a marble monument to his parents in Dolgellau Church, alongside his grandfather's armorial plaque, which noted:

Underneath lyeth the Body of Robt Nanney, late of Llwyn in this Parish, Attorney at Law who dy'd the 26th day of November 1751 aged 71. During the course of his practice he acted with more than common lenity uprightness and integrity, as his sweetness of temper and humanity made him beloved and respected by all his acquaintance, so his death was much lamented; in gratitude to the memory of one of the best Fathers Lewis Nanney of Llwyn Esq, his only Son by Mary Wynne daughter of Howel Wynne late of Llangower Esq deceased, caused this Monument to be erected. Underneath also lyeth the body of Mary Nanney daughter of the said Lewis Nanney by Anne his Wife who dyed the 8th of May 1751 aged one.

JUSTICE LEWIS NANNEY OF LLWYN

Justice Lewis Nanney undoubtedly worked with his attorney father building up their legal practice, although it is clear that Lewis's preoccupation was focussed on running the family's expanding estate. In 1748, Lewis Nanney

369. **Dolgellau Great Bridge** *circa 1800*

Underneath lie the Remains of
LEWIS NANNEY of Llwyn Esq.
One of his Majesty's Justices
Of the Peace for this County;
Who, having lived much respected
And belov'd, died sincerely regreted,
By his Family and Neighbours
In particular. His Acquaintance
And the Publick in general,
On the 27. of Aug 1779, aged 65
This Monument, small Tribute
Of her Esteem, was erected by
Order of his Mournful Widow
ANN NANNEY.

purchased the Llwyn from the Anwyl heiress, Lady Anne Prendergast and her husband Sir Thomas. The Anwyl estate had devolved to the Prendergasts and was, through prolonged litigation, heavily encumbered by this time. As a result the Prendergasts were eagerly seeking buyers for their Merioneth lands. Lewis Nanney, being closely connected to the family, was well-placed to expand his portfolio and avail himself of the Anwyl estate lands in Mawddwy, adding another 15 farms to the Llwyn estate. Although a successful attorney, Robert Nanney had not the entrepreneurial drive of his son, being a very benevolent soul. He was willing to assist family members financially with loans and advances, leaving his son to ultimately recoup loans and mortgages, some advanced decades previously.

Well established in his family seat at Llwyn, Lewis Nanney enthusiastically took on the role of Justice of the Peace in 1760 and became, over his 19-year tenure, one of Merioneth's most active Justices, his legal background greatly assisting his work on the bench.

Through the surviving pages of Elizabeth Baker's diaries we get fleeting glimpses of the social life of Dolgellau in the latter part of the 18th century, with Lewis Nanney regularly appearing in her colourful entries, referred to as either 'Justice Nanney' or simply 'Mr Nanney'. Her entries portray Justice Nanney as an upright public figure, well respected in his locality.

In May 1779, at the height of Hugh Vaughan's financial troubles, Dolgellau was in turmoil, with huge uncertainty in the area created by the imminent sale of the Hengwrt estate. The population of the town, many of them Hengwrt tenants, showed great resentment towards

Robert Lloyd (who was attempting to foreclose on Hugh Vaughan) as such an action would directly threaten their livelihoods. When Robert Lloyd's agent, an individual named Lever, made an appearance in the town he was mercilessly stoned by the populace. An entry in Elizabeth Baker's diary informs us that:

> *Mr Nanney voluntarily took him under his protection, yet the Justice's dignity and oratory could not prevent the whizzing of a stone passing his nose and striking Lever's neck. Mr Nanney held the bridle as Lever rode along through the crowd.*

Justice Nanney would have been acutely aware of the growing public disquiet in the town. Previously an enraged group of townspeople had burned an effigy of Lever's wife and there was a strong possibility that riots would break out. In his role as Justice of the Peace, Lewis Nanney would have been expected to maintain public order. The upright Justice, not shirking from his duties, intervened. Whether or not this

371. above: **Llanfwrog Church near Ruthin, a living once held by Rev. Robert Nanney of Llwyn**

disturbing event affected the Justice is not known, but tellingly, by July 22nd 1779 Elizabeth Baker noted that he had been taken seriously ill, and on Friday 27th August she added that Justice Nanney

died this morning about 2 o'clock, a better husband or parent he has not left behind him, or neighbour...

He was buried on the following Tuesday 31st September in Dolgellau churchyard. Elizabeth Baker noted that although the Assizes were being held on the same day,

There were more gentlemen at Mr Nanney's funeral than at the Assize.

He left behind a widow and four sons: Rev. Robert Nanney, eldest son and heir; Rev. Hugh Nanney; Captain Lewis Nanney; and youngest son William. Robert and Hugh had matriculated

Jesus College, Oxford - Robert in 1764 and Hugh in 1765.

REVEREND **ROBERT NANNEY**

Rev. Robert Nanney had married Jane, the daughter and heiress of Thomas and Mary Meredith of the Hendre Eirian estate near Barmouth, in 1773. They took up residence in Hengwrt, which he rented from the lawyer Robert Lloyd, much to the consternation of Elizabeth Baker whose hatred of Lloyd was clearly evident. At one stage in her diaries she categorically vowed never to accept an invitation from Robert Nanney to dine at Hengwrt whilst it was in the hands of the 'usurper Lloyd'!

Robert Nanney began his ecclesiastical career as rector of Llanfwrog Church in Denbighshire in 1776. He held this post until 1792 when, at the behest of the Bishop of St. Asaph, he was given an ultimatum: 'Take up residence in Llanfwrog

372. above: **Haltwhistle Church in Northumberland, where Rev. Hugh Nanney was vicar from 1782-1809**

or be allocated the living of Llanymawddwy Church in Merioneth'- a much poorer living. Unwilling to take up residence in Llanfwrog, he was reluctantly forced to accept the bishop's decree. His brother Rev. Hugh Nanney's clerical career was a great deal more successful, being the vicar of Mitford and Haltwhistle in Northumberland from 1772 until his death in 1809. Rev. Hugh Nanney had married well, taking for his wife Barbara, a daughter of Thomas Middleton of River Green, Northumberland (a son of the powerful Middletons of Belsay Castle).

Rev. Robert Nanney appears regularly on the pages of the outspoken diarist Elizabeth Baker. Initially she portrays him in somewhat glowing terms, but as the diary unfolds she is often less

than complementary to Robert who interestingly is never referred to as Reverend, but simply Robert or Bob Nanney.

Ever the gossip, Elizabeth Baker noted in September of 1779 that the town was buzzing with news of Justice Nanney's will, which she stated

> *is unfavourable to his eldest son and should he die before the Dowager* (Justice's widow – Anne) *more so to Mrs Robert Nanney.*

Justice Nanney had left the entire estate to his wife Anne for her lifetime, and henceforth to his son and heir Rev. Robert Nanney, clearly a controversial decision but one indicating the

Justice's obvious reservation in placing the estate in the hands of his eldest son. His reservations would prove well-founded, as in future years the estate would be shaken to its very core by the actions of this intransigent cleric.

Meanwhile, the Justice's widow was relishing running the family estate and, like her husband before her, worried little about taking radical actions. Elizabeth Baker's first encounter with the cantankerous widow was a rather sullen one, Elizabeth noting that the Nanney Dowager

looked at me as a bull would look at a new gate.

Anne Nanney was a strong-willed individual not afraid to make a stand for what she believed in, regardless of public opinion. Elizabeth Baker thoroughly castigated the widow for employing Lever (the hated agent of Robert Lloyd) to tend the espaliers she had recently purchased from Caernarfon, and was beside herself when she heard that the widow was entertaining Lever in the parlour at Llwyn!

Entertaining Robert Lloyd's agent and bailiff so openly, revealed that the Llwyn family were not taking Hugh Vaughan's side in his battle against his adversaries. Quite the contrary, the Llwyn family, although living on a significant income themselves, were unassuming in their lifestyle and probably frowned upon Hugh Vaughan's wildly extravagant ways, feeling that perhaps he deserved the actions that he precipitated.

Elizabeth Baker had initially come to Merioneth to take up a mining patent, but this had not yielded the anticipated results, leaving her almost devoid of income. She seized the opportunity to become Hugh Vaughan's secretary and was drawn into the financial

mélange that pervaded the area as the crisis developed. Over time she became increasingly dependent on local charity, particularly the charity of the local gentry who regularly invited her to dine at their homes. Surprisingly, by 1784 Elizabeth's diary informs us that she is a regular dinner guest at the home of the widow Nanney of Llwyn!

Many entries recall magnificent meals at the mansion, such as:

Friday, 14th May 1784 - *... turn'd to Llwyn, Mrs Nanney came out to meet me, received me more cordially than the last time I was here, about three years since, ... she then asked me to dine ... the dinner was presently served and an excellent one it proved to be ... tis almost six years that I have not known such a joyous meal ... after the meal a delicious pot of coffee with*

375. above: **Plas Newydd, Eldon Square, Dolgellau, once owned by the Llwyn estate** (postcard circa 1900)

cream from the Alderney cow completed the festivities.

Wednesday 29th September 1784 - ... *Mrs Nanney of Llwyn sent this morning an invitation for my dining with her; accepted it - the curate of the parish, made the fourth at table – the dinner a very good one, and plenty of fruit, plumbs, nuts and peaches and nectarines, which to me is the highest luxury...*

In addition to her fine dining, the Nanney widow was somewhat of a seasoned traveller, as on the 25th June 1784, she set off in the family chaise bound for Northumberland to visit her son the Rev. Hugh Nanney at Haltwhistle. In her absence, the Llwyn had been offered to Robert Howel Vaughan, High Sheriff of the County, as the venue for the Assize Ball which took place on the 11th August that year. Robert Howel Vaughan at this time had taken up residence at Rhûg, near Corwen.

The arrival of the Assizes in Dolgellau was always an occasion for festivities. Tradition dictated that the High Sheriff hosted the main event and on successive nights the gentry, singly or in groups, organised other functions. Tragically, on the 7th November 1784, Rev. Robert Nanney's wife died only a short while after the return of the Nanney widow from Nothumberland. She was interred in Llanaber Church on the 10th November amid very heavy rain. The grieving widower at this point seemed to have taken to drinking heavily, although he was not a moderate drinker prior to this sad event.

Elizabeth Baker's diaries clearly portray the upper classes as carefree, highly privileged individuals, who often drank to excess, and in this respect Rev. Robert Nanney emulated his class. There are many references to his drinking excesses, and she often describes him as 'intolerably drunk'.

On the 21st January 1785, Elizabeth Baker vividly portrayed a typical night of gentry revelry in the house of Mr Thomas Meredith (Rev. Robert Nanney's father-in-law) in Dolgellau:

Last night there was at Mr Thos.
Merediths a Xmas night as they call it
here, and according to custom the company
beastly drunk – then Mr. Anwyl attacked
Robin Owen for pretending to fish from
hence to Barmouth, having no right, it
being Mr. Vaughans; that quarrel ended,
Captain Nanney began one with Mr. Anwyl
for detaining a fowling net of his fathers,
which by the way he had given to my Ld.
Chancellor, but that the Capt. pretended to
be ignorant of, said his mother had
demanded it, and that demand was not
comply'd with. Upon hearing that Mr.
Anwyl told him that his Mother was a
D ... d Liar... Now to refuse this company
the name of Gentlemen would be
unpardonable, but to reconcile their
behaviour with that appellation is
IMPOSSIBLE

It is quite likely that Rev. Robert Nanney and his drinking companions partook of a home-brewed beer from Corsygedol known as 'Caesar's Blood'; it had been highly prized in Hengwrt in the time of Hugh Vaughan, and freely available to these heavy drinkers.

Elizabeth Baker noted in March 1785 that Captain Nanney of the Llwyn had left for Chester in search of a house for his mother and himself. It was with great regret that the widow and son quitted the Llwyn on the 26th June 1785, leaving the son and heir Rev. Robert Nanney to return to the family home from his lodgings at Hengwrt.

Although now comfortably installed at the Llwyn with his young family, Robert Nanney was unable to settle. With a travelling companion called L'Anson, he selfishly embarked on a ten week journey to the Isle of

Man and Ireland, leaving his three young children (Mary aged 11, Lewis 6 and Jane 4) in the charge of servants. In the eyes of Elizabeth Baker and no doubt other inhabitants of Dolgellau it was considered very irresponsible to abandon his vulnerable young family in such circumstances.

Throughout the latter part of the 18th century, despite holding livings in two different parishes, Rev. Robert Nanney continued his itinerant lifestyle, travelling extensively in the south of England. Whilst installing his only son Lewis at Blundell's School in Tiverton, he embarked on a tour of Devon, where a chance meeting with a tallow chandler in Dartmouth set in motion a chain of events that would be catastrophic for the Llwyn estate and the entire family. The unimaginable consequences of this liaison would reverberate throughout the tight-knit community of Dolgellau and beyond.

A certain Captain John Jenkin Jones retold the tragic tale of the Llwyn estate's troubles in his diary of a tour he undertook in 1819:

A Mr Nanney of Llwyn, a quarter of a mile
from Dolgelley, was a Clergyman, but had
not for many years done duty as he lived
on his estate of about £2,000 per annum.
He had one son and two daughters, and the
eldest daughter married a Mr Hartley and
is now living with her husband at
Dolgelley. When travelling in Devonshire
about 20 years ago, at Dartmouth Mr
Nanney fell in with a chandler of the name
of Matthews in very indigent
circumstances, with a wife and several
children. He took the man, as his steward,
and otherwise assisted the whole family. In
a few years this fellow gained such a

perfect ascendancy over his master as to make the house very uncomfortable to young Lewis Nanney, a high spirited boy, and he got his father's permission to enter the Navy, in which he served till the short peace of Amiens. On his return home he found things so unpleasant that he determined on travelling in France, and set off accordingly. When the war broke out, he was among the détenu, and continued in prison until the peace of 1814. When liberated he set off for Wales but at Aberystwyth he by chance fell into a company of men to whom he was unknown, and who were talking of Miss Nanney's insanity and being confined in a mad-house.

Without disclosing himself he learnt this horrid story that Matthews had seduced his sister and when she found herself pregnant they had made the father drunk and put him into his daughter's bed persuading him that he had committed incest; that under this belief Matthews command of him was confirmed, that the daughter was taken to Swansea where she was delivered of a boy, who is now at Wells in Somerset and that her compunction had driven her mad; that she had been many years in a mad-house in London; that on going to see her Matthews had introduced a designing female relation of his to old Nanney who had married her, but soon growing disgusted had parted, but not before she had obtained a settlement of £200 a year.

Horrified as he was the young man had sufficient command of himself to go home and convince himself that all this was too true, the first thing his father did was to refer him to Matthews to know whether his residence in the house for a few weeks would be convenient. Fired with rage, young Nanney on the morning after his return fired his fowling piece at the Steward, which however only grazed his head and knocked the crown of his hat out. The young man supposing it had taken effect, fled the country.

The distraught fugitive fled to Belgium and, from then on, travelled under an assumed name, living off money sent to him by his cousin in Haltwhistle.

LIEUTENANT **LEWIS NANNEY** R.N.

Lewis had joined the Navy in 1793 at the tender age of 15. Entering as an able seaman, he quickly moved up the ranks. Within three weeks he was a midshipman serving on HMS Diadem, under Captain Towry. On the 14th February 1797, he saw action at the Battle of Cape St. Vincent, part of the French revolutionary war, an action that saw the British Naval Fleet crush the enemy, although greatly outnumbered.

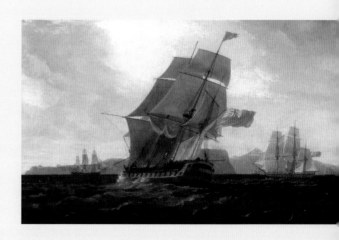

378. above: 'The Battle of St. Vincent' by Richard Brydges Beechey (1808-1895)

By 1800 Lewis, having served for more than six years, sat the Lieutenant's examination, successfully completing the testing course, only to pass out during the short-lived Peace of Amiens. In 1806, however, Lewis was serving aboard HMS Glatton off the Calabrian Coast. Whilst endeavouring to recover Sicilian gunboats that had fallen into enemy hands, he took part in a daring attempt to assist HMS Delight, which had run aground. Lewis and some of his crew were unfortunately captured by the French and were initially imprisoned in Valenciennes in Northern France, to be later moved to Verdun.

Officer captives were on the whole treated well, as opposed to the rank and file who experienced a harsh regime. Lewis Nanney's internment was in many respects rather civilised. Being sent to Verdun, Lewis would have been billeted in reasonable comfort, not incarcerated, but free to move around the town, needing only to report to the authorities once every five days. The British captive community at Verdun were able to set up schools and even had their own racecourse. Officers caught attempting to escape

lost their privileges, and it is reasonable to suppose that Lewis settled down to a fairly leisurely existence, perhaps too leisurely, as records show that he was sent to Arras, a more secure prison for the crime of 'seducing a townsman's wife'!

Whilst imprisoned at Arras, Lewis would have experienced much harsher treatment and, unsurprisingly, in 1807 he made a bid for freedom but sadly was recaptured. Unperturbed, he bided his time and on the 14th August 1809 attempted another breakout. It is very likely that he was apprehended as he only

379. above: A bird's eye view of Verdun in 1638

made a reappearance in Britain at the end of the war in 1814. One can only speculate on the treatment that a double escapee would have been subjected to and the state of his health at the end of his incarceration.

His return to his hometown of Dolgellau after almost a decade of captivity should have been a joyous event; the townspeople certainly celebrated his return in style with great rejoicing for the safe return of the heir of the Llwyn estate. Most of the town illuminated their windows with candles to mark the occasion - such a contrast to the welcome poor Lewis received from his father and the scheming Matthews! Now the bedraggled heir became a fugitive, moving through the shadows, living from hand to mouth.

Rev. Robert Nanney made a number of attempts to contact his fugitive son. One surviving letter

graphically illustrates the plight of poor Lewis and in some ways the hapless and misguided figure that the once proud cleric had become:

Lewis Nanney ... As you gave no answer to my last letter when your draft was returned, I again write to you, for I cannot rest until I know whether you have any plan to proceed on in your present unhappy position to keep yourself safe from the power of the law. I must now tell you that the Judge at the last Bala Assizes about a fortnight ago mentioned to the Grand Jury your case as a most outrageous offence and said that you might be apprehended at any time or place. You can never think of living in Wales with any credit, should you be so fortunate as to make it up with Mr Matthews, nor will you, I am informed be able to receive the rents of the estate when I am no more. After a prosecution commences if you fly from trial, another thing is, will not the Admiralty in such a case, stop your pay? But alas having brought yourself into this horrible situation what is best to be done? I say make it up with Mr Matthews that is the grand point, do it before things are too far-gone. You might by this means and no other have enough to live upon comfortably, nay plenty in France or even England after a few years. If you intend to do this it must be while I am alive as my influence over him, his family and all who can give evidence against you, will induce him to accept terms less heavy than can be expected to be done hereafter.

Parson Thomas called here lately, all desirous that some negotiation might be set on foot – this affair has nearly sunk me to the grave, as all my hopes are now blasted of you ever coming to your inheritance. God knows, I propose what follows only to prevent you in your dreadful state from selling your interest for a trifle and coming to want at last. As you cannot succeed me here, I will if you choose, join with you and sell the estate, for I confess unless you married a person of fortune, it is so much encumbered it will always keep you poor, as it has me – the money may be placed in the funds I secured for the same uses as before. In this case you would have after my decease which in the course of nature cannot now be long and trouble now will hasten it, from £800 to £1800 a year, by doing this you may be comfortable and in time by leading a virtuous life, may reconcile yourself to the great disposer of all events, for surely nothing but his arm which almost visible saved you from being a murderer and the gallows. Seriously consider what I have written, for should you be condemned or even fly from justice, the estate will escheat to the Crown after my death, for such an offence and it requires no great legacy to know, which way the interest of the next heir will be, he being no relation to you but by marriage, whose great advantage to keep you abroad under the terror of the law and pray the Crown to return the lands to him.

This I am told is the law in such a case and into whose hands the deeds and writings of the estate will fall when I die, consider this, I most anxiously wish you had some true friends to advise you, he certainly would recommend to lose not a moment to embrace the offered satisfaction as far as it can be done or such as the injured person will accept of, and think yourself a most fortunate being having committed such a deed to escape so well.

Good heavens what could have induced you to such a deed. This man never injured you in any way whatsoever, but quite the contrary. This poor Jane and myself conscientiously know, and Mr Humphrey Williams (Solicitor), that as far as relates to the property, not a man of a thousand would have born the calamities he has done in quietness for the sake of any man or family whatsoever – I think he will accept a remuneration of such a kind which would be but little felt by us though of great advantage to him. Let me instantly hear from you, for there is not a moment to lose.

Your unhappy father, Robert Nanney

Llwyn, April 29ᵗʰ 1816

(A Letter from Rev. Robert Nanney to his son Lt. Lewis Nanney in Brussels)

The hoped-for friends so desperately needed by Lewis appeared in the persons of Sir Robert Williames Vaughan, 2ⁿᵈ Bart, and Lewis's best friend the attorney T. Longueville Jones of Oswestry, who did their utmost to assist the family in the dark days that followed. Lewis never replied to his father but we can gauge his level of desperation from a short note he penned to his friend Longueville Jones:

30ᵗʰ August 1816
From London Hotel, Bruxelles

My dear Friend,

I have reviewed both your letters, for the kind advice they contain. Accept my most grateful thanks. At the moment my injured feelings and conception is at variance with both my reason and understanding. I to my misfortune forfeited myself to the laws of my country and so to the joined pact of both relative and friends. Being inspired by you that I am not forgotten by my friends is to my feelings the highest consolation added to an inward disgrace which stands in full conviction of my heart, that I yet possess so notable a need to protect the last remnants of my wounded birth right, to afford this is a portion of its full value. I have to request of you immediately on receipt of this to forward me a power of attorney giving the highest strength authority that the law admits on as much to allow me my dear friend to place in your hands the destiny of my existence by your decision I will be governed. I have returned no answer. Added to my absconded condition my health is declining fast, be pleased your self and family to all my relatives and friends to accept the grateful recollection of a sincere but unfortunate friend.

Lewis Nanney

Address your letter undercover to Madam St. Amour, Ostend.

382. above: 'A view of the Thames and St. Paul's' by Maclure, Macdonald and Macgregor

This was the last letter received from Lewis and, despite extensive searches, his whereabouts continued to be a mystery. In January 1817, reports were received of him circumspectly meeting a contact in St. Paul's Cathedral churchyard in London. There were other accounts received of him contemplating travelling to Constantinople, Egypt, Bordeaux and even South America!

In the meantime Rev. Robert Nanney had taken up residence in a fashionable part of London and soon after had been 'induced' to marry an acquaintance of Matthews, a certain Mrs Lone, who had allegedly paid Rev. Nanney £1200 as part of a marriage settlement so as to secure a widow's annuity of £80 a year. The 'contrived' marriage took place at St. Marylebone Church on the 25th October 1816. Robert Nanney, no doubt in a state of confusion, had also made over a number of leases of Llwyn estate property at Bala, Mawddwy, Llanuwchllyn and Dolgellau to Matthews.

On the 18th December 1818, Matthews communicated to Thomas Hartley (son-in-law of Rev. Robert and husband of Mary Nanney) that:

... poor Mr Nanney had departed life on the 5th of December at half past eight in the evening... he is to be interred in St.

George's Vault under the Church ... he is remembered in the Parish Book by his name Revd. Robert Nanney of Llwyn, Merionethshire. The coffin is handsome and will cost near £20 – he will be drawn by four horses in a hearse with plumes of feathers and followed by a mourning coach drawn also in the same manner.

Matthews wasted no time in informing the family of the heavy debts left by Rev. Nanney in London and of the annuity for the now Mrs Nanney. He further stated that he would be sending proper authority for himself to receive rents due to him from the leases drawn up by Robert Nanney and the costs to cover his funeral expenses.

The news of Matthew's intention to receive the rents of the Llwyn and Hendre Eirian estates caused a huge flurry of legal activity. Sir Robert Williames Vaughan, 2nd Bart of Nannau was crucially involved, and at one time stated that he was not at all willing that Matthews should have any rents. Thomas Hartley's solicitor G. Griffiths believed that Rev. Nanney had been incapable of drawing up a new will, or for that matter leases, and that the £1200 marriage settlement money was probably Rev. Nanney's own money!

By the 19th December 1818, G. Griffiths wrote to T. Longueville Jones fearing that 'our unfortunate friend Mr Lewis Nanney is dead'. He went on to suggest that his clients should take possession of the Llwyn estate as rightful heirs.

On the 23rd December 1818, Thomas Hartley wrote to Longueville Jones, communicating the

melancholy intelligence of poor Lewis Nanney's death.

It was thought that Lewis got seriously ill whilst staying in a hotel in Brussels, and when his money ran out he was turned out on to the streets with a raging fever, and that he died on the roadside penniless.

Attempts were made to collect rents on behalf of Matthews, but the tenants had been forewarned and cooperated with the Hartleys who had swiftly taken up residence at the Llwyn. Fortunately for the Llwyn family, Thomas Hartley had an immense amount of experience in estate management, having been Sir Watkin Williams Wynn's land agent for the Llwydiarth estate, and having received legal training.

Despite many years of litigation, the complete control of the Llwyn estate was not handed back to the family for more than a decade, and poor Miss Jane Nanney remained under the control of Matthews until 1823, when he died. Jane Nanney continued to live in London with Rev. Nanney's widow (Mrs Lone) with the Llwyn family having no idea of their whereabouts. Matthews had been in control of Jane's affairs and her annuities since Rev. Nanney had moved to London. On being appointed High Sherriff of Merioneth in 1828, Thomas Hartley used his connections to find Jane's whereabouts, which his agent accidentally stumbled upon in 1829. At the instigation of the Hartleys, a Commission of Lunacy sat in 1829 to determine whether Jane Nanney was of a sound mind.

The Commission, a highly respected group of Middlesex magistrates, listened to much evidence. Mr Carrington opened the case by observing that he appeared for:

Mrs Hartley, the sister of the alleged lunatic. Mrs Hartley and the object of the present inquiry were the only daughters of the Rev. Mr. Nanney a gentleman of an ancient family who owned a great deal of property in North Wales … Miss Nanney

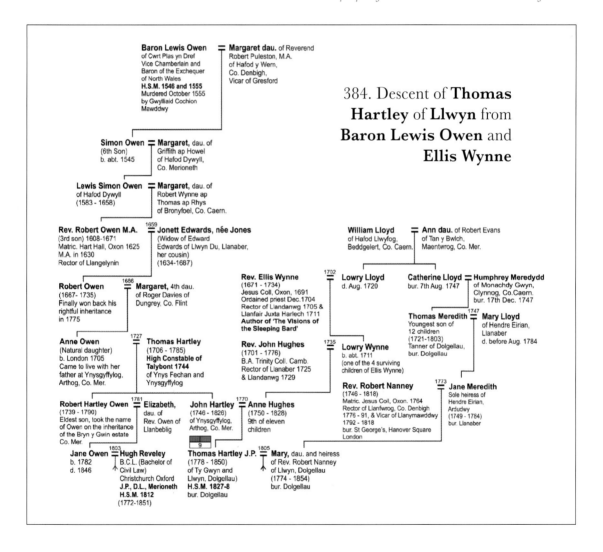

384. Descent of **Thomas Hartley** of **Llwyn** from **Baron Lewis Owen** and **Ellis Wynne**

385. *Llwyn Hall, Dolgellau (2014)*

YN Y TY HWN
Y CANED Y BU FYW Y BU FARW
ELLIS WYNNE
1671-1734
AWDUR GWELEDIGAETHEU
Y BARDD CWSG
"A DDARLLENNO YSTYRIED
A YSTYRIO COFIED"
ER COF AMDANO AC ER PARCH
I'W ENW Y GOSODWYD YMA'R
GARREG HON AWST MCMXXII

was born in the year 1781, and received an education in every respect befitting a young lady. During the latter part of his life Mr. Nanney became infirm in mind, and at that time a man, named Matthews, a bankrupt tallow chandler, was received by him into his service and confidence, and soon achieved a great ascendancy over him. This man, in 1803, accomplished the seduction of Miss Nanney, and ever since that period this unfortunate victim had been insane.

The Jury expressed a verdict that Miss Nanney had been of unsound mind ever since September 1824. The family made arrangements for her to be transferred to an institution at Aberystwyth, where she stayed until her death in February 1833. She was buried in St. Michael's churchyard, Aberystwyth.

Thomas and Mary Hartley endured many years of litigation before the estate was finally restored to the rightful owners. Family tradition has it that the final action of the whole sad affair was reviewed in the Quarter Sessions at Bala, where a verdict was returned in favour of the Llwyn family. It is related that a certain F. P. Evans of Hendreforion brought the joyful news to Dolgellau in an hour, his horse dropping down dead on the lawn in front of the Llwyn! The jubilation was so great that the loss of the hunter was not thought of amid the church bells ringing, and later, every window in the town was illuminated.

THE HARTLEYS OF LLWYN

Llwyn under the Hartleys entered a new era of gracious living, and once more the venerable hall echoed to the sounds of celebration and genuine hospitality.

The Hartley family were revered for their kindness to the poor and needy of Dolgellau. A local newspaper, *Y Dydd*, reminiscing about Thomas Hartley's kindness, stated:

> You only had to tell Mr Hartley that so and so was rather poor and experiencing difficulties, to which he instantly replied, Take this half sovereign to him at once!

The family's kindness and consideration to servants and their many tenants was renowned. Edward Griffiths, an antiquarian of Dolgellau, wrote of the Llwyn family in the 1840s, in an article of 1912:

> The old tenants were never to be removed nor did they ever think of paying rent, and little, if anything was ever done in the way of improvement. The servants at this time were getting on in years – Sion Prys, the gardener, and Huw Sion, Iram Jones and William of Llwyn - from 70 years upwards. There were four big horses at the Llwyn in magnificent condition and when a team of three head of these horses came to town there was an old servant at the head of each. The old family was proverbial for its kindness to the poor –

> Living in peace and contentment, and paying tribute to the Muse that was the chief characteristic of this epoch of the Llwyn's history.

A worthy tribute to a gentry family, who understood the responsibilities associated with the privilege of land ownership. Successive generations of the Llwyn family continued to adhere to this worthy ideal, through good times and bad.

Thomas Hartley was of a famous poetic line, his grandmother Lowry being the fourth daughter of the Rev. Ellis Wynne, the noted author of *Gweledigaethau y Bardd Cwsg* (The Visions of the Sleeping Bard). Thomas adopted for himself the poetic pen name of 'Llewelyn Idris' and became well-known for his 'poetic effusions' as they were similarly described; no Christmas celebration at Nannau was complete without Thomas's poetic interludes.

*386. opposite left: **Las Ynys Fawr, Harlech, the home of Ellis Wynne, author of 'Gweledigaethau y Bardd Cwsg' (1671-1734)***
*387. opposite inset: **Plaque at Las Ynys Fawr***
*388. above: **East Gate of Caernarfon Castle, site of the Exchequer Tower in Baron Lewis Owen's time***
*389. top right: **East Gate of Caernarfon Castle from the road below***
*390. top right inset: **Plaque designating the tower as the site of the Exchequer in the 16th century***

Thomas Hartley's descent can also be traced back directly to Baron Lewis Owen of Cwrt Plas yn Dre, Dolgellau, the infamous Baron of the Exchequer of North Wales, who was reputedly murdered by the legendary 'Gwylliaid Cochion of Mawddwy' (The Red Bandits of Mawddwy) in 1555.

Residing at the Llwyn, Thomas was living in the house of the eldest son of the Baron, and he would have felt a strong attachment to the old family home built by John Lewis Owen in 1578.

BARON LEWIS OWEN

Baron Lewis Owen was the son of Owen ap Hywel ap Llywelyn of Dolgellau, an old Welsh family boasting a pedigree that stretched back to Gwrgan ap Ithel, the 11th-century ruler of Glamorgan. Lewis had married Margaret Puleston, the niece of Sir John Puleston, and rose to prominence under the patronage of the powerful Puleston dynasty.

Lewis Owen held high office under the Crown, rising to Deputy Chamberlain and Baron of the Exchequer of North Wales. He was Sheriff of

Merioneth in 1545-6 and 1554-5, holding this important post at a time when few Welshmen rose to such height. He represented Merioneth as the Member of Parliament in 1547, 1553 and 1554. As Baron of the Exchequer, he would have had responsibility for leasing Crown lands and collecting revenues.

Baron Owen built up a considerable estate in Merioneth, capitalising on the dissolution of the monasteries in 1536-40 and managing to 'acquire' lands in Nannau, Llanegryn and Talyllyn, together with a number of leases in Dolgellau, which he no doubt passed to his son. He was a hugely ambitious man who capitalised on all the opportunities that the 1536 Act of Union provided to the gentry for advancement and, in the process, built up great resentment in his local area, becoming increasingly more unpopular and alienated in his community.

As part of his remit, Lewis acted as a judge officiating at the Exchequer Court where debts and duties to the Crown were collected and arbitrated. In this important role Lewis was paid £13 a year in addition to a £2 attendance fee. The Exchequer of North Wales was housed in the East Gate House of Caernarfon town, a gate often referred to as 'Porth Mawr'. As an important official at the Exchequer, Lewis was provided with an apartment within the tower, which he used when on court business.

As Sheriff of Merioneth and a Justice of the Peace, Lewis was charged with the responsibility for safeguarding the shire from the ravages of thieves and outlaws. Unfortunately for Lewis, Mawddwy was one of the most lawless areas of the country and had recently come under his jurisdiction. Mawddwy

at this time was notorious for gross disorder and general turmoil permeated this remote mountainous area where many of the inhabitants were engaged in cattle rustling and indiscriminate raiding.

At the height of his powers, on Saturday 12th October 1555, whilst travelling home to Dolgellau from the Assizes in Montgomeryshire, Baron Owen was ambushed in a dark wooded ravine and brutally murdered by the Gwylliaid Cochion of Mawddwy. The site of this grievous act was immortalised as 'Llidiart-y-Barwn' (The Baron's Gate).

The Baron's great great grandson, the celebrated Antiquarian Robert Vaughan of Hengwrt, recounted the whole tragic event, with much of the detail taken from the testimony of Sir John Wynn of Gwydir:

Lewis Owen, esquire: vice chamberlain and Baron of the Exchequer of North Wales, lived in great credit and authorite in the time of King Henry VIII, Edward VI, and Queen Mary, as it appeareth by their letters under sign manual directed him and John Wynn ap Meredith of Gwydir, esquire touching matters that concerned the peace and quiet government of the country, as the apprehending of and punishing of felons and outlaws. And they in performance of the dutie required by some of these letters, (being authorised to call to their aid the power of the counties, and also to keep sessions of jail delivery when occasion required) raised a great company of tall and lusty men, and on a Christmas eve took above 80 felons and outlaws, whom they punished according to the

nature of their delinquencies... Afterwards the said Lewis Owen being High Sheriff of the county of Merioneth, and having occasion to go to Montgomeryshire Assizes to treat with the Lord of Mawddwy, about the marriage to be had between John Owen, his son and heir and the daughter of the said Lord of Mawddwy, was in his return met by a damned crew of thieves and outlaws, who in the thick woods of Mawddwy lay in wait for his coming, and had cut down long trees to cross the way and hinder his passage, and being come to the place, they let fly at him a shower of arrows, whereof one lighted in his face, the which he took out with his hand and broke it, then they all fell upon him with their bills and javelins and killed him – his men upon the first assault fled and left him only accompanied with his son-in-law John Lloyd of Ceiswyn esquire who defended him till he fell down to the ground dead, where he was found having above 30

bloody wounds in his body. This cruel murder was committed about allhallowstide in the year of our Lord 1555. And the murderers soon after were for the most part taken and executed, some few fled the land and never returned. And so, with the loss of his life, he purchased peace and quietness to his country, the which God be praised we enjoy even to our days.

The brutal event passed into local folklore and embellishments to the gruesome tale were added by other commentators. Edward Lhuyd, the noted Antiquarian, was the first to allocate the name of 'Gwihiaid Kochion' to the Baron's assailants in his 'Parochialia' written around 1700, some forty years after the death of Robert Vaughan. In 1784, Thomas Pennant's version of the tragedy had incorporated the idea of the Baron being slain by the Red-Haired Bandits of Mawddwy in revenge for hanging eighty of their men folk and recounts the story of a mother's curse upon the Baron and her revenge that was taken at his death:

> ... *the mother, in rage, told him (baring her breast) these yellow breasts have given suck to those who shall wash their hands in your blood.*

Henceforth it became one of the best-known legends in Wales.

There is no actual evidence of any hangings taking place prior to the murder of the Baron. Although the area was lawless, the Sheriff would be required to follow the law by arresting suspected felons and would have relied on the courts to pass judgement. Owen Wynn, Sheriff of Merioneth in 1570, was given exceptional powers to pursue felons and outlaws in Montgomeryshire and Cardiganshire, but was required to imprison them and ensure that they were brought before the Court of the Great Sessions.

Actual evidence of a roaming band of red-haired bandits terrorising the countryside is non-existent. Court records reveal the Baron's assassins as being, overwhelmingly, respected yeoman farmers, namely:

Gruffudd Wyn ap Dafydd ap Gutun, yeoman (carried a billhook)
Ellis ap Tudur, yeoman, of Nannau (carried a sword)
John Goch ap Gruffudd ap Huw, yeoman, of Mawddwy
Robert ap Rhys ap Hywel, yeoman, of Mawddwy (bow and arrow)
Jenkyn ap Einion (bow and arrow)
David Gwyn ap Gruffudd ap Huw, yeoman, of Mawddwy (bow and arrow)
Morus Goch, yeoman, of Cemais, Mont. (carried a sword)
Ieuan Thomas, yeoman, of Llanwddyn (carried a dagger)

According to the indictment it appears that John Goch ap Gruffudd ap Huw was the person who actually dealt the death-blow to the Baron, allegedly striking Lewis Owen in his stomach, below the ribs, and killing him instantly. All eight of the assailants were convicted and summarily hanged for the crime.

A consideration of the main assailant's name, John Goch, leads one to deduce that he was red-haired, ('goch' meaning red) which could account for the origin of the red-haired bandits myth.

Why respected yeomen of standing in the community would resort to such a grievous crime is difficult to determine. Gruffudd Hiraethog, one of the many poets who lamented the Baron's demise, intuitively summed up how unpopular the Sheriff had become:

> *There is a cold rumour among us; on a dreary Saturday in the month of October, when a sheriff was killed, a cold chill was felt; many are his enemies.*

As the Crown's chief representative of a perceived oppressive regime, the Baron was a natural target for the dissatisfied elements of Mawddwy society, who not only opposed the new order and its punitive taxation, but disapproved of his far from subtle land acquisitions which added to their deep sense of injustice.

Parliament House of Owen Glyndŵr, Dolgelley.

393. above: **'Parliament House of Owen Glyndŵr Dolgelley** engraved by A. Le Petit (1804-1896)

An interesting but poignant inventory exists of the Baron's possessions left behind at the Exchequer. Made by Robert Puleston, it notes the following items:

five bedstedes
hangings of buckram about the bedd in the chamber
half pewter vessel
12 gret platters of pewter
12 saucers
one pan and one pot of 4 gallons apiece
a turnell to salt beef
a payr of goblets
a broche & brand iron
a cupborde in the buttery
half a dozen cussions
a carpet
two board clothes – old and very ragged
one towel

From information presented by E. D. Jones, who drew the conclusion from the inventory that

The exchequer could not be described as well-appointed.
(Susan C. Passmore Collection)

The Baron's once salubrious abode at Cwrt Plas yn Dre, which the bards waxed lyrical about, remained in the possession of his family for generations. Miraculously it was still standing in the latter part of the 19th century, when it once more became the focus of much attention, having languished unnoticed for centuries.

In the 1880s, threats to demolish what had become a rather ramshackle building spawned a movement that aimed to preserve it as a public museum. A committee was formed headed by Mr Holland, M.P. for Merioneth, and Mr Beale the High Sheriff, together with a group of public-spirited gentlemen (with John Vaughan of Nannau and Thomas Humphrey Williams of Llwyn notably amongst their number).

An architect was commissioned to survey the building and prepare plans for its remodelling,

GREAT HALL

394. Cwrt Plas Yn Dre (Renovation Plans)
Plans prepared for the refurbishment of
Cwrt Plas Yn Dre, Dolgellau, in 1875, by
Birmingham architect A.B. Phipson

Detail of wooden
hinges on doors
and
windows

One surviving relic from Thomas Hartley's farming days exists in the guise of a stuffed sheep's head that has been in the family since at least the middle of the 19th century, known simply as 'Captain Bligh'. The mounted sheep's head was once part of a flock of black sheep that were bred at the Llwyn by Thomas Hartley and his descendants for several generations. The black sheep were kept in the fields surrounding the Llwyn, akin to the manner of white cattle kept in parklands. Family tradition recounts that 'Captain Bligh' in his time was something of a pet and well-liked by the family, hence the taxidermy and subsequent gracing of his presence on the walls of their ancient home.

but unfortunately through lack of funds the scheme fell through, with the Dr. Williams's School Project taking precedence.

In 1885, Sir Pryce Jones, a wealthy merchant of Newtown, purchased the whole building which was dismantled and subsequently re-erected in the grounds of his mansion at Newtown, in a rather reduced form, and given the erroneous name of 'Owain Glyndŵr's Parliament House'. The vacant site became occupied by an Ironmonger's shop, 'T. H. Roberts', and the only clue to the existence of the old house is a street at the rear, which perpetuates its name.

THOMAS HARTLEY THE AGRICULTURALIST

Thomas Hartley had received a good education, attending St. John's College, Cambridge, in 1796. Throughout his life he was an avid agriculturalist, paying particular attention to sheep breeding, and keeping up to date with advances in the field. He worked closely with Sir Robert Williames Vaughan, a like-minded fellow, who cared passionately about agricultural improvements.

In an attempt to discover the origin of the Llwyn sheep, we made initial enquiries to the Rare Breeds Society who were unable to come up with a definitive answer. They suggested that Captain Bligh was of an extinct primitive stock, possibly a cross between an old Welsh and a multiple horned type, stating that:

The multiple horned breeds were used in gladiatorial games and there is a theory that it was brought over to Britain in the 1st Century A.D. for use in sheep breeding programmes. As the Romans had a strong presence in Wales they could have easily been used on Welsh estates and might be one of the many examples of regional type sheep that has either become extinct or was used in the creation of modern breeds.

Then later, whilst trawling an article in 'The Cambro-Briton' of 1820, a chance discovery unveiled Captain Bligh's possible pedigree.

The article in question was a description of a walk from Dolgellau to Nannau in 1820. The author reveals that as he approached the Nannau mansion:

The house is not visible till nearly the extremity of the avenue is gained, and then it presents itself to view in all its substantial neatness and simplicity. In front is a small lawn, decorated with some fine specimens of many horned sheep, the Oves Polyceratae of Linnaeus.

This old Icelandic breed could well have been of the same type as the Llwyn sheep, as the description given in an early encyclopaedia fits them perfectly. Possibly the Nannau flock 'migrated' to Llwyn on the death of Sir Robert Williames Vaughan, 2nd Bart in 1843. Thomas

Hartley, being a keen breeder of sheep, might have rescued the flock for posterity.

On May 24th 1869, Thomas Humphrey Williams of Llwyn, a grandson of Thomas Hartley, took the Llwyn sheep to the Merioneth Agricultural Show. *Y Dydd* newspaper reported that the famous many-horned sheep of the Llwyn were there and many people were fascinated by them.

Many references to the unique multi-horned Llwyn sheep exist from the middle of the 19th century. It seems they were somewhat of a crowd puller, and in the 1870s, a cleric visiting Dolgellau commented that:

the sheep are unique and their like is not seen anywhere in the country.

A handsome reward was given to each of the above and 5s. to each of the others that had started. There was a respectable party at the Ship Hotel in the evening.

Thomas Hartley, J.P., D.L. of the Llwyn, died on the 28th August 1850 in his seventy first year, leaving behind his widow Mary (née Nanney). He was succeeded by his son, Robert Nanney Hartley.

An article written in the *North Wales Chronicle* encapsulates this distinguished old gentleman and the values he held so dearly:

THOMAS HARTLEY, ESQ., LLWYN

This gentleman was born in this County ...and on his maternal side descended from Rev. Ellis Wynne, (author of Bardd Cwsg) Rector of Llandanwg, and Llanfair juxta Harlech (1670-1734).
Mr Hartley succeeded to the Llwyn estate, in right of his wife, (being the only surviving issue of the late Rev. Robert Nanney), and resided at the family mansion at Llwyn, up to the period of his death. Mr Hartley was appointed by the late Lord Lieutenant, Sir W. W. Wynn, Bart, Deputy Lieutenant for the County and Commissioner for Dolgelley Green. (The Commissioners being, by appointment, forever the heirs of Nannau, Hengwrt, Caerynwch, Llwyn, and the Rector of Dolgelley). He held the Commission of the Peace from the year 1821, but did not act as Magistrate until much later, and filled the office of High Sheriff in 1827. The chair of the Dolgelley Auxiliary Bible Society becoming vacant by the death of the late highly respected

In March 1847, the annual ploughing matches for the parishes of Dolgellau, Llanfachreth and Llanelltyd took place in a meadow on Llwyn land near Dolgellau. The area to be ploughed consisted of half an acre and ten ploughs entered the competition which began at 10.40 am, the whole area being ploughed by 3 pm.

The results were:

1st – Sir Robert Williames Vaughan, Bart, ploughman – Cadwaladr Thomas
2nd - Mr Watkin Anwyl, ploughman, Richard Williams
3rd - Mr G. Griffiths, Tyddyn Bach, ploughman, E. Griffith
4th – Thomas Hartley, Esq. , ploughman, Hugh Rees

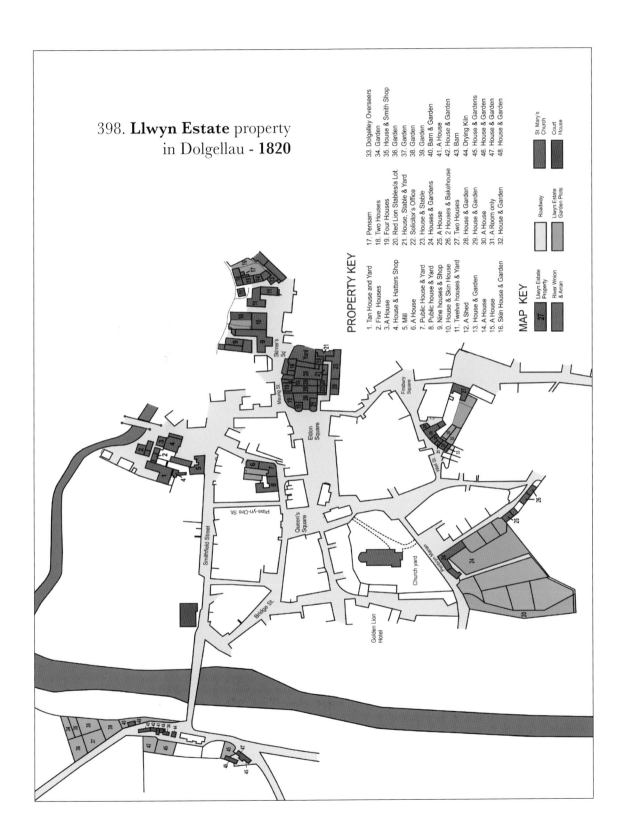

398. **Llwyn Estate** property in Dolgellau - **1820**

PROPERTY KEY

1. Tan House and Yard
2. Five Houses
3. A House
4. House & Hatters Shop
5. Mill
6. A House
7. Public House & Yard
8. Public house & Yard
9. Nine houses & Shop
10. House & Skin House
11. Twelve houses & Yard
12. A Shed
13. House & Garden
14. A House
15. A House
16. Skin House & Garden

17. Pensam
18. Two Houses
19. Four Houses
20. Red Lion Stables/a Lot.
21. House, Stable & Yard
22. Solicitor's Office
23. House & Stable
24. Houses & Gardens
25. A House
26. 2 Houses & Bakehouse
27. Two Houses
28. House & Garden
29. House & Garden
30. A House
31. A Room only
32. House & Garden

33. Dolgelley Overseers
34. Garden
35. House & Smith Shop
36. Garden
37. Garden
38. Garden
39. Garden
40. Barn & Garden
41. A House
42. House & Garden
43. Barn
44. Drying Kiln
45. House & Gardens
46. House & Garden
47. House & Garden
48. House & Garden

MAP KEY

27 Llwyn Estate Property

River Wnion & Arran

Roadway

Llwyn Estate Garden Plots

St. Mary's Church

Court House

He was a conscientious and regular and devoted member of the Church of England, and died in full faith in its embrace. In early life, he cultivated an acquaintance with the Muse (thoughtful meditation), and still to the last years of his life was fond of his Awen, (poetic inspiration). At every annual meeting of the Bible Society, his Englyn was greeted with applause, his bardic name being 'Bardd Idris'. On the 28th August, 1850, died this good and kind gentleman, lamented and respected by all around. He is succeeded by his son and heir, R. Nanney Hartley, Esq., a kind and esteemed gentleman, worthy of his sire.

ROBERT NANNEY HARTLEY OF LLWYN

Robert Nanney Hartley matriculated St. John's College, Cambridge in 1836 and returned to Dolgellau to assist with the running of the family estate. He was appointed a Commissioner of the Turnpike Trust, but seemed to have taken little interest in public affairs, being a very private and quiet individual who followed his father in showing great concern for the poor and the needy in society.

Robert Nanney Hartley died on the 6th April 1860 aged 45, having survived his father by less than ten short years. He was buried in the family vault at Dolgellau Church. The funeral procession moved from the Llwyn with the mourning coach followed by the hearse and four pallbearers on each side, and 24 tenants, two by two abreast. The mourning coach contained Griffith Williams Esq. (brother-in-law), Thomas

Humphrey Williams, Esq., in 1826, Mr Hartley was elected President.

He was a thorough kind hearted, liberal, and generous person – very unostentatious and retired. His greatest attractions were those of home, of which he was the centre and joy. His household he never changed, unless removed by death or marriage. Many advantages were taken of his extreme kindness, as a landlord, by unprincipled tenants; he never put in a distress for rent, in consequence of which he frequently suffered losses. He was always the great friend of the poor, his ears were always open to their call, and during the last 18 years was the greatest opponent of a Poor-house in the district. No arguments could persuade him to it.

*400. above: **Caegoronwy, Llanaber - once the home of the Williams family whose ancestry descends from Osbwrn Wyddel***

Humphrey Williams Esq., Robert Nanney Williams Esq., and Master Meyrick Meredith Williams, all nephews to the deceased.

The North Wales Chronicle of Saturday 14th April 1860 reported that:

> *The funeral being a public one, was joined at the Llwyn gate by nearly all the inhabitants of the town and neighbourhood, anxious to show their respect for the deceased lamented gentleman. All the shops were closed throughout the town and the bells rang muffled peals at intervals throughout the day.*

Griffith Williams, Attorney-at-Law, was the youngest son of Humphrey Williams, Clerk of the Peace for Merioneth (a well-respected

attorney whose father was William Williams of Plas Issa, Dolgellau, a member of the Caegoronwy family). Three of Humphrey's sons had followed their father into law: the eldest John Jones Williams, who became Clerk of the Peace after his father; Griffith Williams of Llwyn, a practicing attorney in Dolgellau, and Humphrey Lloyd Williams, attorney of Llanfyllin (Master in Chancery in 1833).

John Jones Williams's life had been tragically cut short by a horrific accident at Barmouth in May of 1842 when, on his way to finalise the sale of a schooner, *The Cambrian Maid*, he was thrown from his carriage when his horse was spooked. Two others in the carriage jumped clear but John, holding on to the reins, attempted to bring the carriage under control. The carriage wheels struck the rocks and he was hurled head first into the cliff. His injuries were so great that

he died at three o'clock later that day, at the age of 38 years. The tragedy was particularly sad as he left a widow with two young children.

A regular visitor to the Llwyn in the time of Griffith Williams was the Rev. John Williams, known widely to every lover of Welsh literature by his bardic name 'Ab Ithel.' Ab Ithel was a noted antiquarian and Anglican priest who became the rector of Llanymawddy.

Taking the pseudonym Ab Ithel from the surname of his grandfather, William Bethell, Ab Ithel went on to publish many books, some ecclesiastical, and many concerned with Welsh antiquities. In 1860, he published the *Chronicles of the Princes* and *Annales Cambriae*, and was widely regarded by many of his contemporaries as one of the leading Welsh scholars of his day. He had been, along with Harry Longueville Jones, another leading cleric and antiquarian, one of the founders of 'The Cambrian Archeological Association' in 1846. He edited the associated journal *Archaeologia Cambrensis* until 1853, when he relinquished the post to establish *The Cambrian Journal*. Ab Ithel is known to have spent much time visiting the

Llwyn, having married into the Williams family and revelled in the stories and mysteries associated with the old mansion.

Ancestors of the Williams family had settled at Caegoronwy in Llanaber parish as early as the 15th century, and had built up a significant estate in the parish encompassing much property in the village of Bontddu near Dolgellau. The driving force of the family's later wealth was a certain William Willliams, who propelled the family's standing in the community through his impressive entrepreneurial efforts and rose to be one of the richest men in the county. He held extensive shipping interests and land speculations, even financing the improvement of Barmouth harbour in 1804. William Williams died in 1836, and his great wealth was distributed amongst eight cousins, Humphrey Williams's siblings being half of the fortunate beneficiaries.

One cousin, another William Williams, inherited the family estate and was fundamental in developing the Clogau Gold mine. He also rebuilt the mansion of Bryntirion at Bontddu on the proceeds of the initial flush of gold from the famous mine. Bryntirion later became the 'Bont Ddu Hall Hotel'. The Caegoronwy estate records highlight the huge expenditure William Williams was willing to lavish on his newly erected mansion - over £700 alone on plants for his garden!

He oversaw huge investments in the Clogau goldmine, which unfortunately came to nothing and the company crashed. The serial speculator immediately switched his attention to slate mining. He died in 1867 at the age of only 49, shortly before the coming-of-age of his son, Dr. William Williams M.D.

Griffith Williams of Llwyn's son-in-law, the Rev. Lewis Jones, wrote an interesting account of the folly of investing in gold mines, which appeared in the Western Mail on Saturday 17th December 1887:

Forty years ago an old gentleman of the name of Harvey bought the Vigra and Clogau Mines, which in those days were worked for lead. He brought, I believe, into the country the sum of £30,000 in hard cash, spent it all, and died in the Denbigh Lunatic Asylum. Poor old Mr. Harvey, I remember him well, living at a place within a mile of Dolgelley, called Dol'rhyd. He always used to say there is enough gold in the mountain to clear the National Debt, but it would require the amount of the National Debt to work it. However, some years afterwards these mines fell into the hands of Mr Williams, of Bennar (one of the Cae Goronow Williamses), and it was a miner of the name of John Parry, of Bontddu – to whom 'Geologist' (Lagan) in the Western Mail of Thursday refers – who actually first found the gold, or at least brought it to light, in these latter years. As long as Mr Williams and John Parry and Parry's sons worked the gold with hand-machines they, as the 'Geologist' mentions, did get gold, which was sent every fortnight for some months, per mail cart as far as Tycoch Station, on the Great Western Railway, and thence by rail to London. It was sent in tin cases – two cases containing about 20oz. each. Mr Williams cleared in a short time the mortgage on his own property, the gold find happening just in time to save a foreclosure, and besides clearing the mortgage, he also had sufficient money to buy Bryntirion, the place where Mr.P. Morgan now lives. In those days Bryntirion was a ruin of what once was a very beautiful villa, built by a Mr. Harford, and burnt down about 45 years ago, old Mr. Harford and Mr. Page his agent escaping with their lives. Williams was a speculator by nature; he was not satisfied with the daily golden egg produced by the little hand-machines worked by John Parry and his sons. He formed a limited company, and they launched out in machinery, which did to the ruin of the mine. They got a Mexican Austrian down, whose name has escaped my memory. He lived at Tyn y Coed, Dolgelley and managed the crushing machines, which turned out quite a failure in all respects other than crushing the

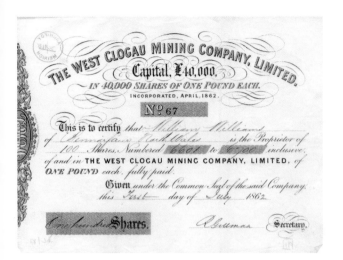

company and the gold mania of 1862-1863. It is a well-known fact that old Parry, of Bontddu, used to get the gold in the stream below the crushers which had escaped the Austrian.

Mr Williams died very shortly after the collapse of the company. My advice to all who have money to spare is that they be not in a hurry to invest in the Merionethshire gold mines ... there is gold, but not sufficient to pay, unless worked economically ...

Lewis Jones

Cadoxton Vicarage, near Neath

Reverend Lewis Jones married Margaret, Griffith Williams's eldest daughter, on Tuesday 19th January 1869 at Dolgellau, amid huge rejoicings in the town. The *Wrexham Advertiser* of Saturday 23rd reported:

Tuesday last was quite a gala day in this charming little town and the immediate neighbourhood, consequent on the

marriage of the late curate of St.Mary's, the Rev. Lewis Jones, Minor Canon of Bangor Cathedral and eldest son of Griffith Jones, Esq. late coroner for the county of Merioneth, to Margaret, eldest daughter of Griffith Williams, Esq. of Llwyn. The family of both bride and bridegroom being highly respected in the town and neighbourhood, great preparations had been going on in order to give due éclat to the occasion.

From early in the morning salvoes of artillery rang out from fields near Llwyn and virtually every window was illuminated in the town. Llwyn's mansion entrance had been transformed by a large triumphal arch constructed of ivy and laurel branches and gaily festooned with 'unusual flowers' and the motto of:

Long life and happiness to Mr and Mrs Jones.

(in Welsh and English)

Similar arches had been erected along the route to the town, all being the work of Llwyn servants and estate workers. The town was gaily decorated with banners, flags and arches all wishing the young couple health and happiness.

The wedding party arrived about eleven o'clock in four broughams with a pair of greys each. A carpet was put down from the carriage to the church and the interior of the church presented a tasteful appearance ... the bride was dressed in dove coloured silk with hermit jacket and bonnet with orange blossoms and veil. She was attended by four bridesmaids, whose dresses were of similar texture, but a shade

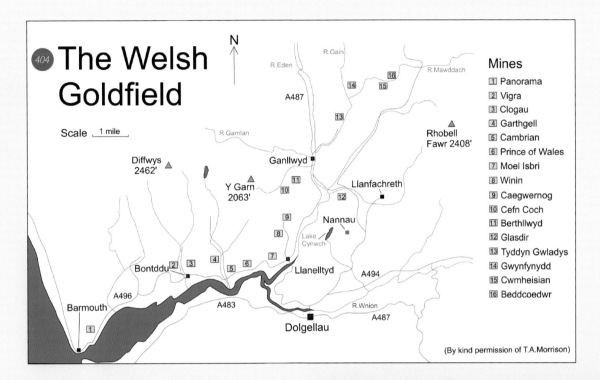

404 **The Welsh Goldfield**

N

Scale 1 mile

R.Gain

R.Eden

R.Mawddach

A487

14 16 15

13

R.Gamlan

Rhobell Fawr 2408'

Diffwys 2462'

Ganllwyd

11

Y Garn 2063'

10

Llanfachreth

12

9

Nannau

8

Lake Cynwch

7

Bontddu 2 3 4 5 6

Llanelltyd

A494

Barmouth

A496

A483

R.Wnion

A487

1

Dolgellau

Mines

1 Panorama
2 Vigra
3 Clogau
4 Garthgell
5 Cambrian
6 Prince of Wales
7 Moel Isbri
8 Winin
9 Caegwernog
10 Cefn Coch
11 Berthllwyd
12 Glasdir
13 Tyddyn Gwladys
14 Gwynfynydd
15 Cwmheisian
16 Beddcoedwr

(By kind permission of T.A.Morrison)

*darker, and with bonnets without veils...
Mrs Ellis presided at the harmonium, and
Mendelssohn's wedding march was well
played.*

The bridal party left the church, driving off amid
huge cheers and cannon fire and the church
bells rang out for the rest of the day. The family
went to Llwyn to enjoy what was referred to as
a very recherché wedding breakfast and at five
past three the newly weds departed the town on
a train bound for Chester,

amidst a shower of old slippers and boots.

At three o'clock teas were enjoyed at many
street parties throughout the town with several
hundreds partaking of the fare. The town band
which played throughout the day was enjoyed

by all. At six o'clock a large bonfire was lit on the green and fire balloons launched with hundreds in attendance.

At night an excellent supper was given at Llwyn for the servants and friends, and the usual toasts were the prelude to further revelry and songs, adding to the pleasant occasion. When the happy couple returned on Friday, fireworks were let off and the rejoicing continued.

On the death of Robert Nanney Hartley in 1860, the Llwyn estate devolved to his sister Miss Anne Hartley and her nephew Thomas Humphrey Williams. Thomas had already lost both his father, Griffith Williams, attorney of Llwyn, and his mother Mary, within a year of each other. Nine years later, the marriage of Thomas Humphrey Williams and Sarah Watkins was a distinctly low-key event as it took place in the bride's hometown of Teignmouth in Devon, and deprived the locals of an occasion to celebrate.

Robert Nanney Williams, Thomas Humphrey's younger brother, had other ideas. Marrying a local girl, Miss Elizabeth Miles, enabled the town to rise to the occasion and mark the

esteem in which the family of the bride and groom were held. Early on the morning of Thursday 20th June 1872, the town awoke early, with many attending to the finishing touches of the numerous decorative arches that had sprung up around Dolgellau. The wedding took place at St. Mary's Church at ten o'clock, and departure of the happy couple from the church was heralded by a merry peal of bells and cannon fire, and the town band paraded through the streets,

discoursing sweet music in honour of the occasion.

(*North Wales Chronicle*, Saturday 22nd June, 1872)

The newly weds left the town by the 2 o'clock train, and in the evening a large bonfire was lit on the Marian Mawr and a dinner took place at the Golden Goat Inn to celebrate the joyus event.

Robert Nanney Williams and his aunt, Anne Hartley, appear to have had a rather stormy relationship. In her perceived role as matriarch of the family, perhaps she exerted too much control over the headstrong Robert, who apparently did much to antagonise his aunt. Thomas Humphrey Williams's approach to his aged aunt was more conciliatory, possibly even pandering to her whims.

Monday the 30ᵗʰ March 1868 had started as an ordinary spring day, until rumours spread like wildfire that the Cambrian Railway would, in their construction of the new railway, enter land belonging to the Llwyn estate. The powers that be had decided that this important milestone for the town should be celebrated. About four o'clock in the afternoon the town crier was sent to announce:

That the first sod on the Llwyn estate for the railway would be cut at five p.m. by Thomas Humphrey Williams Esq. of Llwyn.

The whole town began to gather at the appointed time in a field in front of Llwyn. Amongst the hundreds gathered were Miss Anne Hartley, her nephews and family. The sod was cut by T.H. Williams and wheeled away in a barrow amid huge cheers from the multitude assembled.

Mr Pryce, the local railways company line engineer, made the following speech:

You all know that we were called together at a very short notice, but in accordance with what we hope was the general wish of the townspeople, that the railway works should not be commenced in these grounds without some sort of demonstration taking place. It was said some time ago that the railway would not come nearer to Dolgelley than two miles, but I am glad to be able to tell you that such is not the fact. The railway will be carried on to the town

408. above: **'Dolgellau cottage in Autumn'** *Watercolour. Robert Nanney Williams. Circa 1880*

at once, or to the nearest point possible to it. It was rumoured that the company were not met as well as might be desired by the representatives of the Llwyn estate. I am here to tell you that such was not the case. (Cheers) We could not have been met in a more handsome manner than we have been. (Cheers) ...

Thomas Humphrey Williams responded:

I assure you that I had very great pleasure in being deputed by my aunt, Miss Hartley, to cut the first sod of the Bala and Dolgelley Railway on this, the Llwyn estate. You scarcely need any reassurances from me that our little town of Dolgelley and the welfare of its inhabitants are always our deepest desire. We feel grateful for the very kind and generous way in which the company have met us, and we earnestly hope that the 'sinews of war' may

never be found wanting to further a scheme which will promote in every way the trade and commerce of our little town of Dolgelley and prove a lasting benefit and great boon to its inhabitants (Loud Cheers).

After making a few remarks in Welsh, Mr. J. Chidlaw Roberts called for three cheers for the Llwyn family, and for the Railway Company which were heartily given. The Volunteer Band was in attendance, and the bells of the parish church rang forth a merry peal during the afternoon.

(*North Wales Chronicle*, Saturday 4th April, 1868)

For the next eighteen years stability returned to the family with Anne Hartley and Thomas Humphrey Williams seemingly running the estate together, but in reality, the spinster aunt was very much in the driving seat.

Robert Nanney Williams contented himself with a life of leisure, living off a family annuity. He was known to have frequented many of the local hostelries and on one occasion even took up residence in one, to the total dismay of his aged aunt! There was however another side to this rebellious character, an artistic side that was to develop throughout his life. He painted a large number of scenes around Dolgellau: mills, rivers, estate cottages, and he was particularly fond of depicting thunderstorms and lightning. He was equally at home in differing media and had received some professional training in this field. So prolific was his output that cupboards and storerooms of his artwork overflowed the old mansion at Llwyn.

Anne Hartley died on the 24th February 1886 and was buried in Dolgellau. Her nephew Thomas Humphrey Williams inherited the Llwyn and Hendre Eirian estates. It would prove to be a short tenure as his death followed only five years later, and dying without issue, both estates devolved to Robert Nanney Williams.

Both obituaries reveal how diligently they attended to the needs of the poor in their community, and how the name of Hartley had become synonymous with poor relief for more than half a century. Thomas Humphrey Williams was singled out for particular praise for his dealings with his tenants:

> *He owned a large estate and was much liked by his tenants for his kindness and considerate actions towards them.*

(*The North Wales Chronicle*, Saturday 21st March, 1891)

It would have been quite a shock for Robert to find himself as heir of the whole estate, but he seemingly found his feet, launching himself headlong into local politics, church and community work of all kinds. He became a truly public-spirited landowner and a Guardian of the Workhouse, somewhat of a change from his belligerent past. His tenure was also to be very short, as he died only five years after his brother in 1896. In his wake catastrophic changes would befall the Llwyn estate, with his son and heir Ludovic left to pick up the pieces of an estate disintegrating about his ears.

Anne Hartley had not been the only forceful character in Robert Nanney Williams's life. His mother-in-law, Mrs Elizabeth Miles, was a person to be reckoned with. Her story comes to life through the words of an aged inhabitant of Dolgellau who remembered this unique individual of Upper Mill, Dolgellau:

> *Any history or information about old mills should be of great interest to all. In the past Dolgellau area was notable for its mills. It's a pity that none remain in*

EXHIBITION OF THE WORKS OF INDUSTRY OF ALL NATIONS, 1851.

UNITED KINGDOM, CLASS XII & XV, No: *253*

I hereby certify that
Elizabeth Mills
was an Exhibitor.

Exhibition
Hyde Park. London. 15th Oct. 1851.

President of the Royal Commission.

existence, especially when they were so important to the economy of Wales. The only thing that remains are bare walls of the old mills, reminding us of the service that they gave to the past, many of them having been converted to other uses.

This time I only have time to provide a little history of one old mill of the town this being Upper Mill.

Upper Mill was built over a hundred years ago. It would be easy to find out the exact date if we had sight of the owners deed's. I'm going to attempt to give a little of the history as it was about a hundred years ago. The owner then was John Miles, he was a miller by trade and was married to Elizabeth Miles, she was in business manufacturing household cloth for garments for both men and women. Mrs Miles also made fancy vests with pearl buttons. There was a big demand for these items in those days. Mrs Miles also had another speciality which was a shoulder shawl. Both John and Elizabeth Miles were thoroughly Welsh. John Miles descended from one of the old families of the county. One of his brothers had the Clywedog Mill and another owned the King's Mill. He was a small quiet man with little business in him. Mrs Mills was the daughter of Griffith Davies, Landlord of the Unicorn Inn. A brother of hers was a surgeon, Griffith Davies who died at the young age of 40 in 1853. Mrs Miles was totally different to her husband as far as business was concerned. She spent a number of years in London learning the trade of tailoress and returned to Dolgellau to open a business at the Mill. I got a description of her from a local who remembers her well. She was a tall woman

with a charming personality, kind eyes and a slippery tongue and full of business, always on the go. The towns people admired and respected her a great deal. She lost her husband relatively young, at the age of 66 in 1870, her son John took over from the husband. Her son John died in 1900 the same age as his father had died. I'm afraid that nobody remembers John Miles senior as it has been some 75 years since he died, but there are many who remember Mrs Miles and her son.

In 1850 she employed 150 workers in the Mill and her business, mostly women. I saw a card of the time advertising her business. On the front there was a picture of the Mill in the year 1851, it showed a handsome building with a wide road leading to it and tidy low walls along the road. Under the picture was printed the following:

UPPER MILL, DOLGELLEY.

(Patronised by the Queen)
Mrs. E. M. Miles, Manufacturer of Ladies' Welsh Woollen Dresses. Also Aprons, Gentlemen's Waistcoatings and Woollen Welsh Cloths.
Mrs Miles received a Gold Medal from the Commissioner of the Great Exhibition of 1851, and a Diploma signed by H.R.H. Prince Albert.

THE COMING OF AGE
OF MR.
LUDOVIC NANNEY WILLIAMS
OF LLWYN

19th AUGUST, 1895

ATHLETIC SPORTS

&C., WILL BE HELD ON THE
MARIAN

Commencing at 3-30 o'clock.   Entries for the same are to be made to
Mr. Fichard, Bridge Street, Not later than 11 a.m. on that day.

MISS   FLETCHER

Has kindly consented to distribute the prizes after each event..

PROGRAMME OF EVENTS :-

	1st	2nd	3rd		1st	2nd	3rd
120 yards Handicap	4s.	2s.		Boot Race 100yds, Boys over 15yrs	5s.	3/6	2/6
1 Mile	7/6	5s.		Ditto Boys under 15yrs	3s.	2s.	1/6
100 yards, Men over 40 years of age	5s.	3/6		Bicycle Slow Race, distance 120yds	10s.	5s.	2/6
High Jump, Boys under 15	2/6	1/6		Obstacle Race, Boys under 15yrs	5s.	3/6	2/6
Ditto Open	5s.	3/6		Egg & Spoon Race, Boys under 14	3s.	2s.	1s.
Girls Race, 12 to 20 years 100yds	5s.	3/6		Ditto Girls under 14	3s.	2s.	1s.
Boys ditto under 14 years	3/6	2/6		Donkey Race	10s.	5s.	3s.
Three Legged Race				Open 5s. 3s. 2s.			

Dolgelley : Printed by EDWARD WILLIAMS.

This remarkable woman passed away in June 1888 and was buried with her husband in Dolgellau churchyard.

COMING OF AGE OF **THE HEIR OF LLWYN**

It was with an air of optimism for the future that the Llwyn family made preparations for the coming-of-age of the heir, Ludovic Nanney Williams in 1895. Dolgellau townsfolk would not have wanted to miss the opportunity for revelry that such an occasion provided. *Y Dydd* newspaper alerted the population to the occasion:

Llwyn Heir

We understand that he is to come of age in the middle of August. A meeting was held on Monday night in Dolgelley Town Hall to consider how to celebrate this event. It was decided to make a collection as the Llwyn Estate has many tenants and they are likely to do their best assist.

(*Y Dydd*, August 2nd, 1895)

On the 16th of August they reported:

Llwyn Heir II

Next Monday, 19th August is the Coming of Age of the heir of Llwyn, Mr Ludovic Nanney Williams, eldest son of Mr Robert Nanney Williams, Llwyn.

It is unnecessary to outline to the readers the virtues of this ancient family, their kindness to the poor is widely known in the locality.

The family has been held in high regard for generations down to the present head of the family Mr R. Nanney Williams who is noted for his kindness and generosity to everyone.

It is pleasing to see that the family's generosity of spirit had been passed down to the present heir, he being exceedingly kind and a true gentleman.

A considerable sum of money has been collected and we understand that Sports will be held next Monday on the Marian.

Our wish for the young heir is a long and happy life during which he continues to do his best for his home town and country.

The celebration got underway on Sunday 18th August, when a delegation of the townsfolk gathered at Llwyn to present the young heir with a handsome inscribed silver salver

obtained through the spontaneous and willing subscriptions of the friends of the family and tenants of the estate. The salver was elaborately inscribed, and included the arms of the family, a lion rampant.

Speeches were made and the young heir responded by expressing his hope that he could live up to their expectations and was sorry that his father could not attend the celebrations, his poor state of health precluding him from joining in with the festivities.

The following morning the town of Dolgellau awoke to a remarkable transformation: banners, bunting and flags in profusion echoed the sentiments of all the inhabitants:

Long life and happiness to the heir of the Llwyn.

The church bells rang merrily throughout the day and the Idris Brass Band marched through the town playing their stirring tunes. In the afternoon Athletic Sports were held on the Marian Mawr with many youngsters coming from Bala and Barmouth area to take part in the events. The organisers had carefully formulated the programme for maximum interest and enjoyment, the bicycle slow race and donkey derby appealing most to the hundreds of onlookers.

Tables laden with bara brith and all manner of cakes and refreshments were liberally set up in many streets of the town, and all were encouraged to partake of the delicacies so generously provided.

The Llwyn family had not forgotten the inmates of the Workhouse, and had provided a magnificent feast for them to enjoy.

Later in the afternoon Ludovic was hauled through the town in a carriage pulled by a host of strong youths, being led by the town band still issuing forth their lively music. The musical procession progressed through the town to the Workhouse where the young heir alighted to the delight of the inmates who thanked him profusely for remembering them.

As evening fell a bonfire was lit on the fields of Staylittle, and a display of fireworks was held

on the fields in front of Llwyn. The celebrations concluded with balloons being let off just above the great bridge.

The tenants of the Llwyn estate at Dinas Mawddwy sat down to a dinner at the Red Lion Hotel which had been arranged by Robert Nanney Williams.

It had been a day to remember; the town had risen to the occasion and provided Ludovic with fond memories, in stark contrast to the dark shadow that would soon envelop the estate and its benevolent family.

Less than a year later, the death of Robert Nanney Williams on the 2nd April 1896, heralded

413. below: **Elizabeth, wife of Robert Nanney Williams, in the gardens at Llwyn,** *circa 1896*

415. above: **Tyn y Coed, Arthog, home of Mr William Simms Bull (son of Joseph Bull - Iron Master of Birmingham)**

the beginning of a swathe of litigation that would eventually lead to the break-up of the ancient estate. It emerged that Miss Anne Hartley, Robert's aunt, had written a will ten years previously, bequeathing her half-share of the Llwyn estate to the third son of Griffith Williams, namely Meyrick Meredith Williams. In reality Thomas Humphrey Williams had only been entitled to pass on his half of the estate to his brother Robert, and hence to Ludovic.

Dr. Meyrick Meredith Williams was at this time a surgeon, living in Dalbeattie, Scotland. Having undertaken his medical training in Glasgow, he naturally took up residence in Scotland. It appeared that a family solicitor, who had died, had hidden the contentious will and his widow had intervened and alerted Meyrick to his rightful inheritance. Not wanting to feel the wrath of his elder brother Robert, Meyrick had held back the legal challenge until his brother had passed away and only then unleashed the

full force of the law on his young nephew Ludovic.

Ludovic was immediately launched into litigation that would be the hallmark of his tenure for the next decade as a string of court cases saw his estate whittle away to nothing. It must have been totally perplexing for the young, naive heir: on the one hand, legal advice encouraged him to fight the claim made by his uncle, as he was assured 'he could not lose'; and on the other, his uncle decried the folly of his ways. Although he initially fought the claim, Ludovic was forced to yield as the Chancery Court awarded half the estate to his uncle Meyrick and loaded the costs onto the defendant.

In September 1897, Ludovic resigned his commission in the 4th Battalion, the Royal Welsh Fusiliers, to concentrate on running the Llwyn estate together with his uncle. Such a fickle

416. above: **Ludovic Nanney Williams,** *circa 1910*

417. above: **Mary Emily Maud with her first child,**
Ethel Mary *(Chester 1900)*

partnership was doomed to failure from the beginning, and the uneasy venture began to unravel in 1899, when Dr. Meyrick Meredith Williams once more dragged his young nephew through the court for a share of a family settlement he perceived was his due. On this occasion the court dismissed the claim on the grounds of statutes of limitation.

On a happier note on the 16th September 1899, Ludovic married Mary Emily Maud, the daughter of William Simms Bull, a wealthy industrialist whose wife Mary was the daughter of William Adams of the well-known potting dynasty of Stoke-on-Trent. William Simms Bull, Deputy Mayor of Cheltenham, seemingly disapproved of this union, fearing it unwise for his daughter to get involved with such a litigious family. The young couple, however, were deeply in love and 'absconded' and married in St. Pancras Church, London. At the very last minute they got the approval of her father, the bride being only 19 and a minor, but William

Simms Bull did not attend the young couple's wedding.

Years of litigation were taking their toll on young Ludovic, who by 1900, aged 26, withdrew from Dolgellau, taking up residence in Chester with his growing family. Mary, who could see the imminence of a break-down, probably instigated the move. For the next decade Ludovic built a life for himself and his family in Chester, joining in with local charities and church events. At this point in time he appears to have turned his back on his family estate, and although he still had a part-time agent to collect rents, he was drifting further and further away from his uncle.

In 1906, when living at Prestatyn, Ludovic made a request in court to sell his half of the estate. Court records show that at this time the Llwyn estate consisted of 4,615 acres and many houses, pubs and shops in Dolgellau. The whole estate was valued at approximately £50,000, with a

418. *The Nanney Williams Family,* (Chester 1904)

419. below: *Poster announcing the Llwyn Estate sale of 1912*

420. below: *Sale catalogue of the remnants of the Llwyn Estate in 1941, on the death of Dr. M. M. Williams (Uncle to Ludovic Nanney Williams)*

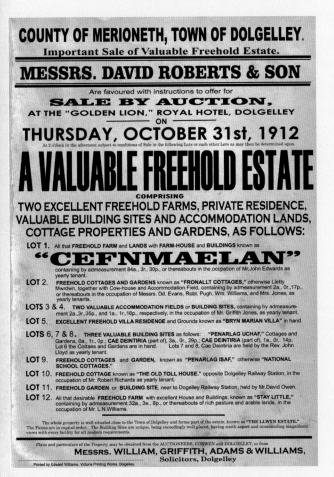

COUNTY OF MERIONETH, TOWN OF DOLGELLEY.

Important Sale of Valuable Freehold Estate.

MESSRS. DAVID ROBERTS & SON

Are favoured with instructions to offer for

SALE BY AUCTION,

AT THE "GOLDEN LION," ROYAL HOTEL, DOLGELLEY

ON

THURSDAY, OCTOBER 31st, 1912

At 2 o'clock in the afternoon subject to conditions of Sale in the following Lots or such other Lots as may then be determined upon.

A VALUABLE FREEHOLD ESTATE

COMPRISING

TWO EXCELLENT FREEHOLD FARMS, PRIVATE RESIDENCE, VALUABLE BUILDING SITES AND ACCOMMODATION LANDS, COTTAGE PROPERTIES AND GARDENS, AS FOLLOWS:

LOT 1. All that FREEHOLD FARM and LANDS with FARM-HOUSE and BUILDINGS known as

"CEFNMAELAN"

containing by admeasurement 84a., 3r., 30p., or thereabouts in the occpation of Mr. John Edwards as yearly tenant.

LOT 2. FREEHOLD COTTAGES and GARDENS known as "FRONALLT COTTAGES," otherwise Lletty Mwrdwn, together with Cow-house and Accommodation Field, containing by admeasurement 2a., 0r.,17p., or thereabouts in the occupation of Messrs. Dd. Evans, Robt. Pugh, Wm. Williams, and Mrs. Jones, as yearly tenants.

LOTS 3 & 4. TWO VALUABLE ACCOMMODATION FIELDS or BUILDING SITES, containing by admeasurement 2a.,3r.,35p., and 1a., 1r.,16p., respectively, in the occupation of Mr. Griffith Jones, as yearly tenant.

LOT 5. EXCELLENT FREEHOLD VILLA RESIDENCE and Grounds known as "BRYN MARIAN VILLA" in hand.

LOTS 6, 7 & 8. THREE VALUABLE BUILDING SITES as follows: "PENARLAG UCHAF," Cottages and Gardens, 0a., 1r., 0p.; CAE DEINTIRIA (part of), 3a., 0r., 29p.; CAE DEINTIRIA (part of), 1a., 0r., 14p. Lot 6 the Cottages and Gardens are in hand. Lots 7 and 8, Cae Deintiria are held by the Rev. John Lloyd as yearly tenant.

LOT 9. FREEHOLD COTTAGES and GARDEN, known as "PENARLAG ISAF," otherwise "NATIONAL SCHOOL COTTAGES."

LOT 10. FREEHOLD COTTAGE known as "THE OLD TOLL HOUSE," opposite Dolgelley Railway Station, in the occupation of Mr. Robert Richards as yearly tenant.

LOT 11. FREEHOLD GARDEN or BUILDING SITE, near to Dogelley Railway Station, held by Mr. David Owen.

LOT 12. All that desirable FREEHOLD FARM with excellent House and Buildings, known as "STAY LITTLE," containing by admeasurement 32a., 3e., 8p., or thereabouts of rich pasture and arable lands, in the occupation of Mr. L.N.Williams.

The whole property is well situated close to the Town of Dolgelley and forms part of the estate, known as "THE LLWYN ESTATE." The Farms are in capital order. The Building Sites are unique, being exceedingly well placed, having south aspect and commanding magnificent views with every facility for all modern requirements.

Plans and particulars of the Property may be obtained from the AUCTIONEERS, CORWEN and DOLGELLEY, or from

MESSRS. WILLIAM, GRIFFITH, ADAMS & WILLIAMS,
Solicitors, Dolgelley.

Printed by Edward Williams, Victoria Printing Works, Dolgelley.

PARTICULARS

OF THE

Desirable Freehold Properties

FORMING THE

Hendre Eirian and Llwyn Estates

IN THE DISTRICTS OF

Dyffryn and Barmouth, Dolgelley and Dinas Mawddwy,

EXTENDING TO AN AREA OF ABOUT

1444 Acres

AND INCLUDING

7 WELL-KNOWN FARMS, EXTENSIVE SHEEP WALKS, RESIDENTIAL PROPERTIES, ACCOMMODATION LAND, GROUND RENTS, &c.

TO BE SOLD BY AUCTION AT

The Golden Lion Royal Hotel, Dolgelley,

On Wednesday, August 27th, 1941,

at 3 o'clock in the afternoon PUNCTUALLY,

and subject to conditions to be produced (Unless previously Sold by Private Treaty)

To view apply to the Tenants and for further particulars to the Solicitors,

Messrs. ELDRIDGE & JONES-WILLIAMS, Dolgelley,

and also (as to Lots 1, 2, 3 and 4) to

Messrs. GUTHRIE JONES & JONES, Dolgelley,

and (as to Lots 1 and 2) to

Messrs. FOULKES-JONES & SON, Llangollen,

or the Auctioneers,

MORRIS, MARSHALL & POOLE, Welshpool (Phone 10).

---

rental income of £1920 per year. Whilst Ludovic wanted to sell his part, Meyrick indicated that he wished to keep his intact. It was decreed that a sale be arranged and the estate partitioned.

In 1907, the sale of part of Llwyn estate ended many years of uncertainty as far as a number of tenants were concerned, as a significant number were to buy their own properties. After paying off a great deal of his accrued debt and mortgages, Ludovic was left with the ownership of 15 farms in Dinas Mawddwy, a scattering of farms and properties in Dolgellau, and the co-ownership of the Llwyn mansion and farm.

Ludovic's continued absence had a detrimental effect on what was left of his dwindling estate and, still with mounting debt and mortgage demands, he sold his Mawddwy holdings to Sir O. M. Edwards in 1912, for £7995. Sir O. M. Edwards had, at the eleventh hour, stepped in at the behest of one of the tenants to save the whole valley of tenant farmers from losing their homes and livelihoods.

In a further sale of 1912, the last of Ludovic's holdings went under the hammer, and he bought back the farm of Staylittle where the family remained until his death in 1947.

Dr. Meyrick Meredith Williams, as tenant for life, continued to run his half of the Llwyn and Hendre Eirian estates profitably until his death in 1940, aged almost a hundred, when he passed it to his sister's children. They petitioned the court to sell the remainder of the estate in 1941, which comprised the Llwyn mansion and some 1444 acres.

The selling of the family mansion had a devastating effect on Ludovic and sadly he never recovered from the ordeal. In later life his thoughts often drifted back to an era when the Llwyn's ancient walls echoed to the sounds of a more joyful time. True to the spirit of the old family, though devoid of his estate, Ludovic in old age regularly called on many of his old tenants as if to check on their welfare. They for their part still held the old family in high regard: a worthy tribute to a true gentleman who strongly adhered to the beliefs so firmly held by his family throughout the centuries. He was one of the last truly beneficial landowners of Merioneth and a most perfect gentleman.

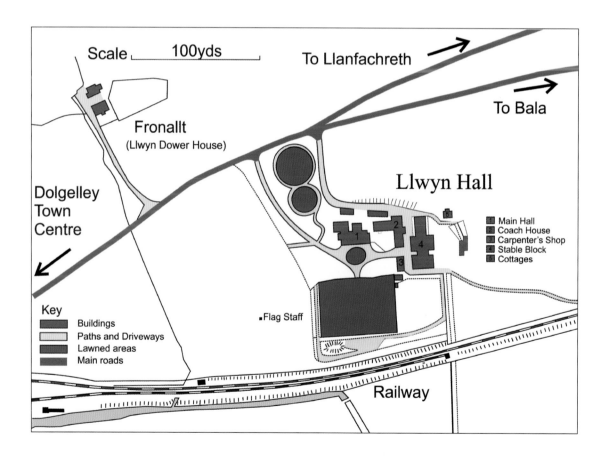

Scale ⌐____100yds____⌐

To Llanfachreth

To Bala

Fronallt
(Llwyn Dower House)

Dolgelley
Town
Centre

Llwyn Hall

1 Main Hall
2 Coach House
3 Carpenter's Shop
4 Stable Block
5 Cottages

Key

Buildings
Paths and Driveways
Lawned areas
Main roads

Flag Staff

Railway

422. **Williams** of **Caegoronwy** Estate

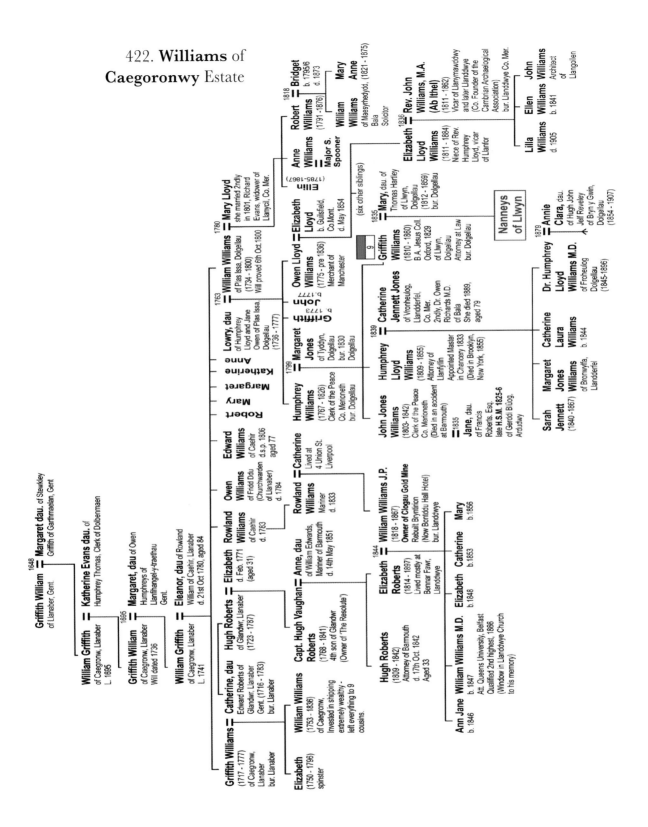

NANNEYS
OF MAESYPANDY, LLANFENDIGAID AND MAESYNEUADD

The history of the Nanneys of Llanfendigaid and Maesyneuadd have been well researched and comprehensively outlined by Miles Wynn Cato in his books *Old Blood of Merioneth* (1989) and *A Perfect Patriarch* (1993). Therefore what follows here is effectively a summary for the purpose of historical continuity.

This branch of the family, in common with the Llwyn, descend from Lewis Nanney of Maesypandy, but through his eldest son and heir John Nanney I. Over the next century no fewer than four John Nanneys, all following successively in lineal descent, headed up the family.

John Nanney I married Elizabeth, daughter and heiress of John Anwyl of Llanfendigaid, and seems to have lived most of his life at Llanfendigaid as his mother Jane, having married secondly John Lloyd of Ceiswyn, still occupied the family mansion of Maesypandy. By 1693, two years after the death of his mother, documents reveal him to be residing at Maesypandy and enjoying the benefits of both estates.

John Nanney II married Blandina, daughter of Vincent Corbet of Ynysymaengwyn, a nearby estate, and in all probability took up residence at Llanfendigaid. He sadly predeceased his father in 1681 at a relatively young age, leaving behind

a widow with three young children, the oldest, John Nanney III, aged only 8yrs.

John Nanney III of Maesypandy's tenure was fortunately longer. He married Mary the daughter of Humphrey Pugh of Aberffrydlan, a local gentry family. The marriage produced five children and he rose to be High Sheriff of Merioneth in 1701, emulating most heirs in his immediate family with the exception of his father. His son and heir, John Nanney IV, is accredited with the rebuilding of Llanfendigaid, although curiously he continued to live at Maesypandy, forgoing the pleasure of occupying his fashionable new seven-bayed house and seemingly content to let it to tenants. A possible explanation might lie in the relative size of the two estates: Maesypandy was the largest estate by far, making it wholly appropriate to reside there. He possibly had thoughts of retiring to Llanfendigaid in his later years.

The last of the John Nanneys died in 1764 and was buried in Talyllyn. The failure of the male

423 above: Coat of Arms of the Nanney-Wynn family

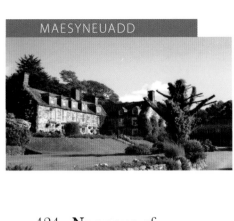

MAESYNEUADD

424. Nanneys of Maesypandy, Llanfendigaid & Maesyneuadd

LLANFENDIGAID

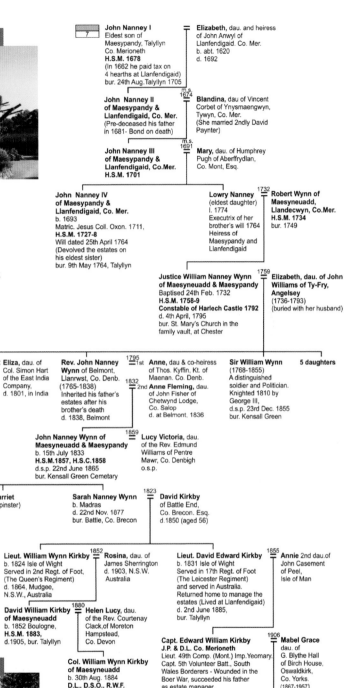

John Nanney I
Eldest son of
Maesypandy, Talyllyn
Co. Merioneth
H.S.M. 1678
(In 1662 he paid tax on
4 hearths at Llanfendigaid)
bur. 24th Aug.Talyllyn 1705

Elizabeth, dau. and heiress
of John Anwyl of
Llanfendigaid. Co. Mer.
b. abt. 1620
d. 1692

— m.s 1674 —

John Nanney II
of Maesypandy &
Llanfendigaid, Co. Mer.
(Pre-deceased his father
in 1681- Bond on death)

Blandina, dau of Vincent
Corbet of Ynysmaengwyn,
Tywyn, Co. Mer.
(She married 2ndly David
Paynter)

— m.s 1691 —

John Nanney III
of Maesypandy &
Llanfendigaid, Co.Mer.
H.S.M. 1701

Mary, dau. of Humphrey
Pugh of Aberffrydlan,
Co. Mont, Esq.

John Nanney IV
of Maesypandy &
Llanfendigaid, Co. Mer.
b. 1693
Matric. Jesus Coll. Oxon. 1711,
H.S.M. 1727-8
Will dated 25th April 1764
(Devolved the estates on
his eldest sister)
bur. 9th May 1764, Talyllyn

Lowry Nanney
(eldest daughter)
l. 1774
Executrix of her
brother's will 1764
Heiress of
Maesypandy and
Llanfendigaid

— 1732 —

Robert Wynn of
Maesyneuadd,
Llandecwyn, Co.Mer.
H.S.M. 1734
bur. 1749

Justice William Nanney Wynn
of Maesyneuadd & Maesypandy
Baptised 24th Feb. 1732
H.S.M. 1758-9
Constable of Harlech Castle 1792
d. 4th April, 1795
bur. St. Mary's Church in the
family vault, at Chester

— 1759 —

Elizabeth, dau. of John
Williams of Ty-Fry,
Anglesey
(1736-1793)
(buried with her husband)

Capt. Robert Wynn
(1760-1803)
(pedigrees say he died
unmarried in 1803, but
record of his marriage
in India to Eliza may have
been deliberately destroyed)
Returned to England in
where he died,
bur. St. Marylebone.
London

Eliza, dau. of
Col. Simon Hart
of the East India
Company,
d. 1801, in India

Rev. John Nanney
Wynn of Belmont,
Llanrwst, Co. Denb.
(1765-1838)
Inherited his father's
estates after his
brother's death
d. 1838, Belmont

— 1795 1st —

Anne, dau & co-heiress
of Thos. Kyffin, Kt. of
Maenan. Co. Denb.

— 1832 2nd —

Anne Fleming, dau.
of John Fisher of
Chetwynd Lodge,
Co. Salop
d. at Belmont, 1836

Sir William Wynn
(1768-1855)
A distinguished
soldier and Politician.
Knighted 1810 by
George III,
d.s.p. 23rd Dec. 1855
bur. Kensall Green

5 daughters

John Nanney Wynn of
Maesyneuadd & Maesypandy
b. 15th July 1833
H.S.M.1857, H.S.C.1858
d.s.p. 22nd June 1865
bur. Kensall Green Cemetary

— 1859 —

Lucy Victoria, dau.
of the Rev. Edmund
Williams of Pentre
Mawr, Co. Denbigh
o.s.p.

Rev. Simon Hart Nanney Wynn
10
(1799-1865)
Rector of West Barkwith, Lincs.
Adm. St. John's Coll. Camb. 1819
Matric. Lent 1820 - migrated to
Magdalene Coll. 1822, B.A. 1824
d.s.p. 15th Nov. 1865

Harriet
(Spinster)

Sarah Nanney Wynn
b. Madras
d. 22nd Nov. 1877
bur. Battle, Co. Brecon

— 1823 —

David Kirkby
of Battle End,
Co. Brecon. Esq.
d.1850 (aged 56)

Lieut. William Wynn Kirkby
b. 1824 Isle of Wight
Served in 2nd Regt. of Foot,
(The Queen's Regiment)
d. 1864, Mudgee,
N.S.W., Australia

— 1852 —

Rosina, dau. of
James Sherrington
d. 1903, N.S.W.
Australia

Lieut. David Edward Kirkby
b. 1831 Isle of Wight
Served in 17th Regt. of Foot
(The Leicester Regiment)
and served in Australia.
Returned home to manage the
estates (Lived at Llanfendigaid)
d. 2nd June 1885,
bur. Talyllyn

— 1855 —

Annie 2nd dau.of
John Casement
of Peel,
Isle of Man

David William Kirkby
of Maesyneuadd
b. 1852 Boulogne,
H.S.M. 1883,
d.1905, bur. Talyllyn

— 1880 —

Helen Lucy, dau.
of the Rev. Courtenay
Clack,of Moreton
Hampstead,
Co. Devon

Col. William Wynn Kirkby
of Maesyneuadd
b. 30th Aug. 1884
D.L., D.S.O., R.W.F.
(Under him the
estates failed and
had to be sold in
the 1920s and 30s)

Capt. Edward William Kirkby
J.P. & D.L. Co. Merioneth
Lieut. 49th Comp. (Mont.) Imp.Yeomary.
Capt. 5th Volunteer Batt., South
Wales Borderers - Wounded in the
Boer War, succeeded his father
as estate manager.
M.B.E. 1919 (Changed his name by
deed-poll to Nanney-Wynn in 1925
and bought back Llanfendigaid)
d. 1932

— 1906 —

Mabel Grace
dau. of
G. Blythe Hall
of Birch House,
Oswaldkirk,
Co. Yorks.
(1867-1957)

Lieut. Col. Edward Roger Nanney-Wynn
b. 1907
Educ. Imperial Service College, Windsor
R.M.C., Sandhurst
(Distinguished army career - retired 1950)
D.L. Mer. 1958 & H.S.M. 1967
Knight of St. John
d. 1982 (aged 75)
bur. Rhoslefain, Co. Mer.

— 1936 —

Marjorie dau. of
Major W. Freese
-Sheffield, D.S.O.
of Farthings,
Nr. Horsham,
Sussex
(1911-2012)

3 daughters

line, the first for over 600 years, saw his entire estates devolve to his eldest sister, Lowry Nanney. Lowry had married Robert Wynn of Maesyneuadd in 1732, and on the death of John Nanney IV, this union resulted in the merging of the three estates (Maesyneuadd, Llanfendigaid and Maesypandy) under one owner. The family chose to live at Maesyneuadd, but on the death of Robert Wynn in 1749, the formidable widow seems to have spent much of her time at her childhood home of Maesypandy. In 1768, she was described as

adhering firmly to the feudal system, she exercises it's arbitrary maxims over her dependents with unlimited sway, holding her tenants, her vassals, and her household in absolute subjection as if she were

another homage Catherine, and, I doubt not would have shown as much in manly and martial enterprises, had fortune created her an Empress over subjugated kingdoms, as she had placed over a limited domain, peopled with farmers, subordinate to her will, with their labouring appendents strengthened and augmented by the numerous freeholders attached to her interest by the impulse of patronage.

(John Jackson, 1960-67)

On the death of Lowry sometime after 1774, her son and heir William Wynn inherited all three estates: Maesyneuadd from his father, and Llanfendigiaid and Maesypandy from his mother, and adhering to the terms of his uncle's

426. below: **William Nanney Wynn.** *Oil on canvas. 30 x 25 inches. James Fellowes. Circa 1759*

427. top left: **Justice William Nanney Wynn, aged 36.** *Oil on canvas.*
8 x 7 inches. Attributed to William Parry A.R.A. Circa 1768
428. below left: **Portrait of Rev. John Nanney Wynn (1765-1838)**

will, added Nanney to his name, becoming William Nanney Wynn. He chose Maesyneuadd as his home, and Maesypandy and Llanfendigaid were occupied by tenants of their home farms. He rose to the rank of a major county landowner, with a total of 75 farms and a 10,000 acre estate. William Nanney Wynn married well, taking the beautiful Elizabeth Williams of Ty-fry, Anglesey, for his wife. Elizabeth was the daughter of John Williams, an eminent barrister, and she came with a handsome marriage settlement.

William, a cultured man with a good education, fully conversant in the Welsh language, served as High Sheriff of Merioneth in 1758 and was later appointed Constable of Harlech Castle in 1792. In 1779 he was elected a member of the Druids Society, an old body that celebrated ancient Welsh traditions. William also had a passion for country sports and was a keen supporter of cock fighting.

Through the diaries of Elizabeth Baker, we gain many insights into William's life and character. She finds him charming, referring to him always as 'Mr Wynn Nanney', as opposed to William's distant cousin of Llwyn, Lewis Nanney, who she called 'Mr Nanney' or 'Justice Nanney'. Both Nanneys figure in Elizabeth's diaries, both were landed proprietors with substantial estates and both diligent Justices of the Peace; in her eyes both were thoroughly upright pillars of the community. Both were also descendants of Lewis Nanney of Maesypandy, Lewis being a great-grandson and William a three times great grandson. Both had legal training and were well acquainted, and, significantly, Justice Nanney of Llwyn chose his distant cousin as trustee for his own will in 1779.

The marriage of William and Elizabeth produced seven children, three boys and four girls. The eldest son and heir Robert caused his father much heartache and torment. Whilst at Oxford, the wayward individual took to gambling and incurred substantial debts, which William was expected to settle. Such behaviour undoubtedly put a strain on their relationship, and in 1782 Robert was sent to India to take up employment with the East India Company. The joyful celebrations of Robert's coming-of-age in 1781 were to become a dim reflection of long lost aspirations.

Robert's initial career in India might well have given his father some cause for optimism. He took part in the campaign against the King of Mysore as adjutant to the 18th Battalion (of Sepoys) and gained subsequent promotion to Captain. All too soon aspirations were shattered when, in 1794, Robert wrote to his father from Madras stating that although he was still a bachelor, he had fathered four children by a European woman - devastating news for the beleaguered father and catastrophic for the future of the estate! A further letter in September 1795, arriving seven months after the death of his father, informed the family that he had been married in January 1790 to Miss Eliza Hart, the second daughter of the late Colonel Hart of the Madras Establishment. It is thought that Robert became addicted to opium, and this would, to a certain extent, explain his erratic and often confused communications, leaving his family uncertain of his true circumstances.

Meanwhile, Robert's younger brother William was dispatched to India in 1802, with strict instructions to bring his brother back and, in the process, to search for any record of the alleged marriage. Robert returned to England in 1803, accompanied by his brother William and three children (Simon Hart Wynn, Sarah and Harriet Wynn), but he did not long survive the gruelling journey, dying intestate soon after returning to England. Under the will of William Nanney Wynn, Robert had remained heir, but his children were effectively disinherited, as no proof of their legitimacy existed. Robert Wynn would therefore have no legal heir and his brother would effectively inherit. The estate passed to his brother, Rev. John Wynn, who became a Nanney-Wynn upon inheriting the estate. His main interest was horse racing, and he ran a major stud on his own account with very considerable success.

William Nanney Wynn's third son, William, had taken up a commission in the King's Dragoon Guards during the Napoleonic Wars. He was badly wounded by a musket ball but due to the skill of a Scottish surgeon, Dr John Hunter, he survived and made a complete recovery. He was honoured by a knighthood circa 1810 and given the command of Sandown Fort on the Isle of Wight. The added advantage of marriage to an heiress, Miss Long of Tubney, brought him a fortune.

When Rev. John Nanney-Wynn died in 1838 (after catching a cold when out hunting), under the terms of his will his estates were left in trust for his son John. Life remainders were left successively to his brother Sir William and his nephew the Rev. Simon Hart Wynn and Simon's sister Sarah, who had married David Kirkby of Brecon. The next twenty years witnessed a period of protracted litigation and long Chancery suits between John Nanney-Wynn II and the other benefactors of his father's will concerning the right and title to the Maesyneuadd

estate and the legitimacy of Rev. Simon Hart Wynn, as eldest son of Robert Wynn. In a desperate attempt to prove conclusively that his father had married Elizabeth Hart, Rev. Simon travelled to Madras to elicit the proof. He became convinced that original entries of his and his sisters' births in a Madras church had been changed from 'legitimate' to 'illegitimate' in an attempt to deny the rightful heirs their inheritance. He also found that the page of the marriage register that should have contained his parent's marriage had been torn out!

Over the years Sir William Wynn became increasingly fond of his nephew (Robert's son Rev. Simon Hart Wynn) and was moved by his nephew's pleas for justice. Shortly before his death in 1855, Sir William is said to have told his nephew:

> *I declare before God that I look upon you as head of the Maesyneuadd family. I have very different feelings towards you to what I had when you were an infant, and I am willing to make you every recompense in my power. A man who had wronged another generally hates him but that is not my feeling towards you.*

In 1865, when John Nanney-Wynn II died childless, Simon Hart Nanney-Wynn finally came into his inheritance, but it was to be tragically short lived, as he too died later that year. His sister Sarah Kirkby succeeded to the combined Maesyneuadd and Maesypandy estates, together with lands in Denbigh, Flint and Caernarfon: a total of 16,022 acres and an annual rental of £4,988. Henceforth the Kirkbys became heirs of these ancient Welsh estates.

Nanneys
of Cefndeuddwr and Gwynfryn

The cadet branches of Cefndeuddwr and Maesypandy grew out of the Nannau main line in the 16th century, the former in the middle of the century and the latter at the end.

The founder of the collateral branch that established themselves in Cefndeuddwr was Richard Nanney, son of Howel Nanney of Nannau (1480-1540) by his second wife, Lowry, daughter of William ap Gruffudd ap Ieuan of Rhiwgoch, Trawsfynydd. Richard Nanney married Elizabeth, the second daughter of Baron Lewis Owen, Vice Chamberlain of North Wales, and when the Nannau/Llwyn feud broke out in the 1590s, he sided with the Owen faction against his own blood relations, an alignment that did much to distance the Cefndeuddwr branch from the main line.

Little is known of the Cefndeuddwr family until the beginning of the 18th century, when one family member rose to prominence, the Rev. Richard Nanney. He was a very evangelical cleric and vicar of Clynnog in 1718. His mother was a daughter of Richard Edwards of Nanhoron, a prominent Puritan squire in the Restoration. Rev. Richard Nanney became a strong supporter of Griffith Jones's circulating schools, and often allowed the organisation to use his church at Clynnog. His preaching must have been inspirational as accounts exist of crowds travelling to listen to him preach at Clynnog, many journeying from adjoining parishes. He cared little for worldly possessions,

it being noted by one of his contemporaries that:

> *He never knew any horse but the one he rode on.*

When he died in 1768, he passed his lands to his son, the Rev. Richard Nanney of Bachwen who, dying without issue in 1812, passed his Cefndeuddwr property to his nephew, David Ellis.

In accordance with the will of his uncle, David changed his name to Ellis Nanney. Known as

CEFNDEUDDWR

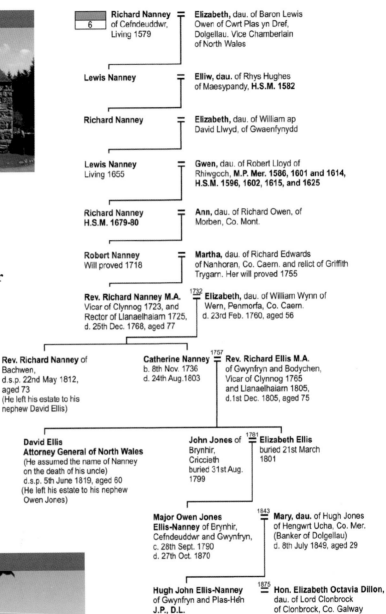

Richard Nanney
of Cefndeuddwr,
Living 1579

6

= Elizabeth, dau. of Baron Lewis
Owen of Cwrt Plas yn Dref,
Dolgellau. Vice Chamberlain
of North Wales

Lewis Nanney

= Elliw, dau. of Rhys Hughes
of Maesypandy, **H.S.M. 1582**

Richard Nanney

= Elizabeth, dau. of William ap
David Llwyd, of Gwaenfynydd

Lewis Nanney
Living 1655

= Gwen, dau. of Robert Lloyd of
Rhiwgoch, **M.P. Mer. 1586, 1601 and 1614,
H.S.M. 1596, 1602, 1615, and 1625**

Richard Nanney
H.S.M. 1679-80

= Ann, dau. of Richard Owen, of
Morben, Co. Mont.

Robert Nanney
Will proved 1718

= Martha, dau. of Richard Edwards
of Nanhoran, Co. Caern. and relict of Griffith
Trygarn. Her will proved 1755

Rev. Richard Nanney M.A.
Vicar of Clynnog 1723, and
Rector of Llanaelhaiarn 1725,
d. 25th Dec. 1768, aged 77

1732 = **Elizabeth**, dau. of William Wynn of
Wern, Penmorfa, Co. Caern.
d. 23rd Feb. 1760, aged 56

Rev. Richard Nanney of
Bachwen,
d.s.p. 22nd May 1812,
aged 73
(He left his estate to his
nephew David Ellis)

Catherine Nanney
b. 8th Nov. 1736
d. 24th Aug.1803

1757 = **Rev. Richard Ellis M.A.**
of Gwynfryn and Bodychen,
Vicar of Clynnog 1765
and Llanaelhaiarn 1805,
d.1st Dec. 1805, aged 75

**David Ellis
Attorney General of North Wales**
(He assumed the name of Nanney
on the death of his uncle)
d.s.p. 5th June 1819, aged 60
(He left his estate to his nephew
Owen Jones)

John Jones of
Brynhir,
Criccieth
buried 31st Aug.
1799

1781 = **Elizabeth Ellis**
buried 21st March
1801

**Major Owen Jones
Ellis-Nanney** of Brynhir,
Cefndeuddwr and Gwynfryn,
c. 28th Sept. 1790
d. 27th Oct. 1870

1843 = **Mary, dau.** of Hugh Jones
of Hengwrt Ucha, Co. Mer.
(Banker of Dolgellau)
d. 8th July 1849, aged 29

Hugh John Ellis-Nanney
of Gwynfryn and Plas-Hên
J.P., D.L.
b. 16th February 1845
H.S.C. 1870 and H.S.M. 1877
Created a Baronet,1897

1875 = **Hon. Elizabeth Octavia Dillon,**
dau. of Lord Clonbrock
of Clonbrock, Co. Galway

432. **Nanneys
of Brynhir,
Cefndeuddwr
& Gwynfryn**

PLAS GWYNFRYN

the 'Learned Lawyer', David Ellis Nanney rose to become Attorney General of North Wales. He married Henrietta Watts, a daughter of the Rev. Watts, vicar of Uffington in Berkshire. Similarly dying without issue, he passed his estate to his sister's son, Owen Jones, who with predictable regularity assumed the Nanney name and became Owen Jones Ellis-Nanney. Now a possessor of a landed estate, Owen immediately set about purchasing any available land in the locality of his estate at Gwynfryn. 'The Old Major' as he became affectionately known, used to delight in wandering about the area pretending to be an out of work farm-worker, asking strangers if there was any chance of getting work at the Plas (his own hall), a strategy employed to elicit their comments on the 'Lord of the Manor'.

At the age of 53, he decided that he needed an heir to pass on his estate to and quickly set about finding a wife, settling on the 23-year-old Mary, daughter of Hugh Jones of Hengwrt Uchaf, a wealthy banker of Dolgellau. Within a year of his marriage, the adjoining Plas-Hên estate came up for sale. Ellis-Nanney was able to purchase a significant part of this extensive estate, his father-in-law putting up the purchase money of £50,000! The following year, in 1845, a son and heir was born. The son and heir was christened Hugh John Ellis-Nanney, and the Plas Hên estate was settled on him, with trustees appointed to manage it until he came of age.

Young Hugh was educated at Eton and Oxford and, at the age of 25, on the death of his father, inherited the Gwynfryn estate to add to his other landholdings. Using wealth accumulated during his minority, he demolished the old house of Gwynfryn and employed architect George Williams to design a fashionable house commensurate with his standing in the community. By 1876, at the huge cost of £70,000, the new castellated 'Plas Gwynfryn' stood resplendent in its own parkland with Snowdonia as a backdrop.

Hugh John Ellis-Nanney was now squire of Gwynfryn, Plas Hên and Cefndeuddwr, and moved into his palatial new home with his recently acquired wife, the Honourable Elizabeth Octavia Dillon, youngest daughter of Lord Clonbrock of Clonbrock Castle, County Galway in Ireland. Hugh settled down to a life befitting a country gentleman and was appointed as Justice of the Peace for Caernarfonshire and Merioneth, Deputy Lieutenant of Caernarfon and High Sheriff of Caernarfon (and later Merioneth).

Hugh was also very active in local politics, and was drawn into a fight with the people's champion David Lloyd George in the Caernarfon Borough election of 1895. Losing narrowly to the future prime minster (by only 194 votes) he entered into the historical record. By way of some consolation Hugh was created a baronet in 1897, and lived out his life at Plas Gwynfryn, dying on the 7th June 1920. As his only son had died at the age of eight, the house and estate devolved to his daughter. In 1959, the estates were finally broken up and sold almost entirely to tenants.

433. **Plas Gwynfryn** (2014)

NANNAU: An Epilogue

Nannau is a house renowned for many reasons; its ancient origins, its attraction to medieval bards, its elevation of over 700ft, which with its superb views suggest that for once a Welsh house builder appreciated the majesty and beauty of his native land.

(Royal Commission on the Ancient and Historical Monuments of Wales)

Nannau's importance in Welsh history is immense, its ancient story indelibly etched on its beautiful Snowdonia setting. Through nine hundred years, twenty-five generations of Nanneys and Vaughans have left a unique legacy in their wake.

Once aptly described as the 'Jewel in the Meirionydd crown', Nannau now stands desolate and forgotten - a melancholy sentence for such a noble house.

With the inevitable twentieth-century decline and break-up of the estate, Nannau was sold to a succession of owners, each one with their own vision for the future of this important house. From Country House Hotel to proposed Leisure Complex and Chalet Park, the schemes seemed destined to fail.

Two decades of neglect took its toll on the mansion. It became badly infected with dry rot, which tragically led to the once grand Georgian interiors being completely stripped out, with the exception of the staircase and its decorative iron balusters. Bromfield's magnificent plaster work, the marble fireplaces and moulded door cases have all disappeared, leaving a gutted shell - a sad reminder of the once illustrious house.

In recent times, despite being issued with a repair notice, the ancient edifice languishes in a time warp, condemned to slip down the slippery slope of neglect to the unthinkable ... dilapidation and ruin ... becoming another grim statistic in Wales's register of lost heritage.

All images circa 2000

THE FORSAKEN

The peace which others seek they find;
The heaviest storms not longest last;
Heaven grants even to the guiltiest mind
An amnesty for what is past;
When will my sentence be reversed?
I only pray to know the worst;
And wish as if my heart would burst.

O weary struggle! Silent year
Tell seemingly no doubtful tale;
And yet they leave it short, and fear
And hopes are strong and will prevail.
My calmest faith escapes not pain;
And, feeling that the hope in vain,
I think that He will come again.

William Wordsworth

PHOTOGRAPHIC CREDITS

Every effort has been made to secure the permission of the copyright holders of images used and credits listed as requested. Any deficiencies brought to our attention will be corrected in subsequent editions.

For the many individuals and institutions who allowed images to be used free of charge, the author would like to offer sincere thanks for their generosity and support.

* All numbers are references to images in the book

AP, HP & **CM** 277
Airborne Assault Duxford 310, 314, 315, 316, 320, 326, 327, 328, 329
Author's Collection 22, 39, 43, 48, 49, 54, 57, 62, 71, 72, 75, 106, 110, 116, 119, 128, 132, 133, 134, 153, 163, 164, 165, 176, 178, 181, 182, 189, 190, 194, 215, 221, 222, 225, 227, 228, 229, 230, 231, 236, 237, 241, 247, 248, 249, 252, 253, 255, 259, 260, 261, 262, 263, 270, 271, 274, 275, 276, 278, 279, 280, 281, 282, 292, 296, 299, 300, 330, 334, 342, 352, 358, 375, 376, 381, 393, 394, 395, 396, 401, 406, 407, 408, 411, 414, 416, 417, 418, 419
Bangor University Archives and Special Collections 144, 210
Richard Bebb (Welsh Antiques) 143, 204,
The British Library 15, 217
David Brown 433
Stuart Brown (Skipper Press) 312
Canadian War Museum 273
Miles Wynn Cato (Welsh Art) 105, 122, 123, 124, 125, 127, 154, 158, 162, 179, 205, 211, 423, 425, 426, 427, 428, 429, 430
Gwynedd Archives, Caernarvon 198, 220, 223, 283, 284, 369, 402, 403, 405, 413, 415, 420
Guildhall Art Gallery, City of London 81
Paul Hett 206, 295, 344
Horse Power, the museum of the King's Royal Hussars, Winchester 297
The Armstrong Papers at the University of Limerick Glucksman Library 254, 267, 268, 269
T.A.Morrison 258, 346
The Museum Of London 382
Nannau – (Family collection) 301, 302, 303, 304, 305, 306, 308, 309, 311, 313, 317, 318, 323, 324, 331, 336, 337, 338, 339, 340, 341, 345, 347, 348, 349, 350, 351
National Library of Scotland 272
National Library of Wales 2, 11, 18, 45, 46, 47, 117, 120, 121, 126, 135, 145, 146, 147, 151, 159, 160, 161, 167, 180, 184, 187, 365, 368, 380, 391, 409, 431
National Museum of Wales 131, 141, 142, 150, 152, 196, 197, 200, 293
National Portrait Gallery 155, 201, 239
National Trust 38
Richard Pillinger 264, 265, 266
Powysland Club 59
Christopher Quail 285, 286, 287, 288,289, 290, 291

BIBLIOGRAPHY by chapters

This initial list of publications were extensively utilised during the writing of this book and are clearly identified as sources that relate to a number of different chapters:

J.E. Griffith, *Pedigrees of Anglesey and Caernarvonshire Families with their Collateral Branches in Denbighshire and Merionethshire, and other parts* (Horne Castle, 1914)

E.D. Jones, 'The Family of Nannau (Nanney) of Nannau', *Journal of the Merioneth Historical and Record Society (1953)*

Brynle Rees Parry, *The History of the Nannau Family (Merionethshire) to 1623,* unpublished M.A. Thesis, University of Wales (1958)

J. Beverley Smith and Llinos Beverley Smith (eds.), *History of Merioneth Vol. II : The Middle Ages* (Cardiff, 2001)

Bangor University: Archives and Special Collections, *Nannau Manuscripts*

Philip Nanney Williams, Pauline Ann Williams (eds.), *The Nanney Williams Collection: Covering Nannau, Dol'rhyd and Hengwrt Estates and the written communications between the major participants (19th and 20th Century)* (2010, unpublished catalogue – 582 items)

CHAPTER 1. A Royal Dynastic Descent (1018-1128)

P.C. Bartrum (ed.), 'Achau Brenhinoedd a Thywysogion Cymru', *Bulletin of the Board of Celtic Studies,* 19 (1960-2)

P.C. Bartrum (ed.), *Early Welsh Genealogical Tracts* (Cardiff, 1966)

P.C. Bartrum, 'Some Studies in Early Welsh History', *Transactions of the Honourable Society of Cymmrodorion* (1948)

P.C. Bartrum, *Welsh Genealogies A.D. 300-1400,* 8 vols. (Cardiff 1974), *and supplement* (Cardiff 1980)

Thomas Jones (ed. & trans.) *Brut y Tywysogion, or the (Chronicle of the Princes): Peniarth MS 20* (Cardiff, 1952)

Thomas Jones (ed. & trans.) *Brut y Tywysogion,* or the (Chronicle of the Princes): *Red Book of Hergest* (2nd edition - Cardiff, 1973)

A.D. Carr, *Medieval Wales* (London, 1995)

B.G. Charles, *Old Norse relations with Wales* (London, 1934)

John Davies, *A History of Wales* (London, 1993)

R.R. Davies,   *The Age of Conquest: Wales 1063-1415* (Oxford, 1991)

R.G. Vaughton Dymock, 'The Policy of the Princes of Powys after Bleddyn',
                  Montgomeryshire Collections, 36 (1910-12)

T.P. Ellis,   *The Story of Two Parishes, Dolgelley and Llanelltyd*
                  (Newtown, 1928)

T.P. Ellis,   *Welsh Tribal Law and Custom in the Middle Ages* (Oxford, 1926)

J.E. Lloyd,   *A History of Wales, from the Earliest Times to the Edwardian
                  Conquest* (London, 1939)

J.Y.W. Lloyd,   *The History of the Princes, The Lords Marcher, and the Ancient
                  Nobility of Powys Fadog* (London, 1884)

K.L. Maund,   'Cynan ab Iago and the Killing of Gruffudd ap Llywelyn',
                  Cambridge Medieval Celtic Studies, 10 (1985)

K.L. Maund,   *Ireland, Wales and England in the eleventh century*
                  (Woodbridge, 1991)

K.L. Maund,   'Trahaearn ap Caradog: Legitimate Usurper?', *Welsh History
                  Review*, 13 (1987)

Kari Maund,   *Princess Nest of Wales: Seductress of the English* (Stroud, 2007)

Kari Maund,   *The Welsh Kings* (Stroud, 2000)

W.J. McCann,   'The Welsh view of the Normans in the 11th and 12th Centuries',
                  Transactions of the Honourable Society of Cymmrodorion (1991)

David Moore,   *The Welsh Wars of Independence c.410 - c.1415* (Stroud, 2005)

Edward Owen,   *A List of those who did Homage & Fealty to the First English
                  Prince of Wales in A.D. 1301* (1901)

T. Jones Pierce, 'The Age of the Princes' in *The Historical Basis of Welsh
                  Nationalism* (1950)

A.J. Roderick,   'Marriage & Politics in Wales, 1066-1282', *Welsh History
                  Review*, 4 (1968-9)

D. Stephenson,   *The Governance of Gwynedd* (Cardiff, 1984)

R. Turvey,   *The Welsh Princes 1063-1283* (London, 2002)

John Williams,   Ab Ithel (ed.), *Annales Cambriae* (London, 1860)

D. Wyatt,   'Gruffudd ap Cynan and the Hiberno-Norse World',
                  Welsh History Review, 19 (1999)

CHAPTER 2. Foundation of the House of Nannau (1129-1400)

P.B. Ironside Bax, *The Cathedral Church of St. Asaph* (1896)

E. Breese,   *The New Kalendars of Gwynedd 1284-1993* (Denbigh, 1994)

A.D. Carr,   'An Aristocracy in Decline: The Native Welsh Lords after the Edwardian
                  Conquest', *Welsh History Review*, 5 (1970-71)

R.R. Davies,   'Kings, Lords and Liberties in the March of Wales', *Transactions of the
                  Royal Historical Society*, 29 (1979)

Ruth C. Easterling, 'Anian of Nannau, O.F.P.', *Journal of the Flintshire
                  Historical Society* (1914-15)

J.G. Edwards,   'The Battle of Maes Madog and the Welsh Campaign of 1294-5',
                  English History Review, 39 (1924)

J.G. Edwards,	'Madog ap Llywelyn: the Welsh Leader in 1294-95,' *Bulletin of the Board of Celtic Studies*, 13 (1950)
Canon J. Fisher,	'Three Welsh Wills', *Archaeologia Cambrensis* (1919)
C.A. Gresham,	*Medieval Stone Carving in North Wales: Sepulchral Slabs and Effigies of the Thirteenth and Fourteenth Centuries* (Cardiff 1968)
J. Griffiths,	'The Revolt of Madog ap Llywelyn, 1294-95', *Transactions of the Caernarvonshire Historical Society*, 16 (1955)
A. Jones,	'Estates of the Welsh Abbeys', *Archaeologia Cambrensis* (1937)
Arthur Jones (ed. & trans.),	*The History of Gruffudd ap Cynan* (Manchester, 1910)
F. Jones,	'The Dynasty of Powys', *Transactions of the Honourable Society of Cymmrodorion* (1958)
E.A. Lewis,	'The Decay of Tribalism in North Wales', *Transactions of the Honourable Society of Cymmrodorion* (1902-3)
Kari Maund,	*The Welsh Kings* (Stroud, 2000)
J.E. Morris,	*The Welsh Wars of Edward I* (Oxford, 1901)
National Library of Wales,	'Madog ap Llywelyn', *[1]* *(http://yba.llgc.org.uk/en/s-MADO-APL-1294.html)*
T. Jones Pierce,	'Ancient Meirionydd', *Journal of the Merioneth Historical and Record Society* (1949-51)
T. Jones Pierce,	'Einion ap Ynyr (Anian II) Bishop of St. Asaph', *Flintshire Historical Society Publication*, 17 (1957)
A.J. Roderick,	'The feudal relations between the English Crown and the Welsh Princes', *History*, 37 (1952)
F.A. Seebohm,	*The Tribal System* (2nd edition, 1904)
J. Beverley Smith and L.A.S. Butler,	'The Cistercian Order: Cymer Abbey' in *History of Merioneth, Vol. II* (J. Beverley Smith and Llinos Beverley Smith, eds.) (Cardiff, 2001)
J. Beverley Smith,	'Owain Gwynedd', *Transactions of Caernarvonshire Historical Society*, 32 (1971)
D.R. Thomas,	*History of the Diocese of St. Asaph*, Vol. I (1908)
R. Vaughan,	'Notes on the House of Nannau', *Archaeologia Cambrensis* (1863)
David H. Williams,	'The Cistercians in West Wales', *Archaeologia Cambrensis* (1981)
David H. Williams,	*The Welsh Cistercians* (Pontypool, 1969)
Gruffydd Aled Williams,	'The Literary Tradition to c.1560' in *History of Merioneth, Vol. II* (J. Beverley Smith and Llinos Beverley Smith, eds.) (Cardiff, 2001)
Stephen W. Williams,	'Some Monumental Effigies in Wales', *Archaeologia Cambrensis* (1890)
K. Williams-Jones,	'Llywelyn's Charter to Cymer Abbey in 1209', *Journal of the Merioneth Historical and Record Society* (1957)

CHAPTER 3. Nannau's Blasted Oak (1401-1402)

S. Baring-Gould,	*A Book of North Wales* (London, 1903)
William Bingley,	*Excursions in North Wales* (London, 1839)
Jim Bradbury,	*The Medieval Archer* (Suffolk, 1985)
G.J. Brough,	*Glyn Dŵr's War* (Cowbridge, 2002)
Louisa Stuart Costello,	*The Falls, Lakes, and Mountains of North Wales* (London, 1845)
T.P. Ellis,	*The Story of Two Parishes, Dolgelley and Llanelltyd* (Newtown, 1928)
Rev. John Evans,	*Topographical and historical description of North Wales* (London, 1812)
Richard Fenton,	*Tours in Wales: 1804 - 1813*, edited by John Fisher (London, 1917)
Douglas B. Hague, Cynthia Warhurst,	'Excavations at Sycharth Castle, Denbighshire, 1962-63', *Archaeologia Cambrensis* (1966)
George Agar Hansard,	*The Book of Archery* (London, 1841)
D.R. Johnston (ed.),	*Gwaith Iolo Goch* (Cardiff, 1988)
E. A. Kilner,	*Four Welsh Counties* (London, 1891)
H. Lewis, T. Roberts, I. Williams,	*Cywyddau Iolo Goch ac Eraill* (Cardiff, 1937)
J.E. Lloyd,	*Owen Glendower: Owain Glyn Dwr* (Oxford, 1931)
A. Morris,	*Merionethshire* (Cambridge, 1915)
Thomas Pennant,	*A Tour in Wales*, 2 vols. (London, 1784)
R. Vaughan,	'Notes on the House of Nannau', *Archaeologia Cambrensis* (1863)
Gruffydd Aled Williams,	'The Medieval Welsh Poetry associated with Owain Glyndŵr' (*Sir John Rhŷs Memorial Lecture*, 2010)

CHAPTER 4. The Emergence of a Gentry Family (1403-1573)

W. Watkin Davies,	*A Wayfarer in Wales* (London, 1931)
T.P. Ellis,	'Merioneth Notes', *Y Cymmrodor* (1927)
T.P. Ellis,	'The Founding of Cymmer Abbey' (Chapter 8) in *The Story of Two Parishes, Dolgelley and Llanelltyd* (Newtown, 1928)
H. T. Evans,	*Wales and the Wars of the Roses* (Cambridge, 1915)
W.J. Hemp,	'The Tale of a Bucket', *Journal of the Merioneth Historical and Record Society* (1960)
Trevor Herbert, Gareth Elwyn Jones (eds.),	*Tudor Wales* (Cardiff, 1998)
G. Jones,	*The Gentry and the Elizabethan State* (Llandybie, 1977)
J.G. Jones,	'The Merioneth Gentry in the Social Order: Bardic Evidence c.1540-1640', *Journal of the Merioneth Historical and Record Society* (1984)
J.G. Jones,	'The Welsh Poets and their Patrons c. 1550-1640', *Welsh History Review*, 9 (1979)
J. Gwynfor Jones,	*Concepts of Order and Gentility in Wales 1540-1640* (Llandysul, 1992)

J. Gwynfor Jones,	*The Welsh Gentry 1536-1640* (Cardiff, 1998)
Thomas H. Lewis,	'The Justice of the Peace in Wales', *Transactions of the Honourable Society of Cymmrodorion* (1943-4)
Hugh J. Owen,	*Treasures of the Mawddach* (Bala, 1950)
Hugh J. Owen,	'The Romance of the Chalice and Paten of Cymer Abbey', *Journal of the Merioneth Historical and Record Society* (1955)
Peter R. Roberts,	'The Act of Union in Welsh History', *Transactions of the Honourable Society of Cymmrodorion* (1972-3)
D.M. Robinson,	*Cymer Abbey* (Cadw, 1990)
Colin Thomas,	'Patterns and Processes of Estate Expansion in the Fifteenth and Sixteenth Centuries', *Journal of the Merioneth Historical and Record Society* (1972)
D.R. Thomas,	'Merionethshire Six Hundred Years Ago', *Archaeologia Cambrensis* (1886)
D.H. Williams,	'Cymer Abbey', *Archaeologia Cambrensis* (1981)
Ivor Williams, J.L. Williams (eds.),	*Gwaith Guto'r Glyn* (Cardiff, 1939)
David H. Williams,	'The Cistercians in West Wales', *Archaeologia Cambrensis* (2010)
W.W.E. Wynne,	'Cymmer Abbey', *Archaeologia Cambrensis* (1847)
W.W.E. Wynne,	'Will of David ap Meuric Vychan', *Archaeologia Cambrensis* (1873)

CHAPTER 5. Huw Nanney Hên (1573-1623)

G. Davies,	*Noddwyr Beirdd ym Meirion* (Dolgellau, 1974)
Ifan ap Owen Edwards (ed.),	*Star Chamber Proceedings Relating to Wales* (Cardiff, 1929)
T.P. Ellis,	'The Founding of Cymmer Abbey' (Chapter 8) in *The Story of Two Parishes, Dolgelley and Llanelltyd* (Newtown, 1928)
E.D. Evans,	'Politics and Parliamentary Representation in Merioneth 1536-1644', *Journal of the Merioneth Historical and Record Society* (2007)
J. Foster,	*Alumni Oxoniensis 1500-1714* (Oxford, 1891)
A. Jones,	'Estates of the Welsh Abbeys at the Dissolution', *Archaeologia Cambrensis* (1937)
E.D. Jones,	'An Account Book of Sir Thomas Myddelton', *National Library of Wales Journal* (1939)
J.G. Jones,	'The Merioneth Gentry in the Social Order: Bardic Evidence c.1540-1640', *Journal of the Merioneth Historical and Record Society* (1984)
E. Rosalie Jones,	*The History of Barmouth and its Vicinity* (Barmouth, 1909)
Thomas H. Lewis,	'The Justice of Peace in Wales', *Transactions of the Honourable Society of Cymmrodorion* (1946)
Lewis W. Lloyd,	'Corsygedol, Ardudwy's Principal Estate', *Journal of the Merioneth Historical and Record Society* (1977/8)
H. Gareth Owen,	'Family Politics in Elizabethan Merionethshire', *Bulletin of the Board of Celtic Studies* 18 (1960)

Bryn R. Parry,   'Hugh Nanney Hên (c.1546-1623), Squire of Nannau', *Journal of the Merioneth Historical and Record Society* (1967)

Bryn R. Parry,   'A Sixteenth century Merioneth Ironworks', *Journal of the Merioneth Historical and Record Society* (1963)

Peter Smith,   'Corsygedol', *Journal of the Merioneth Historical and Record Society* (1956)

C. Thomas,   'The Corsygedol Estate during the Age of Improvement', *Journal of the Merioneth Historical and Record Society* (1971)

C. Thomas,   'Patterns and processes of estate expansion in the 15th and 16th centuries', *Journal of the Merioneth Historical and Record Society* (1972)

C. Thomas,   'The Township of Nannau, 1100-1600 A.D.', *Journal of the Merioneth Historical and Record Society* (1965-8)

Colin Thomas,   'Enclosure and the rural landscape of Merioneth in the sixteenth century', *Journal of the Merioneth Historical and Record Society* (2007)

M. Vaughan,   'Nannau', *Journal of the Merioneth Historical and Record Society* (1961-4)

W.W.E. Wynne,   'The Vaughans of Cors y Gedol', *Archaeologia Cambrensis* (1875)

CHAPTER 6. The Turbulent 17th Century (1624-1701)

Miles K. Wynn Cato,   'Nannau and Early Portraiture in North Wales', *Journal of the Merioneth Historical and Record Society* (1991)

A.H. Dodd,   *Studies in Stuart Wales*, 2nd edition (Cardiff, 1971)

E.D. Evans,   'Politics and Parliamentary representation in Merioneth 1644-1832', *Journal of the Merioneth Historical and Record Society* (2007)

E.D. Evans,   'The Revolution of 1688 and its aftermath in Merioneth', *Journal of the Merioneth Historical and Record Society* (2002/5)

Peter Gaunt,   *A Nation under siege: the Civil War in Wales 1642-48* (HMSO 1991)

Daniel Huws,   *Medieval Welsh Manuscripts* (Cardiff, 2000)

Philip Jenkins,   'Wales and the Order of the Royal Oak', *National Library of Wales Journal* (1985/6)

E.D. Jones,   'Robert Vaughan of Hengwrt', *Journal of the Merioneth Historical and Record Society* (1949-51)

John Lloyd,   'Colonel John Jones, Maesygarnedd', *Journal of the Merioneth Historical and Record Society* (1953-6)

Richard Morgan,   'Robert Vaughan of Hengwrt (1592-1667)', *Journal of the Merioneth Historical and Record Society* (1980)

Owen Parry (ed.),   'The Hearth Tax of 1662 in Merioneth', *Journal of the Merioneth Historical and Record Society* (1953-6)

Peter R. Roberts,   'The Merioneth Gentry and Local Government: circa 1650-1838', *Journal of the Merioneth Historical and Record Society* (1965)

Gregory Carl Seyfer, *Colonel John Jones: Puritan regicide from Merioneth* (M.A. Dissertation, Aberystwyth, 1991)

Peter Smith,	'Ynysmaengwyn, Merioneth', *Archaeologia Cambrensis* (1960)
John Steegman,	*A Survey of Portraits in Welsh Houses, Vol. 1: Houses in North Wales* (Cardiff, 1957)
Ben Bowen Thomas,	'Elizabeth Baker and her diary', *National Library of Wales Journal* (1943)
Colin Thomas,	'Estate Surveys as sources in Historical Geography', *National Library of Wales Journal* (1965-6)
G. Tibbott,	'William Watkin Edward Wynne', *Journal of the Merioneth Historical and Record Society* (1949-51)
N. Tucker,	*North Wales in the Civil War* (Denbigh, 1958)
G. J. Williams,	'The Quakers of Merioneth During the Seventeenth Century', *Journal of the Merioneth Historical and Record Society* (1978-9)
W.W.E. Wynne,	'Funeral of Hugh Nanney, Esq., of Nanney A.D. 1647', *Archaeologia Cambrensis* (1860)

CHAPTER 7. The Vaughans of Nannau (1702-1783)

Bangor University: Archives and Special Collections, *Mostyn Manuscripts*
E. Griffith,	'The Friends in Wales', (1895)
Richard Haslam (ed.)	*The Buildings of Wales*, Gwynedd (London, 2009)
R.T. Jenkins, H.M. Ramage,	'A History of the Honourable Society of Cymmrodorion and of the Gwyneddigion and Cymreigyddion Societies (1751-1951)' *Y Cymmrodor* (1951)
Alun R. Jones,	'Lewis Morris and Honest Mr Vaughan of Nannau and Corsygedol', *Journal of the Merioneth Historical and Record Society* (1998)
Ieuan Gwynedd Jones,	'Merioneth Politics in Mid Nineteenth Century: The Politics of a Rural Economy', *Journal of the Merioneth Historical and Record Society* (1967)
Sir Lewis Namier, John Brooke,	*The House of Commons, 1754-1790* (HMSO 1964)
Peter R. Roberts,	'The gentry and the land in eighteenth-century Merioneth', *Journal of the Merioneth Historical and Record Society* (1964)
Peter R. Roberts,	*The Landed Gentry in Merioneth, circa 1660-1832* (M.A. Dissertation, University of Wales, 1963)
John Steegman,	*A Survey of Portraits in Welsh Houses, Vol. 1: Houses in North Wales* (Cardiff, 1957)
Colin Thomas,	'Merioneth Estates, 1790-1850', *Journal of the Merioneth Historical and Record Society* (1967)
Peter D.G. Thomas,	'The Parliamentary Representation of Merioneth during the Eighteenth Century', *Journal of the Merioneth Historical and Record Society* (1958)
Rhiannon Thomas,	'William Vaughan (1707-75) of Corsygedol', *Journal of the Merioneth Historical and Record Society* (1998)
Arthur Young,	*Annals of Agriculture* (London, 1803)

CHAPTER 8. The Baronets of Nannau (1723-1859)

Judith Alfrey,	'Rural Building in Nineteenth-Century North Wales: The Role of the Great Estates', *Archaeologia Cambrensis* (2001)
M.J.B. Baddeley, C.S. Ward,	*North Wales: part 2* (London, 1891)
Elizabeth Baker's Diary	(Peniarth MS 416, National Library of Wales)
Richard Bebb,	*Welsh Furniture: A Cultural History of Craftsmanship and Design, 1250-1950* (Kidwelly, 2007)
Miles Kirkby Wynn Cato,	*Old Blood of Merioneth: A short History of the Nanney-Wynn Family and their Estates over Ten Centuries* (Llandysul, 1989)
Miles Wynn Cato,	Parry: The Life and Works of William Parry A.R.A (1743-1791) (2008)
L. Twiston Davies, A. Edwards,	*Welsh Life in the Eighteenth Century* (London, 1939)
M. Escott,	'How Wales lost its Judicature: the making of the 1830 Act for the Abolition of the Courts of Great Sessions', *Transactions of the Honourable Society of Cymmrodorion* (2007)
Richard Fenton,	*Tours in Wales 1804-1813,* edited by John Fisher (London, 1917)
Mary Corbett Harris,	*Craft, Customs and Legends of Wales* (London, 1980)
Mary Corbett Harris,	'History of Religion in the Parish of Llanfachreth', *Journal of the Merioneth Historical and Record Society* (1961-4)
Mary Corbett Harris,	*Llanfachreth: Bygones of a Merioneth Parish* (Dolgellau, 1973)
Christopher Hill,	*The Century of Revolution: 1603-1714* (London, 1961)
The Honourable Society of Cymmrodorion,	*The Dictionary of Welsh Biography down to 1940* (London, 1959)
Elizabeth Inglis-Jones,	'A Blue-Stocking Lady in Wales', *Journal of the Merioneth Historical and Record Society* (1961-4)
W. Fergusson Irvine,	'Notes on the History of Rug', *Journal of the Merioneth Historical and Record Society* (1949-51)
D.C. Jones,	'The rural economy and society of Wales between 1790-1815 with special reference to the manuscripts of Walter Davies (Gwallter Mechain)', *Board of Celtic Studies Research Project,* (2000-1)
Griff R. Jones,	*The Rock Cannon of Gwynedd* (2002)
E.A. Kilner,	*Four Welsh Counties: Brecknock, Caernarvon, Merioneth and Pembroke* (London, 1891)
Mostyn Lewis,	*Stained Glass in North Wales up to 1850* (Altrincham, 1970)
Samuel Lewis,	*A Topographical Directory of Wales: Llanfachreth* (1849)
T. Alwyn Lloyd,	'The Georgian Period in Welsh Building', *Archaeologia Cambrensis* (1957)
'Mervinius',	'Walks around Dolgellau', *The Cambro-Briton* (1820)
A. Morris,	*Merionethshire* (Cambridge, 1915)
Donald Nicholas,	'The Welsh Jacobites', *Transactions of the Honourable Society of Cymmrodorion* (1948)

Thomas Nicholas,	*Annals and Antiquities of The Counties and County Families of Wales* (London, 1872)
H.J. Owen,	*Merioneth Volunteers and Local Militia during the Napoleonic Wars (1795-1816)* (Dolgellau, 1934)
Trevor M. Owen,	'Llwyddiant i Etifedd Meillionydd', *Transactions of the Caernarvonshire Historical Society* (2002)
Brenda Parry-Jones,	'The Journals of H.J. Reveley (1812-1889) of Bryn-y-gwin, Dolgellau', *Journal of the Merioneth Historical and Record Society* (1969-72)
Liz Pitman,	*Pigsties and Paradise: Lady Diarists and the Tour of Wales, 1795-1860* (Llanrwst, 2009)
T.W. Pritchard,	*The Wynns at Wynnstay* (Caerwys, 1982)
Peter R. Roberts,	'The Social History of the Merioneth Gentry, circa 1660-1840', *Journal of the Merioneth Historical and Record Society* (1963)
P.F. Robinson,	*Rural Architecture: A series of Designs for Ornamental Cottages* (London, 1838)
The Royal Commission on the Ancient and Historical Monuments and Constructions in Wales and Monmouthshire:	*An Inventory of the Ancient Monuments in Wales and Monmouthshire: County of Merioneth* (London, 1917)
Geoffrey B. Seddon,	*The Jacobites and their Drinking Glasses* (Woodbridge, 1995)
Peter Smith,	*Houses of the Welsh Countryside: A Study in Historical Geography* (London, 1975)
Ben Bowen Thomas,	'Elizabeth Baker and her diary', *National Library of Wales Journal* (1943)
Colin Thomas,	'Colonization, Enclosure and the Rural Landscape', *National Library of Wales Journal* (1975)
Colin Thomas,	'Estates and the Rural Economy of North Wales; 1770-1850', *Board of Celtic Studies* (1978-80)
M.W. Thompson (ed.),	*The Journeys of Sir Richard Colt Hoare through Wales and England, 1793-1810* (Gloucester, 1983)
R.G. Thorne,	*The History of Parliament: the House of Commons, 1790-1820* (London, 1986)
Herbert Vaughan,	'Some Jacobite Relics of Peniarth in Merionethshire', *Y Cymmrodor* (1926)
Herbert Vaughan,	'Welsh Jacobitism', *Transactions of the Honourable Society of Cymmrodorion* (1920-21)
Mary Vaughan,	The Mary Vaughan Papers – Z/DBM/1-93 (Gwynedd Archives)
Peter Howell Williams,	'A bathing company on a reading holiday in Barmouth in 1831', *Journal of the Merioneth Historical and Record Society* (2002/5)

CHAPTER 9. The Victorian and Edwardian Era (1863-1917)

Byegones (supplement) *A complete record of the Royal Visit to Wales, 1889*
(Oswestry, 1889)

R.J. Colyer, 'The Land Agent in nineteenth-century Wales',
Welsh History Review (1977)

Mary Corbett-Harris, 'Cwm School, Llanfachreth', *Journal of the Merioneth Historical
and Record Society* (1977-80)

Mary Corbett-Harris, 'Heather Hid a Silver Fortune', *Country Quest* (January, 1973)

Mary Corbett Harris, *The History of Llanfachreth Church* (booklet, Barmouth, 1974)

Mary Corbett Harris, *Llanfachreth: Bygones of a Merioneth Parish* (Dolgellau, 1973)

Mary Corbett-Harris, 'In Service With The Family', *Country Life* (November, 1972)

V. Challinor Davies, G.W. Owen, 'Goldmines of Merioneth', *Journal of the Merioneth
Historical and Record Society* (1961)

David Egan, *People, Protest and Politics: Case Studies in Nineteenth Century
Wales* (Llandysul, 1987)

David.W. Howell , 'The Land Question in nineteenth-century Wales, Ireland and
Scotland: A Comparative study', *Agricultural History
Review* (2013)

Illustrated London News, *The Queen's Visit to North Wales, August 1889* (London, 1889)

B.Ll. James, 'The great landowners of Wales in 1873',
National Library of Wales Journal (1965-6)

Gareth Elwyn Jones, *Modern Wales: A Concise History* (Cambridge, 1994)

L.A. Rees, 'Middleton Hall and Aberglasney: Two Carmarthenshire Landed
Estates and their Families, c.1780-1875' (Ph.D.
Aberystwyth, 2009)

CHAPTER 10. Major-General John Vaughan (1871-1956)

Roger L. Brown, 'The Great Row of Dolgellau Church, 1933-4', *Journal of the
Merioneth Historical and Record Society* (1990-3)

John Davies, 'The End of the Great Estates and the Rise of Freehold Farming
in Wales', *Welsh History Review* (1974)

Dictionary of Welsh Biography, 'John Vaughan (1871-1956)' (yba.llgc.org.uk)

Robert Graves, *Goodbye to All That* (London, 1929)

R.J. Moore-Colyer, 'Field Sports, Conservation and the Countryside in Georgian
and Victorian Wales', *Welsh History Review* (1992-3)

Richard Pillinger, *Major Roland Pillinger: A soldier of the British Empire,
1879-1922* (majorpillinger.com)

Shell-shock (www.spartacus-educational.com)

Brian Slyfield, 'The Nannau Officers' Auxiliary Hospital in 1919' – from the
pages of Moel Offrwm, its house journal, *Journal of the
Merioneth Historical and Record Society* (2002-5)

Major-General John Vaughan, *Cavalry and Sporting Memories* (Bala, 1954)
Wikipedia,   '7th (Queen's Own) Hussars' (www.wikipedia.org)
Wikipedia,   '10th (Prince of Wales's Own) Royal Hussars' (www.wikipedia.org)
Wikipedia,   ' John Vaughan (British Army major-general)' (www.wikipedia.org)
Wikipedia,   'Shell Shock' (www.wikipedia.org)

CHAPTER 11. Charles Hilary Vaughan Pritchard (1905-1976)

Charles Bremner,   'Heroes of forgotten D-Day land again' *(The Times*, Saturday 16 August, 2014)
Col. Thomas R. Cross, 'The Airborne Invasion of Southern France: Operation Dragoon', (www.517prct.org/documents/airborne_invasion)
Robert Elphick,   'The Liberation of Fayence – August 1944' (www.rivierareporter.com/local_living/171)
Peter Harclerode,   *Wings of War – Airborne Warfare 1918-1945* (London, 2005)
Cliff Meredith,   'The Sinking of HMS Abdiel - 9th/10th Sept. 1943', *Journal of The Royal Welch Fusiliers*
G.G. Norton,   *The Red Devils: the story of the British airborne forces* (London, 1973)
Lt. Col. T.B.H. Otway, *Airborne Forces: The Second World War 1939 - 1945* (London, 1990)
Hilary St. George Saunders, *The Red Beret: The story of the Parachute Regiment at war 1940 -1945* (London, 1950)
John C. Warren,   *Airborne Missions in the Mediterranean*, 1942-1945 (USAF Historical Study, 1955)
Wikipedia,   '2nd Parachute Brigade in Southern France' (www.wikipedia.org)
Wikipedia,   '2nd Parachute Brigade (United Kingdom)' (www.wikipedia.org)
Wikipedia,   '6th (Royal Welch) Parachute Battalion' (www.wikipedia.org)
Steven Zaloga,   *Operation Dragoon 1944: France's Other D-Day* (Oxford, 2009)

CHAPTER 12. Cadet Branches (1579-1941)

John Goldworth Alger,   *Napoleon's British visitors and captives, 1801-1815* (New York, 1904)
Elizabeth Baker's Diary (Peniarth MS 416, National Library of Wales)
Miles Kirkby Wynn Cato, *A Perfect Patriarch: William Nanney-Wynn – A Life in Georgian Merioneth* (1993)
Miles Kirkby Wynn Cato, *Old Blood of Merioneth: A short History of the Nanney-Wynn Family and their Estates over Ten Centuries* (Llandysul, 1989)
Gwynedd Archives,   The Caegoronwy/Bennar Fawr Collection: 1581-1970 Z/DC (1956)
G.W. Hall,   *The Gold Mines of Merioneth* (Gloucester, 1971)
Richard Haslam (ed.),   *The Buildings of Wales, Gwynedd* (London, 2009)

M. Hartley,	'The Hartleys of Gwynedd, 1725 - 1968', *Gwynedd Family History Society* (1984)
John Hodgson,	*A History of Northumberland* (Newcastle-upon-Tyne, 1858)
Letters from and relating to North Wales,	*Journal of the Merioneth Historical and Record Society* (1960 -67)
J.G. Jenkins,	'Rural Industry in Merioneth', *Journal of the Merioneth Historical and Record Society* (1977)
J.G. Jenkins,	*The Welsh Woollen Industry* (Cardiff, 1969)
Emyr Gwynne Jones,	'Manuscripts relating to Merioneth at Bangor, 1- The Maesyneuadd Collection', *Journal of the Merioneth Historical and Record Society* (1957-60)
E. Rosalie Jones,	*The History of Barmouth and its Vicinity* (Barmouth, 1909)
J. Gwynfor Jones,	'Lewis Owen, Sheriff of Merioneth and the Gwylliaid Cochion of Mawddwy in 1554-5', *Journal of the Merioneth Historical and Record Society* (1994-7)
Capt. Jenkins Jones RN,	'Captain Jenkins Jones's Diary', *Historical Society of West Wales* (1912)
M.J. Jones,	'Merioneth Woollen Industry from 1750-1820', *Transactions of the Honourable Society of Cymmrodorion* (1940)
W.H. Jones,	*Sixpenny Illustrated Guide to Barmouth and Dolgelley* (Bangor, no date)
James Kenward,	'An account of the life and writings of John Williams – Ab Ithel', *Cambrian Journal* (1862)
Philip H. Lawson,	Margery M. Anwyl, and Thomas Anwyl-Davies, *The Anwyl Familes* (1982)
Michael Lewis,	*Napoleon and his British Captives* (London, 1962)
J. Lindsay,	*A History of the North Wales Slate Industry* (Newton Abbott, 1974)
Lewis W. Lloyd,	'Early Nineteenth-Century Ships and Shareholders of the Barmouth River-Parts 1 and 2', *Journal of the Merioneth Historical and Record Society* (1992)
Lewis W. Lloyd,	'Profiles of Mawddach Square-Riggers', *Journal of the Merioneth Historical and Record Society* (1981)
Lewis W. Lloyd,	*The Unity of Barmouth* (1977)
'Mervinius',	'Walks around Dolgellau', *The Cambro-Briton* (1820)
T.A. Morrison,	*Goldmining in Western Merioneth* (Llandysul, 1975)
National Library of Wales,	Griffith family of Garn papers – NLW MS 16632D
North Wales Chronicle,	'Thomas Hartley, Esq., Llwyn' (Friday 29 April, 1853)
A.J. Parkinson,	'Fulling Mills in Merioneth', *Journal of the Merioneth Historical and Record Society* (1984)
Susan C. Passmore,	'A fresh look at the diary (1778–86) of Elizabeth Baker, Dolgellau – Parts 1 and 2', *Journal of the Merioneth Historical and Record Society* (1999-2000)

Susan C. Passmore Collection	(Gwynedd Archives)
R.T. Pritchard,	'Merionethshire Roads and Turnpike Trusts', *Journal of the Merioneth Historical and Record Society* (1961)
H.A.C. Sturgess,	*Register of Admissions to the Honourable Society of the Middle Temple* (London, 1949)
Ben Bowen Thomas,	'Elizabeth Baker and her diary', *National Library of Wales Journal* (1944)
Ben Bowen Thomas,	*The Old Order, based on the diary of Elizabeth Baker (Dolgelley, 1778 – 1786)* (Cardiff, 1945)
Wikipedia	'Battle of Cape St. Vincent (1797)' (www.wikipedia.org)
Wikipedia,	'John Williams (Ab Ithel)' (www.wikipedia.org)
Ellis Wynne,	*Gweledigaetheu y Bardd Cwsc*, 1703 (translated by T. Gwynn Jones) (Gregynog Press, 1940)
W.W.E. Wynne	'Anecdotes Characteristic of the Lawless State of Society in Merionethshire in the Reigns of Edward IV and Henry VIII', *Archaeologia Cambrensis* (1847)

NANNAU:
Family Tree Colour Coding System

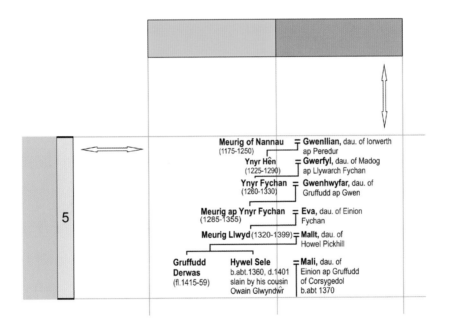

Meurig of Nannau (1175-1250) = Gwenllian, dau. of Iorwerth ap Peredur

Ynyr Hên (1225-1290) = Gwerfyl, dau. of Madog ap Llywarch Fychan

Ynyr Fychan (1260-1330) = Gwenhwyfar, dau. of Gruffudd ap Gwen

Meurig ap Ynyr Fychan (1285-1355) = Eva, dau. of Einion Fychan

Meurig Llwyd (1320-1399) = Mallt, dau. of Howel Pickhill

Gruffudd Derwas (fl.1415-59)

Hywel Sele b.abt.1360, d.1401 slain by his cousin Owain Glwyndŵr = Mali, dau. of Einion ap Gruffudd of Corsygedol b.abt 1370

5

Example :   Identifies Hywel Sele's position on Nannau Lines of Descent

5